国家出版基金项目
NATIONAL PUBLICATION FOUNDATION

THE
CHINESE
PATH

INNOVATION OF SOCIAL GOVERNANCE IN CHINA

GONG WEIBIN ET AL.

Translated by
RUAN XIANYU, LIU QINJUN

Proofread by
ZHANG JIE

中国财经出版传媒集团
经济科学出版社
Economic Science Press
·北 京·

图书在版编目（CIP）数据

中国社会治理创新之路 = Innovation of Social
Governance in China：英文 / 龚维斌等著；阮先玉，
刘秦君译. --北京：经济科学出版社, 2025. 5.
（《中国道路》丛书：英文版）. -- ISBN 978-7-5218
-6084-9

Ⅰ. D63

中国国家版本馆 CIP 数据核字第 2024P8B789 号

责任编辑：刘　博
责任校对：易　超
责任印制：张佳裕

中国社会治理创新之路
ZHONGGUO SHEHUI ZHILI CHUANGXIN ZHILU
Innovation of Social Governance in China

龚维斌　等著

阮先玉　刘秦君　译
经济科学出版社出版、发行　新华书店经销
社址：北京市海淀区阜成路甲 28 号　邮编：100142
总编部电话：010-88191217　发行部电话：010-88191522
网址：www.esp.com.cn
电子邮箱：esp@esp.com.cn
天猫网店：经济科学出版社旗舰店
网址：http://jjkxcbs.tmall.com
固安华明印业有限公司印装
787×1092　16 开　20.75 印张　525000 字
2025 年 5 月第 1 版　2025 年 5 月第 1 次印刷
ISBN 978-7-5218-6084-9　定价：92.00 元
（图书出现印装问题，本社负责调换。电话：010-88191545）
（版权所有　侵权必究　打击盗版　举报热线：010-88191661
QQ：2242791300　营销中心电话：010-88191537
电子邮箱：dbts@esp.com.cn）

Preface

The Chinese path refers to the path of socialism with distinctive Chinese characteristics. As Chinese President Xi Jinping points out, it is not an easy path. We are able to embark on this path thanks to the great endeavors of the reform and opening up over the past 30 years and more, and the continuous quest made in the 60-plus years since the founding of the People's Republic of China (PRC). It is based on a thorough review of the evolution of the Chinese nation over more than 170 years since modern times and carrying forward the 5,000-year-long Chinese civilization. This path is deeply rooted in history and broadly based on China's present realities.

A right path leads to a bright future. The Chinese path is not only access to China's development and prosperity, but also a path of hope and promise to the rejuvenation of the Chinese nation. Only by forging the confidence in the path, theory, institution and culture can we advance along this path of socialism with Chinese characteristics. With this focus, *The Chinese Path Series* presents to readers an overview in practice, achievements and experiences as well as the past, present and future of the Chinese path.

The Chinese Path Series is divided into ten volumes with one hundred books on different topics. The main topics of the volumes are as follows: economic development, political advancement, cultural progress, social development, ecological conservation, national defense and armed forces building, diplomacy and international policies, the Party's leadership and building, localization of Marxism in China and views from other countries on the Chinese path. Each volume on a particular topic consists of several books which respectively throw light on exploration in practice, reform process, achievements, experiences and theoretical innovations of the Chinese path. Focusing on the practice in the reform and opening up with the continuous exploration since the founding of the PRC, these books summarize on the development and inheritance of China's glorious civilization, which not only display a strong sense of the times, but also have profound historical appeal and future-oriented impact.

The series is conceived in its entirety and assigned to different authors. In terms of the writing, special attention has been paid to the combination of history and reality, as well as theory and practice at home and abroad. It gives a realistic and innovative interpretation of the practice, experience, process and theory of the Chinese path. Efforts are made on the distinctive and convincing expression in a global context. It helps to cast light on the "Chinese wisdom" and the "Chinese approach" that the Chinese path has contributed to the modernization of developing countries and solutions to human problems.

On the basis of the great achievements in China's development since the founding of the PRC, particularly since the reform and opening up, the Chinese nation, which had endured so much and for so long since the modern times, has achieved tremendous growth—it has stood up, become prosperous and grown in strength. The socialism with distinctive Chinese characteristics has shown great vitality and entered a new stage. This path has been expanded and is now at a new historical starting point. At this vital stage of development, the Economic Science Press of China Finance & Economy Media Group has designed and organized the compilation of *The Chinese Path Series*, which is of great significance in theory and practice.

The program of *The Chinese Path Series* was launched in 2015, and the first publications came out in 2017. The series was listed in a couple of national key publication programs, the "90 kinds of selected publications in celebration of the 19th CPC National Congress", and National Publication Foundation.

Editorial Board of The Chinese Path Series

Contents

Chapter 1
Introduction

Since China implemented the reform and opening-up policy in 1978, tremendous changes have taken place in all aspects of the economy, society, politics, and culture. In this process, the way society is organized and managed has also undergone adjustments and reforms. Traditional social administration has evolved into modern social governance. The continuous reform and innovation of the social governance system are mainly manifested in several aspects such as the concept, the main body, the methods, and the focus.

1.1 The innovation of the concept of social governance

In 2012, the 18th National Congress of the Communist Party of China (CPC) put forward an important idea of "the modernization of the national system and capability for governance". As an important part of the idea, the term "social governance" was introduced into the nation and Party's discourse for the first time after its long use in academia. With the maintenance and realization of the public's legitimate rights and interests the people as the core, social governance involves fairness and justice, coordinating social relations, handling social problems, resolving social conflicts, preventing social risks, promoting social identity, ensuring public safety, and maintaining social harmony and stability. Social governance is a concept with strong Chinese characteristics, both relevant to and different from the internationally accepted concept of "governance". In a certain sense, it can be regarded as an aspect or part of "governance". Therefore, the concepts, principles, methods, and means of "governance" are equally applicable to social governance to a large extent.

Literally, social governance consists of two sides: society and governance. In this context, "society", if interpreted as "multiple social forces and social subjects", may be regarded as a subject, that is, governance by the society, or as an object, i.e., governance of the society. Whether "society" is a subject or an object, social governance is only part, not all, of the governance. Therefore, the main difference between social governance and governance is that governance is a larger concept. The objects, scope, and tasks of governance are broader, more complex, and more arduous than those of social governance, while social governance is relatively simple compared to governance. Social governance is a theory or concept with Chinese characteristics as it is a combination of Chinese tradition and reality.

1.1.1 From social administration to social governance

Social governance evolves from social administration. The Chinese people have long been accustomed to social administration, a concept born and bred in China, but are very unfamiliar with governance or social governance. Where there is a human society, there is social administration. In the 21st century, with the rapid development of China's economy and urbanization, profound changes can be seen in the economic and social structure and people's class and demand structure. As new and old social problems and conflicts, intertwine and occur more frequently than ever, there is an urgent need to strengthen and innovate social administration. In 2004, the Fourth Plenary Session of the 16th CPC Central Committee emphasized the need to strengthen social construction and administration and promote innovation in the social administration system. Since then, social administration has become an important task of the Party and the government, a mission going along with economic development and management. In the meantime, social administration has been valued by the academic community and has become an important academic research field, where numerous and valuable academic achievements have been made. However, at that time, social administration still followed the traditional mindset and methods, where "maintenance of social stability" was the sole goal and "social management and control" the main means. Inspired by governance theory and social administration practice, the Party and the government, with an open mind and courage to innovate, put forward the new idea of social governance. Social governance, developed from social administration theory, is in line with the requirements of the times, featuring a humanistic spirit and more scientific than social administration.

1.1.2 Respect for fairness and justice

Social governance requires respect for fairness and justice, which are not only an important principle of social governance, but also a benchmark for the methods used in social governance, and a yardstick for judging the effect and quality of social governance as well.

"Injustice leads to mental imbalance, hence grudges and ultimately social disharmony." Unfairness and injustice are the roots of many social problems, contradictions, and conflicts. In recent years, the Chinese government has been endeavoring to promote justice in rights, opportunities, and rules, and is committed to reforming the household registration system to narrow the gap between urban and rural areas. China is also reforming employment, education, and social security policies to reduce inequities; In addition, the government strives to deepen the reform of the judicial system, standardize judicial behavior to build a fair, efficient, and authoritative judicial system, and to ensure fairness and justice in the entire society.

1.1.3 Adherence to the people-centered philosophy

Social governance requires adhering to the people-centered philosophy and protecting citizens' legitimate rights and interests. Adhering to the people-centered philosophy is to maintain human dignity, meet human needs, and protect human rights. It is the most important principle in social governance. In adhering to the people-centered philosophy, the priority is to protect the underprivileged. Only when their rights are protected can society truly progress and become better civilized. Farmers, migrant workers, the poor, and those with employment difficulties in urban areas are included as the underprivileged. They are disadvantaged in terms of wealth, social status, and social influence, with more difficulties in work and life, which could hardly be handled by themselves. In recent years, the protection of rights of the ordinary people represented by the above-mentioned groups has been the focus of the work of the Party and the government. While embodying inclusiveness, China's series of public policies are committed to making up for the shortcomings of social development by implementing favorable and targeted protection policies for targeted groups. The Fifth Plenary Session of the 18th CPC Central Committee proposed that during the 13th Five-year Plan period, we must insist on shared development, so that all people have a greater sense of gain from the reform and development. The session also called for vigorous development of social undertakings, efforts to safeguard and improve people's wellbeing, to ensure universal access to childcare, education, employment, medical services, elderly care, and housing. Only when the actual difficulties in the work and life of the people have been truly solved, will the room that gives rise to social problems and contradictions be greatly reduced.

1.1.4 Integration of order and vitality

Social governance seeks the integration of order and vitality by emphasizing not only stability and order, but also the stimulation of social vitality. This integration is a manifestation of how social governance evolves from social administration. We must not one-sidedly emphasize the maintenance of social order while neglecting the promotion of the social vitality, and we must prevent the emergence of a situation where "if strictly administered, it would be in stagnancy; if let be free, it would be in chaos." Since the newly-elected central government took office, it has always regarded "streamlining administration and delegating power, improving regulation, and upgrading services" as the central task of deepening the administrative review and approval system and even the reform of the administrative structure. The government has delegated to the market and the community the affairs that should not be, or cannot be, or are not well managed by the government. Relationships between the government and the market, the government and society, the society and the market, and the central government and local governments have been well handled. All these efforts help to stimulate the vitality of the market and society, as well as to encourage and support public entrepreneurship and innovation, so that creativity for wealth is given full play and talents and materials are made the best use of, and everyone feels content.

1.1.5 Addressing problems at the source

Social governance requires an emphasis on addressing problems at the source, rather than remedial actions. It is not about waiting for problems to emerge and then trying to solve them, nor is it about simply controlling and suppressing them, but to prevent and relieve possible problems in advance. It also requires the protection of citizens' rights, efforts to improve people's wellbeing, and an effective social risk assessment, so that any signs of contradictions, problems, hidden dangers, and possible risks are identified early.

1.2 Extended entities in social governance

Generally speaking, the main entity of social governance is diverse. Multiple forces participate in social co-governance. Prior to 1978, China adopted a highly centralized planned economic system, with the government overseeing everything: economy, politics, and culture, etc. The government (public authority including the Party) in a certain sense represents the state (state power). Therefore, more radical views even believe that before the reform and opening up, China only had the concept of the state, excluding that of a market or society.

In the framework of "state-market-society", the state was so overwhelming that the market and society were deprived of any room for survival and development. The state (or the Party and the government) was the sole provider of public affairs, products, services, and order. Since there was little space for social power, the social administration (governance) before the reform and opening up was more of political management (governance).

Since the reform and opening up, China has strived to break free from the planned economic system to establish a socialist market economic system, where the government encourages entrepreneurs and market forces, and strives to give full play to the role of the market in allocating resources. Direct intervention from the state in economic life has been in decline. The relationship between the government and the market is scientifically relevant. However, in contrast, the relationship between the government and society still needs improvement. To be specific, on the one hand, the government intervenes too much in social affairs. On the other hand, the government is often absent from real problems that members of society face, leading to a situation where social problems and contradictions are not resolved in a timely and effective manner, and demands of the people cannot be reflected. This situation not only overburdens the government, but also hinders the role of social forces. Therefore, establishing a new pattern of social governance under the leadership of the Party and the government is an inevitable choice for the reform and innovation of China's social governance system.

1.2.1   The leading role of the Party and the government

The social governance system with Chinese characteristics calls for strengthening the leadership of the Party committee, giving play to the leading role of the government, and encouraging participation from all sectors of society so that a conducive interaction can be reached among governance by the government, self-regulation by the society, and self-governance of the public. The social governance system is the continuation and development of social administration system, and it is a sublation in persistence and innovation. The participation of multiple entities is carried out under the leadership of the Party and the government. Therefore, to innovate social governance, the Party's leadership must first be strengthened, and the government's leading role should be fully exerted. However, the way the Party and the government participate in social governance cannot simply follow the traditional methods, instead, it must be reformed and improved with the times. The leadership of the Party helps ensure that social governance does not deviate from the right direction and moves forward on the right track.

For China, it is impossible to mechanically copy the experience and practices of social governance from any other countries. Instead, China should explore a social governance model compatible with its historical and cultural traditions and socialist market economic system. The leadership of the Party is conducive to uniting, organizing, and mobilizing all forces to participate, because the Communist Party has strong cohesion and integration to coordinate various forces. Under the new historical conditions, the Party's leadership in social governance is mainly reflected in the assessment of the social governance situation, in the formulation of major guidelines and policies, and in the mastery and guidance of social thoughts, values, public opinion, psychology, and in the selection, use and training of social governance talents. The government's leading role in social governance is mainly manifested in regularly studying and judging social development trends, formulating special plans for social development, formulating social policies and regulations, coordinating institutional design and overall management of social governance, raising, and rationally allocating social governance resources. In recent years, Party committees and governments at all levels have strengthened the research on macro-policies and the top-level design of social governance, and continuously improved the social governance responsibility system, strengthened the evaluation of social governance, and established a more detailed and strict evaluation system for social governance.

1.2.2 Diversified participation

In the modern complex society, people's social needs are diverse, and social affairs are complicated with numerous problems and conflicts. The Party and the government cannot afford to take all the responsibilities. Social governance requires full participation from market sectors, social organizations, and other social forces. In China's construction of a diversified co-governance structure, the first is to enhance self-governance by developing urban and rural organizations. In this regard, the Party and government have introduced a series of policies and measures in recent years. The second is to leverage the people's organizations in mobilizing targeted groups to enhance their vitality and give play to their important role in social governance. Such organizations include trade unions, women's federations, and the Communist Youth League. In July 2015, the Central Committee held a work conference with the people's organizations and proposed that their work should be centered on grassroots organizations. It is necessary to vigorously develop organizations at the community level, establish new ones in new industries, contact, and guide relevant social organizations so that they can play a better role in social governance. In the same month, the central government issued the Opinions on Strengthening and Improving the Party's Work on People's Organizations, pointing out the direction of reform and development of the people's organizations such as trade unions, women's federations, and the Communist Youth League, revitalizing and motivating the people's organizations for effective participation in social governance. In addition, the most important and urgent thing is to standardize and develop such organizations and encourage these organizations to participate in social governance.

1.2.3   Development of social organizations

Social organization is a concept indigenous to China, an integration of traditional non-governmental organizations, non-profit organizations, the voluntary sector, and civil organizations. There are two main types: One is the social organizations under the supervision of the civil affairs department, including associations, foundations, and private non-enterprise units. As of the end of 2015, there were more than 600,000 social organizations in China. The other is unregistered social organizations, which are usually small in scale, relatively simple in internal structure, or even not very formal in organization, such as community-level elderly volunteer service organizations, fishing associations, chess, and card associations, etc. It is estimated that the number of such organizations, often very vigorous, far exceeds the number of organizations registered in state agencies.

The Chinese government has adopted a two-step approach towards the reform and development of social organizations. The first step is to tap the full potential of existing organizations, that is, to regulate the behavior of existing social organizations and stimulate their vitality through reform. Since the 18th CPC National Congress, the reform of social organizations has entered a new historical stage, with the goal of separating government functions from social organizations, encouraging social organizations, industry associations, and chambers of commerce to truly operate independently according to the requirements of social organizations, establishing a sound corporate governance structure, and improving their service. The Second Plenary Session of the 18th CPC Central Committee decided to decouple industry associations and chambers of commerce from administrative agencies within a fixed time. After two years of research and analysis, in 2015, the General Office of the CPC Central Committee and the General Office of the State Council issued the Framework Plan for the De-affiliation of Administrative Agencies from Industry Associations and Chambers of Commerce, expounding the overall requirements and basic principles of the reform, and clarifying the subject, scope, and tasks of decoupling. Related regulatory policies and implementation methods were also explained in detail. Among them, the core content is the "Five Separations and Five Norms" between industry associations, chambers of commerce, and administrative organs in terms of institutions, functions, assets and finance, personnel, and Party-building and foreign affairs. At present, the decoupling of industry associations and chambers from administrative organs is underway. The second step is to establish more social organizations. The number of social organizations in China is far from enough compared with developed countries, which can hardly meet the requirements in social governance innovation. So, there is an urgent need for vigorous development of social organizations. In 2013, the Chinese government clearly requested a reform on the registration system of social organizations. Social organizations such as chambers of commerce, science and technology organizations, public welfare and charity organizations, and urban and rural community service social organizations, can directly apply for registration to the civil affairs department without the approval of a supervisor, unless the law mandates them to obtain pre-registration approval or the State Council's approval. This is conducive to the development of social organizations to a certain extent.

1.3   Reform on social governance model

The social governance model refers to the methods and tools used to govern society. Whether it is carried out under the rule of law is one of the most important differences between social governance and social administration. While emphasizing the rule of law, social governance must also leverage effective methods and tools in social administration, such as moral restraint, citizen conventions, village regulations, industry regulations, and unit management.

1.3.1   Application of the rule of law

Since the 18th CPC National Congress, the rule of law has become the main theme of the reform and innovation in social governance. The Fourth Plenary Session of the

18th CPC Central Committee put forward the major task of advancing the construction of a society under the rule of law, requiring that social governance be brought into the track of the rule of law to improve the governance by the law. Among which, the leading officials are the key. General Secretary Xi Jinping has repeatedly emphasized that leading officials at all levels must advance various tasks with the rule of law guiding their thinking and work. Leading officials at all levels are also required to effectively implement social governance by taking the lead in abiding by the law, using the rule of law in their thinking and work so that people can express their demands in a rational way, to safeguard their rights and interests in accordance with laws and procedures, thus preventing and resolving contradictions. The leading officials are required to have the idea that the rule of law is for "administering officials" rather than "administering the people". The severe crackdown on corruption and the comprehensive and strict governance of the Party since the 18th CPC National Congress are both powerful guarantees and important manifestations of promoting social governance in accordance with the law.

The rule of law requires regulation to constrain government power and protect citizens' rights. Since the 18th CPC National Congress, the Party and the government have been committed to establishing mechanisms for the expression and protection of people's interests and for resolution of conflicts and disputes in accordance with the law. The first is to build a mechanism for people to express their interests and a mechanism for consultation and communication. Governments at all levels are required to establish a decision-making hearing system. Under this system, all major decisions concerning the people's vital interests should seek their advice. People's voices can also be heard through improving the mechanism for the deputies of National People's Congress (NPC) to contact them. By constructing a system of consultation democracy with relevant and rational procedures, consultation channels can be broadened in the Chinese People's Political Consultative Conference (CPPCC) organizations, Party groups, grassroots organizations, and social organizations. Consultative democracy can be conducive to the expression of the interests of the people and in consultation and communication. Democracy at the community level should be improved to safeguard the interests of the people. Democratic administration of enterprises and public institutions featuring workers' congresses should be improved to safeguard and guarantee the democratic rights and interests of workers. Reform in petition system can be improved by establishing legal conclusion system in the cases involving legal issues. Legislation can effectively guide petition into the track of the rule of law, so that the public are able to express their demands rationally in accordance with the law, and to safeguard their legitimate rights and interests through legal channels. The second is to focus on building an early warning mechanism for social conflicts. Experiences acquired in digital management for a matrix of urban communities and commercialized service in some places should be widely promoted. Efforts should be dedicated to building primary-level Party organizations, political and legal comprehensive governance institutions, and people's mediation organizations to give play to their advantages of being rooted in communities and connected with the public, and timely understanding people's sufferings and their needs. Early detection of signs about social contradictions provides a basis for decision-making and management of the Party committee, government and relevant departments. The third is to improve the mechanism for the prevention and resolution of social conflicts and disputes. Local governments should pay more grassroots visits, investigate, and settle disputes on a large scale in the grassroots communities so that they can catch small signs early and resolve problems on the spot in a timely manner, resolving the contradictions at the grassroots level and preventing conflicts from escalating. In this regard, China has established dispute resolution systems including mediation, arbitration, administrative adjudication, administrative reconsideration, and litigation. These systems have their own characteristics and advantages, and each plays a unique role in resolving conflicts and disputes. The Fourth Plenary Session of the 18th CPC Central Committee proposed that it is necessary to further improve various dispute resolution systems and strive to establish a diversified dispute resolution mechanism in which different dispute resolution systems operate smoothly and complement each other. Specifically, it is required to further improve the mechanism of docking between litigation and mediation, coordination between arbitration and trial, and connection between reconsideration and litigation. Different dispute resolution systems not only can play a role in their respective fields, but can also smoothly connect, cooperate, support each other, all contributing to effective dispute resolution. For example, mediation is a dispute resolution system with Chinese characteristics. The People's Mediation Law of the People's Republic of China stipulates a system for the People's Courts to confirm and enforce the validity of mediation agreements. Effective implementation of this system is of great significance for improving the credibility of mediation and preventing mediated disputes from flooding into the courts again, thereby reducing the pressure on court cases. Therefore, it is necessary to uphold and improve mediation system; at the same time, we must seek coordination between mediation, punishment and litigation. Disputes should be properly resolved in accordance with the law.

1.3.2 Application of information technology

China is witnessing the in-depth development of information technology, the Internet and the Internet of Things. Expanded access to information technology and the Internet has provided great possibilities and conveniences for information exchange, resource sharing, and social cooperation. This brings both challenges and opportunities to social governance. The Chinese government is fully aware of the importance of integrating "Internet Plus" technology and social governance services and regards it as a powerful support for refined social governance. The model of digital management for a matrix of urban communities that has emerged in recent years is one of the applications of information technology in social governance. The digital management for a matrix of urban communities is essentially a social governance model, using digital and information methods to operate in communities and matrices, with events as the content and relevant unit as the responsible Party. Through managing the information platform, the units in the matrix interact with each other and share resources. In July 2015, the State Council promulgated the Guiding Opinion on Vigorously Advancing the "Internet Plus" Action, which put forward 11 tasks, many of which involve social governance. Information technology such as big data and cloud computing related to "Internet Plus" has increasingly become an important tool for social governance. In August 2015, the State Council issued the Action Outline for Promoting the Development of Big Data, which outlined the creation of a new model of social governance featuring precise governance and multi-party collaboration in the next 5 to 10 years. It is increasingly becoming a trend to build smart cities, smart communities, smart policing, and implement "sunshine petition".

1.4 Adjustment of focus in social governance

The focus of social governance refers to the scope, fields, and key tasks of social governance. With the deepening of industrialization, urbanization, information technology, marketization, and internationalization, the status quo and tasks of social governance in China have undergone tremendous changes. Accordingly, the key areas of social governance and the focus of work have also shifted.

1.4.1 Stress on Internet governance

Since the 21st century, Internet technology has developed rapidly, forming a huge and complex network society. The network society develops so rapidly that it is far beyond people's imagination due to its anonymity, equality, universal participation, and interaction. It is both independent and closely connected with the real society, creating a new space and way of living and interaction in human history. In 2010, the number of Chinese netizens was 457 million. By December 2015, it had jumped to 688 million, an increase of more than 200 million in just a little more than five years. With the advent of internet society comes the great convenience for people's work and life, learning and shopping, communication and friends-making. However, hazardous information involving violence, pornography, fraud, and rumors, tends to go hand in hand with the internet information, making it difficult to distinguish between true and false. Information security is at stake as some information is irrational, irresponsible, and even carries political purposes, posing a threat to social order and political stability. Therefore, it is urgent to coordinate the governance of the society and the Internet has become an urgent task. In May 2011, the General Office of the State Council established the National Internet Information Office (now known as Cyberspace Administration of China), responsible for implementing guidelines and policies for Internet information dissemination and promoting the establishment of a legal system for Internet information dissemination. The office is also responsible for guiding, coordinating, and urging relevant departments to strengthen Internet information content management. In August 2014, the Cyberspace Administration of China promulgated and implemented the Interim Provisions on the Administration of the Development of Public Information Services Provided through Instant Messaging Tools, to regulate the behaviors of service providers and users of instant messaging tools. In 2015, the Standing Committee of the National People's Congress drafted the Cybersecurity Law (Draft) to solicit public opinions on related matters. Since 2014, special campaigns have been waged against online rumors and cybercrimes. The government has established special management organizations and formulated special policies and laws to implement Internet governance in accordance with the law, and to promote a healthy and orderly development of the network society.

1.4.2 Stress on urban governance

In 2011, China's urbanization rate reached 51.27%, marking the point where the urban population surpassed the rural population. It also meant that China was no longer a country dominated by rural areas and farmers, but one dominated by urban areas and urban populations. By the end of 2015, China's urbanization rate increased to 56.1%, and it is projected to reach 60% in 2020. During this process of rapid urbanization, many rural residents have moved into cities. Statistics show that in 1978, China's urbanization rate was less than 18%. Over the past 30 years, China's urbanization rate has increased by 38 percentage points. Hundreds of millions of rural residents have left the countryside for urban areas. China's rapid urbanization process has resulted in two polarizing effects. The first is that the population of cities, especially large cities, has expanded rapidly, resulting in "overpopulation", which in turn brought relevant problems such as shortage of public resources, insufficient public services, and inability for migrants to integrate into local society. As a result, social governance faces many dilemmas. This problem is particularly serious in the metropolises such as Beijing, Shanghai, Guangzhou and Shenzhen. The second is the "hollowing" of the rural population, especially in the economically underdeveloped areas of the central and western regions. With many "hollow villages" and "empty villages", there are more than 100 million "left-behind children", "left-behind women" and "left-behind elderly" after young and middle-aged people leave to cities, becoming a new vulnerable group. New changes and challenges brought about by urbanization have put forward a brand-new topic for China's social governance. On the one hand, we must establish a social governance system that adapts to the characteristics of the city, and on the other hand, we must strengthen and innovate rural governance. At the end of 2015, the central government held the first city affair conference after 37 years of the reform and opening up. It requested the Party committees and governments at all levels to attach great importance to the work in the cities, such as scientific planning, construction, and management of cities. The conference also called to strengthen the construction of urban management institutions, and reform urban law enforcement to improve social governance. The position of urban governance in the urban and rural governance structure will further be heightened.

1.4.3   Stress on social governance at the grassroots level

Social governance starts on the grassroots level, that is, in urban and rural communities. Community governance has become the main form of social governance at the grassroots level. Party committees and governments at all levels have become more and more aware that the focus and challenge of social governance lies in grassroots level. It takes efforts from basic-level communities to implement any policy issued by the government. Community organizations in the townships and neighborhood committees directly face and serve the people. The level of grassroots social governance directly reflects and determines the level of social governance of the entire country. In recent years, various localities have promoted the reform of sub-district and community's management system in accordance with the requirement of "empowering communities in social governance". In many places, social services and urban functions have been further delegated to primary-level communities to provide public services, coordinate the governance of the jurisdiction, organize comprehensive law enforcement, and guide community construction. Sub-district offices play a comprehensive role in coordinating social service and urban management of the jurisdiction, and promoting the construction of the sub-district government service center. Community development has been further strengthened through burden reduction. To be specific, a task list is formulated for each community, where community has the right to refuse any work outside the list. In this way, community work is better regulated. In accordance with the requirement of "resources go with duty", the government has invested and transferred more resources to communities. At the same time, a platform can be built for community members to communicate and exchange ideas by adhering to the rules of community governance. The platform plays a significant role in mobilizing neighborhood committees, social organizations, property companies, proprietor's committees, and organizations in the community. With the platform, it is possible to encourage and support community members to help each other, strengthen democratic management of community public affairs, improve the connection of community members, and ultimately enhance community identity and a sense of belonging among community members.

1.4.4 Stress on public safety and emergency management

Public safety concerns people's live and work, social stability, and order. Therefore, social governance sees it vital to improve public safety system and emergency management to ensure public safety. Since the 21st century, China has entered a period of frequent occurrence of natural disasters, major accidents and disasters have occurred from time to time. The prevention and control of public health incidents is growingly difficult. In terms of anti-terrorism and safeguarding stability, the situation is grim, and the task is arduous. Some large-scale key equipment, chemical industrial parks face more major risks with the backdrop of acceleration in industrialization and urbanization, more skyscrapers, more lifeline engineering in hydropower, oil and gas transportation. Once an accident occurs, it may cause major economic and social losses and casualties, leading to social chaos. After the fight against the SARS epidemic in 2003, the Chinese government began to build a modern emergency management system with "contingency plan with relevant laws, systems and mechanisms" as the core. After many years of construction and development, China's emergency management institutions and systems have been gradually established and improved, with greater ability to prevent and deal with emergencies. As a non-normality in governance, emergency management has received unprecedented attention. Relevant departments are formulating the plan for the national emergency response system, which is committed to weaving a strong public safety net to make up for shortcomings in emergency management, and to improve public safety and the ability to respond to emergencies.

Chapter 2
Diversification of Social Governance Actors

"Diversification" is a basic trend as well as an important feature of modern social governance. Aiming to advance the modernization of China's system and capacity, the Third Plenary Session of the 18th CPC Central Committee put forward the strategy of innovating the social governance system that involves positive interaction among government governance, social self-regulation, and self-management of residents, emphasizing the leading role of Party committees, encouraging, and supporting participation of all social sectors in social governance. The 19th CPC National Congress further proposed to improve the social governance system, implemented by the government under the leadership of Party committees, based on social coordination, public participation, and the rule of law, and to establish a social governance model based on collaboration, participation, and shared benefits. The establishment of such social governance "system" and "model" indicates the concept transformation from social administration to social governance and embodies the diversification of social governance participants.

2.1 Upholding the leadership of the CPC and playing its core role

The CPC is the core of leadership for the cause of socialism with Chinese characteristics. The Party's nature fundamentally determines its central leadership in the national political life. To strengthen the Party's leadership in social governance is to always uphold the Party's core leadership, give full play to its role in governance and coordination, and express the Party's will and propositions in laws and regulations. Meanwhile, we should support diversified people to participate in social governance and fully play the role of community-level Party organizations and Party members in serving the public and achieving solidarity. Thus, the Party can play the leading role and serve the society more effectively.

2.1.1 Social governance：a key factor affecting the CPC ruling

Sound social governance will help realize the Party's ruling goals. Innovating social governance is an essential requirement and important guarantee for adhering to and developing socialism with Chinese characteristics, as well as the inexorable requirements for the modernization of the national governance system and governance capacity. People are the creators of history. Always upholding people's principal status is the basic principle for the Marxist view of the people as well as one of the fundamental differences that distinguish Marxist political parties from other parties. The key for a ruling party to govern for long, thoroughly implement its program and realize its goal fundamentally lies in whether it can effectively mobilize society and win people's recognition. As a Party governing for the people, the CPC holds as its ultimate ruling goal to safeguard people's happiness, as pointed out by Xi Jinping at the Standing Committee of the Central Political Bureau meeting the press on November 15, 2012 that "our people's expectation for a better life is our goal". Social governance involves all aspects of people's life. The concept, approaches, capacity and effect of social governance will determine social stability and order, the vitality of social development, the resolution of social contradictions, the provision of public services, and public security, all of which are closely related to people's happiness. Since the reform and opening up, the CPC has led all ethnic groups to make unremitting efforts to build a moderately prosperous society in all respects and achieved great progress in social development focusing on people's wellbeing, and rapid development in social public services. However, its social governance capacity needs further improvement. To sum up, innovating and improving the Party's social governance leadership and capacity bears on the realization of its ruling goals.

Social governance bears on the consolidation of the Party's ruling foundation. The ruling foundation of the CPC, based on public's support, is embodied in its role as the vanguard of the working class and Xi Jinping pointed out that "we have always been and will always be obligated to do everything for the public, rely on them in every task, carry out the principle of 'from the public, to the public, and translate its correct views into action by the public of their own accord and follow the mass line in its work".[1]

---

[1] Xi Jinping, Speech at the Symposium to Commemorate the 120th Anniversary of Mao Zedong's Birth.

Generally speaking, China's social governance has synchronized with social development since the reform and opening up. However, in the new historical period, especially after the establishment of the socialist market economy system, the CPC's ruling foundation has undergone and will continue to undergo major changes due to the coexistence of different economic sectors and the complexity and diversification of the social structure. In the meantime, profound changes have taken place in the scope, content, objects, and external environment of social governance. The traditional governance approach is incompatible with the new social environment, so some contradictions emerge quickly, and various mass incidents including petitions occur frequently. Therefore, the government must innovate its social governance and coordinate the interests among all social groups. Otherwise, the ruling foundation of the Party will be weakened or even be undermined.

Social governance directly reflects the ruling capacity of the Party. The Third Plenary Session of the 18th CPC Central Committee proposed the overall goal of accelerating the modernization of the national governance system and capacity, reflecting the Party's new understanding of the development laws of the socialist cause and national governance, and it is the intrinsic requirements for strengthening the CPC's governance capacity. Social governance is one of the major tasks of the social construction and a major part of national governance. The quality of social governance reflects the governance level, the leadership and ruling capacity of the Party. In the new era, to strengthen and improve the Party's governance capability, we must meet the essential requirement of the Party's commitment to serving the public good and exercising power in the interests of the people, fully respect the law of social development and safeguard people's interests. Efforts should also be made to correctly handle current social contradictions, constantly improve social fairness and justice, and create a stable and orderly social environment. These major practical issues are major tests for the Party's ruling capacity. We should further improve the Party's leadership over social governance, and accelerate the reform of the social governance system, to improve the Party's governance capacity scientifically, democratically and in accordance with law.

2.1.2 History of social governance under the leadership of the CPC

As the ruling Party after the founding of the People's Republic of China (PRC), the CPC has been deepening its understanding of the law of social development and governance, and improving its theory and practice in social development and governance.

In different historical periods and backgrounds, the CPC has actively explored the rules of social development, innovated social administration, improved people's lives, and maintained social harmony and stability.

The social administration led by the Party before the reform and opening up. On September 30, 1949, in the declaration Long Live the Great Unity of the Chinese People, Mao Zedong called on the compatriots across the country to "further organize" the whole society. In the early days of the People's Republic of China, the primary tasks for the CPC were to consolidate the new power and transform the old social structure, learn from the experience and practices of the socialist construction of the Soviet Union, completely monopolize economy and social resources, and control the society in an all-round way. Social members were planned to be allocated in a fixed social space. Individuals interacted with each other in an organizational system demanding obedience. People's social life (food, clothing, housing, transportation, birth, aging, illness, death, etc.) was supported and supplied by the state. Institutionalization, the people's commune system, the household registration system, the class stratification system and the highly unified ideology were the foundation for the basic institutional arrangements in this period. Under this national and social framework, social development was affiliated to the political power of a country, thus forming a unique social governance model in China.

The social administration led by the Party after the reform and opening up. The Third Plenary Session of the 11th CPC Central Committee opened a new chapter for starting the great historical journey of reform and opening up, which has become a key choice to determine the future of contemporary China. The CPC has taken as its work focus exploring the socialist modernization with Chinese characteristics. "We should carry out reform in those aspects and links of the production relations and the superstructure that do not conform to the development of the productive forces and transform ways of management, activities and thinking that do not catch up with times."[1] During this period, economic construction was prioritized as the main focus of the Party and the government in their work, which served economic construction. In the process of market-oriented reform, the policies of management and control were gradually loosened. At that time, the Party did not take the exploration of social administration system into the key area of reformation, and social development was subordinate to

---

[1] Party Literature Research Center of the CPC Central Committee, *Selected Key Documents Since the Third Plenary Session of the 11th CPC National Congress,* Vol. Ⅰ, Beijing: People's Publishing House, 1982.

economic development. So social administration system reform was not included in government's primary works. With administrative interventions, the government mainly takes management and control as its social administration approaches. However, the market-oriented reform also had a profound impact on the Party's strategic ideas and major decisions on social construction, which had invisibly promoted the reform of the social administration system. The government has begun to pay attention to the quality and efficiency of public services. Non-governmental organizations have also developed rapidly.

Strengthening and innovating the Party's leadership over social administration. After the 16th CPC National Congress, in line with the development and changes of national and international situations, the CPC has seized the strategic opportunity period, implemented scientific development and promoted social harmony, improved the social market economic system, incorporated social construction into the overall layout of the cause of socialism with Chinese characteristics, and established a socialist social administration system with Chinese characteristics. In 2002, the requirement of "enhancing social harmony" was put forward in the report to the 16th CPC National Congress for the first time, emphasizing "management being implemented in services, and services being reflected in management", thus equating importance of social administration and social services. The Fourth Plenary Session of the 16th CPC Central Committee in 2004 emphasized that "we should adapt to the profound changes in our society, put the construction of a harmonious society in an important position, pay attention to stimulating social vitality, promote social fairness and justice, enhance the legal awareness and integrity awareness of the whole society, and maintain social stability and unity", and proposed "strengthening social construction and management, and promoting the innovation of social administration system". In 2006, the Decision of the CPC Central Committee on Several Major Issues Concerning the Construction of a Harmonious Socialist Society was passed at the Sixth Plenary Session of the 16th CPC Central Committee, which further confirmed "the law-based social administration model under which Party committees exercise leadership, government assumes responsibility, non-governmental actors provide assistance, and the public get involved", and establish a social governance model constructed, governed and shared by all the people. The Report to the 17th CPC National Congress in 2007 first included the concept of "social construction" in the overall layout of the cause of socialism with Chinese characteristics, and proposed the concept of "accelerating social construction with the focus on improving people's wellbeing". In 2012, the 18th CPC National Congress incorporated the "rule of law" into the social administration system with Chinese characteristics.

The birth of the concept of social governance. The Decision of the CPC Central Committee on Some Major Issues Concerning Comprehensively Deepening the Reform was passed at the Third Plenary Session of the 18th CPC Central Committee in 2013. For the first time, the concept of "innovating the social governance system" was proposed, emphasizing that "we must focus on safeguarding the fundamental interests of the overwhelming majority of the people, maximizing the factors of harmony, enhancing the vitality of social development, and improving social governance quality". The shift from "social administration" to "social governance" represents the great transformation and sublimation of the ruling ideas of the CPC.

2.1.3 Challenges in social governance under the leadership of the CPC

At the beginning of the 21st century, the ruling environment of the Party underwent profound changes. Contemporary China not only enjoys a period of important development opportunities, but also faces a period of multiple social contradictions, leading to ever more arduous task of social governance under the leadership of the CPC. At present, problems still exist in social governance, such as vague understanding of governance ideas, inefficiency of governance system and mechanism, and insufficient governance capacity of the government, etc. We need to make innovations in social governance system and improve governing methods based on problems and needs.

The concept of social governance was put forward at the Third Plenary Session of the 18th CPC Central Committee, which reflects the transformation and renewal of the Party's ruling ideology. Due to the lack of diversified actors highlighted by social governance and absence of social forces, social governance cannot adapt to the new changes of the era, nor meet the new expectations of the majority of the people. In practice, especially in the social governance of primary-level streets (towns) and communities, the ideology of maintaining stability and control still prevails, awareness of social service does not suffice, the foundation of social self-governance is weak, and the vitality of social development is low.

Like what the Party does in economic reformation, it should do the same in social governance reformation to improve the top-level design, initiate social policy reform, advocate the idea of "crossing the river by feeling the stones", carry out the pilot projects for comprehensive social reform, and constantly improve and innovate the concepts, systems, means and methods of social governance.

Talent is a key factor for the modernization of social governance capacity, where the essence lies in improving the governance capacity of leading officials and talents for the primary-level governance. At present, leading officials at all levels can not adapt themselves to the current social governance situation. On the one hand, officials' governance concept needs be improved, because their outlook on power is not updated. As a result, they are reluctant to streamline administration and delegate power. On the other hand, officials are used to solving social problems via top-down management, rather than through laws and public participation. At the same time, they are inexperienced in dealing with complex social problems and short of methods and mechanisms in responding to emergencies. The governance capacity at primary level does not suit the current social situation. The urban and rural "Two Committees" (the Party branch committee and residents committee) tend to be weak in governance capacity. It is important and urgent to cultivate more social governance talents for accelerating the modernization of social governance capacity.

2.1.4 Work system of social governance under the leadership of the CPC

Constitution of the Communist Party of China stipulates that "The Party must, acting on the principle of guiding the overall situation and coordinating the work of all sides, assume the role of leadership core among all other organizations at the corresponding levels." The concept of "guiding the overall situation and coordinating the work of all sides" serves not only as the embodiment of the Party's core role in leadership, but also as an important way for the Party to lead social governance. To innovate the social governance system and improve governance capacity, we should institutionalize the Party's core leadership and Party committee's leadership in social governance.

Strengthening the Party committee's leadership system in social governance. The leadership of the Party committees over social governance is mainly reflected in their clear institutional responsibilities at all levels in social construction and social governance. As the central government puts more weights on social construction and social administration innovation, all localities have fresh experiences and practical models of social construction and management that are in line with national and local conditions, thus continuously enriching and developing social construction with Chinese characteristics. For example, provinces and cities, like Beijing, Shanghai, Guangdong, Nanjing, Guiyang, Daqing, have improved the Party committee's leadership of social construction and social administration innovation by establishing working organs. Beijing, Shanghai and Guangdong are most typical examples. Shanghai takes the lead. In August 2003, the Party committee for social work was set up to promote social progress in line with the Party development of "two new" organizations (new economic organization and new social organization). Beijing's effort is believed to be most comprehensive and systematic. In December 2007, the Municipal Committee of Social Work and the Municipal Office of Social Construction were set up, and the Social Construction Leading Group and its office were set up the next year. To meet the requirements of the Five-sphere Integrated Plan to promote socialism with Chinese characteristics encompassing economic, political, cultural, social, and ecological development, the social construction of Beijing was designed and promoted in a systematic and all-round way. Since the provincial Social Work Committee was established in August 2011, Guangdong has made great efforts to promote the reform of social system by taking the advantage of separating the government from social organizations and transferring government functions.

Improving the working mechanism of social governance led by the Party committee. Efficient and smooth working mechanism is an important foundation and guarantee for social governance led by the Party. In recent years, various localities have established corresponding working mechanisms based on leading organs' responsibilities. For example, Beijing has comprehensively innovated the leadership system and working mechanism of social governance, and constructed a three-level social governance leading working mechanism of "upper, middle, and basic levels". For the upper level, the social construction leading group, responsible for overall planning, is headed by the main leaders of the municipal Party committee and the government; for the "middle" level, the municipal and district social work committees and social affairs offices take the lead in coordination; while for "basic" level, the intricate network has been established to cover sub-districts and "new economic organizations and new social organizations" for implementation. At the same time, Party committees of social work have been set up in sub-districts (townships), thus forming a regional pattern of Party development; the management of community service is deepened, establishing a three-sphere integrated governance mechanism of community Party development, community self-governance and community services. A "hub" work system is built, forming a classified and hierarchical service management pattern of social organizations. "Five stations" (Party development workstation, social workstation, trade union workstation, Youth League workstation and women's federation workstation) are established in all commercial areas to create an all-round governance pattern and social governance working mechanism covering communities and "two new" organizations.

Consolidating rule of law for social governance under the leadership of the Party committee. As an ancient philosopher put it, "No country is permanently strong, nor is any country permanently weak. If conformers to laws are strong, the country is strong; if conformers to laws are weak, the country is weak." Xi Jinping emphasized in the Report to the 19th CPC National Congress that we must commit to the organic unity of Party leadership, the people running the country and law-based governance, and put the Party's leadership into the whole process of law-based governance. To speed up the modernization of the social governance system and governance capacity, we must continue to improve social construction and social governance policies and institutional innovation, so as to form a strong system for legal protection. A case in point is the exploration and practice by Beijing, where a three-level "tower-shaped" policy system has taken shape for social construction and governance. The "top" is the programmatic document to coordinate the city's social construction, including the "program" for social construction, social governance planning, etc., the "middle" is the special documents in all fields of the "six major systems" of social construction; for "basic level", there are special supporting policy documents and management measures, etc. Centered on these three levels, Beijing has issued nearly 100 policy documents on social construction and social governance, which are being transformed into legalization.

2.2 Implementing government's responsibility and innovating administration mechanism

The government takes main responsibilities in social administration and plays a leading role in national and social affairs. As one of the basic functions of the government, sound social administration can maintain social fairness and justice, enhance people's well-being, resolve social contradictions and maintain social stability. With the deepening of reform and opening up, profound changes have taken place in the economic system, social structure, interest pattern, and ideology. The government has assumed an increasingly heavier task of fulfilling its social administration responsibilities. The government is required to fulfill its responsibility for social administration and continuously promote the reform of social administration system and improve the way of social governance, mobilize the whole society to form a governance pattern with diversified participants.

2.2.1   Social administration: an important part of government functions

Social administration, with promoting social harmony as its core, regulates social behaviors, coordinates social relations, promotes social identity, upholds social justice, solves social problems, resolves social conflicts, maintains social order, and copes with social risks under the guidance of the government and participated by various parties. It creates an orderly and vital basic operating condition and social environment for the survival and development of the human society.[1] It can be seen that fully implementing social administration functions is necessary to strengthen the government's self-construction and build a service-oriented government. It is of great significance to ensure stable social order, promote social equity and justice, and realize people's peace and contentment in work and lives.

Sound social administration helps to ensure social stability. The development of a country is inseparable from its social stability and order. China's national conditions determine government's leading role in social administration. Contemporary China is not only developing in an important period of strategic opportunities, but also in a period of prominent social conflicts. There are increasing factors affecting social stability, such as the insufficient supply of public services, accelerated urban-rural mobility, widening income gap, increasing interest demands, frequent mass incidents, and increasing social risks, etc. If effective social administration is absent, China will lack a stable and favorable environment on the road to modernization. Therefore, if the government wants to effectively perform its social administration functions, it should, aiming at real problems, accelerate the innovation of social administration systems and mechanisms, actively resolve social conflicts, and prevent social risks, in an aim to build a governance pattern of joint contribution and sharing by all the people, and ensure that its functions, work and responsibilities are in place.

Sound social administration is conducive to promoting social equity and justice. Confucius proposed that "a nation or a family does not worry about scarcity or poverty, but inequality or instability, as fairness relieves poverty, harmony covers scarcity, and peace alleviates peril". Fairness and justice are central to the development and stability of modern societies. Fairness and justice mean that the interests of all social sectors are properly coordinated, contradictions among the people and other social contradictions

---

[1] Ma Kai, "Striving to Strengthen and Innovate Social Administration", *Qiushi*, Oct. 16, 2010.

are properly handled, and social fairness and justice are effectively maintained and realized. Therefore, to perform social administration functions, the government should formulate social policies to safeguard social fairness and justice and take the fundamental interests of the overwhelming majority of the people as the basic focus in formulating and implementing the Party's principles and policies. The government should take into account the interests of different social strata and groups. In accordance with the law, we should gradually establish a social equity guarantee system featuring fairness in rights, opportunities, rules and distribution, so that fairness and justice can be embodied in the purposes, opportunities, processes and results of people's activities, thus allowing all people to share the fruits of reform and progress towards common prosperity through joint development.

Sound social administration is conducive to stimulating the vitality of social development. One of the goals of strengthening and innovating social administration is to build a society with vitality. Government dominance does not mean that the government is in charge of everything, but rather the government, the market and the society should develop in a coordinated and balanced way. Otherwise, enthusiasm will be absent in the society. Since the 18th CPC National Congress, the central and local governments have comprehensively strengthened innovation in social administration, accelerated the reform of the social system, and made it clear that they will speed up the formation of a modern social organization system featuring separation of government administration from social organizations, clear powers and responsibilities, and law-based self-governance. The government management functions in promoting the development of social organizations. With the deepening of reform in social organization management, the government itself has been reformed and its public service approaches have been innovated. Meanwhile, it is conducive to reflecting social demands, resolving social contradictions, and creating more employment opportunities.

2.2.2 Changes of the government function in social administration

The social administration functions of the government must be improved with the development of the economy and society. Since the founding of the PRC, the development and changes of government functions show different characteristics and functional orientation in different stages and periods. The social administration functions transformed from "omnipotent government" to "administrative government" and then to the current "service-oriented government" under construction.

During the period between the founding of the PRC and the reform and opening up, the government played an omnipotent role. In the early days of the PRC, the country focused on consolidating political power and maintaining social order and stability. In that period, the national productivity was low, and the economy and society suffered havoc due to the long-term wars. In order to resume production and carry out economic and social construction as soon as possible, China followed the Soviet model to implement a highly centralized system. During this period, all social resources were produced and provided by the government. Political ruling was the main function of the government. The "state-society" power was centralized, while the state and the government monopolized all social resources. The government functions were all-inclusive and highly overlapped with those of the society. The government manages society mainly by strong control without effective governance and services. "The government rationally designs the order of social operation through planning and control, engages social activities and manages them to the end, and strives to bring the disorderly economic and social life into the scope of order through this plan with the minimum profit and losses and the best effect."[1]

During the period from the reform and opening up to 1992, the social administration of the government was subject to the economic administration. After the reform and opening up, the CPC Central Committee timely adjusted the national development strategy and central tasks, shifted the focus of work to economic construction, and the government paid more attention to economic management functions. In order to adapt to the new situation of economic construction, the administrative system reform with the transformation of government functions as the core was put on the agenda. In 1988, the institutional reform was proposed for the first time to transform government functions. Through the reform, the government agencies were streamlined, the intervention by the government of enterprises was reduced, and the government management of micro-economic activities was changed. However, the government public power did not loosen its control over the society, still dominating all social affairs. Although the government promoted the development of social undertakings such as education, healthcare, culture and sports and maintained social stability, its social administration mainly served economic development. "This kind of reform method has enabled China's management of economic affairs to be increasingly

---

[1] Ma Jingren, "The Administration of Chinese Government, Enterprises and Society in the Transitional Period: Decoding of Chinese Administration Problems", *Chinese Public Administration*, 1996(1).

mature. At the same time, it also leads to the serious lag of the reform of social administration departments".[1]

From 1993 to 2002, maintaining stability was one of the focuses of social administration for governments. In October 1992, The Report to the 14th CPC National Congress clearly proposed establishing a socialist market economic system as the reform goal. Since then, with the deepening of China's socialist market economic system, comprehensive social transformation commenced. In addition to the sustained growth of the country's economic aggregate, social contradictions and risks emerged such as the intensified social differentiation and the widening wealth gap. The idea of strengthening macro-control, comprehensive coordination and social administration was proposed at the Report on the Work of the Government 1994. The Report on the Work of the Government 2000 emphasized the idea of "building a sound social security system and maintaining social stability". During this period, the government strengthened the function of social administration and began to put more weight on the construction of social security system, with government's focus of social administration being on the comprehensive social security and the maintenance of social stability.

Since 2003, social construction has been accelerated comprehensively and social administration has been innovated through ensuring and improving people's wellbeing. With the development and improvement of the market economic system, unbalanced, uncoordinated and unsuited economic and social development has become increasingly noticeable. The government functions have gradually shifted from putting equal emphasis on economic development and social administration. The institutional reform of the State Council in 2003 clearly stated that the functions of the government should cover economic regulation, market supervision, social administration and public service, taking social administration as one of the basic functions of the government in a socialist market economy. In 2007, the 17th CPC National Congress proposed to accelerate six major tasks of social construction focusing on improving people's wellbeing, which shows that strengthening social administration has become a major strategic choice for our government to accelerate the transformation of functions and build a harmonious society. The Report on the Work of the Government 2011 proposed that the government should strengthen the social administration function, extensively mobilize and organize the public to participate in social administration according to law, make use of the

---

[1] "Government Social Management" Research Group, "Analysis of the Current Situation and Problems in Chinese Government's Social Administration", *Southeast Academic Research*, 2005(4).

positive role of social organizations, and improve the structure of social administration, in an aim to realize the effective connection and positive interaction between the government administration and the primary-level public self-governance. In 2012, the report to the 18th CPC National Congress further stressed the need to strengthen social construction in improving people's wellbeing and innovating management, accelerate the reform of social system, promote the science-based social administration, and strengthen the construction of laws, systems, mechanisms, capabilities, talent teams and informatization in social administration. The Third Plenary Session of the 18th CPC Central Committee in 2013 proposed the idea of social governance. The Report on the Work of the Government 2014 further proposed to promote the innovation of social governance and improve the methods of social governance. In short, during this period, the government put more emphasis on its function of social administration, by focusing on ensuring and improving people's wellbeing, and effectively promoting the development of social undertakings, so as to build a social governance model with diversified participants.

2.2.3 Achievements by the Chinese government in social administration

Since the founding of the PRC, the social administration functions of the government have evolved and gradually adapted to economic and social development. Especially since the reform and opening up, to adapt to the transformation from the planned economy to the socialist market economy, China has carried out a series of reforms on social administration system, by vigorously developing social undertakings, and innovating social administration methods, thus achieving remarkable results.

(1) *People's lives are constantly improving*

Before the reform and opening up, China's urban and rural residents were basically living in scarcity, with 250 million rural impoverished population. With 40 years of rapid economic development, residents' living standards and quality in urban and rural areas have improved significantly, and the wealth owned by the residents has increased rapidly. According to the classification standard released by the World Bank, China has leaped from a low-income country to a lower middle-income country in the world. In 2016, the per capita disposable income of Chinese residents was RMB23,821, the per capita disposable income of urban residents was RMB33,616, and the per capita disposable income of rural residents was RMB12,363.[1] Rapid economic growth

---

[1] National Bureau of Statistics, Statistical Bulletin on the National Economic and Social Development of the People's Republic of China for the Year 2016, http: //www. stats. gov.cn /tjsj/zxfb/201702/t20170228_7424.html.

synchronized with increase in employment, which reached 776.03 million by the end of 2016. At the same time, the urban and rural social security system has been gradually established and improved. A basic framework for a social security system has been put in place, including old-age pensions, medical insurance, unemployment insurance, work-related injury insurance and maternity insurance with widening coverage. As many as 972 million residents hold security cards as of 2016. The government's poverty alleviation work has achieved remarkable results. The impoverished population in Chinese rural areas has decreased from 98.99 million in 2012 to 43.35 million in 2016.

(2) *Social undertakings are booming*

After the reform and opening up, China's economic strength has been continuously enhanced, and the development of social undertakings has received great attention. Especially since the beginning of the 21st century, social undertakings have shown a tendency of accelerated development. Through reforming educational, medical, cultural and other institutions, the government has vigorously increased the supply of public goods and services, which has greatly met the growing needs of the general public in education, medical care and cultural life. Specifically, education has been popularized significantly, approaching the average level of education of middle-income countries. The nine-year compulsory education has been fully popularized; disparity between urban and rural education development has been effectively shortened. The national financial budget on education has continued to increase, reaching a total of RMB3,137.3 billion in 2016.[1] In terms of the medical and healthcare sector, the construction of the public healthcare service system has been continuously strengthened. By the end of July 2016, a total of 990,000 medical and healthcare institutions and 928,000 primary medical and healthcare institutions have been established. The average life expectancy of residents has increased from 67.8 years in 1981 to 76.3 years in 2016.

(3) *Social administration is continuously innovated*

The evolution and development of the government's functions of social administration attract the central and local governments' increasing attention. The transformation of the government function is speeding up, together with a deepening reform of the administrative system, a changing concept of social administration, and a better relationship between the government and the society. Efforts are made to strengthen innovation in public services and social administration, protect public's

---

[1] Xinhua Net, National Fiscal Expenditure on Education Exceeds RMB3 Trillion for the First Time in 2016, http://www.xinhuanet.com/politics/2017-10/25/c_1121855952.htm.

legitimate rights and interests, as well as prevent and resolve social contradictions. To strengthen the innovation of social administration at primary level in urban and rural areas and give full play to the functions of urban and rural communities, Beijing, Shanghai, Guangdong and other places have shifted the focus of social administration to villages and communities. Efforts are made to establish corresponding daily system norms and operation mechanisms, and eliminate a large number of social contradictions at the primary level from the source, thus effectively maintaining social and political stability and promoting the construction of a harmonious society. We should build and improve the management system of modern social organizations, by vigorously cultivating and developing social organizations, and giving full play to the role of social organizations in social administration, so that they will become an important force to stabilize and serve the society.

2.2.4   Deepening system reform in social administration

With modernization speeding forward, profound changes have taken place in all fields of the economy and society in China, and more and more people have changed from "*Danwei man*"[1] to "*Shehui man*"[2]. With an increasingly complex interest structure and diversified needs of the masses, the rapid changes of society have resulted in the complexity and difficulty of social administration; the government's perception, function, system and mode of social administration are lagging behind and incompatible with social development. It is necessary to further straighten out the relationship between government and society, develop the social governance system, innovate the idea and mode of social administration, perfect the system and mechanism of social administration, and improve the ability and level of the government's social administration.

(1) *Innovating the idea of social administration*

The key to the innovation of social administration lies in the innovation of ideas. To transform traditional idea of social administration and establish the social administration ideas of social standards, common governance, limited government and

---

[1] "*Danwei man*" means individuals who worked for the national enterprises for their lifetime during the planned economy period. They received low wages but high benefits. Danwei was obliged to supply a full set of facilities including housing, schools, canteen and medical care, etc. —*Tr.*

[2] "*Shehui Man*" means individuals who can switch jobs now and then in the market economy period. They earn high wages but receive low benefits. The facilities including housing, schools, canteen and medical care, etc., are not for them, and people need to pay for these services. —*Tr.*

service-oriented government, it is inevitable to speed up the reform of the government system, clarify the functional orientation of the government, and answer the questions of what to manage and how to manage. Therefore, we must establish the philosophy of "put people and services first, coordinated management and law-based administration", uphold people's principal position in China, and always take ensuring and improving people's wellbeing as our immutable goal. Efforts should also be made to actively guide the people to participate in social administration in an orderly manner according to law, let go of the management-over-service mindset, and properly tackle housing, education, medical care, employment and other livelihood issues, so as to achieve the organic unity of management and service. At the same time, the government should strengthen social administration in accordance with the law, make better use of legal thinking and legal means to coordinate social relations, regulate social behavior, resolve social contradictions, and maintain social stability, so as to ensure that laws are fully observed and strictly enforced.

(2) *Improving the method of social administration*

The way of social administration is an umbrella term for the indispensable methods, means and skills adopted by the government and its civil servants in order to implement administration ideas, perform administration functions, improve administration efficiency and achieve administration objectives.[1] At present, the Chinese government implements a top-down administration, where the government imposes strict administrative control on the society. The Third Plenary Session of the 18th CPC Central Committee proposed to improve governance with complete laws and regulations, systematic and comprehensive measures and an emphasis on addressing the root causes of issues. It is necessary to straighten out the relationship between the government and the society, accelerate function transformation of the government, strive to construct a service-oriented government, encourage all the parties of the society to participate and increase self-governance of residents in urban and rural communities, so that government's governance efforts on the one hand and society's self-regulation and residents' self-governance on the other will reinforce each other. Chaoyang District of Beijing has greatly improved the efficiency of primary-level social administration by exploring the approach to innovate community-level social administration, carrying out coordinated projects by the Party, the government and the public, setting up information platform to

---

[1] Sheng Meijuan, "The Study on China's Social Transition and the Innovation of Its Social Administration Modes", *Lanzhou Academic Journal*, 2008 (12): 77-80.

"consult the people on governance, learn about their needs and seek their advice" and organizing government, urban and rural communities, enterprises, social organizations, residents (villages) and other participants to work together on community-level service administration affairs.

(3) *Improving the mechanism for social administration*

The primary purpose of the government to conduct social administration is to tackle issues of the most direct and practical interests that people are most concerned about. The core task lies in the improvement of the mechanism led by the Party and government for safeguarding the rights and interests of the public, as well as the formation of scientific and effective mechanisms to coordinate interests among different parties, express interest demands, resolve interest disputes, protect the rights and assess the risks. With these mechanisms, we can coordinate the interest relations among all parties and strengthen the source governance of social contradictions so that the legitimate rights and interests of the masses are effectively safeguarded. In addition, we should strengthen the construction of public security system to establish a system of social security prevention and control, production safety, food and drug safety, disaster prevention and relief, and emergency management, which combines active prevention and control with emergency disposal, as well as traditional methods with modern means.

2.3   Promoting social synergy and stimulating vitality in development

Social synergy refers to the harmonious relationship and cooperative actions of mutual support between different groups in the society.[1] It is proposed in the Third Plenary Session of the 18th CPC Central Committee that the overall goal of comprehensively deepening the reform is to achieve the modernization of the national governance system and capacity and that we should innovate and improve social governance. Social synergy is an important support of the social governance system, and plays a critical role in the construction of social governance system and capacity. To realize "good governance" requires concerted participation by all social forces, giving full play to the role of people's organizations, social organizations and the public composed of workers, youths, and women in social administration, the establishment of

---

[1] Zhu Li, Ge Liang, "Innovative Social Governance Research: Social Collaboration as Great Innovation of Social Administration", *Social Science Research*, 2013(5): 1-7.

an effective collaborative governance mechanism, and the full stimulation of the vitality of social development.

2.3.1 Social synergy: an innovative change in social administration

Since the reform and opening up, China has adjusted the relationship between the government and the market as well as between the government and society under the leadership of the CPC. With the transformation of government's functions and reform in social system, all the participants, not only administered by the government, begin to regulate themselves and become partners in government governance. They are taking more responsibilities in social service management including public service, community construction, charity, environmental protection, social stability and conflict resolution.

(1) *Social synergy is the intrinsic requirement for improving social administration system*

Since the founding of the PRC, the reform of China's social administration system has undergone a long historical evolution. Along with the requirements of economic and social development, the social administration system under the Party's leadership has been constantly improved in practice, gradually changing from a highly centralized social control system to a modern social administration model with diversified participants, realizing the transformation from Party-government integration to the law-based social governance system led by Party committees, implemented by the government, based on social coordination, public participation and the rule of law. To improve the social administration system, it is necessary to give full play to the collaborative role of social organizations, establish a social synergy network that effectively interacts with and complements the social administration functions and forces of the government, and gradually change the traditional mode of "strong government and weak society".

(2) *Social synergy is an inevitable choice to strengthen and innovate social administration*

Under planned economy, the traditional social administration means the Party and the government administering public social affairs. Due to the underdevelopment of various social players, social forces are extremely weak, with the government being in charge of everything and highly depended by the whole society. In the market economy, especially since the 1990s, China's social structure has been changing constantly; various interest gainers and their demands are increasingly diversified; social contradictions and risks are gradually increasing, and the traditional single social administration mode dominated by the government was unsuited to new problems and new situations. It is urgent to make up the inadequacy of social organizations and public participation ideologically and systematically. To modernize governance, we must give full play to the synergistic and complementary roles of the Party committee, government, market and society in social administration, embodying the philosophy and ideas of multi-party participation and common governance, and realize the transformation from comprehensive government administration to cooperative governance by government, society and citizens.

(3) *Social synergy is an effective approach to improve social administration*

The construction of a cooperative society should be a conscious social reform.[1] Modern social governance attaches more importance to the cooperative governance of society, featuring diversity, equality, coordination and order of governance participants. Social synergy reflects the transformation of government dominance to diversified participation, and realizes the organic combination of top-down government departments and bottom-up social fields. On the one hand, the government withdraws from where it does not administer well or where it should not administer, and strives to build a service-oriented government that the people are satisfied with. On the other hand, the society carries out self-organization and self-management of public social affairs during its growth. At the same time, social synergy also further strengthens the public spirit and citizen identity, mobilizes all social parties to participate in social administration more actively and effectively, gives play to the role of multiple participants, and shifts from the traditional administration mode to the "good governance" mode which is adapted to the times.

2.3.2 Promoting social synergy among diversified participants

Social synergy is an important part of the social governance mechanism. To fully realize the role of social synergy, communities, social organizations and the public must get involved in social administration under the guidance and with the mobilization of the Party committee and the government. They make full use of their resources to participate in improving people's livelihood, public services and social administration. Social synergy not only emphasizes the leading role of the government as well as mobilization and integration of social resources, but also lays stress on the role of social multi-subjects in social affairs.

(1) *The government is the leading force of social synergy*

The government is the major subject to promote social synergy. In order to give

---

[1] Zhang Kangzhi, *Towards a Collaborative Society*, Beijing: China Renmin University Press, 2015.

full play to the role of the government in social synergy while innovating social governance, we must first coordinate the relationship between governmental and non-governmental actors, with the former assuming responsibility and the latter providing assistance. Under the leadership of the Party, the government, which plays a leading role, is the key to the new social administration system. Similarly, among the multiple participation of social synergy, the government also needs to continuously promote the realization of social collaborative governance as a leader, an organizer, a supporter and a regulator, so as to maximize the overall interests of the society. In the process of social governance with the participation of non-governmental actors, the government, through the formulation of social policies and laws and regulations, provides a necessary institutional environment for market players, social organizations, communities and the public to participate in social governance, through which the government vigorously cultivates and guides social organizations. By allocating social public resources, the government then guides, serves and manages social organizations, realizing its functions in coordination.

(2) *Social organization is the foundation of social synergy*

The self-administration of society relies on social organizations, whose emergence and development is a major change in China since the reform and opening up. They play an indispensable role in China's national political, economic, cultural and social activities. They are becoming an important force in national governance. By the end of 2015, there were 662,000 social organizations nationwide, increasing by 9.2% over the year before. These organizations provided 7.348 million jobs, up 7.7% from a year earlier. They generated a total annual income of RMB292.9 billion, while spending RMB238.38 billion, accumulating fixed assets of RMB231.11 billion, and receiving RMB61.03 billion of donations.[1] Social synergy by nature is to give full play to social organizations in the management of social services. The positive roles of social organizations are mainly manifested as the complementary role that provides social services for market failure; the role as a bridge between government and the society in social administration; the role as a safety valve as they represent the public demands and maintain social stability; the role as a reservoir since they organize public welfare charity and pool social resources.[2] It is precisely because social organizations act as

---

[1] Ministry of Civil Affairs of People's Republic of China, Statistical Bulletin on the Social Services Development of the People's Republic of China for the Year 2014.

[2] Zhou Aiping, "The Role of Community Social Organizations in Social Governance Innovation: A Case Study of Nanhai, Guangdong", *The Journal of Yunnan Administration College*, 2014(3): 96-99.

"generalists" in social governance that the government actively guides social organizations to participate in social governance, increasing its support and cultivation. All kinds of social organizations have sprung up, playing an irreplaceable role in integrating social resources, undertaking the government's function transfer, providing diversified social services, preventing and resolving conflicts and disputes, collecting public opinions, reflecting public sentiment, and maintaining social fairness and justice.

(3) *Grassroots self-governing organizations are an important force in social synergy*

Self-governing organizations like community committees, villagers' committees, house owners' committees and social organizations in community are the most grassroots organizations directly connected with the public. They are organized in their living areas by locals according to their own will to manage their own affairs. As an important part of social synergy, grassroots self-governing organizations get deeply involved in grassroots public services through self-management, self-education, self-supervision and self-service. They not only effectively make up for where the Party committee falls short and the market malfunctions, improve the quality and efficiency of public services, but also greatly stimulate the vitality of the society, thus becoming powerful supplements for the function of the Party and the government and promoting the innovation of social governance. Meanwhile, these organizations have gathered scattered individuals to jointly handle the common social affairs, so as to achieve social self-governance. They play an important role in spreading and promoting the implementation of the policies issued by the Party and the government, advocating the healthy development of grassroots democracy, solving practical difficulties and problems, resolving conflicts and disputes, and maintaining social harmony and stability.

2.3.3 Challenges in enhancing social synergy

As the Party puts more emphasis on social construction and social administration in an era of deepening economic system reform and government function transformation, the vitality of social development has been further unleashed, the room for social organizations' development has expanded, and these organizations have been fully utilized. However, due to insufficient self-construction and institutional guarantee, social organizations still face many challenges in social synergy.

(1) *The transformation of government functions is not thorough*

Such a transformation is the premise to straighten out the relationship between government and society and clarify their demarcation, which can fundamentally promote social governance innovation. "The market economy requires the modern government to switch its role from the political ruler to the manager of social public affairs, and requires it to transform from maintaining political governance to fully performing social public management in its government functions."[1] Since the reform and opening up, China has made significant progress in administrative system reform and sped up the pace of building a service-oriented government. Nevertheless, shackle of traditional management philosophy and impact of traditional model and institutional inertia lead to disparities between the government and its social administration functions. Problems still exist such as incomplete transformation of government functions, the government's overstepping border, mismatch of government functions, absence of the government in providing public services and low capacity of social administration and public service. Furthermore, there also exist unreasonable structure of the administrative organizations, vague definition of administrative responsibilities, the discrepancy between powers and responsibilities and buck-passing, the inadequate construction of legal government and delayed disclosure of governmental affairs, and failure to meet people's demands. The oversight and restriction mechanism of administrative power still needs to be improved.

(2) *The inadequacy of participants in social synergy*

The people's organizations, community-level self-governing organizations, industry organizations, social groups, social service institutions, voluntary service organizations are the important participants in social synergy. In recent years, various social organizations in China have developed rapidly, with 662,000 organizations by the end of 2015. However, compared with developed countries, Chinese social organizations are still in their infancy and face many problems. As far as social organizations properly are concerned, there are problems like limited scale, difficulty in raising funds, lack of competitiveness and professional personnel, non-standardized operation, weak self-discipline among the industries, imperfect internal structure and tendency of social organizations becoming quasi-government institutions. Besides, blockaded by the governmental management system, social organizations are barred by imperfect policies and regulations, underdeveloped management system, weak government supervision, etc., which to some extent hinder social organizations' participation in social service management affairs and weaken the foundation of social synergy.

---

[1] Su Jiayi, Chen Yu, "The Analysis of Government's Social Governance Functions in a Harmonious Society", *Red Flag Manuscript*, 2006(5): 10-12.

(3) *The mechanism of social synergy remains to be perfected*

It has been an urgent task for various participants to realize social synergy, effectively integrate scattered functions and leverage their strength, and work together to achieve synergy among various systems, departments, and strata in the governance of social affairs. The specific implementation mechanism is a must for the realization of social synergy.[1] However, the current theoretical research and practical exploration of social synergy mechanisms are relatively underdeveloped. The information-sharing mechanism, service undertaking mechanism, responsibility-sharing mechanism, supervision and evaluation mechanism have not been established, which affects the improvement of the social administration structure and the effective performance of social synergy functions. Additionally, social organizations, still in their inception, are low in their capacity and credibility. Furthermore, the government is still cautious about the development of social organizations. Lack of cultivation of social administration subjects' construction results in the incompetence of these subjects when participating in social administration.

2.3.4 Approaches to promoting social synergy

The purpose of social synergy is to actively mobilize all positive factors and forces to jointly govern the society; the core is to improve the scale of social participation; and the key is to figure out appropriate approaches and modes, which are also the preconditions for achieving a good social governance.

(1) *Vigorously cultivate the public spirit of the society*

Public spirit refers to citizens' active participation in public affairs, recognition of basic social values, and maintenance of public norms. It is not only a virtue of the public, but also a kind of social capital. A strong sense of public spirit can lay a good foundation for the development of democratic politics, which will, in turn, provide favorable conditions for public spirit.[2] Cultivating public spirit based on public interest is an important cornerstone for social synergy and conducive to improving citizens' sense of public responsibility and enhancing the spirit of mutual benefit and cooperation of multiple social subjects. Therefore, we should respect people's principal position, give full play to their initiative spirit, cultivate the public's awareness of their responsibility

---

[1] Shao Jingye, Lai Limei, "The Construction of a Social Collaboration Mechanism in the Innovation of Social Governance Systems", *Journal of Northeast Normal University (Philosophy and Social Sciences Edition)*, 2014(1): 204-206.

[2] Zhang Yang, "Rational Guidance of Civic Spirit", *People's Daily*, Jul. 18, 2012.

and the law, and enhance their willingness to participate in social governance. At the same time, a social community is highly required in social service management for guiding social subjects to form subjective awareness, legal awareness, sense of responsibility and rule awareness, hence, formulating a public spirit with a broad sense of identity. For example, the booming community academies in Xiamen, Fujian Province, have integrated many original cultural activity spaces and resources. After a period of learning and consultation, these academies not only incubated social organizations conducive to community level self-governance, but also cultivated the common spirit of the community, becoming a new platform for exploring the innovation of grassroots social governance.

(2) *Support various social organizations*

Social organizations, an important embodiment of the vigorous social development, are the indispensable participants in modern social governance. At present, social organizations cannot develop without the support and cultivation of the government. The government should give more freedom to social organizations through enabling policies, flexible management and all-around guarantee. Demarcation between government and society should first be clarified, where we need clear separation of the two to promote the transfer of government functions, improve the development environment of social organizations and improve the system for purchasing social services. By doing so, we create a good atmosphere for the growth of social organizations, fully protecting their legitimate rights and interests. Simultaneously, we should speed up the establishment of a modern system for social organizations with clear rights and responsibilities, and legitimate self-governance. Considering the current situation of social organizations, we should also reform the management system, lower the threshold for registration, and accelerate de-administration reform for trade associations and commerce organizations, etc. Moreover, the construction of self-governing organizations is expected to expand its scope and path for public participation. By building platforms for diversified participation, we shall enhance the function of social self-governance, and finally realize the active interaction in governance between the government and the public.

(3) *Improve mechanism of social synergy*

Efficient social coordination can integrate public resources for intensive and extensive participation in social organizations, and thus leverage their initiative and enthusiasm. Consequently, a sound interaction between social governance and social coordination can be set up. Information communication is the basis of social synergy.

The openness and transparency of information communication can not only make the interaction between the government and social participants smooth, but also guarantee the timely implementation of the government's policy, and feedback to public opinions. Improving the operating mechanism of social coordination is crucial to the realization of governance goals. By deepening the supply-side reform of social services and optimizing the ways in which all social sectors participate in service supply, we can see that numerous social forces interact and form joint forces and bring social organizations into the public service supply system in accordance with the law. To establish the supervision and evaluation mechanism of social coordination, we should not only strengthen government supervision by the means of laws, regulations and policies, but also actively encourage people to do mutual supervision. We should also strengthen the legal guarantee of social coordination and clarify responsibilities and rights of various participants in social coordination for a good institutional environment to promote social coordination.

2.4   Encouraging broad social participation and jointly contributing to shared benefit

Citizens are the foundation of the country and society. Public participation is an important trait of modern social governance, which requires effective participation and extensive support by the public. The Report to the 18th CPC National Congress proposed to "mobilize and organize as many people as possible to manage state and social affairs as well as the economy and cultural programs in accordance with the law and to devote themselves to socialist modernization." Public participation demonstrates people's principal position and their initiative in social governance. It breaks through the traditional social administration mode, promotes the innovation of social governance, and effectively reduces the cost of social governance as well as stimulates the vitality of society. By doing so, we can better achieve sound interaction between government's governance, and society's self-regulation and residents' self-governance.

2.4.1   Realistic significance of social governance with public participation

Social administration is to administer and serve people. The public is both the entity to be administered and the administer. With the deepening of the reform of the market economy system, Chinese society has entered a period of rapid transformation, with increasingly diversified and complex social interests. At the same time, the public is more aware of democratic participation, and is more eager to express their own demands and participate in the management of social public affairs. The public has gradually become an important force in modern social governance.

(1) *Public participation essentially demonstrates that the people are the masters of the country*

The people being the masters of the country constitutes the essential requirement of socialism. The Report to the 18th CPC National Congress stressed that "socialism with Chinese characteristics is a cause for the people in their hundreds of millions" and "we must maintain the people's principal position in the country". The majority of the people are the source of strength for social construction. Under the leadership of the CPC, public participation in social governance is to always maintain the people's principal position in the country, and give full play to the basic role of the people's participation, firmly establishing the governance concept of people-centered philosophy. In order to uphold the fundamental interests of the overwhelming majority of the people, we should ensure that the people exercise democratic election, decision-making, management and supervision in accordance with the law. And we should give full play to the principal role of the public in self-management, self-service, self-education and self-supervision.

(2) *Public participation is inherently required for joint contribution to shared benefits*

As the ancient Chinese sage said, "justice and fairness is the underpinning of a country", fairness and equity are the core of national governance and social development. With the deepening reform of the economic system, market competition results in allocation of social resources according to merits instead of in an average way, accompanied by accelerated splitting of social interests. As such, the diversification of interest subjects becomes the basic feature of the society in transition and public interest demands have also become diversified. In particular, the public has stronger demands for fairness and justice due to the gradually increasing gap between the rich and the poor. In recent years, accelerating the protection and improvement of people's wellbeing has become an ardent expectation of the people. Social security, income, medical reform, education equity, housing, environmental protection and other issues of great concern to people's wellbeing have become hot topics of discussion, stimulating public participation in public policy formulation and public affairs management. Social governance that welcomes public engagement can speed up the transformation of government functions and improve the running efficiency of society and ensure that the people can also better share the fruits of economic and social development and achieve social harmony and stability.

(3) *Public participation is an important way to stimulate the vitality of social development*

The people are the creators of history and the essential driving force for social development. "If you want a tree to grow taller, you must strengthen its roots; if you want the spring to flow far, you must dredge its source." The people have unlimited creativity, and their participation in social administration brings continuous vitality for social development. Especially against today's interests of different social groups, public participation has become an important basis for promoting social governance innovation in the new era. It has played an important role in community construction, conflict resolution, mutual assistance, charity, voluntary services, elderly care, and assistance to people with disability, and environmental protection. The rich experience has been a vital force for social development. At the same time, expanding public participation is also an important goal for deepening the reform of social governance system. It is of great significance to improve the way of social governance, cultivate the spirit of social tolerance and consultation, and shape citizens' subject awareness. It is greatly significant in meeting the interest needs of the majority of social members to rationally and legally express the interest demands, and promoting the coordinated development of social interest relations for the public. It is the inevitable path to stimulate the vitality of social development.

2.4.2   The past and present of public participation

The people are the creators of history. Mao Zedong once vividly described the people as "a true bastion of iron". The CPC attaches great importance to mobilizing the people to participate in both the revolutionary period and modernization period. It is fair to say that mobilizing the people and relying on them are the "heirlooms" of the CPC. In retrospect, the development history of the CPC is a history of public participation. In the context of the new era, mobilizing public participation remains a major task in social governance innovation.

In different historical periods, the people have played an important and pivotal role in national and social construction. Before the founding of the PRC, China was a semi-colonial and semi-feudal country. Oppressed by the imperialism, feudalism and bureaucrat-capitalism for a long time, the Chinese people were in great suffer. It was urgent for the people of all ethnic groups to completely break away from the old society, realize national independence, make the people the masters of the country, and make the country prosperous and strong. Under the leadership of the CPC, hundreds of millions of the Chinese people were involved in the revolutionary torrent of fighting against foreign invaders and reactionary forces. With 28 years of heroic fighting, we won the great victory of the New Democratic Revolution, opening a new page of the Chinese history.

From the founding of the PRC to the reform and opening up, the CPC, drawing on the Soviet model of the planned economic system, strove to change the backwardness of China before 1949, which was "poor" and "underdeveloped". The Party extensively mobilized the people to participate in socialist transformation and construction, and focused on restoring and developing economy. By highly "organizing" the people, the country mobilized the human and material resources. The people participated in various social construction activities by the means of social movements. As such, in the planned system period, political mobilization, in terms of the organization and mobilization mechanism of social construction, was the most powerful and effective driving force as every social construction was deployed as a political task, and every specific social development achievement demonstrated a strong political significance.[1] Top-down political mobilization has become the basic path for public participation.

Since the reform and opening up, the central work of the Party and the country has rapidly shifted from "the policy of taking class struggle as the key link" to the development of the national economy. Promoting economic development and unleashing and developing the productive forces have become the primary tasks of national construction. In the Third Plenary Session of the 14th CPC Central Committee, the Party proposed to "build a socialist market economy, with an income distribution system where distribution according to work is the mainstay, and efficiency is given priority to with due consideration to fairness. The Party encourages some areas and some people to become rich first and achieve common prosperity; establishes a multi-level social security system, provides social security for urban and rural residents that is appropriate to our national conditions, and promotes economic development and social stability." The establishment of market economy has completely broken the mono interest structure under planned economy. The diversified interest pattern has been formed with increasing competitive contradictions between interest subjects, and

---

[1] Lu Xueyi, *Sixty Years of Social Construction Development in Beijing*, Beijing: Science Press, 2008, p. 16.

changing interest gap. These changes promote the formation of public interest awareness and self-awareness, and provide the most direct drive for the public to participate in social governance, especially in the government's public policy decision-making.[1] In the 21st century, with the market-based drive, globalization, urbanization and informatization going forward, China's economic and social development has continued to undergo profound changes; many new situations and problems have emerged in the social field, making the government-led governance unsustainable. The role of "public participation" as an important component of the social governance in promoting the modernization of social governance system and governance capacity cannot be ignored.

At this stage, mobilizing the public to participate in social governance has become an important approach and way of innovation. It is playing an important role in public service, social assistance, public welfare, grassroots governance, urban management, environmental protection, etc. At present, as the fundamental support of social governance, public participation is still in the preliminary stage without corresponding system. Development plights still exist, such as weak subject awareness and responsibility awareness of public participation, and the relatively limited breadth and depth of public participation. Lack of corresponding system and legal support, the public cannot participate in social administration normally and systematically. The channel of public participation in social governance is not readily accessible, and the participation procedure is not standardized. Social organizations develop slowly while the public needs to be further organized to participate in social governance. These problems often lead to in-depth defects and formalism for public participation in practice, which greatly impacts public enthusiasm in participation and the effect of social governance.

2.4.3   Carriers and forms of social governance with public participation

Public participation is the source of power to develop new forms of social governance and stimulate social vitality. Since the reform and opening up, China's rapid economic and social development have provided rich soil for public participation. In the long-term practice and exploration, the carriers of public participation in social governance have been constantly multiplied with more flexible forms. "Many hands make light work". How to further play the initiative spirit of the people, improve the

---

[1] Song Yuping, "Public Participation in Social Governance: Foundations, Barriers, and Solutions", *Philosophical Research*, 2014(12): 90-93.

way of public participation, increase the channels of public participation, and improve the efficiency of public participation have become the urgent requirements of innovative social governance in the new era.

The self-management of residents in urban and rural areas is the basic form of public participation in social governance. Urban and rural communities are the common foundation for people's life. The sub-district (village) committee is an organization with self-management, self-education, self-supervision and self-service of residents. By the end of 2015, there were 681,000 community-level self-governing organizations. Self-governing organizations are of vital importance for realizing public participation in social governance, in which democratic election, decision-making, management and supervision are the basic ways for residents' participation. As the reform of the social governance system deepens, the Party committee and the government have fully exerted their leadership. Local governments have generally strengthened the community-level governance, and innovated the ways and methods, building a platform for residents' participation, which then fully mobilized the enthusiasm of residents and reinforced residents' self-management. After years of exploration, valuable experience has been accumulated. For example, the "Community Residents' Executive Meeting" has built up a platform in the community to reflect social situation and public opinions, discussing and negotiating, evaluating and supervising, which stated the dominant position of community residents and smoothed the expression channel of residents' demands. With the mode of "Community Multi-parties Consultation", a joint meeting system is established, which is composed of community Party organizations, neighborhood committees, house owners' committees, property companies and community-based organizations, through which they can jointly handle major community issues under the guideline of "coordination, consultation, collaboration and cooperation". To tackle the troubles in service management in old communities, communities organize and mobilize their residents to help each other, thus solving the problems herein. Matrix of urban communities facilitates the establishment of information service management platform and information channels to collect public opinions and create interactions with the public, enhancing the interaction between the government and society. In addition, many communities make full use of information network technology to improve the working methods of residents' committees, creating new information carriers such as community forum, community micro-blog, community WeChat official account, etc., which have greatly strengthened their communication with residents. Thus, residents' needs are better understood while the democratic self-governance function of residents' committees has gotten enhanced as well.

Social organizations act as significant channels for the public to act in social governance. As the important actors of social governance, social organizations can effectively implement the function of aggregating, contacting and communicating, reflecting and expressing the demands of the public. Meanwhile, they spread the message of the Party and the government to the public, acting as crucial platforms for the public's participation in social governance. Democratic election, decision-making and management within grassroots social organizations have not only improved the people's capacity to understand democratic rules, election procedures, self-organization and self-management, but also promoted them to safeguard their legitimate rights and interests by democratic means.[1] As of 2015, there were 329,000 social organizations, 4,784 foundations of various types, and 329,000 private non-enterprise organizations, employing 7.348 million people of all kinds. In addition, social organizations play an indispensable role in industrial and commercial services, social services, care for the elderly and disabled persons, scientific and technological education, poverty alleviation, charity and public welfare, and environmental protection, etc. As social organizations get more involved in social governance, they provide more paths for citizens to participate in social governance. With the help of social organizations, citizens not only transformed their ideas, enhanced their awareness of participation, but also improved their ability of participation and self-governing.[2] Social organizations are individualized, professionalized and socialized, so they can flexibly coordinate all social resources, encourage social workers and volunteers, and mobilize the public to act in social governance. These activities can meet people's need to participate in social public affairs and heighten the norms and efficiency for people's participation in the social governance.

People's organizations are the bridge between the Party and the public. They play an important role in mobilizing citizens to act in social governance. The 18th CPC National Congress proposed that we should support people's organizations such as trade unions, the Chinese Communist Youth League and women's federations in fully playing their roles as bridges linking the Party and government with the people, voicing public

---

[1] Gou Junli, "The Construction of Social Organizations: An Indispensable Component of Grassroots Democracy", *Xinhua Net*, Feb. 4, 2008.

[2] Gong Weibin, *Social System of Governance with Chinese Characteristics*, Beijing: Economy and Management Publishing House, 2016.

concern and protecting people's legitimate rights and interests. By the end of 2012, there were about 6.683 million community-level organizations in the eight major league organizations including trade unions, Communist Youth League, women's federation, and association for science and technology, etc., far exceeding the total number of social organizations registered in civil affairs departments. Moreover, an intensive and extensive grid network covering all social aspects has been formed. Their political and social attributes ensure their high competence of mobilization. An important way for the people's organizations to participate in social governance is to mobilize various social groups like workers, young people, and women, etc. Meanwhile, it is also necessary to create platforms for the public to participate in social governance when serving and gathering them, further broadening the pathway of social governance. Community Youth Club is the Communist Youth League Beijing Municipal Committee's innovative exploration and effective practice regarding participation in social governance. It actively guides and organizes young people to participate in social governance by carrying out activities like volunteering, self-employing and job-seeking, internship, law popularization and rights protection, sports, match-making, etc. It not only innovates the means but also provides a broad platform for the people's organizations to participate in social governance.

2.4.4   Impetus and guarantee for public participation in social governance

Under the new social governance system, the public participation largely depends on economic and social development foundation, while it is also subject to factors such as the motive mechanism and institutional guarantee. Public participation in social governance can be enhanced by factors including the cultivation of civic spirit, the improvement of grassroots democratic systems, the development and expansion of social organizations, the openness of government information and the legal guarantee, etc.

Improving community-level democracy. As the basic guarantee and foundation for the public to participate in public social affairs, social democracy reflects the openness of the society and accessibility of social governance. The 18th CPC National Congress stated that "an important way for the people to directly exercise their democratic rights in accordance with the law is for them to conduct self-management, self-service, self-education, and self-oversight in exercising urban and rural community governance, in managing community-level public affairs and in running public service programs. We should improve the mechanism for community-level self-governance under the leadership of community-level Party organizations to make it full of vitality. We should broaden the scope and channels of such self-governance and enrich its content and forms, with the focus on expanding orderly participation, promoting transparency in information, improving deliberation and consultation on public affairs, and strengthening oversight of the exercise of power, to ensure that the people have greater and more tangible democratic rights." An integral system of community-level democracy is of importance for cultivating public spirit and understanding of democracy. Such a system would enable the public to understand their principal position in the political and public affairs, strengthening their initiative and ability to exercise rights and undertake responsibility. By doing so, the public will internalize their awareness of participating in social governance. With the continuous improvement of the system of socialist consultative democracy with Chinese characteristics, grassroots consultative democracy has become an important means for the public's participation, which has greatly diversified the approaches for the public to participate in social affairs.

Promoting the transparency in government information. The government plays a leading role in social administration and enjoys an absolute advantage in the acquisition of information and resources. However, due to some limits and inadequate transparency of information, the public lose their opportunities for and enthusiasm in participating in social governance. Therefore, information transparency is the premise for cooperative governance between the government and the society, as well as the foundation for public participation in social governance. To create "sunshine government" "law-based government" and "transparent government", and to establish open and transparent administrative system, the priority is to ensure that the government information is legally available to the public. Guarantee should be made to the public for full participation in decision-making, democratic management and oversight, improving the effect of public participation. On May 1, 2008, the Regulation on the Disclosure of Government Information was put into force. For the first time, the regulation proposed a comprehensive system with specified requirements for the scope, subject, methods and procedures of information disclosure, protected the public's right to know, created a mechanism for the government and public to communicate and established an institutional channel for information collection. The regulation, hence, have become the basic guarantee for the public to participate in the management of social affairs.

Enhancing institutional guarantees for public participation. The key measure to ensure orderly and effective public participation is to establish a long-term system of public participation in social governance. The absence of institutional and mechanical guarantee for public participation impeded the public from participating in the traditional social administration. This caused a lot of social conflicts because not only did it hinder the interaction between the government and society and lower the efficiency of the government's social administration, but it also delayed public's expression of interests. Therefore, the government should further improve the poll system, the system of keeping the public informed and the system of public hearings, the expert consulting system, and the system of feedback and response. Only by these means can the government stimulate the public's enthusiasm in participation in social governance and timely acknowledge the public's interest demands. This will make the government's decision-making more scientific and win public's understanding and support for the government's decisions, so that a good two-way communication and sound interaction between the government and the public will be achieved. In the meantime, it is also essential to nurture various social organizations. The government should strengthen the building of system and laws for public's participation in social organizations, so that the public can be better organized to participate in social affairs in accordance with the law, express their demands of interest and conduct consultative democracy.

Chapter 3
Diversification of Social Governance Modes

3.1 Historical evolution

Social governance can be achieved through administrative, legal, economic, moral and technological approaches. Social conflicts vary with different social forms and at different development stages, as do social structures, forms of power, and technological conditions. These differences require different solutions to social problems and different governance approaches for the maintenance of social order. In traditional societies, social order was maintained mainly by state administration through a complex bureaucratic system, but the growth of social power was neglected. With the progress of modernization, public social affairs have significantly increased, highlighting the limitations of the traditional management and calling for legal, economic, and technological approaches in social governance. Social governance in contemporary China has undergone a transformation from traditional social administration to modern social governance, evolving from managing mainly through administrative and moral approaches to diversified modes with multiple measures and innovation.

3.1.1 All-round management and control by state administration (1949-1978)

The founding of the People's Republic of China in 1949 was the essential prerequisite for China to achieve state prosperity, national rejuvenation, and people's happiness. Due to the weak industrial foundation and shortage of capital, technology and talents, China chose a strongly government-oriented planned economic system and a strategy that gives priority to heavy industry development. This development strategy ensured that the state had a strong capacity to mobilize and allocate resources so as to advance modernization with limited resources. As a result, China quickly transited from a new democratic society to a socialist society, and created a social administration system controlled by the state in all aspects. Social governance then was mainly social mobilization for strengthening ideology by means of top-down administrative instructions and administrative measures through a bureaucratic state organization; few economic and legal measures were used. The main features of governance are as follows:

Firstly, a social administration system of an omnipotent government. A highly centralized system of planned economy was established. An omnipotent social administration system centered on the state government was established. This system centralized and unified deployment of officials, occupation identification, placement of personnel, management of social affairs, and organization of all social activities. Secondly, a personnel management system based on "danwei" (workunit). State organs, enterprises and public institutions, and people's communes were all "large and comprehensive" or "small but comprehensive" organizations. They were both work organizations and primary-level organizations that provided basic public services, tackled various social affairs and implemented social administration and control. Thirdly, a subdistrict-community-committee based management system of urban residents. The unemployed, the idlers, and recipients of government relief and preferential treatment were managed through this system. Since the majority of citizens belonged to certain institutions, this system functioned as an auxiliary in social administration. Fourthly, a social mobility management system based on the institution system, the household registration system, occupation identification system and archive system. The employment and residence of urban citizens are generally fixed, resulting in a highly organized and orderly society. Fifthly, transformation of people's ideology through public opinion guidance, morality development, ideological and political education as well as political pressure so that social administration and control was realized through changing people's behavior.

At a time of relatively low productivity and economic and social conditions, such unified social administration system relied on public movement and ideological mobilization, and integrated the "scattered" Chinese society and equipped the nation with strong social mobilization. In 1972, in his dialogue with Japanese scholar Daisaku Ikeda, British historian Arnold J. Toynbee commented on the Chinese people, "For thousands of years, the Chinese people have more successfully united hundreds of millions of people politically and culturally than any other nation in the world. They have achieved an unparalleled success in political and cultural unification."[1] However,

---

[1] Arnold J. Toynbee, Daisaku Ikeda, *Forecast 21st Century,* Chinese Edition, translated by Xun Chunsheng, Zhu Jizheng and Chen Guoliang, Beijing: International Culture Press, 1985, p. 294.

the biggest drawback of this management system and model was the over-centralization of power and social thought, which led to stagnation in economic and social life and thus hindered the development of the economy and society.

3.1.2   Adjustment and transformation in the reform and opening up (1978-1992)

In 1978, the Third Plenary Session of the 11th CPC Central Committee initiated the reform and opening up, and in 1992, the 14th CPC National Congress declared that the goal of China's economic reform was to build a socialist market economy. During this period, China's social structure, social organization and social values underwent profound changes. The traditional social administration system with the power highly centralized and the all-round government control, was no longer compatible with the new reality, and a large number of social conflicts and disputes arose but unsettled. With this transformation, "the relations of production and superstructure that are unsuited to the development of productive forces should be reformed, and all unsuited modes of management, activities and thinking should be reformed."[1] A reform that streamlined government administration was implemented to the national management system, which was highly centralized and politically and economically integrated. This reform separated the Party from government functions, government administration from the management of social groups, and enterprises. In rural areas, the people's commune system was abolished, and town governments were established to separate government administration from the management of social groups. In urban areas, government administration was separated from the management of enterprises, reinvigorating enterprises by implementing ownership and management separation, and the system of management contract responsibility.

Since the reform and opening up, the identity system has been improved. As economic construction became the center of all work, the political elements in social life began to decrease, and the sense of class identities weakened and gradually disappeared. The reform of the rural economic system featuring "all-round contract" (also known as the household contract responsibility system) has given farmers greater rights in production and distribution. The household registration system and the ticket system were gradually weakened. In cities, the private economy developed, officials

---

[1] Party Literature Research Office of the CPC Central Committee, *Selected Key Documents Since the Third Plenary Session of 11th CPC National Congress,* Vol. I , Beijing: People's Publishing House, 1982, p. 4.

and workers within the national economic system were driven by interests to new jobs outside the system. The identity system was also weakened, and new social groups gradually emerged. In 1985, the Interim Regulations on the Management of Temporary Registered Residence was issued, and temporary residence permit system for the floating population was implemented. In the same year, the system of residents' identity cards was implemented. In 1990, the floating population in China exceeded 30 million. Since the reform and opening up, the reformation of the economic system and the regulatory system resulted in changes in the status and roles of enterprises. The separation of governmental functions and enterprise management made enterprises the main entities of interests, so that enterprises operate on their own, assume sole responsibility for their profits and losses, and bear less responsibility for government instructions. New organizational forms began to sprout, mainly including industry associations, chambers of commerce, cultural and sports associations, academic associations, foundations, and sororities/fraternities, etc. These organizations began to separate from other danwei (workunit). The centralized and unified social governance mode began to change; various social organizations and market players began to participate in social governance. The practice of the all-round management by the Party and the government shifted to that of stimulating social vitality. The management system was replaced by a new legalized management mode. The dual household registration systems in rural and urban areas were increasingly loosened. Danwei transformed from social control cells and welfare providers to pure workplaces.

The adjustment and reform of the social administration system promoted the reform and opening up, and brought market and social vitality. Social productivity was liberated, a stable and unified political situation was consolidated, the problem of the most basic needs of the 1.1 billion people was basically solved, and the whole nation was moving towards a moderately prosperous society. However, as the planned economic system was not fundamentally reformed, many aspects of social administration were not accordingly reformed. More importance was attached to laws and regulations in social administration, and market and laws were playing increasingly important roles, but administrative management of economy and society did not change, and social administration is still under administrative control.

3.1.3 The transition from social administrative management to the market-oriented social administration (1992-2002)

In 1992, the 14th CPC National Congress clearly put forward the goal of establishing a socialist market economy for the first time. The transformation and legalization of the economic system started to gather speed. Comprehensive social development was promoted on the basis of economic development, and the reform of the social system permeated all aspects of the society. During this period, social administration changed to market-oriented social governance when serving the market-oriented reform of the economic system. The process of legalization of social governance accelerated, too. Structural differentiation and a downward shift of governance focus appeared. More legal and economic means were adopted for social governance.

With the advancement of the socialist market economy reform and the financial pressure brought by the expansion of the social administration functions of governments at all levels, market principles were introduced into the field of social administration, whose efficiency and effectiveness have been improved as government public services and social undertakings management absorbed and applied market elements, market mechanisms and market means. The marketization of social administration varied in forms. One form was the marketization of public services, and the other was the marketization reform of social institutions.[1] The market-oriented and business-oriented development of social administration led to some effective instrumental approaches such as contract outsourcing, franchise, user fees, and internal markets, etc.[2] These approaches improved management efficiency, but problems occurred such as the tendency of "corporatization" of government, "rent-seeking" by government departments, and abuse of market mechanisms in redistribution.

The disintegration of the danwei (workunit) system, the common institutions that were previously responsible for production and operation, social order and livelihood, put forward requirements for reform of grassroots social administration, social security management and social group management. The reforms made some positive progress. Firstly, the legalization of grassroots social administration has been strengthened. In 1998, the Standing Committee of the National People's Congress promulgated the

---

[1] In 1993, the CPC Central Committee issued the Scheme for the Reform of the Party and Government Institutions and Opinions on the Implementation of the Scheme of the Reform of the Party and Government Institutions. These two documents clearly stated that the focus of public institution reform is to separate the government from the administration of public institutions. In 1996, the General Office of the CPC Central Committee and the General Office of the State Council issued Opinions on the Central Institution Establishment Committee on Some Issues Concerning the Reform of Public Institutions, making a comprehensive deployment for the reform of public institutions in the new stage.

[2] Lu Hanlong et al., *Research on the Social Management System of New China*, Shanghai: Shanghai People's Publishing House, 2009, pp. 90-96.

Organic Law of the Villagers Committee of the People's Republic of China. In 2000, the General Office of the CPC Central Committee and the General Office of the State Council forwarded the Opinions by the Ministry of Civil Affairs on Promoting the Construction of Urban Communities in the Whole Country. Urban social administration at the grassroots level was brought into community construction, and self-governance for rural villagers has been standardized. Secondly, the legalization of social security management was also steadily advancing. Several documents were issued successively, such as Several Provisions on the Implementation of the Responsibility System of the Leaders in the Comprehensive Management of Public Security (Central Public Security Commission, etc., 1993), Opinions on Strengthening the Work of Rural Governance Committees, Decisions on Intensifying the Improvement of Social Security by Taking Comprehensive Measures (the CPC Central Committee, the State Council, 1996), and Suggestions on Further Promoting Grassroots Safety Building Activities (Central Public Security Comprehensive Management Commission, 1997), etc. In 2001, in Decisions on Further Strengthening Comprehensive Governance of Social Crime Prevention and Control, the State Council proposed to adhere to the policy of "combining attack and prevention and putting prevention first". Thirdly, as integration of government administration and social organizations was dismantled, a large number of social organizations sprang up in China, and legalized management of social organizations stepped onto the right track. In June 1998, the State Council reformed its institutions and established the Civil Organizations Administration of the Ministry of Civil Affairs. In September 1998, the State Council revised Administration Regulations on Registration of Civil Organizations; and in October promulgated the Regulations on the Administration of the Registration of Social Organizations; after the 1990s, the management of civil organization transformed from regular checking to legal registration and administration.

3.1.4   Multi-measures to build a harmonious society (2002-2012)

In 2002, the 16th CPC National Congress proposed the goal of building a moderately prosperous society in an all-round way. The congress identified a harmonious society as an important goal of building a moderately prosperous society, clarified the position of building a harmonious socialist society in the overall plan for building socialism with Chinese characteristics, considered social administration as one of the four major functions of the government, and proposed to maintain social stability by "improving social administration and maintaining good social order".

In 2004, Decisions of the CPC Central Committee on Strengthening the Party's Governing Capacity proposed the policy "to establish a sound social administration system led by the Party committee, taken charge by the government, coordinated by the society and participated by the public".[1] It also clarified the leadership system of social administration. In 2007, the report to the 17th CPC National Congress demanded to build a sound social administration system for building a well-off society in an all-round way. It also demanded to "stimulate social creativity to the greatest extent, increase harmonious elements to the greatest extent, and minimize the unharmonious elements to the greatest extent". It demanded that all people carry out social construction with people's livelihood as priority. The reform of social administration system is officially written into the work agenda of the Party committee and the government, indicating the gradual maturity of social administration thoughts.

In July 2011, the CPC Central Committee and the State Council issued Opinions on Strengthening and Innovating Social Administration, aiming at building a harmonious socialist society, and realizing social construction and social administration to improve social order and social development. After long exploration and practice, a sound social administration system led by the Party committee, taken charge by the government, coordinated by the society and participated by the public was formed. While employing administrative means, more legal regulations, economic adjustments, moral restraints, psychological guidance and public opinion guidance were adopted to achieve the development of social services and social undertakings.

3.1.5 Integration and innovation to promote governance modernization (2012 to the present)

The 18th CPC National Congress, held in November 2012, comprehensively elaborated on the social administration system with Chinese characteristics, and proposed to build a socialist social administration system with Chinese characteristics and accelerate the formation of a social administration system with "led by Party committee, implemented by the government, based on coordination, broad participation and the rule of law." The "rule of law" was supplemented into the social administration system, reflecting the combination of social administration and law-based governance of the country. The rule of law became the basic guarantee for social administration.

---

[1] "Decisions of the CPC Central Committee on Major Issues in Building a Harmonious Socialist Society", *People's Daily*, Oct. 19, 2006.

In November 2013, the Third Plenary Session of the 18th CPC Central Committee approved Decisions of the CPC Central Committee on Some Major Issues Concerning Comprehensively Deepening the Reform, which officially put forward the concept of "social governance" for the first time. "Social governance" became an important part of the national governance system and governance capacity modernization, symbolizing the transformation from the traditional social administration system to a modern, up-to-date social governance system. Xi Jinping pointed out, "The difference between governance and management is reflected in systematic governance by law, governance at source, and comprehensive policy." [1] Traditional social administration focuses more on single-entity government management and top-down government control. Social governance places more emphasis on multiple participation and joint governance, on democratic coordination and management according to law, and on people-centered philosophy and rights protection. It is the combination of co-governance and self-governance, and of law-based governance and moral governance. The Fourth Plenary Session of the 18th CPC Central Committee pointed out that the state and social governance need to give play to both law and morality, so that law and morality complement each other, and law-based governance and moral governance complement each other.

After the 18th CPC National Congress, social governance mode became increasingly diversified. Law thinking and legal approaches were used to do jobs and solve problems. Approaches such as economic regulations, administrative management, legal regulations, moral cultivation, psychological guidance and public opinion guidance were coordinated to enhance the effectiveness of social governance. After years of exploration and innovation, a "vertical and organic combination" of "top-down" social governance and "bottom-up" social self-governance and a "horizontal and organic combination" of "external-internal" law-based governance and "internal-external" moral governance, as well as the "vertical governance" and "horizontal governance" had been gradually formed. Source governance, dynamic management and emergency response combined with one another. In terms of social governance means, "the invisible hand of the market, the visible hand of the government, and the hidden hand of the society" form an organic combination. In terms of the links and key points of social governance, both symptoms and root causes were addressed, and post-event

---

[1] Publicity Department of the CPC Central Committee, *Readings of General Secretary Xi Jinping's Keynote Speeches* (2016), Beijing: Xuexi Press, People's Publishing House, 2016.

relief and source prevention were planned reasonably. Meanwhile, active efforts were made to explore the application of emerging technologies such as Internet, big data and mobile social media in social governance, and to build modern governance technology that is suitable for the information society.

Since the 18th CPC National Congress, China has placed greater emphasis on the use of multiple means. The Fourth Plenary Session of the 18th CPC Central Committee pointed out that the governance of the state and society requires both law and morality to function together. Chinese history tells us that we should "governing by both rites and the law" and that "law alone is not enough for ruling". In the transformation from an agricultural society to an industrial society, from a rural society to an urban society, from a closed society to an open society, and from a traditional society to a modern society, especially under the impact of informatization and globalization, the environment in which people's values, especially young people's outlook on life and worldview are formed has undergone profound changes, which requires us to pay more attention to cultural construction to guide people to form correct values. The Fourth Plenary Session of the 18th CPC Central Committee proposed that we should vigorously promote the core socialist values, promote traditional Chinese virtues, cultivate public morality, professional ethics, family virtues and personal integrity. We should pay attention not only to the normative role of law, but also to the role of moral education. We should include our visions in the rule of law and strengthen the role of law in promoting moral construction; we should nourish the spirit of the rule of law with morality and strengthen the role of morality in supporting legal culture; so that we can make law complement morality, the rule of law complement moral governance, and thus achieve both moral constraints and legal norms.

Social governance makes full use of multiple rule systems. Modern society is complex with plural and heterogeneous rule system for social governance, which is a collection of social norms of different categories, levels and effects. In addition to national laws and regulations, social norms such as resident codes of conduct, industry rules and regulations, and group charters can also regulate, guide and restrain the organizations and their members. Therefore, we should pay more attention to the use of other social norms in social governance innovation, guide and support public through the development and improvement of resident codes of conduct, industry regulations, group regulations, self-restraint, self-management, regulate members' behaviors, and give active play to social norms. In order to resolve social disputes and social contradictions, we should employ both mediation and punishment to improve the interactive work system of people's mediation, administrative mediation and judicial mediation, establish the cohesion mechanism of conflict and dispute mediation, give full play to the unique role of mediation, a dispute resolution system with Chinese characteristics, and properly resolve conflicts and disputes according to the law.[1]

3.2　Guarantee by the rule of law

The rule of law is the basic form of national governance, and social governance is an important part. To promote the modernization of national governance, we must accelerate its process of legalization and improve the level of legalization. Since the 18th CPC National Congress, the CPC Central Committee with Xi Jinping at the core, has attached great importance to the construction of the rule of law, and proposing the integration of the law-based country, the law-based government and the law-based society. It also sets new goals and requirements for the innovation of the social governance system. The Third Plenary Session of the 18th CPC Central Committee made a strategic plan to innovate the social governance system by improving and developing the socialist system with Chinese characteristics and promoting the modernization of the national governance system and capacity. The rule of law is the basic form of state governance, and the modernization of social governance necessarily requires the realization of law-based social governance.

3.2.1　The progress of legalization of social governance

Since the founding of the People's Republic of China, the Party and the state have always attached great importance to the construction of the rule of law, and have conducted long-term exploration and practice for the formation and development of a legal system of social governance suitable for China's conditions. Especially after the reform and opening up, major deployment has been made in the management of social innovation, social governance has made remarkable achievements and valuable experience in legalization, which contributed greatly to the reform, development and stability of China's socialist cause with Chinese characteristics.

(1) *The first stage: foundation (1978-1997)*

In 1978, the Third Plenary Session of the 11th CPC Central Committee established the goals of strengthening socialist democracy and improving the socialist legal system.

---

[1] Gong Weibin, "Eight Features of the New Normal of Social Governance", *Chinese Cadres Tribune*, 2014 (12).

The communique of the Session pointed out that "in order to safeguard people's democracy, we must strengthen the socialist legal system, to institutionalize and legalize democracy, to institutionalize and legalize democracy, to give stability, continuity and great authority to such a system and laws, and to see to it that there are laws to go by, the laws are observed and strictly enforced, and law-breakers are prosecuted".[1] It re-established the supreme position of law in social governance. During this period, the focus was on legislation, and the socialist legal system basically took shape. This fundamentally changed the situation where there is no law to go by in many important fields, and provided a strong guarantee for economic construction and social development. In order to improve the whole nation's quality of the law and sense of rule of law, in 1986 China implemented a five-year plan of law publicity. Through publicizing the law to all the people with leadership, plans and procedures, it has strongly promoted the process of building China's law-based governance and started the transformation of China's social administration from policy-based management to law-based governance.

The deepening of reform and opening up and the establishment of the socialist market economy have greatly promoted the steady progress of the legal system construction. A legal system that can satisfy the needs of economic development and national governance gradually took shape. In 1993, the Third Plenary Session of the 14th CPC Central Committee approved Decisions of the Central Committee of the Communist Party of China on Some Issues Concerning Establishing Socialist Market Economy, which set forth: "governments at all levels should administer and act in accordance with the law." This was the first time to clearly state "administration by law" in an official document of the Party. The construction of a law-based government was set out as the focus of the law construction, which further enriched the implications of law-based governance.

(2) *The second stage: development (1997-2012)*

In the 1990s, China began to comprehensively promote the construction of a socialist market economy, which further laid the economic foundation for the rule of law and set forth higher requirements. In 1997, the 15th CPC National Congress officially set out the basic strategy of governing the country by law. The Amendment to the Constitution of the People's Republic of China adopted in 1999 stipulates that, "The

---

[1] Party Literature Research Office of the CPC Central Committee, *Selected Key Documents Since the Third Plenary Session of 11th CPC National Congress,* Vol. Ⅰ, Beijing: People's Publishing House, 1982.

People's Republic of China shall practice law-based governance and build a socialist state under the rule of law." It made clear the direction of the governance of the country and society in the future. Despite the similar dictions, "rule of law" and "legal system" show big differences in their implications. "Law" is no longer only a governance tool, but the basis and foundation of the national system, and the basic strategy of state governance and an important goal of socialist modernization. Since then, "legal system" has reclaimed its literal meaning and become the cover term for all laws, underlining the integrity and unity of the legal system in terms of legal rules. As a governance strategy opposite to "rule by man", "rule of law" emphasizes governance by law, which not only requires the institutional arrangement and operation mechanism of "act in accordance with the law", but also emphasizes the spirits and values individual's equality before the law, regulated power, guaranteed rights, procedural justice and good law. By 2010, China has basically established a socialist legal system with Chinese characteristics, led by the Constitution, with relevant laws, civil laws, and commercial law, etc. as stems, and composed of various levels of laws, administrative regulations, and regional regulations, etc. On the whole, there are laws to follow in all aspects of national and social life.

In this period, by constructing rule of law, through special, systematic and regulated social policies and regulations, we managed and regulated organizations, reasonably structured modern society, adjusted social interest relations, responded to social demands, resolved social conflicts, maintained social justice, social order and social stability, nurtured a rational, tolerant, harmonious and civilized social atmosphere, and ensured a social environment where the economy, society and nature developed in a harmonious manner.[1] Throughout this period, the core of the rule of law lies in the pursuit of "procedural justice". The pan-politicization and pan-moralization in laws gradually faded. Laws began to reclaim their own principles. The legislative, administrative and judicial systems also kept intensifying their independence, so that the whole society substantially strode towards "rule of law". These efforts not only met the requirements of the development of the socialist market economy, but also decreased the negative influence of social regulation and ensured the rapid development of society.[2]

---

[1] Chen Zhenming, "What is the Social Management Function of the Government", *XinHua Digest*, 2006(3).

[2] Guo Xinghua, Shi Renhao, "From Social Regulation, Social Management to Social Governance: Changes in the Construction of Modern Rule of Law in China after the Reform and Opening Up", *Social Sciences in Heilongjiang*, 2014(6).

(3) *The third stage: improvement (2012 to the present)*

Since the 18th CPC National Congress, the strategy of governing the country by law has been further developed, centering on the promotion of comprehensive reform measures. The comprehensive rule of law has been incorporated into the Four-pronged Comprehensive Strategy.

The Third Plenary Session of the 18th CPC Central Committee proposed to let the market play the decisive role in resource allocation, streamline administration and delegate powers, and transform the government functions, which inevitably requires clarifying the relationship between government and enterprise, and between the government and public institutions, which has laid a sound foundation for the construction of an efficient and clean service-oriented government ruled by law. The Fourth Plenary Session of the 18th CPC Central Committee made overall arrangements and comprehensive planning for the rule of law, setting forth the general goal of building a socialist legal system and a socialist country under the rule of law. In order to achieve this goal, the plenary session determined to create "five systems", namely a complete system of laws, a highly effective enforcement system, a stringent scrutiny system, effective supporting measures, and a sound system of Party regulations. It also stressed pursue coordinated progress in law-based governance, exercise of state power, and government administration, and integrate the rule of law for the country, the government, and society. We must work to ensure sound lawmaking, strict law enforcement, impartial administration of justice, and the observance of law by everyone. We must modernize China's system and capacity for governance. Compared with the building of the socialist legal system proposed in the 15th CPC National Congress in 1997, the legal system proposed at the Fourth Plenary Session of the 18th CPC Central Committee focuses on the legislative level, and the rule of law system covers the whole process of scientific lawmaking, strict law enforcement, impartial administration of justice, and the observance of law by everyone, covering law-based governance, law-based exercise of state power, and law-based government administration, and rule of law for the country, the government, and society, etc.

In 2014, the Fourth Plenary Session of the 18th CPC Central Committee decided to "promote the construction of a society based on the rule of law" as an important content of comprehensive law-based governance, and further take "adhering to systematic governance, law-based governance, comprehensive governance, and source governance" as the basis for improving the level of legalization of social governance, and take "accelerating the efforts to safeguard and improve people's wellbeing, promoting the innovation of social governance system and the construction of legal system" as the prerequisites to improve the level of social governance legalization. By improving the level of the rule of law in social governance, we should bring social governance into the track of the rule of law, and work hard to realize the rule of law and institutionalization for social governance system and operation mechanism.[1] In the Notes on the Decisions of the CPC Central Committee on Major Issues Pertaining to Comprehensively Promoting the Rule of Law, Xi Jinping stressed the importance of promoting the building of a law-based society should start from four aspects: promoting the whole society to establish the awareness of the rule of law, promoting multi-level governance in various fields, building a complete legal service system, and perfecting the rights protection mechanism and resolving disputes mechanism in accordance with the law.[2]

3.2.2 Characteristics and advantages of the rule of law

Xi Jinping pointed out that, "our national governance system and governance capacities are generally good with unique advantages, and they can adapt themselves to China's national conditions and development requirements. The rule of law in China's social governance has distinctive Chinese characteristics and unique edges."

3.2.2.1 Focusing on the big picture for steady development

Promoting coordinated economic and social development is an inevitable requirement for building socialism with Chinese characteristics, as well as for the construction of socialist rule of law. Economic development and prosperity can not necessarily solve the existing social contradictions. Their solutions lie more in accelerating the social development focusing on people's wellbeing and social governance. With the development of society and economy, themes of social governance are constantly updating from social stability and social development to social harmony. During the socialist construction, we established a socialist legal system framework under the guidance of the 1954 Constitution, realized social integration and social mobilization, and resolved the disputes between the enemy and ourselves, and the disputes among people by legal means. We mobilized all positive elements, consolidated the new power, restored and developed the national economy, and helped people live a stable and

---

[1] Shen Xiaofang, "The Innovation of Social Governance Concept since the 18th CPC National Congress", *Chinese Cadres Tribune*, 2017(5).

[2] Xi Jinping, "Notes on the Decisions of the CPC Central Committee on Major Issues Pertaining to Comprehensively Promoting the Rule of Law", *People's Daily*, Oct. 29, 2014.

orderly social life. During the reform and opening up, we launched the basic strategy of law-based governance, and worked hard to build the law-based socialist country. The socialist legal system with Chinese characteristics was basically formed. Decisions on Comprehensively Promoting Law-based Administration issued in 1999 requires governments at all levels to "administrate according to law and strictly govern according to law". The goal of social governance gives priority to economic development. We should correctly handle the relationship between reform, development and stability, combine reform promotion and maintaining social harmony and stability, and unify reform depth, development speed and social power of endurance, so as to achieve social stability and people's well-being. In a new era of comprehensively deepening reform, we will adhere to the integration of the law-based country, the law-based government and the law-based society, and build the overall social governance goal of a safe China. We will advance a society governed and shared by all. We will comprehensively promote the modernization of social governance system and governance capacity, and achieve social justice and fairness and people's happiness.

The themes of social governance should be updated with time, but its fundamental goal is all the same. The rule of law of social governance always revolves around the central work and serves the overall development, handles the relationship between reform, development and stability, and ensures the people living and working in contentment, and social harmony and stability. Since the reform and opening up, we issued a series of laws and regulations, gradually established and improved the mechanism of safeguarding people's rights and interests, the mechanism of safeguarding people's interests, the coordination mechanism of social interests, the mechanism of the people's demand expression, the mechanism of social conflict and dispute investigation and warning, the mechanism of social contradiction adjustment and resolution, the social risk assessment mechanism of the government's major decisions, the monitoring and early warning mechanism of emergency events, and the mechanism for comprehensive virtual society management, etc. We continuously improve social governance system and its capacities. Through effective comprehensive social security management and risk prevention and control, we can ensure a vital, harmonious and orderly society, and realize the long-term stability of the country, people's living and working in peace and contentment, and sustainable development of society and economy.

3.2.2.2 People-centered philosophy and combination of regulation and services

Adhering to people's principal status is not only the concrete embodiment of the people-centered development thought in the field of rule of law, but also the basic feature of the legalization of social governance. In China, people are the major players and the source of strength of law-based governance. The socialist rule of law with Chinese characteristics adheres to the principles for the sake of the people, relies on the people, benefits the people and protects the people. Taking the protection of the people's fundamental rights and interests as the starting point and foothold, it ensures that the people enjoy a wide range of rights and freedoms according to law, undertake their due obligations and responsibilities, safeguard social fairness and justice, and promote common prosperity. The Legislation Law of the People's Republic of China stipulates that "legislation should reflect people's will, carry forward socialist democracy, and ensure that the people participate in lawmaking by various channels". People-centered and making laws for the people, the construction of the rule of law in social governance reflects the people's will and is supported by the people. Socialist laws guarantee that the people, under the leadership of the Party and in accordance with the law, manage state affairs, economic and cultural undertakings and social affairs through various channels and forms.

Social governance is the management of and service for people. Managing the society is not the ultimate goal, it is serving the society that is the fundamental requirement. Construction of law-based social governance is characterized by service priority and combination of management and service. Since the 18th CPC National Congress, a series of laws and regulations have been promulgated to protect and improve people's wellbeing, such as the Charity Law of the People's Republic of China. Adhering to the priorities of people and service, focusing on protecting and improving people's wellbeing first and promoting social fairness and justice, we have vigorously developed social undertakings, improved the public service system, strengthened and innovated social governance, and promoted people's living and working in peace and contentment. The society is stable and orderly. China promulgated and implemented the Implementation Outline for Building a Government Ruled by Law (2015-2020). The outline pinpointed the goals and action programs for building a law-based government by 2020. China kept promoting the policy of "the reform of streamlining administration, delegating power, strengthening regulation and improving service", striving to achieve the organic unity of management and service, and solving those prominent problems affecting social harmony and stability.

3.2.2.3　Adherence to the Party's leadership and coordination of diverse elements

Implementing the Party's leadership in the whole process and all aspects of the rule of law is a basic experience in the construction of socialist rule of law in China. The Fourth Plenary Session of the 18th CPC Central Committee launched the major strategic task of comprehensively promoting the rule of law. The CPC is the strong core of leadership to comprehensively promote the rule of law. The Party's leadership is the fundamental guarantee for the people to be the masters of the country and the rule of law. The people being the masters of the country is the essential requirement of socialist democratic politics. Law-based governance is the basic strategy for the Party to lead the people to govern the country. Law-based exercise of power is the basic way for the Party to govern the country. Law-based administration is the basic principle for exercising government's administrative power. Adhering to the organic unity of the Party's leadership, the people being the masters of the country and the rule of law ensures to give full play to people's enthusiasm, initiative and creativity in building and managing the country.

Since the 18th CPC National Congress, through legislation, we have continuously improved the social governance system led by the Party committee, dominated by the government, coordinated by the whole society, participated by the public, and guaranteed by the rule of law. We have improved the mechanism for the public to participate in the construction of the rule of law in social governance, attentively listened to the opinions of all parties, continuously improved the mechanism of interest expression, interest coordination, and interest protection. We have achieved the benign interaction between government governance, social adjustment and residents' self-governance. We have given full play to both the leading role of the Party and the government and the role of various social forces and social organizations in social governance, so that they could jointly participate in social governance, share development fruits, solve social problems economically, efficiently and fairly. We have brought out the overall effect of the state, promoted government action, realized the collective will of the state, and promoted coordinated social and economic development.

3.2.2.4   Law-based management and comprehensive implementation of policies

China's social governance is also characterized by law-based governance and comprehensive implementation of policies. The Report to the 18th CPC National Congress proposed that we should pay more attention to the guarantee of the rule of law in social administration, make good use of law thinking and law approaches to solve plights in social administration, improve the innovation level of social administration, and intensify social construction through improving people's wellbeing and innovating social administration. Xi Jinping pointed out that "the difference between governance and management lies in the systematic governance, law-based governance, source governance and comprehensive implementation of policies". After the 18th CPC National Congress, to tackle the new situation, new tasks and new requirements faced by the comprehensive rule of law, the Party proposed the new principles of sound lawmaking, strict law enforcement, impartial administration of justice, and the observance of law by everyone. These principles not only cover four basic areas of the construction of the rule of law: lawmaking, law enforcement, justice and law-observance, but also make clear the key requirements of each area, thus forming the basic situation for comprehensive law-based governance in the new period. We should do our work and solve problems following legal thinking and approaches, and coordinate economic regulation, administrative management, legal norms, moral education, psychological counseling, and public opinion guidance, etc. to enhance the effectiveness of social governance. We put more weight on the mediation and resolution of social conflicts and disputes, resulting in a dispute resolution system that is increasingly sound and diversified. We should improve the law-abiding credit reward mechanism and the punishment mechanism for illegal and dishonest behaviors, and strengthen the construction of social credit. Leading officials have improved their ability and level of taking the lead in respecting, studying, observing and using laws. Their law-based governance ability and law thinking have been significantly improved.

3.2.3   Challenges and opportunities for law-based governance

Currently, China is at the primary stage of socialism, at the decisive stage of building a moderately prosperous society, and at the critical period of overcoming the "middle-income trap" and moving towards a high-income country, but the international situation is complicated and changing. China has experienced industrialization, urbanization, marketization, informatization and internationalization. At the same time, it has undergone the transformation from traditional society to modern society and from a planned economy to a socialist market economy. If the former is the universal law of development in the world, the latter is endowed with Chinese characteristics, especially the unprecedented transformation from a planned economy to a socialist market economy, which imposes difficulty on China's modernization. [1] With the further advancement of comprehensive deepening reform, the task of reform, development and stability is unprecedentedly heavy, the number of contradictions and risks are

---

[1] Gong Weibing, "Correct Judgment of Social Situation and Scientific Promotion of Social Management", *Administration Reform*, 2012(11).

unprecedentedly large. We cannot escape from realistic contradictions but we have to satisfy people's reasonable demands. So, it is urgent to further the legalization of social governance. In the face of the new situation and new tasks, we need to better maintain and use the important strategic opportunity period in China's development, better coordinate social forces, balance social interests, adjust social relations, and regulate social behavior, so as to make our society vibrant and orderly in profound changes. To achieve the strategic goal of China's peaceful development, we must give full play to the leading, regulating and guaranteeing role of the rule of law in social governance.

Since the reform and opening up, especially since the 18th CPC National Congress, great progress has been made in comprehensively promoting the rule of law and the construction of a law-based society, improving the level of law-based social governance, bringing social governance into the orbit of the rule of law, and striving to realize the legalization and institutionalization of the social governance system and operation mechanism. It should be noted that the construction of the rule of law in social governance still faces many challenges with problems that do not adapt to and conform to the economic and social development. The first problem is the small quantity, low rank, and insufficient systematicity of legislations. Giant gap exists between the legislations and the actual needs of innovating the social governance system and people's expectations. They are not targeted and practical enough, especially contradictions and lack of coordination still exist between laws, between laws and regulations, and between regulations. Furthermore, some important legislation has not been planned yet, such as Laws on Social Organization, Laws on Petitions of the People's Republic of China, etc. The second problem is laws are not properly observed and strictly enforced, and lawbreakers are not prosecuted. In the law enforcement system, powers and responsibilities are not in balance, and the same law is enforced by different departments or selectively. The enforcement of law and administration of justice are not procedure-based, not strict, not transparent nor civilized. Unfair law enforcement and corruption are strongly repugnant to people. The third problem is some people have weak sense of respecting the law, believing in the law, observing the law and practicing the law, and of safeguarding their rights in accordance with the law. Some state staff members, especially leading officials, do not have a strong sense of acting in accordance with the law or they lack the ability to do so. Law violations remain, such as deliberately breaking the law, overriding the law by fiat, placing their own authority above the law, and abusing the law. We must work hard to solve these problems.

3.2.4 Promoting the legalization of social governance

3.2.4.1 Scientific lawmaking and improving the legal system of social governance

Good law is a prerequisite for sound governance. To advance the modernization of social governance, we must start by creating laws based on sound principles, improving regulations across different sectors, and ensuring that laws are timely, systematic, targeted, and effective. Firstly, we should give more prominence to legislation in the social field, adhere to scientific and democratic lawmaking, make overall planning, implement it step by step, clarify responsibilities, revise incompatible laws, regulations, systems and mechanisms, speed up legislation in key areas, and strive to form a relatively perfect legal system of social governance with Chinese characteristics in three to five years. Secondly, we should delimit social governance entities' rights, responsibilities and procedures in accordance with the law. We should closely follow the functional scope confirmed in the Implementation Outline for Building a Government Ruled by Law (2015-2020), draw a power list, clarify the relationship between the government and society and their respective roles, clarify and legalize the relationship between rights and responsibilities of social governance, and improve the efficiency of social governance. We should build a good situation of good governance by the Party and the government, co-governance by the whole society and primary-level self-governance. Thirdly, we should always pay close attention to the new issues concerning people's wellbeing, social security and ecological protection, constantly improve the relevant laws and regulations, provide a legal basis for solving the new problems in society, and ensure the legitimacy of social governance. Fourthly, while making laws, we should listen to as many public opinions as possible, integrate views from different interest groups, safeguard vulnerable groups' interests, and in the end form a feasible scheme recognized by the majority of social members. The laws can represent most people's interests and reflect majority's wishes. Fifthly, we should refine the experience of social governance to systems through legislation, and improve laws and regulations to provide legal basis for the entities, objects, modes and scopes of social governance.

3.2.4.2 Law-based governance and building of a social security protection
          network

The Third Plenary Session of the 18th CPC Central Committee reviewed and approved the Decision of the CPC Central Committee on Some Major Issues Concerning Comprehensively Deepening the Reform. The decision states, "we should adhere to the rule of law, strengthen the guarantee of the rule of law, and resolve social contradictions by the means of the rule of law." We should promote the rule of law in social governance, innovate the law enforcement system, improve the law enforcement procedures, advance comprehensive law enforcement, strictly enforce the law responsibility, establish a unified and authoritative and efficient law-based governance system, and construct a social security protection network. We should evaluate officials on whether they observe the law and act according to law. The leading officials of the Party and the government must follow the principle of the rule of law and must not go beyond the bottom line of the law. The state administration organs shall operate in accordance with law, undertaking their legal responsibilities, and not acting beyond law so that standardization and legalization of governance procedure for the government at all levels is promoted. Judicial organs should be impartial in justice, and further improve their quality, the level and the credibility of law enforcement. We should solve the livelihood issues closely related to people's immediate interests by the rule of law, breaking the current situation of interest solidification, stimulating the vitality of society, and ensuring the relatively harmonious state of society by law. The law-based thinking can also help analyze public opinions, so that people can build a harmonious society together, share the economic development fruits, and form the spirit of respecting law in the whole society. Thus, we can finally build a law-based society. The law-based social governance is not only an effective way to implement the strategic policy of rule of law, but it can also achieve positive effects by social governance.

3.2.4.3 Respecting and observing the law, and enhancing people's awareness of the rule of law

The authority of law stems from the people's heartfelt support and sincere faith. Xi Jinping pointed out, "the law can function only when the whole society believes in it".[1] First of all, we should take law popularization and law observance as the long-term basic work of law-based governance, carry out in-depth publicity and education of the rule of law in an all-round way, wipe off the long-standing thinking of management and control, strengthen the awareness of cooperation and consultation, and enhance the awareness of studying, respecting, observing and using the law, so as to make law rooted in our mind and embodied in our action. We should cultivate the belief and spirit of the rule of law in the whole society, and make law-based thinking imprinted in the minds of all the

---

[1] Party Literature Research Office of the CPC Central Committee, *Selected Key Documents Since the 18th CPC National Congress*, Vol. I, Beijing: Central Party Literature Publishing House, 2004, p. 721.

members of society. Secondly, we should guide the people to consciously observe the law, resort to the law in case of trouble, solve problems by the law, express their demands and claim rights in accordance with the law, safeguard their legitimate rights and interests, improve their ability to act in accordance with the law, so that the awareness of the rule of law permeates into the whole process of social governance and the law-based governance takes a dominant position. Finally, we should act on this awareness of the rule of law, respect the authority of the law, believing that everyone is equal before the law. Only when people act within the law framework, can their reasonable demands get satisfied legally.

3.2.4.4 Shifting the focus to the community and promoting the legalization of primary-level governance

Comprehensively promoting the rule of law has its foundation and focus at the grassroots level. The Fourth Plenary Session of the 18th CPC Central Committee proposed that we should strengthen the construction of grassroots law institutions, strengthen grassroots law teams, establish a law working mechanism with focus and strength at the primary level, improve the infrastructure and equipment conditions at the grassroots level, and encourage law officials to work at the grassroots level. This clarifies the direction of promoting the legalization of grassroots governance and puts forward the basic requirements. First, we should enhance grassroots officials' awareness of the rule of law and the rule of law for the people, and improve their ability to act according to the law so that the grassroots Party organizations play a leading role. Second, we should strengthen the construction of grassroots law institutions, strengthen the grassroots law teams, establish a law working mechanism with focus and strength shifted to the grassroots level, and improve the infrastructure and equipment conditions. Third, we should take the initiative and improve the ability to prevent and solve social contradictions, establish and improve the mechanism of investigation and mediation of contradictions and disputes, and properly solve the emerging and tendentious problems in grassroots society in accordance with the law. Fourth, we should encourage law officials to work at the grassroots level, actively guiding and recommending excellent law officials to assume a temporary post, take a position or serve at the grassroots level so as to create convenient legal aid service systems, expand the scopes of legal aid, and improve the quality of legal aid.

The government should regulate its administration through taking responsibility for its actions, with violations of law being severely punished. We should strictly follow the requirements by the Decision of the CPC Central Committee on Major Issues

Pertaining to Comprehensively Promoting the Rule of Law, Principles for Integrity and Self-discipline, and Disciplinary Regulations. In case of major misdecisions or severely delayed decisions, the chief executive, other responsible leaders, and relevant responsible personnel shall be strictly prosecuted according to the law. We should strictly implement laws and regulations that regulate administration to ensure that power runs according to the law.

We should work hard to improve the ability of judicial departments and administrative departments to participate in social governance. Meanwhile, we should carry out legal education via new media and improve public awareness of participating in social governance and expressing demands and safeguarding legitimate rights and interests in accordance with the law. We should make great efforts to construct legal service centers (stations and offices), innovate and promote the work of "one village (community), one legal adviser", launch legal service for the Belt and Road Initiative, and legal risk evaluation and prevention for enterprises. We should provide legal services for all kinds of social organizations by building a three-dimensional and multi-level legal service system.

3.3   Moral restraints

As a country of etiquettes with thousands of years of cultural tradition, China attaches importance to and gives full play to the influence of morality in national governance and implements "ruling the country by virtue", which has long been the basic philosophy for China to integrate social forces. The modernization of social governance is a combination of the modernization of system as well as human. Although the modernization of social governance should be guaranteed by the system, the fundamental solution to problems in social governance lies in human's self-restraint on morality. With the advancement of social governance practice, morality, as a non-mandatory and flexible constraint involved in all aspects of social governance, penetrates into social governance practice, and is gradually internalized into an indispensable constituent element in the social governance system. It plays an indispensable role in social governance practice. It is of great significance to study the relationship between morality and social governance and to explore moral constraints on the formation of social governance mechanism and the modernization of national governance.

3.3.1　The implications of moral governance

Human morality is a premise of integrated social life. A society with virtues is a sound society; on the contrary, a society without virtues is an evil one. In an evil society, whatever punishment mechanism cannot fundamentally prohibit the occurrence of evil. Therefore, at every historical stage of human society, motivating people's virtue is the guarantee of successful social governance.[1]

The implications of moral governance can be interpreted as follows: First, instrumental interpretation. By this interpretation, "morality" serves as a tool for social control and the establishment of social order. Moral governance includes social system moral construction and people's moral construction. Some scholars believe that moral governance is a kind of social governance activity in which the ruling class uses morality through state power to maintain social order.[2] Second, the interpretation of philosophical implications. Moral governance is to correct misconducts according to moral value orientation, underlining the inner spirit of morality while emphasizing the normative form of morality, and regarding moral principles as the value foundation for social governance. Some scholars believe that the key to moral governance lies in "governing the mind", and ultimately arriving at "sound governance".[3] This interpretation defines moral governance in terms of moral values. Third, the combination of instrumental and philosophical interpretation. Moral governance is interpreted "as a governance opposite to authoritarianism", which includes two dimensions: "governance of morality", i.e. the measure, approach and power for morality to play its role; and "moral governance", that is, governance with moral nature and tendency.[4]

Different entities of moral governance result in three views in the theory of moral regulation. The first is the "state-centered theory". This theory emphasizes the role of the state and the government in moral regulation. It is mandatory and effective. This view regards moral regulation as an important approach for social governance, represented by Durkheim's "state-centered theory". The second emphasizes "social

---

[1] Zhang Kangzhi, "Choices of Ethical Behaviors in Social Governance Activities", *Hebei Academic Journal*, 2004(4).

[2] Lin Ligong, "Justice: The Main Clue of Western Thoughts on Moral Governance", *Studies in Ethics*, 2006(2).

[3] Zhu Yiting, "The Debate over 'The Origin' and 'The End' on Morality: An Issue Concerning Current Moral Governance", *Morality and Civilization*, 2013(2).

[4] Li Jianlei, "Moral Governance and Moral Culture Construction: Review of the Academic Symposium on the 30th Anniversary of the First Publication of Moral and Civilization", *Studies in Ethics*, 2013(1).

centralism" and holds that moral regulation is a way to regulate people's behavior by using various social forces, represented by Dean's theory of multiple entities. The third focuses on the cultivation and internalization of individual morality. For example, they advocate to transform social members' cognition through moral regulation, so that they can form a consensus and accept the rules.[1]

Moral governance is a way of national governance with a unique operating mechanism, and its realization is a gradual process with notable stages. Moral governance should start from the actual moral level of the society. At the same time, it should also set up a higher moral ideal, so as to provide guidance for people's behavior choice, and constantly lead people's behavior to a more harmonious and orderly level. The hierarchy of moral governance objectives and the diversity of moral governance means determine the gradual process of realization of moral governance, which cannot be achieved overnight. The primary stage of moral governance should focus on the governance of external moral norms, which will regulate individuals in ethical relations; in the intermediate stage, we should pay attention to the transformation from the governance of external moral norms to the governance of internal moral consciousness, so as to ensure that moral governance is timely and targeted; in the advanced stage, we should focus on cultivating the internal adjustment mechanism, so that the governance actors will have self-consciousness and internal constraints. The moral governance will transform from governance actors' internal moral consciousness to external moral behaviors, and thus promote their overall development and improvement.[2]

To sum up, by moral governance, multiple social entities flexibly solve social problems in many fields through their moral influence. It has a dual value of affirmation and negation; that is, punishment of "evil" and promotion of "good". In fact, morality itself is a flexible way of governance in that it is the means to adjust the relationship between people, and between people and society, between people and nature, between people and themselves. It maintains social order and realizes social stability through restraints, incentives, evaluation and guidance. However, compared with the adjustment of social relations by morality, moral governance is a weakened compulsory way of governance.

3.3.2 The history of moral governance

After the founding of the People's Republic of China, the CPC promoted moral

---

[1] Guo Xiajuan, Yang Qijun, "From Periphery to Center: The Trinitarian Moral Regulation in Social Governance", *Zhejiang Social Sciences*, 2017(1).

[2] Wang Le, "On the Three Stages of Moral Governance", *Studies in Ethics*, 2016(5).

construction centered on "what kind of society to build", and "how to conduct social governance". It has played an extremely important role in uniting the people, gathering strength and ensuring social stability. It can be seen that the choice of moral means and key points of moral construction in each period and stage was based on the moral situation as well as a response to the prominent moral problems at the time. With the changes in national development strategy and economic and social development, the objectives, tasks, approaches and means of moral governance in different historical periods varied, which can be roughly divided into three stages.

3.3.2.1 Social control (1949–1978)

Due to the weak industrial foundation and extreme shortage of capital, technology and talents, China chose planned economic system led by a strong government and a strategy of heavy industry first. This strategy ensured the national government's strong ability to mobilize and allocate resources, and promote modernization with limited resources, rapidly resulting in a social governance system under the overall control by the state. After the founding of the People's Republic of China, a socialist value system was established based on the public economy, with collectivism as the core and communism as the goal. This system aimed to eliminate private ownership and its affiliated ideology mainly through the socialist revolution and class struggle. The Party required all Party members and officials to "serve the people wholeheartedly" and "be selfless". In this situation, communist moral model spirits sprang up, such as the "Spirit of Lei Feng", "Spirit of Jiao Yulu", and "Spirit of Iron Man: Wang Jinxi". Moral construction in this stage was an important part of ideological and political education, and is characteristic of moral idealism. During the exploration of the socialist road, the government transformed people's ideology and constantly strengthened and consolidated the dominance of socialist ideology through guidance of social public opinions, moral construction, ideological and political education and political pressure, etc. The government then worked to further change people's behavior to realize social control.

3.3.2.2 Social administration (1978–2012)

During this period, China was undergoing profound social changes from the reform and opening up in 1978 to the establishment of the socialist market economy. With great changes in social structure, forms of social organization and social values, social conflicts were prone to occur. The established model of social administration, in which the state government was granted highly concentrated power and managed and controlled society all round, could no longer adapt to the new situation. To facilitate the transition from planned economy to market economy, the whole society was centered on economic construction, and China's social administration had been continuously evolving with the rapid economic growth. The pace of economic system transformation and rule of law construction had been accelerated. Economic development being a priority, China pushed forward the overall development of society: social governance and the market-oriented reform supporting economic system; the comprehensive control of society shifted to market-oriented social administration. The process of construction of rule of law was also accelerated. Structural differentiation and a shift of the focus of social administration down to the community level promoted the development of reform and opening up. The deregulation brought about market dynamic and social vitality. However, as the planned economic system was not shaken, the adjustment and reform of social administration was done without correspondent reforms in various social sectors and in the circumstance that social economy was still managed by the government through administrative means. Social administration remained to be conducted by the administrative system.

In order to solve newly occurred moral hazards and challenges, close attention has been paid to strengthening cultural and ethical values. In the early 1980s, the nationwide "five things to stress", "four things to beautify", and "three things to love" (stress on decorum, stress on manners, stress on hygiene, stress on discipline, stress on morals; beauty of the mind, beauty of the language, beauty of the behavior, beauty of the environment; love of the motherland, love of socialism, love of the Communist Party of China) moral education campaign brought a fundamental change in the social and moral outlook of China's urban and rural areas. After the CPC shifted its focus to the construction of a modernized China, the Central Committee repeatedly and solemnly pointed out the necessity for promoting socialist cultural-ethical progress while achieving socialist material growth. This was the strategic direction to building socialist China back then. On September 26, 1986, the Sixth Plenary Session of the 12th CPC Central Committee adopted the Resolution of the CPC Central Committee on the Guidelines for Socialist Cultural and Ideological Progress. In October 1996, the Sixth Plenary Session of the 14th CPC Central Committee reviewed and adopted the Resolution of the CPC Central Committee on Several Important Issues Concerning the Strengthening of Socialist Cultural and Ethical Values. The fundamental task of socialist morality drive was to adapt to the needs of socialist modernization, cultivating ideal, moral, educated and disciplined socialist citizens, and thus improving the ideological, moral, scientific and cultural quality of the entire Chinese nation. To do this, it was necessary to mobilize and unite people of all ethnic groups with common ideals, establishing socialist morality, and strengthening the education on socialist democracy, legal system and discipline, as well as popularizing and improving education, science and culture. [1]

In the 21st century, the focus of morality construction shifted to the strengthening of civic morality, with "improving civic morality" as its main content. In 2001, the Program for Improving Civic Morality was promulgated and implemented, proposing that the fundamental task of morality drive was to equip Chinese citizens with ideals, moral integrity, good education and a strong sense of discipline. In 2002, the Report to the 16th CPC National Congress put forward that "it is necessary to establish a socialist ideology compatible with the socialist market economy and the socialist legal standard, and consistent with the traditional virtues of the Chinese nation." From then on, China has vigorously constructed the core socialist values.

3.3.2.3 Social governance (2012 to the present)

The 18th CPC National Congress has started a new journey for the whole country to build a well-off society in an all-round way, fulfilling the Chinese dream of national rejuvenation. The Report to the 18th CPC National Congress put forward the project of solidly advancing civic morality, and at the same time emphasized on "carrying out thorough education to address serious ethical problems, stepping up efforts to enhance government integrity, and reinforcing business and social ethics and judicial integrity."[2] This move once again brought the issue of moral governance to the whole society. Our moral governance mode has changed from the traditional mode of attaching importance to command, movement and mobilization to the mode of rule of law, interaction and standardization, which has significantly improved the social governance with specific rules and regulations.

The Third Plenary Session of the 18th CPC Central Committee put forward the requirement of "innovating the social governance system", replacing the previous formulation of "social administration" with "social governance". Such requirement

---

[1] Party Literature Research Office of the CPC Central Committee, *Selected Key Documents Since the 12th CPC National Congress*, Vol. 2, Beijing: People's Publishing House, 1988, pp. 1273-1278.

[2] Hu Jintao, *Firmly March on the Path of Socialism with Chinese Characteristics and Strive to Complete the Building of a Moderately Prosperous Society in All Respects: Report to the 18th National Congress of the Communist Party of China*, Beijing: People's Publishing House, 2012, p. 32.

placed more emphasis on people-centered philosophy and safeguarding rights, which was the combination of co-governance and self-governance as well as the integration of rule of law and rule of virtue. In the establishment of multiple subjects in social governance, morality was an indispensable basic element. The Fourth Plenary Session of the 18th CPC Central Committee pointed out that law and morality must play a joint role in state and social governance. It is necessary to vigorously carry forward the core socialist values and traditional Chinese virtues, launching a civic morality campaign to raise ethical standards, work ethics, family virtues, and personal integrity of the public. While stressing the normative role of law, attention should also be paid to the educational role of morality. The rule of law embodies social governance concept, and strengthens the role of law in promoting morality, which in turn nourishes the spirit of rule of law and supports the rule of law culture, so that law and morality supplement each other, and rule of law and rule of virtue complement each other, and moral constraints and legal norms work together in social governance.

Xi Jinping pointed out that to realize the Chinese Dream, we must foster Chinese spirit. We must focus on the central task of economic development, firmly hold onto the theme of the great rejuvenation of the Chinese nation, consolidate and strengthen mainstream thinking and public opinion, carry forward the main theme, spread positive energy, so as to inspire the whole society to unite and forge ahead.[1] This created close links between moral construction and the Chinese Dream, endowing the morality construction with a new mission. In 2006, the Sixth Plenary Session of the 16th CPC Central Committee made clear the task of building core socialist values. On this basis, the 18th CPC National Congress refined and summarized the core socialist values into a 24-word norm. In 2014, the Central Committee issued the Opinions on Cultivating and Observing Core Socialist Values. The core socialist values should be implemented into national development practice and social governance through education, guidance, publicity, culture, practice, and institutions. Gradually, the people shall internalize and firmly believe in the core socialist values and purposefully make them the basis for their actions. Efforts should be made toward building intellectual and moral standards to provide a solid moral foundation for the Chinese Dream. Xi pointed out that adhering to Marxist and socialist morality is of vital importance, which can guide people to pursue,

---

[1] Socialist Cultural Development Road with Chinese Characteristics Project Group of Party Literature Research Office of the CPC Central Committee, "Revitalizing the whole Nation's Spirit: New Ideas of the Central Committee on Ideological and Cultural Construction since the 18th CPC National Congress", *People's Daily Online*, Aug. 24, 2015.

respect and abide by morality, forming an upward force for goodness. "As long as the Chinese nation constantly pursue a beautiful and lofty moral realm from generation to generation, our nation will always be full of hope."[1] Xi also stressed in the 13th collective study of the Political Bureau of the CPC Central Committee that the cultivation and promotion of core socialist values must be based on the excellent traditional Chinese culture. Since the 18th CPC National Congress, the Central Committee has attached great importance to the excavation and elucidation of Chinese culture. The creative transformation and innovative development of Chinese traditional culture has become an important source of conserving socialist core values, serving for the practice of realizing the Chinese Dream.

Xi Jinping pointed out that it was necessary to continue to deepen the development of socialist ideology and ethics, carry forward traditional Chinese virtues, advocate new trend of the times, and use core socialist values to gather the nation's soul and strength, so as to better build the Chinese spirit, Chinese values, and Chinese strength, and provide a steady stream of spiritual motivation and moral nourishment for the cause of socialism with Chinese characteristics.[2]

Xi Jinping explained that every era has its own spirit, ideology and moral requirements.[3] Since the 18th CPC National Congress, the CPC Central Committee with Xi Jinping at its core has, on the basis of carrying forward CPC's moral values and in accordance with the requirements of the new era, carried out an overall construction of the "great virtue" to support the development of socialism with Chinese characteristics. Since the 18th CPC National Congress, while advancing economy and legal system, the CPC Central Committee has also attached great importance to the progress in ideology and morality, constructing the nation's "great virtue" with core socialist values, setting the "bottom line" and the "benchmark" of morality. An environment of good virtues was then created through ritual activities, laying the foundation of morality with cultivation and practice. In so doing, basic thoughts and methods on morality governance were constituted.[4]

---

[1] Xi Jinping, "Gathering Up Powerful Positive Energy for Comprehensively Deepening Reform", *People's Daily*, Nov. 29, 2013.

[2] "Xi Jinping Extends Congratulations to the Role Models", *People's Daily*, Oct. 14, 2015.

[3] Xi Jinping, "Speech at the Symposium on Literary and Artistic Work", XinhuaNet, http://news.xinhuannet.com/politics/2015-10/14/c_1116825558.htm.

[4] She Shuanghao, "Expanding Moral Governance through 'Great Virtue' Construction and 'Great Environment' Creation: An Exploration of Xi Jinping's Ideas on Morality Governance", *Decision-Making & Consultancy*, 2016(5).

3.3.3 Morality governance in rapid transition

In response to the transformation in economic and social development, China has attached great importance to the innovation of morality governance, and has made important adjustments in the operation mechanism and manners of moral governance, presenting irreplaceable functions.

3.3.3.1 Cooperative governance by multiple actors

Social governance is not only targeting at the whole society but also requires the participation of the whole society. The greatest strength and the most unique characteristic of China's social governance is cooperative governance by multiple actors led by the Party and the government. In order to participate in the social governance practice, the multiple actors must be authoritative and accepted by the public through their moral judgment rather than under administrative pressure from the Party and government organs. Today in China, the multiple actors involved in moral governance maintain relative self-governance and independence, but cooperate fully to form a harmonious, orderly, self-disciplined institutionalized governance mechanism. This allows morality to exert the flexible restraint and motivation effects in various ways. To deal with the interactive relationship among various actors of this pluralistic system and to take into account the different interests of the multiple social subjects, it is essential to strengthen the guidance and regulation of subjects' behavior through the enhancement of morality. This aims to reach the consensus of social subjects and to promote sound operation and orderly development. However, currently, such good moral governance structure has not yet been established and the function of social self-governance in moral education is relatively insufficient.

3.3.3.2 Facilitating the operation of social systems

Social governance is an important part of national governance. Promoting the sound operation of governance systems has become an important element in advancing the modernization of the national governance system and capacity. Institutions include not only formal written laws and regulations, but also many informal constraints, that is, institutions consisting of informal constraints (sanctions, taboos, customs, traditions and codes of conduct) and formal rules (constitution, laws, property rights).[1] Morality, the flexible constraint that builds a foundation for social governance, cooperates with all kinds of written institutions to guarantee a sound operation of social governance. it

---

[1] Douglas C. North, "On Institutions", translated by Li Fei, *Comparative Economic & Social Systems*, 1991 (6).

is embedded in the social governance system in the form of informal and flexible constraints and norms relying on the strong internal force generated by people's moral conscience; it guides and regulates people's external behavior effectively, and has them consciously pursue the goals of social governance. In addition, morality also plays its unique social governance function with social opinions and moral evaluation influencing all aspects of social life. Promoting institution's reform and innovation, morality complements other written regulations and jointly promotes the practice of social governance. A legal system without internal morality "will undoubtedly lead to a bad legal institution, something that cannot be properly called a legal institution."[1] Moral concepts and moral contents are constantly updated with the development of society, while the written institution is relatively stable. At present, it is important to make efforts to center on the five development concepts, to promote fairness and justice and enhance people's wellbeing, guide and support people from all social levels to carry out self-discipline and self-management by formulating citizen conventions, township regulations, industry regulations and group regulations, and by regulating the behavior of members of all groups so as to give the positive roles of various social norms full play and to provide institutional guarantee for the modernization of national governance system and capacity.

3.3.3.3 Guiding social behavior

During social transition, the current moral situation and moral problems in Chinese society presented a picture of "coexistence of good and bad, condemnation and reflection, anxiety and hope".[2] When people's daily demands are upgraded in an all-round way and people's values have undergone profound changes suited to market economy, the building of social morality and credit system lags behind. In addition, the code of conduct for restricting and supervising the pursuit of personal interests has not been established. Supervision technology cannot meet the needs of this new and more complex governance system. Morality permeates all aspects of social life with its universal applicability, exerting an important influence on people's thoughts and behaviors, and restricting the scope and effect of social governance. Moreover, morality can standardize the actual behavior of social members, and can synergize social

---

[1] Lon L. Fuller, *The Morality of Law*, Chinese Edition, translated by Zheng Ge, Beijing: The Commercial Press, 2005, p. 47.

[2] Qiu Shi, "Recognizing the Mainstream of Morality and Strengthening Moral Confidence: A Re-Discussion on Correctly Understanding the Moral Situation of China at Present", *Qiushi*, 2012(4).

consensus and create an enabling social atmosphere for governance. Moral concepts, principles and norms not only directly regulate people's behavior, but also participate in the construction of social order and go a further step to maintain a reasonable social state. Thus, it provides a foundation for social governance to develop. In the process of promoting national governance system and capacity, various interest demands collide fiercely due to the existence of multiple subjects in social governance, and the fragility of social relations increases, which brings risks to social operation. Morality, as an indispensable and effective means of social regulation, is promoted through moral consciousness and self-discipline, and in turn, helps to promote overall moral standard throughout the society. It enhances harmony and cooperation among various governance actors, eliminates hidden dangers of uncertainty, and resolves social risks, and stabilizes the social structure, and hence ensures the smooth progress of social governance practice.

3.3.4   Innovating the path of moral governance

3.3.4.1   Strengthening moral education, promoting inheritance and innovation

Morality is the cornerstone of social relations and the foundation of interpersonal harmony. During the modernization of national governance, it is necessary to establish a value concept and target system that is compatible with the current political, economic, social and cultural development, and an institutional system that takes into account both instrumental and value rationality. First, the publicity and interpretation of the Chinese Dream must be strengthened. By focusing on firmly grasping the great rejuvenation of the Chinese nation, efforts must be made to advocate the Chinese spirit with new connotations, and the mainstream ideology and spread positive energy so as to inspire the whole society to unite for development. Such measures link the ideological construction with the Chinese Dream closely, offering basic compliance for the moral construction. Second, it is needed to strengthen the ideological and moral construction, for which we should vigorously carry forward the core socialist values, cultivate social morality, professional ethics, family virtues and personal morality so as to guide people to comply with morality in life. Third, setting up role models for higher moral standards. By giving full to play the role of role models' demonstration, people get encouraged to respect morality and deeds of goodness. Fourth, carrying forward traditional Chinese virtues. In learning from the history, it is important to avoid those falling behind the times and bring forth the new from the old. Fifth, great importance should be attached to the betterment of individual family, including family bonding, family upbringing and family traditions, and cultivate the core socialist values in close promotion of the traditional family virtues of the Chinese nation.

3.3.4.2 Improving norms and strengthening management

Deng Xiaoping pointed out in 1992, "It will probably take another thirty years for us to develop a more mature and well-defined system in every field. The principles and policies to be applied under such system will also be more firmly established."[1] The Third Plenary Session of the 18th CPC Central Committee placed special emphasis on system construction. The most fundamental work in modernization of social governance lies in system reform and innovation. Some contradictions and problems at present in morality construction have much to do with the lag-behind of the system and norms during the transformation of society. The moral standard system integrates moral consciousness, concepts and judgment. It exerts influence on the whole society in the entire process of social governance. Modern society is complicated, and the system of social governance rules is not homogeneous, but consists of different categories, different levels and different aspects. The betterment of moral standard system must be carried out in line with the socialist market economy, and at the meantime, the new moral concept of the reform and opening up must be integrated. The moral system should conform to the essential requirements of socialism, embody the spirit of reform and innovation characterized by social criticism and the spirit of the times, and absorb the moral concepts of excellent cultures home and abroad. In addition to national laws and regulations, various forms of social norms (such as citizen conventions, township regulations, industry regulations, and group regulations) play an important role in regulating, directing and restraining organizations and individual members. Therefore, in the innovation of social governance, more attention should be paid to the use of other social norms so that every resident becomes the executor and supervisor of our social norms, through revision and improvement of village rules and regulations, and residents' conventions on the basis of full deliberation and discussion.

3.3.4.3 Co-construction and collaborative practicing

The cooperation and co-governance of multiple social subjects is an important symbol of the modernization of social governance. To strengthen moral restraint and incentives in social governance, we must proceed from China's national conditions. We can neither take the road of concentrating governance power on the government, nor the

---

[1] *Selected Works of Deng Xiaoping*, Vol. Ⅲ, Beijing: People's Publishing House, 1994, p. 372.

road relying entirely on non-governmental organizations as Western countries did. With the gradual improvement of the market economic system, the diversification of the social structure, the increasing of people's awareness of rights and the rapid development of information and communication technology, the long-accumulated market and social energy have been released, which has further laid the foundation and providing possibility for the co-construction of social governance.

The reform of social governance system calls for a reasonable definition of the functions of government, society and individuals. The government and the society have their own functions. Where the government's power cannot reach, social participation comes in. Through participating in social governance, members of society can get further moral education and improve their level of morality and independent individual morality gets developed. Functioning as a coordinator independently, morality plays a role in strengthening the administrative ethics and shaping the social moral system as well. The government has changed from a commander-in-chief to an equal actor to guide and promote the moral innovation in society. Society participants mainly refer to social organizations and civic moral groups, which are in a central position in the new moral regulation mode and have become the major force of moral regulation. Individuals are the participants and practitioners of moral regulation; they are not only the subject of moral regulation, but also the object to be regulated, and an important unit of moral internalization. Since 1997, Deqing County in Zhejiang Province, has tried to regulate and improve morality by granting moral awards, which has become an effective way to integrate various social values to achieve the goal of governance, playing an important role in social governance.[1] Based on Chinese traditional virtues and adapting to the changed social context, Deqing County practice explored ways of moral governance suitable for modern people's mentality and behavioral habits. Through mechanisms of communication, consultation, and expression, the relationship between different interest groups was balanced, thus enabling them to exert their specific function as moral governance actors. The spirit of law and that of the public were emphasized, the positive energy and moral constraints exerted influence in the whole society.

3.3.4.4 The coordination of law and morality

Law is the written form of morality, and morality is the inner law. They support each other in function, cooperate with each other in implementation and absorb each

---

[1] Guo Xiajuan, Yang Qijun, "From the Margin to the Center: The Moral Regulation of the 'Trinity' in Social Governance", *Zhejiang Social Sciences*, 2017(1).

other in content. Improving social governance ability is not a one-man show of law, but requires moral support and cooperation. Only by combining morality with law can we effectively promote and enhance social governance ability. Moreover, combining morality with law is the fundamental way to achieve the modernization of social governance. Effective moral governance depends on orderly legal governance, and the social governance activities must be legal and orderly, and reasonable and moral, rather than adapting only to the law or to moral governance.

Moral governance is the process of realizing moral ideals in human society. In a society ruled by law, morality is the prerequisite for achieving an orderly society, and it is also an important measure to promote the natural formation of social order. We must adhere to the combination of rule of law and rule by virtue. The modernization level of the national governance system and governance capacity can be constantly improved through close combination of the construction of rule of law with moral construction, and close combination of heteronomy with self-governance. Then we can realize the unity of ex-post punishment and ex-ante regulation, the unity of macro-control and micro-regulation, the unity of low cost and high efficiency, the unity of heteronomy and self-governance, the unity of pragmatism and foresightedness, and the unity of purification of the overall social environment and promotion of individual moral level.

3.4   Scientific and technological support

3.4.1   Science and technology development and social governance progress

The innovation of engineering science and technology drives history to move forward rapidly, providing an inexhaustible source of power for the progress of human civilization from ignorance to civilization, from nomadic civilization to agricultural civilization, to industrial civilization and to the information age. Human society has experienced the agricultural revolution, industrial revolution and is currently undergoing the information revolution. The agricultural revolution brought human society from barbarism to civilized society with human beings evolving from feeding and hunting to planting and raising, thus enhancing the survival ability of human beings. The industrial revolution replaced manpower with machines and replaced manual production in individual workshops with large-scale factory production, thus expanding reach of human physical strength. The information revolution, on the other hand, has strengthened man's brainpower, bringing about another qualitative leap in productivity, and exerting profound influence on the development of international politics, economy, culture, society, ecology, military and other fields. When Europe and the rest of the world were going through the industrial revolution, China lost the opportunity to progress, but now China is in the information revolution, the historical process of "information and economic globalization". Xi Jinping pointed out, "This is an important historical opportunity for the Chinese nation, and we must firmly grasp it."[1]

The Internet, one of the greatest inventions in the 20th century, has been integrated into all aspects of social life and has profoundly changed people's production and lifestyle. With the development of mobile Internet, Internet of Things, big data, cloud computing and artificial intelligence, everything in human life is changing. An emerging field, the Internet gives an overtaking opportunity for China's national development. The Internet plays a strong driving role in innovation and development in many fields, bringing historical opportunities for innovation in all walks of life. At the same time, the development of the Internet poses new challenges to national sovereignty, national security and national interests. With the Internet becoming the "maximum variable", the Party has to face up to its challenges for its long-term administration.

This unprecedented era of rapid development provides us with opportunities to enhance social governance with foresight and efficiency and with solutions to problems in social governance, but also brings new challenges to social governance.[2]To grasp the opportunities and to answer the challenges, we must make constant efforts to improve the ability to take opportunities, and to face up to risks and challenges, so that the opportunities become driving forces and the "maximum variable" can release "maximum positive energy".

3.4.2 The development of science and technology and the reform of social governance in China

As pointed out by Xi Jinping, it is necessary to put more stress on cooperation and integration and co-governance, on democracy and law, and technological innovation. Social governance should not only be participated by all under the rule of law, but also

---

[1] Xi Jinping, "Speech at the Symposium on Cybersecurity and Informatization Work", *People's Daily*, Apr. 26, 2016.

[2] Meng Jianzhu, "Deepening Social Governance Innovation to Further Enhance People's Sense of Security: Study and Implement General Secretary Xi Jinping's Important Instructions on Strengthening and Innovating Social Governance", *Chang'an*, 2016(11).

be smart and professional, so as to enhance the ability to predict, prevent and cope with various risks. It is necessary to improve the comprehensive management of social security and speed up the construction of a three-dimensional and information-based social security system. Since the 18th CPC National Congress, we have been adhering to the guidance of science and technology support. And by using modern scientific and technological means like the Internet, Internet of Things, big data and cloud computing, many places in China have realized informatization and precision of three-dimensional and intelligent social governance, laying a high-tech protection network for people's safety, which greatly improved the modernization of China's national social governance.

3.4.2.1   Informatization of social governance

Acceleration of the construction of the basic digitalized social governance system has greatly improved the predictability, accuracy and efficiency of social governance, laying the foundation stone for making full use of modern science and technology. As Xi Jinping pointed out, in the modernization of the national governance system and capacity, information is an important basis for national governance and should play an important role in this process. In recent years, we have made overall plans to develop e-government, online service platforms, and new smart cities, breaking through information barriers and building a national information resource sharing system. Relevant departments have issued a series of regulations on the establishment of citizenship identification number, organization registration code, real estate registration, real name access to the Internet etc. These regulations played an important role in strengthening the basic work of social governance with a national complaint center and a basic comprehensive service management platform. At present, China has achieved the goal of accuracy and exclusivity in citizenship identification number management. The comprehensive and accurate basic information laid a foundation for speeding up the upgrading of the demographic information management system, and for information integration and sharing across departments and regions so as to establish an online inquiry and comparison system for household registration and ID card information that enables citizens to renew or apply for their ID cards and do the fingerprint information registration outside their registered permanent residence.[1] In April 2014, National Public Complaints and Proposals Administration issued Opinions on Promoting

---

[1] Meng Jianzhu, "Deepening Social Governance Innovation to Further Enhancing People's Sense of Security: Study and Implement General Secretary Xi Jinping's Important Instructions on Strengthening and Innovating Social Governance", *Chang'an*, 2016(11).

Digitalization in Work of Public Complaints and Proposals, clearly proposing to build a nationwide information system for public complaints and proposals that connect the grassroots with the national government. In 2015, public complaints and proposals were successfully digitalized, and the information system became the major channel for circulation of public complaints and proposals. In April 2015, the General Office of the CPC Central Committee and the General Office of the State Council issued the Opinions on Strengthening the Construction of Social Security Prevention and Control System, which required the establishment of a national information sharing database of unique citizenship identification number, and of a real-name registration system in relevant fields. After 2015, the central government made deployments and requirements for speeding up the sharing of government data and improving government services with the help of Internet technology, which has accelerated the pace of innovation and changes in corresponding fields with a series of documents such as the Action Outline for Promoting the Development of Big Data, Guiding Opinions on Vigorously Advancing the "Internet Plus" Action, Guiding Opinions on Accelerating the Promotion of the "Internet + Government Services" Work, and Interim Measures for the Administration of Sharing of Government Information Resources. According to the Action Outline for Promoting the Development of Big Data, by 2018, unified data sharing platform will have covered all state-level government organs. The Outline of the 13th Five-Year Plan specifically requires the establishment of a basic national demographic database to strengthen construction of systems of population management, real-name registration, credit system and crisis warning and intervention, etc.; and improvements will be made to the comprehensive service management platform for urban and rural communities to promote the connection of public services, people-friendly services, and voluntary services, and to realize one-stop service. Full coverage of comprehensive service facilities in urban communities shall be achieved and the construction of comprehensive service facilities in rural communities shall be promoted.

3.4.2.2 Social governance refinement

Refined management is a management mode that ensures each unit of an organization operates accurately, efficiently, and cooperatively through systematization and concretization of rules and the use of procedural, standardized and data-based means. At present, refined management has been applied to the field of public management and has expanded into social governance. The Fifth Plenary Session of the 18th CPC Central Committee proposed to strengthen and innovate social governance, promoting the refinement of social governance, and building a social governance pattern that is jointly built and shared by the whole society. The Internet provides a technology platform for equal communication. And the characteristics of interconnection and intercommunication in the network society bring opportunities for refined governance. The sharing and intercommunication of network information platforms improve the accessibility and convenience of public management and services, where the comparative advantages of different governance actors will be highlighted. Information technology improves the accuracy and detail of social governance, and accelerates its transition to a refined social governance.

The exploration and practice of grid management is an important embodiment of social governance refinement. The Third Plenary Session of the 18th CPC Central Committee made a clear requirement to take "networked management and socialized service as our direction, improving grassroots level comprehensive service platforms, reflecting and coordinating in a timely manner the interests and appeals of the people from all walks of life and at all levels." Beijing took the lead in introducing the grid model of urban management in 2004, which was later expanded to social service management and social security management, and then promoted the integration of urban management network, social service management network and social security network. In August 2015, Beijing issued another document of "1+3" gridded management, clearly proposing the "three-step" goal to complete full coverage of information collection in key monitoring areas by 2018 for normalized and institutionalized refinement and gridded management. Guiyang City, in Guizhou Province, on the basis of grid management, explored and made good use of "governance technology" such as blockchain and "identity chain" and realized accurate governance and service through scenario application in social governance.

Standardization is the key to the refinement of social governance and public services, with clear and precise standards for managers and service providers. To implement standardization of social governance, it is necessary to establish a framework for public services covering standard systems, support platforms and evaluation mechanisms. Based on the development of specific function management standards, and the construction of a standardized system for government functions, it is necessary to promote work planning for the standardization of government management and services. As early as December 1988, the Standardization Law of the People's Republic of China was enacted, and the Standardization Administration of PRC was established in 2001 to strengthen the unified management of standardization work. In March 2015, the State

Council formulated and issued the Program on Deepening the Reform of the Work of Standardization, which put forward the general requirements and a series of initiatives for deepening the reform of standardization work in the coming period. Up to now, a system covering the first, second and third industries and various fields of social undertakings has basically taken shape with the total number of 100,000 national standards, industry standards and local standards in China. Standardization has played an increasingly important role in ensuring product quality and safety, promoting economic development and social progress, so that it can regulate management services. Meanwhile, it also serves public the diplomacy of foreign economic and trade cooperation and exchange.[1] The Cybersecurity Law of the People's Republic of China adopted in November, 2016 requires to promote the construction of cybersecurity protection system under the guidance of the standard system, so as to strengthen cybersecurity protection in core areas through mandatory national standards, and to strengthen cyberspace governance under the guidance of national standards and industry standards. This gives unprecedented priority to cybersecurity standardization.

3.4.2.3 Three-dimensional social governance

The Report to the 18th CPC National Congress clearly put forward that we should "intensify efforts to ensure law and order, improve the multi-dimensional system for crime prevention and control". Xi Jinping also pointed out that "with the development of the Internet, especially the mobile Internet, social governance model is shifting from one-way management to two-way interaction, from offline to online-offline integration, from simple government supervision to more-focused collaborative social governance". These changes have put forward new requirements for the multi-dimensional social governance which is a response to the complex social security situation, and to bettering the comprehensive management of social security.

At present, public security incidents are prone to occur more often, and the task of maintaining public security is heavy. In recent years, the comprehensive political and legal governance organs have integrated information resources and network platforms. Supported by big data, cloud computing and "Internet Plus", they integrated modern information means with traditional practices. With concerted efforts of relevant departments and active participation of social forces, an effective multi-dimensional institutional mechanism was established that integrates combat, defense and control,

---

[1] Wei Liqun, "Accelerating Standardization to Promote Modernization of Governance", *China Standardization* (*Overseas Edition*), 2016(1).

and connects online and offline. In 2009, the Ministry of Public Security proposed the construction of "six networks, four mechanisms", which aimed to expand the security system from the city to the countryside. The General Office of the CPC Central Committee and the General Office of the State Council issued the Opinions on Strengthening the Construction of Public Security Prevention and Control System in 2015, calling for the construction of an innovative multi-dimensional social security system and the comprehensive promotion of Peaceful China Initiative. The social security system entered the stage of co-construction by the state government and society. The main body of the social security system has gone through an interactive stage from local to national public security departments, further elevating to the central government, and then a government-led stage with extensive participation of social forces. In November 2015, the Ministry of Public Security, together with Publicity Department of the CPC Central Committee, the Ministry of Industry and Information Technology, the People's Bank of China and other departments, organized a special operation to combat new types of crimes in cyber networks. Through investigations tracing into the origins of criminal activities, and fighting against the entire procedures of criminal activities with multi-dimensional information technology means, effective management over new types of crimes in cyber networks was implemented.

3.4.2.4   Intelligent social governance

Xi Jinping pointed out, promoting intelligent social governance should focus more on scientific and technological innovation. Integrated with modern scientific and technological means such as big data, social governance may take a big leap forward.

Integration of technological revolution with the mechanism reform will bring forth great creativity. As a national strategy, big data is increasingly becoming a core driving force to promote the modernization of national governance system and capacity. Explorations are taking place in deep integration of big data, cloud computing and other applications with social governance innovation to promote function improvement, and mechanism reform so as to enhance social governance intelligence. Guizhou Province integrated and shared social governance data on the unified "Guizhou-Cloud Big Data" platform. They carried out data mining, data research and analysis through cloud computing, which broke the boundaries between regions, departments and police types, and promoted the integration of vertical governance and horizontal governance. The combination of big data and community governance created an ecological, green and intelligent management of the new "cloud community" and improved the quality of life of residents. Shanghai's 12th Five-year Plan sets "smart city" as the most important goal.

They collected, analyzed and integrated data with general information technology and applied them to traffic safety, urban services, and citizen livelihood. The "smart city" is the "business card" of a city's civilization and competitiveness, and of transformation of social governance mode. Guangdong Provincial Public Security Department has built a "video cloud + big data" platform with dynamic face recognition as the core technology with over 70% accuracy in specific environments. They created professional models that judge late-night access and improved the information acquisition, and discovery ability of public security organs through intelligent discovery of suspicious characters. Wuhan, in Hubei Province, has integrated massive information source of a comprehensive social security management system and a database of public security cloud, and has realized the cascading analysis and intelligent application of 50 billion pieces of data in 83 categories.

3.4.3 Risk society in the age of technology

From the perspective of the technological revolution, everything in human life is transforming with the development of mobile Internet, the Internet of Things, big data, cloud computing and artificial intelligence. Such an era of rapid development, unprecedented in human history, provides important opportunities for us to enhance our foresight, accuracy and efficiency in social governance, and to answer social governance challenges, but also brings new challenges to social governance.[1]

3.4.3.1 Scientific and technological progress has brought about increased risk

The secret of the industrial era is the division of labor, as seen in how the assembly line greatly improved production efficiency; the secret of the Internet era is integration, namely information exchange, resource sharing, and method superposition. The Internet is changing all aspects of people's lives, bringing great benefits to people's production and life, along with many risks. The rapid progress of science and technology has put society in a complex intertwined picture of informatization and networking, which worked together with China's economic transition and social transformation, has driven economy and society changes. In this context, various types of contradictions are intertwined and superimposed, risks are more deeply interrelated, and the complexity of social contradictions are deepened and public security risks increase. With short-term and long-term contradictions superimposed, structural factors and cyclical factors

---

[1] Meng Jianzhu, "Deepening Social Governance Innovation to Further Enhance People's Sense of Security: Study and Implement General Secretary Xi Jinping's Important Instructions on Strengthening and Innovating Social Governance", *Chang'an*, 2016 (11).

coexisting, and traditional risks and nontraditional risks increasing, China's economy and society have encountered many unprecedented problems. This has brought China into a risk society. The deeper digitalization develops, the more diverse and complex the information security issues may present themselves. Currently, the most prominent security threats are mainly from cyberspace and the complexity, and the impact of cybersecurity are far beyond traditional security issues. At present, network crimes in China have accounted for one-third of the total number of crimes, with an annual growth rate of more than 30%. Due to globalization and networked information diffusion, the Internet has become an amplifier of criminal activities. A prominent feature of today's society is the increasing scope and speed of population flow. Easier cross-border population flow helps digitalization development break through the original national and geographical boundaries, making cross-border economic cases, criminal cases, terrorism, and infectious diseases worldwide problems.

In the past few years, there have frequently occurred network information security incidents, causing great impact on governments, enterprises and individuals. Network security and information technology are mutually reinforcing. As Xi Jinping pointed out, that we must recognize that, seen from history, many technologies are "double-edged swords". On the one hand, technology can benefit society and people, but on the other hand, it can also harm the interest of the public and people. From a global perspective, cybersecurity threats and risks are becoming increasingly prominent, especially in political, economic, cultural, social, ecological areas. In particular, the critical national information infrastructure is facing greater risks, while the network security defense and control capabilities are weak, making it difficult to effectively respond to national-level and organized high-intensity network attacks.[1]

3.4.3.2 Slower progress in social governance innovation

The governance concept lags behind. The modernization of social governance requires a "data culture" that respects facts and rationality, and emphasizes precision and details. However, in traditional Chinese culture, intuition and emotional thinking are better accepted. Thus, it is customary to make vague generalizations about things, instead of rigorous, rational and systematic empirical researches. This way of thinking tends to lead to oversimplification over sophistication.[2]

---

[1] Xi Jinping, "Speech at the Symposium on Cybersecurity and Informatization Work", *People's Daily*, Apr. 26, 2016.

[2] Meng Jianzhu, "Strengthening and Innovating Social Governance", *People's Daily*, Nov. 17, 2015.

Resources are not sufficiently shared. The increased cross-domain and interrelated nature of the various types of risks necessitates comprehensive measures. Government organs at various levels are actively using new technologies to improve their governance; however, due to the long-term division of the administrative system, there are still unclear definitions of responsibilities and powers among government departments, causing various problems in technology application in governance and difficulties in data security protection. Information resources are closed to each other, and government departments become independent "information islands", so that the information is difficult to interoperate and share and many social governance initiatives and social services are not effectively implemented. However, it is not appropriate to overemphasize technology, thinking that all problems can be solved through technical means, but ignoring the role of government organs as major actor in social governance.

The gap in core technology is not invisible. For more than 20 years, China's Internet development has hit remarkable achievements; big data, cloud computing and other technologies are used in social governance and have some good results. Overall, China's science and technology innovation foundation is still not firm, independent innovation especially originality is not strong enough. Compared with the world's advanced level, there is still a wide gap in many aspects, the biggest of which lies in the core technology and the core technology blockade of China has been the biggest hidden danger. To achieve the modernization of social governance, and to protect Internet security and national security, China must make breakthroughs in core technology for the possibility of "corner overtaking" in certain fields.

3.4.4 Bringing to full play the science and technology support

In order to better adapt to the social situation and the general trend of scientific and technological revolution, we need to be good at using the latest achievements of modern science and technology to solve difficult problems, and at preventing and responding to the risks and challenges brought by them, so as to promote social governance to a new level and further improve social governance work.

3.4.4.1 Tackling the core technology and promoting the leapfrog development of social governance

With the rapid development and widespread application of modern technology, China's economic and social life will undergo profound changes, and the objects, contents, concepts and methods of social governance will also undergo fundamental transformation. At present, China's scientific and technological innovation has entered a new stage. A new round of technological revolution and industrial transformation is gestating. The Fifth Plenary Session of the 18th CPC Central Committee and the Outline of the 13th Five-Year Plan have made arrangements for strengthening the country through the network, the "Internet Plus" action plan and the big data strategy. It is necessary to determine the strategies orientated to problems according to the national conditions: concentrate on core technologies such as high-end general-purpose chips, integrated circuit equipment and broadband mobile communications, striving for major breakthroughs in quantum communication, intelligent manufacturing, robotics, brain science, etc., and innovating "governance technology" such as blockchain and "identity chain". The purpose of scientific and technological innovation is to better serve the people, making full use of the new technology to improve social governance, which will also promote the realization of social governance reform in China. To promote the improvement of social governance functions and mechanisms, a vision of the future and the mentality of innovation are a must to identify the entry point of scientific and technological means to serve social governance innovation, and to deeply integrate technological innovation. With science and technology integrated with social governance, modernization of social governance system and ability is made possible through digitalization that can be applied to improving awareness of social situations, clearing communication channels, supporting decision making, ensuring social security, and to solving social problems. On this basis, we will be able to realize the leap-forward development of social governance in China.

3.4.4.2 Deep integration and strengthening information infrastructure construction

If the keyword of the industrial age is division of labor, then the keyword of the Internet age shall be integration, that is, information exchange and resource sharing. In the information age, economic globalization, regional integration and social informatization result in social risks and threats that are more overlapping and more interrelated, which naturally requires deep integration of scattered information resources and emphasis on information infrastructure construction. First, the construction of information infrastructure may start with building a national information resource sharing system based on a unified for government data sharing and exchange platform so as to promote the vertical and horizontal integration through improved interaction and collaboration among regions, departments, and tiers. Second, multiple social governance resources can be integrated by encouraging enterprises, industry associations, scientific research institutions and social organizations to collect and open access to data. Third, the systematicity, integrity and synergy of social governance can be enhanced with more attention on online and offline interaction and complementarity through facility connectivity, information exchange, resource sharing, and communication between computer programs.

3.4.4.3   Interacting and integrating, enhancing governance synergy through open co-governance

Fundamentally speaking, social governance is to safeguard the interests of people. Without the participation of the people, the reform of social governance cannot be truly realized. The application of the Internet will promote governance to transform from a "government acting alone" to a "society working together" among all parties, and gradually realize a new social governance model of multi-subject. First of all, we should establish and improve the working system and mechanism of linkage and integration; set up a unified leadership or coordination organization, build a good working platform, and coordinate resources of all parties. Then we need to build a "flat and open" management service team composed of professional forces, volunteers, non-governmental organizations and other public welfare forces, generating a new network-like, real-time and multi-dimensional collaborative governance pattern, and forming a joint force in social governance. Secondly, we shall make overall plans to develop e-government by building an integrated online service management platform, promoting the construction of new smart cities. Finally, we should make full use of the achievements of new technologies to expand the ways and means for the people to participate in social governance. In that way, it is possible to promote network democracy, and electronic democracy, optimizing the governance structure, which shall effectively solve the "last mile" problem of contacting and serving the people.

3.5   Integration and innovation

The realization of the Chinese Dream requires generations of Chinese Communists to lead the people in successive struggles. Social governance under the new situation is a complex systemic project that requires a firm position and a scientific approach. Since the 18th CPC National Congress, the Party and the state have been able to open a new chapter, which is fundamentally due to the CPC Central Committee with Xi Jinping as its core. The CPC has been adhering to dialectical thinking, to practical and theoretical innovation, and constantly has enriched and developed Marxist methodology and comprehensively promoted the systematization of social governance.

3.5.1   Innovating ideas, enhancing governance in the overall situation

Promoting the modernization of the national governance system and capacity is a complex systematic project, which cannot be advanced by individuals, but requires planning and coordination. To strive for a Peaceful China, we must make and implement plans in the overall situation of economic and social development and the Overall Plan (the overall plan for promoting economic, political, cultural, social, and ecological progress), so that social governance and develops in step with economic and social development. Adjustment of social governance assessment is required in a timely manner, so that social governance will extend wherever the problems arise.

The concept of social governance comes from the social practice, and in return, it guides the practice and leads the development of social governance methods. First, the overall situation constantly deepens our understanding of the overall work of the Party and the state, and constantly adjusts the overall situation of social governance. At present, to promote the modernization of the national governance system and capacity, we need to find the right point in the overall situation, so as to innovate social governance mechanisms and methods to resolve social conflicts and to promote social harmony. Second, the concept of the people should be emphasized. Social governance is in essence the public work of the Party. We should always adhere to the people-centered philosophy and govern for the people, carrying out the concept of mass work throughout the whole process of social governance, and improving the ability of public work, and actively explore new ways to do social governance well. Third, we must be equipped with the concept of law, using legitimate thinking in social governance, and studying and promoting the legalization of social governance. Fourth, we must promote the scientific and modern social governance under the guidance of scientific concept. Social governance system that not only embodies the scientific concept and spirit, but also generates scientific planning, scientific rules and operation can be established, and social governance can be done through modern science and technology. Fifth, we have to establish the people-centered philosophy. By doing so we can integrate governance and service and promote the transformation from "governance" to "service" by improving services to society, enterprises and grassroots units. In a word, we should lead the innovation of social governance with the new development concept of "innovation, coordination, green, openness and sharing", enhancing the ability and level of co-construction, so that our social governance ability can be comprehensively enhanced and can better coordinate social economic development, urban and rural development, and material and spiritual civilization development.

3.5.2   Open and co-management, enhancing the synergy of social governance

In the context of economic globalization, regional integration and social informatization, various overlapping and interrelated risks have arisen. Therefore, departments, regions and organizations need to coordinate through open co-governance. To establish the working system and mechanism, all relevant departments in various regions must abandon departmentalism, and coordinate resources for facility connectivity, information exchange, strength coordination and resource sharing. Besides, joint efforts must be made for integrity and synergy of social governance, through connection in work and procedure, regional cooperation and vertical and horizontal complementation.

We should form a pattern of cooperation and co-governance with unitary leadership and multi-participation. A large number of social affairs and service functions can be delegated to social organizations and the public under the leadership of the Party and government. Various social forces are welcome to play active roles in social governance. Public institutions, and enterprises should be guided to fulfill their social responsibilities; people's organizations and industry associations should be encouraged to play their role in social governance and public service activities; and social organizations that can undertake social services on the list of government purchase should be encouraged and supported to grow. Moreover, we ought to enhance the construction of people's self-governing organizations in urban and rural communities, improving the new community governance system with people's self-governing organizations as the major actor and extensive participation of all social parties. Thus, urban and rural communities are built into the basic platform of social governance.

3.5.3   Multiple measures to promote the scientific social governance

In the modernization of the scientific social governance, more attention should be paid to comprehensive application, scientific and technological innovation and to democracy and law for the socialization, legalization, and digitalization of specialized social governance. First, it is necessary to effectively develop socialist democracy, enabling citizens' rational and lawful political participation. And social consensus can be achieved through improved internet public opinion collection and consultation mechanism so as to achieve legalization of social governance. Second, it is necessary to accelerate improvement of legislation in the field of social governance, so that a better legal system can be achieved and social interest appeals can be satisfied through lawful measures for greater social governance efficiency. Third, we should focus on the application of scientific and technological innovation in social governance, and advance the ability to predict and prevent various social risks. The Internet technology, big data analysis, etc., may help break the barriers among interest groups through internet resource integration, standard unification and openness and sharing. Fourth, more emphasis should be given to the construction of basic systems to provide support for building an honest society and improving the overall level of social governance. Credit management system, mechanism of trust and responsibility must be established, evaluation and supervision mechanism must be enhanced, and information exchange mechanism must be improved for a transparent and operational social governance model.

3.5.4 Systematically summarizing experience and strengthening top-level design

At present, China's reform and development have stepped into an intricate and complex situation, with difficulties arising and problems intertwined, which requires broader vision, greater wisdom and more refined skills in national governance. Since the 18th CPC National Congress, the CPC Central Committee has attached greater importance to learning and using the basic principles of Marxism,[1] insisting on the use of dialectical thinking, the combination of top-level design and practice in modernizing social governance through correct judgement of reality and trend of development. Xi Jinping stresses the need to constantly enhance the ability of dialectical thinking and improve the ability to handle complex situations. With dialectical thinking, strategic thinking, and bottom-line thinking, we can constantly improve the ability to solve basic problems in China's reform and development. In addition, through combination of top-level design of the central government and specific local practice, we can improve the top-level design of social governance innovation, and establish ways suitable for our national conditions through systematical summarization of local experience through in-depth investigation.

Governance theory is a foreign theory. In order for it to work in China, a governance approach suitable for China's national conditions needs to be established.

---

[1] The eleventh, twentieth and twenty-eighth collective study of the Political Bureau of the 18th CPC Central Committee were themed on the basic principles and methodology of historical materialism, the basic principles and methodology of dialectical materialism and the basic principles and methodology of Marxist political economy.

With situations varying greatly in different parts of China, one lesson learned from practice and proved to be successful in China's reform is to summarize local experience. On the Third Plenary Session of the 18th CPC Central Committee, the Decisions of the CPC Central Committee on Some Major Issues Concerning Comprehensively Deepening the Reform states that it is necessary to "firmly follow the road of socialism with Chinese characteristics" and to "summarize successful domestic practices, draw on beneficial foreign experiences, and courageously promote theoretical and practical innovations" from the practical point of view. Summarization of social governance experience should be based on reality and practice instead of "starting all over again" or "having discrepancy". The advantages of litigation mediation and grand mediation mechanism as a tradition should be given full play in resolving conflicts and disputes in accordance with law.

Chapter 4
People's Organizations in Social Governance

People's organizations such as trade unions, Communist Youth League, Women's Federation, link the Party and the government to the people are a major driving force for advancing the modernization of China's system and capacity for governance. In February 2015, Opinions on Strengthening and Improving the Party's Work on People's Organizations issued by the CPC Central Committee specifies that "the people's organizations are important channels for people's extensive and orderly participation in national and social affairs as well as economic and cultural undertakings in accordance with the law". It also proposed people's organizations' major historical tasks in innovation-oriented social governance. Under new circumstances, the full utilization of the people's organizations' resource advantages and active participation in social governance innovation are of great significance to consolidate the basis of the Party's governance, stimulate social vigor, safeguard social fairness and justice and improve social governance ability.

4.1   Overview

The Chinese socialist development path of people's organizations is a creation of the CPC in carrying out public work and advancing the cause of the Party and an important part of the path of socialism with Chinese characteristics. The people's organizations led by the CPC have made significant contributions to the Party's missions at all historical periods of revolution, construction and reform. In the new era, to realize the Two Centenary Goals[1] and the Chinese Dream of national rejuvenation,

---

[1] The Two Centenary Goals are to complete a moderately prosperous society in all respects by the centenary of the CPC (founded in 1921), and to build China into a modern socialist country that is prosperous, strong, democratic, culturally advanced, and harmonious by the centenary of the People's Republic of China (founded in 1949). —*Tr.*

China needs to do a solid work on people's organizations, give full play to the important role of people's organizations and better pool the strength to forge ahead in unity and overcome challenges.

4.1.1   The formation and development of people's organizations

4.1.1.1   The formation of people's organizations

In the early 20th century, the Revolution of 1911, led by Sun Yat-sen and other pioneers of the democratic revolution overthrew the autocracy of the Qing Government, This brought series of unprecedented changes in China, particularly the emergence of social forces with intellectuals as representatives and numerous association activities. During the May Fourth Movement, with the vigorous development of the New Culture Movement, the establishment of new associations was in full swing. In this context, the term "people's organizations" emerged.

Under the governance of Nanking National Government, a series of laws and regulations were formulated to regulate the development of social associations such as the Organization Plan of People's Organizations (June 1929), the Amendment to Organization Plan of People's Organizations (July 1930), the Organization Plan of Mass Organizations (August 1932), etc. Such regulations divided "people's organizations" into occupational organizations and social organizations.

In the liberated areas under the leadership of the CPC, expressions such as revolutionary organizations, mass organizations and people's organizations were more frequently used to refer to social organizations. Before the War of Resistance against Japanese Aggression, the CPC often referred to social organizations as revolutionary organizations and mass organizations, the former exhibited political orientation while the latter reflected broad representation. In 1942, the Shaanxi-Gansu-Ningxia Border Region government formulated Outline of People's Organizations of Shaanxi-Gansu-Ningxia Border Region and Measures for the Registration of Public Organizations in the Shaanxi-Gansu-Ningxia Border Region, granting legal positions to social organizations. After the victory of the War of Resistance Against Japanese Aggression in 1945, "people's organization" was frequently used in speeches by the leaders of the CPC and in various important documents.

4.1.1.2   The development of people's organizations

From September 21 to 30, 1949, over 600 representatives from 46 institutions of the CPC, other political parties, people's organizations and prominent individuals without any party affiliation attended the First Plenary Session of the Chinese People's Political Consultative Conference (CPPCC) exercising the functions and powers of the National People's Congress (NPC). The conference passed the Common Program of the Chinese People's Political Consultative Conference which functioned as a provisional constitution.

After the conference, changes took place to social organizations in China, and several organizations converted into people's organizations. In September 1950, the Provisional Measures for Registration of Social Organizations passed by the Government Administration Council of the Central People's Government, classified organizations in terms of ranges of activity and function, into mass organization, social welfare organization, arts organization, academic organization, religious organization and other organizations formed in accordance with the laws of people's government. Among them, mass organizations refer to social organizations that extensively undertake public social activities, such as the Federation of Trade Unions, Farmers' Association, Federation of Industry and Commerce, Women's Federation, Youth Federation, Students' Federation, etc. The Provisional Measures for Registration of Social Organizations grants these people's organizations with particular political status including representation in the CPPCC and exemption from registration of social organizations. With broad public foundation, these people's organizations have their own organizations from the central government to grassroots and are major link between the Party and the grassroots people of all walks of life and from all social groups. Historically, they have been assistants of the Party, so their central leading organs are equal to the Party and government departments. Therefore, judging from their origin, people's organizations should be defined at present time as the specified organizations with political missions, vast members and broad representation in society, and whether they are exempted from organization registration and enjoy government funding are not the factors that define "people's organization".[1]

4.1.2 The nature and features of people's organizations

4.1.2.1 The nature of people's organizations

People's organizations led by the CPC are the national people's organizations with their own characteristics that are engaged in specific social activities. They are shaped

---

[1] Gong Weibin, *Social System of Governance with Chinese Characteristics*, Beijing: Economy & Management Publishing House, 2016.

by specific historical, cultural, and political conditions, and have distinct political, progressive, and popular characteristics.

People's organizations, as a unique social organization in China, are organized under the guidance of the CPC or approved by government departments authorized by the State Council, which receive funds for administrative undertakings by the state, consciously accept the leadership of the CPC, play the role of bridge and link, and carry out their work in accordance with the laws and regulations. On October 25, 1989, the State Council issued the Regulation on Registration and Management of Social Organizations, which for the first time gave an authoritative definition of "social organizations" with its connotation close to that of "people's organizations". Regulation on Registration and Management of Social Organizations stipulates that three types of organizations do not fall within the scope of required registration: those that are included in the Chinese People's Political Consultative Conference, those that are approved by the State Council's institutional establishment body, and those that are affiliated to and are approved by government organs, organizations, enterprises and institutions and operate only within the organizations. In December 2000, the Ministry of Civil Affairs of the State Council issued the Notice on Issues Relating to Exemption of Some Organizations from Registration, which clearly defined which organizations can be exempted from registration. Among those that are granted the exemption of registration, eight are included in the CPPCC, which are All-China Federation of Trade Unions, the Communist Youth League of China, the All-China Women's Federation, China Association for Science and Technology, All-China Federation of Returned Overseas Chinese, All-China Federation of Taiwan Compatriots, All-China Youth Federation, All-China Federation of Industry and Commerce. Fourteen social organizations are exempted from registration with the approval of the State Council, which includes China Federation of Literary and Art Circles, China Writers Association, All-China Journalists Association, the Chinese People's Association for Friendship with Foreign Countries, Chinese People's Institute of Foreign Affairs, China Council for the Promotion of International Trade, China Disabled Persons' Federation, China Soong Ching Ling Foundation, China Law Society, Red Cross Society of China, Chinese Society of Ideological and Political Work, Western Returned Scholars Association, Alumni Association of the Huangpu Military Academy, and China Vocational Education Association.

The 22 people's organizations mentioned above are all under the leadership of the CPC and have relatively strict and standardized association constitutions and organizational system. They represent the majority of the people at all levels, in all fields, in all strata, in all fronts and in all groups in China, and basically cover organizational structures of different types, characters and fields. Generally speaking, "people's organizations" can be defined in a narrow sense and in a broad sense. In a narrow sense, it refers specifically to the eight social organizations that are included in the CPPCC. In a broad sense, it refers to social organizations that are not registered and may not need to be registered, and other social organizations whose main tasks, establishment and leadership positions are directly determined by establishment departments.[1]

4.1.2.2 Features of the people's organizations

People's organizations under the leadership of the CPC are neither the non-governmental organizations nor the "third sector" in Western countries, nor the ordinary social organizations in China. They are typical of both "governmental and non-governmental" natures. They not only represent the interests of the people, but also connect the Party and the government with the public. Their basic characteristic is consciously adhering to CPC leadership, uniting and serving the people that they contact, and operating under the organizational constitution and the law.

(1) *Distinctive political nature*

People's organizations are social organizations with Chinese characteristics formed under specific political and historical conditions in China, which consciously follow the leadership of the Party, carry out the Party's proposition, play the function of united front, represent the interests of certain social groups and participate in national political activities, but they are not political parties. Although people's organizations are not state administrative bodies in the traditional sense, in a general sense, they have extremely significant state attributes, functioning as arms of the Party and the government, and undertaking a large number of social management affairs. After the promulgation of the Provisional Regulation of Civil Servant in 1993, Trade Unions, the Communist Youth League, Women's Federation and other people's organizations were included in the administrative establishment. At the national level, except for the Red Cross Society of China, the Chinese Society of Ideological and Political Work, and the China Family Planning Association are administrative establishments, and all other mass organizations are managed with reference to the Civil Servant Law of the People's Republic of China. Their daily funding is allocated by the state treasury, and their leaders are appointed and assessed by the organizational departments of the Party

---

[1] Gong Weibin, *Social System of Governance with Chinese Characteristics*, Beijing: Economy & Management Publishing House, 2016.

committees. It is because of their state attributes that the mass organizations have had a strong administrative tendency for a long time.

(2) *Innate social nature*

People's organizations in China are led by the Party and the government, and at the same time, they represent the interests of the people. Judging from the nature and content of their work, people's organizations' work is organizing, mobilizing, contacting and serving the people. People's organizations such as Trade Unions, the Communist Youth League, Women's Federation are in contact with people of different sectors and in different fields, representing their interests, and conveying their opinions, suggestions and voices, operating on the non-profit and voluntary basis for public welfare and involving the public to a great extent. These characteristics are the same as those of ordinary social organizations registered in the civil affairs department, which suggests their strong social attributes. At the same time, people's organizations focus on the most immediate and practical interests of the general public, and carry out social services and public welfare activities such as entrepreneurship and employment, poverty alleviation and relief, and old-age assistance for the disabled.

(3) *Performing functions in accordance with organizational constitutions and the law*

Although the people's organizations in China are not covered by the Regulations on Registration and Management of Social Organizations, they generally have their own constitutions and functions within the framework of state laws, insisting on carrying out their work and performing their functions and tasks independently in accordance with their constitutions. The constitution of each people's organization clearly stipulates their nature, functions, goals, tasks, organizational principles and rights and obligations of the members. The constitution has a strong binding effect on the people's organizations and their members.

(4) *Sound organizational system*

Due to its unique nature and status, Chinese people's organizations are large in number, broad in their scope and have various functions and numerous members. As a channel for the Party to keep in touch with the public, people's organizations are close to the public, represent the public and serve them. They have broad public basis that no other social organization can reach. People's organizations have a mature work network and organizational system with their grassroots organizations found in urban and rural government offices, communities, enterprises, schools and other fields throughout the country. By the end of 2012, the number of grassroots organizations of the eight people's organizations in China was about 6.683 million, far exceeding the total number of social organizations registered in the civil affairs authorities. An organizational network that reaches the bottom and covers the widest range has been formed.

(5) *Good tradition and extensive influence*

In different historical periods, people's organizations, under the leadership of the Party, have always insisted on centering on and serving the overall situation, serving the public and the society, taking the initiative and actively performing their duties, and creatively carrying out a series of activities with characteristics and effectiveness. At the same time, the people's organizations have a large number of members, who are in contact with the public in different groups and fields, representing, defending and serving the interests of the groups, and have strong social credibility and influence compared with other associations, with the function of "one call for one hundred responses".

4.1.3 The function and status of people's organizations[1]

4.1.3.1 The function of people's organizations

People's organizations have four main functions. First, people's organizations are channels for people's participation in politics. The CPC attaches great importance to the role of people's organizations in the political and social life of the country and regards them as democratic channels for the public to participate in political affairs in an organized, disciplined manner under appropriate leadership, thus enabling them to represent the public in the political and social life of the country and play the role of democratic participation and supervision in state and social affairs. Second, people's organizations are the key organizers and leaders of mass movements. The CPC attaches great importance to the role of people's organizations in the revolutionary mass movement, always pushing them to the front line of the mass movement and to assume the role of organizers and leaders. Third, people's organizations are an important social pillar of China's socialist regime. The CPC attaches importance to the role of people's organizations in the stability and development of state power, and regards them as the reliable social foundation, supporting force and defender of state power. Fourth, people's organizations are an important force for revolution and construction.

---

[1] Gong Weibin, *Social System of Governance with Chinese Characteristics*, Beijing: Economy & Management Publishing House, 2016.

4.1.3.2   The status of people's organizations

(1) *Historical status*

People's organizations are what the Party aims to unite in establishing the united front and building the people's power. People's organizations came into being in response to the trend of China's historical development. From August 1948, various national people's organizations have been set up. The establishment of these people's organizations further organized the public from all walks of life and was one of the important organizational preparations for the convening of the new political consultative conference. After the founding of the People's Republic of China in 1949, all people's organizations have established and improved their institutions, formulated, and perfected their constitutions, expanded their organizations at all levels, focused on the central tasks and work of the Party and the state, carried out various work and activities according to their own characteristics, and gave full play to their roles in socialist transformation and socialist modernization.

(2) *Political and legal status*

People's organizations are an important part of the state political system and an important social pillar of state power. People's organizations are an important social force and a strong pillar for building socialist democracy, especially the people's organizations that are included in the CPPCC. The CPPCC is an important organizational form for other political parties, people's organizations and representatives from all walks of life to participate in the deliberation and administration of state affairs. People's organizations, especially those included in the CPPCC, are endowed by the Constitution with the rights and obligations of political consultation, democratic supervision, and participation in the deliberation and administration of state affairs, and can play the role of democratic participation and democratic supervision in the management of state and social affairs on behalf of specific social groups.

4.1.4   Difficulties in the development faced by people's organizations

Since the reform and opening up, people's organizations like trade unions, the Communist Youth League, Women's Federations and other people's organizations have drawn on their unique strengths and played an important role in organizing and mobilizing the public, educating and guiding the public, contacting and serving the public, and safeguarding their legitimate rights and interests. In recent years, in the face of new situations and tasks, the work of people's organizations has taken on new characteristics, and it is faced with both new challenges for development and new opportunities for reform. First, people's organizations have strong official attributes and weak nonofficial characteristics. Most people's organizations are established under the direct leadership of the Party and the government, and assume certain administrative functions of the state. They are guaranteed in terms of political status, organization, system, personnel, funds, etc., which, to some extent, results in their "administrative" characteristics and weakens their civilian and social characteristics. In particular, the organization setup, personnel allocation, organization funds and main activities of the mass organizations such as the trade unions, the Communist Youth League, the Women's Federation and other people's organizations are essentially part of the Party and government organizations. In terms of interests, the organizations focus more on the interests of the state, society and the general interests, while their work in protecting and representing the specific interests of the group they represent is not in-depth enough due to less frequent and strong enough efforts.[1] Second, the work coverage shrinks and cohesion decreases. The attractiveness and cohesiveness of people's organizations are not strong, and the effective work coverage is not enough, which are two major problems that have long plagued the development of people's organizations, especially the phenomenon of "hollowing out" and "idling" of grassroots organizations.[2] Due to the mindset of "bureaucratic prioritization", the people's organizations are of weak motivation and enterprising and innovative spirit, which leads to the cohesion decrease. Their influence needs to be enhanced especially in the non-public economic organizations, social organizations and various emerging social groups. The rapid development of social organizations after the reform and opening up has provided a channel for the public to express their opinions and participate in social and public affairs. To some extent, this has partially replaced the bridging function of people's organizations, which has brought severe challenges and external competition to the development of people's organizations. Third, people's organizations have a weak foundation at the grassroots level and lack personnel with adequate competence and quality. "Lack of hands, money and materials" is a common problem for grassroots organizations, and the contradiction of inadequate hands and heavy workload is prominent. Some Party members and officials, due to their cognitive limitations, are not aware of the status, functions, tasks and roles of people's organizations, and fail to

---

[1] Shi Xuehua, *Principles of Political Science*, Guangzhou: Sun Yat-sen University Press, 2001, p. 372.

[2] Hu Xianzhong, "A Review of Research on People's Organizations Since the Reform and Opening Up", *The Journal of Yunnan Provincial Committee School of CPC*, 2015(5).

provide effective support and guidance to the work of people's organizations. As a result, they often choose to give priority to central tasks and neglect the work of people's organizations. In practice, there usually exist problems like inappropriate positioning of people's organizations and they tend to be weakened or marginalized, and thus be driven to a "vulnerable" position. Officials cultivation of people's organizations lad behind the requirements of mass work under new conditions. Some officials are lack of research of mass work and work with over-simplification; others with multiple positions, and unclear self-positioning, are often preoccupied with finishing work assignments and tend to avoid difficulties.

Mass work is the important bridge for the Party to understand the social conditions and people's opinions and to coordinate the interests of all parties. Therefore, it is necessary to reform people's organizations. In February 2015, the Opinions on Strengthening and Improving the Party's people's Organization Work was issued by the CPC Central Committee which specifies that Party committees at all levels should encourage people's organizations to reform and innovate, reinforce vitality through creative work, and win the trust of the public. The opinions also suggest measures for people's organizations to play their role and to promote the reform and innovation. In November 2015, the 18th meeting of the Central Leading Team for Comprehensively Deepening the Reform examined and adopted the All-China Federation of Trade Unions Reform Pilot Program, the Shanghai People's Organization Reform Pilot Program, and the Chongqing People's Organization Reform Pilot Program, making clear that the pilot department and local authorities should strengthen coordination, and take effective measures in addressing both the symptoms and root causes of prominent problems, aiming to create replicable experiences. In 2016, with the further reform of people's organizations, the Central Committee of the Communist Youth League and the All-China Women Federation put forward in their reform schemes that the representativeness of the Party congress, Party committees, and standing committees should be promoted and increase the proportion of grassroots officials and ordinary people. At the same time, the Central Committee of the Communist Youth League and the All-China Women Federation have begun to streamline the administrative establishment of their organs, and build a team of leading officials that combines full-time, provisional, and part-time members; they innovate grassroots organs and enhance grassroots strength, and make efforts to address the problems of the undesirable tendency of institutionalization and entertainment of people's organizations, and the problem of detachment from the public.

4.2 The participation of the Communist Youth League in social governance

The Third Plenary Session of the 18th CPC Central Committee proposed that we need to innovate social governance, promote the mode of social governance, invigorate social organizations, and actively participate in the innovation of social governance, which set higher demand for the Communist Youth League of China and brings greater development opportunities. Standing at a new starting historical point, the Communist Youth League of China should actively adapt to the transformation and development of conditions, strengthen the innovation of social governance, advance modes of social governance, continue to promote attractiveness, and cohesion and expand the effective coverage of work.

4.2.1　The history and status quo of the Communist Youth League of China

4.2.1.1　The development course of the Communist Youth League of China

The Communist Youth League of China is a people's organization of advanced young people under the leadership of the CPC; it is a school where a large number of young people learn about socialism with Chinese characteristics and about communism through practice, and as the bridge linking the CPC with the young people, and as an important social pillar of China and the assistant to and a reserve force of China. Since its founding in 1922, the Communist Youth League of China has kept developing and has been playing an active role under the leadership of the CPC in the process of building a new China, establishing and consolidating the socialist system, and in strengthening the socialist economic, political, cultural, social and ecological construction by unifying and leading young people of all ethnic groups.

On the eve of the founding of the CPC, communists all over China first organized the Socialist Youth League in Shanghai in August 1920, in order to educate and unite young people on a wide scale, so as to better carry out social transformation and publicize socialism. Subsequently, early organizations of the Socialist Youth League were created in various places. The First National Congress of the Chinese Communist Youth League was held in May 1922, and a unified national organization was established. In January 1925, the Third National Congress held by the Chinese

Communist Youth League decided to change the name of the Chinese Socialist Youth League to the Communist Youth League of China. In May 1927, the Communist Youth League held its Fourth National Congress, which further clarified the nature of the League as a "revolutionary organization of the proletarian youth". In November 1935, the CPC decided to transform the Communist Youth League into a youth organization dedicated to national salvation and liberation against Japan. After the victory of the War of Resistance Against Japanese Aggression, the Democratic Youth League was proposed in October 1946 to meet the needs of the new situation and new tasks. On the eve of the founding of the People's Republic of China in 1949, the CPC proposed a resolution to establish the New Democratic Youth League of China. In April 1949, the New Democratic Youth League of China was officially established. In May 1957, the New Democratic Youth League of China held its Third National Congress and decided to change the name to the Communist Youth League of China. During the Cultural Revolution, the work of the Communist Youth League was forced to come to a halt. Since the reform and opening up, the Communist Youth League, under the leadership of the CPC and in accordance with the shift of the Party's work focus, has carried out Communist Youth League and youth work closely around the reform and opening up and economic construction, making important contributions to the advancement of socialist modernization and promoting the growth of the younger generation.

4.2.1.2 The nature and basic tasks of the Communist Youth League at the present stage

(1) *The nature of the Communist Youth League*

The Communist Youth League of China bridges the Party and young people, bears the responsibilities of contacting the youth and consolidate and expand the youth support for the Party's ruling. The Communist Youth League of China performs its duties of "organizing, leading, serving and protecting the legal rights and interests of young people," assisting the Party and the government in managing youth affairs, sending talented young people to the Party and the government, providing advice and suggestions, and fulfilling the rights of people's organizations to participate in political consultation, and always maintaining a close relationship with the Party.

The Communist Youth League of China accepts the leadership of the Party, receives funding from the fiscal appropriation of the government, and the major leaders are directly appointed by the Party committee of a higher level. There is no specified government department dealing with youth affairs in China. The Communist Youth League of China manages youth affairs on behalf of the Party committee and the government, coordinating relevant government departments and social organizations to jointly participate in providing services. Therefore, it is characteristic of a quasi-government organization. In addition, the Communist Youth League is also a people's organization organized by the majority of young people to conduct independent activities. It maintains close contact with the young people and is widely supported by them; content and methods of its work are also of strong civic nature. Therefore, it has a strong social attribute. The two attributes complement each other.

(2) *Basic tasks at the present stage*

The Constitution of the Communist Youth League of China states that the basic tasks at the present stage are to hold high the banner of socialism with Chinese characteristics, unswervingly implementing the Party's basic line in the primary stage of socialism, focusing on economic development, adhering to the four cardinal principles and reform and opening up, and educating young people with the core socialist value system. In the great practice of building socialism with Chinese characteristics, the Communist Youth League will bring up successors with ideals, ethics, education and discipline, constantly consolidate and expand the support of young people for the Party, and strive to bring new blood to the Party, training young people for national development, uniting and leading the majority of young people to make efforts and work hard to build a socialist economy, and to make political, cultural, social, and ecological progress, so as to contribute wisdom and strength to the Chinese Dream of building a moderately prosperous society in all respects, accelerating socialist modernization, and realizing the great rejuvenation of the Chinese nation.

4.2.2 The significance of the Communist Youth League's participation in social governance

As a people's organization and an advanced youth organization, the Communist Youth League provides youth support for the Party to consolidate its ruling position, bridging the Party, the government, and the youth. With remarkable progressiveness and civic nature, it plays a central role in the youth social organizations and the youth in China.

4.2.2.1 Consolidating and expanding the Party's ruling basis

It is an important task of the Communist Youth League to consolidate the youth support for the Party and the government. The Communist Youth League has a sound organizational network and extensive social contacts, covering young people from all walks of life, including towns and townships, rural areas, government organs, schools, private enterprises, associations of young entrepreneurs and associations of young scientists and technicians. By connecting with and uniting numerous young people, it maintains the Party's youth and public foundation. The participation of the Communist Youth League of China in social governance is not only an urgent requirement to adapt to the development of the times, but also an inevitable choice to serve as the Party's assistant and reserve force to expand and consolidate the youth support for the Party and effectively perform its functions. It is an important content of the Communist Youth League's service to the harmonious society and the youth. In the new situation, the Communist Youth League of China participates in social governance innovation, maintains the appeal and influence of the Communist Youth League of China on the youth, rallies the youth around the Communist Youth League of China, and strengthens the youth foundation of the Party, which is of great significance to improve the status of the Communist Youth League in the youth group.

4.2.2.2 Stimulating the vitality of social development

Stimulating social vitality to the maximum extent is the Party's overall requirement for social governance in the new era. Youth prosperity is the prosperity of the country. The quality of the youth, and of the management, is closely related to the vitality of social development. The participation of the Communist Youth League in social governance is not only the need of the times, but also the necessity of maintaining social stability and stimulating the vitality of social development. With the rapid economic and social transformation, numerous young people are faced with many pressures in terms of education, employment, marriage, housing, and medical care. The Communist Youth League of China involved in social governance has become an important way to maintain social stability to meet the needs of young people in all fields and provide them with high-quality services for their growth and development while contacting and managing the youth. In recent years, the local Communist Youth League organizations in various places have made great efforts to explore ways of social governance, and have aroused the enthusiasm of young people to participate in social governance. Activities such as "Youth Entrepreneurship Action", "Youth Micro-credit Loan" and "Employment and Entrepreneurship Action for College Students" have been carried out to provide a reliable guarantee for meeting the social needs of young people. It has enhanced the social status of the Communist Youth League of China when serving the youth, strengthened its cohesion and cohesiveness, and has effectively stimulated social vitality.

4.2.2.3 Being the important content of harmonious society building

Building a socialist harmonious society is the requirement of social development in the period of system transition and social transformation. The Communist Youth League of China actively participates in the social governance, fulfills its distinctive functions of contacting the youth, mediates the social affairs, and maintains stability. They change the working concept, innovate the management concept, and find their position in youth social organization management, community function building, expression of interests and settlement of contradiction for the youth, psychological service for the youth and teenagers, and cultivation of youth talents, and build a socialized service system for the youth. Through constantly promoting the level of serving the youth, they undertake the youth affairs transferred from the government, and promote the construction of a harmonious society. For example, in preventing juvenile delinquency and juvenile protection, the local Communist Youth League organizations have explored the establishment of special organizations for juvenile delinquency prevention and juvenile protection committees. China Communist Youth League Xi'an Committee included the funds for juvenile delinquency prevention and juvenile protection in its fiscal budget, and equipped each "Youth Station" with professional working force: no less than two full-time or part-time staff through government procurement of social services. Besides, they set up a dynamic information investigation mechanism of key youth groups at the municipal level for strengthening the education, assistance, and correction and management of the key youth groups.

4.2.2.4 The urgent need to promote the development of the Communist Youth League of China

It is the requirement for the Communist Youth League of China to strengthen its social functions, to promote innovation in the organization and work of the League and enhance its performance in youth work by mobilizing and generating wider participation of the youth in social governance innovation. At present, with the continuous differentiation and diversification of social interest groups, the characteristics of young people in the new era are becoming complex and diverse, with their diversified and individualized social demands. And with the active and frequent movement of young people across regions and industries, a large number of new youth groups have emerged, and a large number of young people are gathering in new economic and social organizations. In the face of new characteristics of new youth groups, new organizations and new media, and new challenges, problems and opportunities they bring about, the

Communist Youth League of China has grasped the characteristics and laws of youth work in the era of transformation, and has made adjustment and improvement of its organizational structure in a timely manner. China Communist Youth League Beijing Committee and other people's organizations actively improved their internal organizational structure, established a social work department to expand and strengthen their social functions, and consolidate their position in the innovation of social governance system and further enhance their vitality and competitiveness.

4.2.3 The major tasks for the Communist Youth League of China in its participation in social governance

In the new era, the Communist Youth League of China has actively adapted itself to the rapid social changes, effectively participated in social governance innovation, and has worked hard to undertake the government's youth affairs, better serving the youth and promoting its own development. It has played an irreplaceable role in improving the social governance system, and promoting the modernization of the social governance system and capacity.

4.2.3.1 Protecting the legal rights and interests of the youth

Safeguarding the legitimate rights and interests of young people is an important task and an effective starting point for the Communist Youth League of China to participate in social governance innovation. As a people's organization under the leadership of the CPC, the Communist Youth League effectively expands the channels for expressing the interests of young people, and constantly improves the protection mechanism for their rights and interests. The Youth League makes efforts to satisfy the actual needs of special youth groups, such as idle adolescents, left-behind children in rural areas, minor vagrants, and minor children of those serving prison sentences, and to give full play to the roles of families, schools, social organizations and communities, and effectively represents and safeguards the legitimate rights and interests of young people, and ensures that young people become an active force in promoting social governance. The Central Committee of the Communist Youth League and local Communist Youth League have set up a network on the rights and interests of the Communist Youth League, carrying out in-depth protection projects, and safeguarding the legitimate rights and interests of young people through laws. These efforts give full play to the role of the Youth League as the main channel for expressing the voice of youth interests, and better represent and safeguard the legitimate rights and interests of youth. Provinces and municipalities such as Beijing, Tianjin, Chongqing, Anhui, Liaoning, and Zhejiang have carried out pilot programs for the protection of the minors, and Yuzhong District of Chongqing has opened a "mobile classroom" in community citizen schools based on the "Yuzhong District Youth Health Base". Through the thematic education activities for minors, they integrated the strength of the Base and carried out education and training programs such as "Escort for Growth" to strengthen the education of adolescents' physical and mental health. At the same time, the "Rights Protection Express" project was extensively operated to provide direct legal assistance to young people.

4.2.3.2 Supporting the vulnerable youth groups

Vulnerable youth groups not only face significant challenges in their growth and development, but also are a factor affecting the social harmony and stability. The new era presents new challenges to the work of the Communist Youth League in helping the vulnerable youth groups solve practical problems and promote their healthy growth. To this end, the Communist Youth League in various places set out solving the most immediate and practical problems of the youth groups, through combination of serving the youth and serving the society. They actively carried out voluntary services and developed public welfare undertakings to promote social equity and justice. For example, through various means, they have helped laid-off and unemployed young people to find jobs, lifted rural youth out of poverty, provided skill training for rural young people working in cities, and helped young people with disabilities. Through partner assistance and aid-in-labor assistance, the Communist Youth League encouraged young people to actively participate in educational undertakings in poverty-stricken areas, deepened the Project Hope and supported education in rural areas, and effectively promoted the equity of education for young people. In addition, they accelerate the promotion of voluntary services for young people, and provide extensive voluntary services such as community services, rural revitalization, public health and legal aid, to help vulnerable groups solve their practical difficulties and make the vulnerable groups of young people fully feel the care of society.

4.2.3.3 Preventing juvenile delinquency

Since the reform and opening up, the number of cases involving juvenile delinquency has been increasing, which has aroused widespread concern in the whole society. The prevention of juvenile delinquency is an important part of the comprehensive management of social security and an important measure to promote the healthy growth of juvenile delinquency. Giving full play to its own advantages, the Communist Youth League, through grasping the ideal and belief of youth and moral and legal education work, optimizing the environment for youth growth, implementing community prevention programs, building a grassroots prevention and control system for delinquency, carrying out youth volunteer action and other effective measures, widely mobilizes youth members, strengthens research on juvenile delinquency, summarizes the experience and practices of preventing juvenile delinquency, strives to master the characteristics and laws of preventing juvenile delinquency under the new situation, better supports and prevents juvenile delinquency, effectively maintains social stability, and makes active efforts to serve the overall situation of reform, development and stability.

4.2.3.4　Managing youth foreign affairs

Youth foreign affairs work, an important part of China's overall diplomacy, non-governmental diplomacy, and a driving force for opening to the outside world, is entrusted to the Communist Youth League of China by the Chinese government. The work of youth foreign affairs should "serve the Party and the government diplomacy, economic development and youth work," give full play to the role of bridges, and explore extensive resources to serve the domestic economic development. The Youth League must strengthen economic dialogues and exchanges with youth from other countries through various channels, and promote cooperation between Chinese and foreign youth. The work of youth foreign affairs can promote the active participation of Chinese youth in global youth affairs, promote publicity, and shape a good image of Chinese youth and youth organizations and expand the international influence of Chinese youth organizations through coordination with the key work of the Communist Youth League. [1]

4.2.4　Mechanism for the Communist Youth League of China to participate in social governance

4.2.4.1　Building an interactive public service platform for young people with new media

The Internet has increasingly become an indispensable tool for young people to obtain information, to study and get employment, entertainment, and communication, and an important way and carrier to communicate with, and to gather, contact and

---

[1] Wu Qing, "On the Role of the Communist Youth League in Building a Harmonious Society", *Youth & Juvenile Research*, 2008(1).

mobilize young people. The Internet is a "double-edged sword". Without proper guidance and regulation, radical and false remarks may appear on the Internet, which may be used by lawbreakers and have negative effects on social stability, which cannot be ignored. Therefore, it has become new tasks for the Communist Youth League of China in the complicated social governance process to cope with the impact of the Internet on the real society, to give full play to the prominent role of the Internet in integrating the opinions of young people, reflecting their voices and expressing their appeals, and to strengthen the analysis of youth public opinion and improve digitalization of youth services.

4.2.4.2 Building a supporting system for young migrant workers to integrate into society through community construction

Young migrant workers, also known as the new generation of migrant workers, have a high degree of education, high professional expectations, high material life enjoyment requirements, and low work tolerance. Young migrant workers have a strong ability to accept new things and long for urban civilization, and their awareness of democracy, equality, rights protection and self-worth is constantly strengthened. However, it is still difficult for the young migrant workers to integrate into the city and they still belong to the vulnerable groups. And, urban community is the socialized organizational channel and effective way for the young migrant workers to integrate into the city. Therefore, it is necessary to establish a supporting system for the integration of young migrant workers into urban communities economically, socially and psychologically.

4.2.4.3 Youth League organizations dispatched by municipal-level organizations as channels to enhance the coverage of Youth League organizations in non-state-owned enterprises

The conference on promoting the overseas organization construction held in August 2011 emphasized that in order to realize the goal of "two ensures for all young people"[1], it is necessary to enhance the Youth League organization construction in non-state-owned enterprises to organize young migrant workers well. The Youth League organizations in non-state-owned enterprises will become an important organizational channel for the Youth League to serve young migrant workers and to participate in strengthening and innovating social governance. Through the establishment of the

---

[1] The "two ensures for all young people" aim to ensure that the Youth League's grassroots network reaches all youth and that its activities and initiatives have an impact on every young person. —*Tr.*

mechanism of cooperation and co-management between the Youth League organizations in areas of labor inflow and outflow organizational construction of Youth League in non-state-owned enterprises was strengthened, and overseas Youth League organizations were set up on the basis of shared affection for hometown, an important social mechanism. These efforts contribute to the extensive and effective organizational coverage and work coverage for young migrant workers, a huge group of young people whose coverage by the Communist Youth League is very weak.

4.2.4.4   Building a professional team of public youth affairs management through the cultivation of youth leaders

Youth leaders are those who have taken responsibility in various fields, created their own businesses, and made a positive impact on the development of society on a whole. The "National Top Ten Outstanding Youth" selected by the All-China Youth Federation as the representative "official" accreditation standard, and the local elites selected by *Southern People Weekly*, are both young people who have an important impact on youth development and even a demonstrative effect. Under the new situation, the Communist Youth League of China should proceed from the requirements of "two all-young people", use talents in a more flexible way, innovate the incentive mechanism, give full play to the organizational cohesion, and cultivate youth leaders and provide a resource platform for the development of young elites, especially local youth leaders.

4.2.4.5   Building a long-term management system for social public services based on youth self-organization

Youth self-organization refers to the non-governmental organizations that are established spontaneously, developed independently, operated independently and governed by youth themselves with a certain scale, constitution and an organizational framework. In recent years, domestic youth self-organizations have played an important role in social governance, such as safeguarding the rights and interests of adolescents, strengthening communication between youth and society, vocational training for the unemployed, assistance to the disabled and vulnerable groups, and development education. They have actively guided the youth to participate in poverty alleviation, poverty assistance, rights protection, culture, environmental protection and other social welfare undertakings, achieving a beneficial supplement to the government's service function. Compared with traditional organizations, the self-organization formed by young people with shared interests or characteristics is more dynamic and cohesive with distinctive characteristics.

4.2.5 Community Youth Club: the exploration and practice of the Communist Youth League's participation in social governance

The Community Youth Club is an active exploration and effective practice of the China Communist Youth League Beijing Committee's participation in the innovation of social governance. In 2011, China Communist Youth League Beijing Committee found through the "Where Are the Youth" survey that there were 4,487,800 non-Beijing permanent adolescents aged 6-35, accounting for nearly 50% of the total in the city, and showing a growing trend. In order to strengthen the service to the migrant youth, Beijing decided that the Communist Youth League will start with activities based on Community Youth Club to serve the young migrant population. To this end, China Communist Youth League Beijing Committee, based on the building of a composite organizational system, enhanced the effective coverage and the attraction and cohesion of the Youth League. By the end of 2013, 500 Community Youth Club have been set up in the whole city in batches, and a grassroots network covering the whole city, embedded in the grassroots administrative system and providing services for young people was formed.

4.2.5.1 Addressing youth needs, enhancing social integration of youth groups

In response to the needs of the youth, the Beijing Community Youth Club serve the youth in training and education, volunteering for public welfare, visits and practice, entrepreneurship and employment, law enforcement, sports and health, dating, and literature and art and entertainment. In the training and education activities represented by the "New Youth School", university student volunteers are invited to provide free courses preparing interested migrant youth for the adult college entrance examination; the "New Youth City Experience Camp", a representative visits and practice activity, organizes young people to visit special police and fire fighting training bases, milk and automobile enterprises, and museums, so as to enhance their sense of community integration.

4.2.5.2 Building a service system, extending the new front of youth work

Based on the construction of the compound organization system of the Communist Youth League, the Community Youth Club has gradually become another important front for the organization of the Communist Youth League to contact the youth. By providing "life scenarios", the Community Youth Club explored and established a youth activity front within the community, in addition to the traditional organization system mainly based on the "workplace". It has effectively expanded the coverage and influence of the Youth League, and expanded the service of the Youth League. Focusing on "hobbies and public services", the Community Youth Club explored and established the youth social organizations in the community. The more than 1,300 youth social organizations in Beijing apply for purchase of social organization services on the Community Youth Club platform, actively undertake government youth affairs, and assist residential district and township Youth League committees in organizing education and guidance for young people and serving key youth groups.

4.2.5.3   Exploring "the Communist Youth League + social worker" model, providing social services for the youth

The advantages of the Communist Youth League's organizational network, combined with the professionality of social work institutions, have gradually formed a social work situation with unlimited vitality and long-term sustainability for young people. With the core working model of "the Communist Youth League + social worker", Community Youth Club has formed a complementary team of professional youth social workers and the Communist Youth League, showing a strong dynamic. China Communist Youth League Beijing Committee actively explores the use of professional methods of social work to make social workers an important force for the league organizations to provide youth services in a more specialized and stable manner, helping youth with psychological guidance, behavior correction and personal and environmental adaptation at the social level in terms of promoting youth career development, physical and mental health, social integration and family building.

4.2.5.4   Developing a comprehensive social work network, fostering professional social work institutions

The Community Youth Club has set up a comprehensive network of social workers for young people in the whole city. Social workers provide services in grassroots communities seven days a week, which is an important social work force supported, managed and fostered by the Communist Youth League. The team not only engages in professional community, group work and case work, but also plays an important role in regional youth league construction, supporting youth league organizations, professional social work agencies and voluntary service organizations at all levels to carry out activities in the community. China Communist Youth League Beijing Committee actively promotes the development of more professional youth social work agencies, which carry out the initial intervention of social workers in the stages of investigation and interrogation, examination and approval of arrest, investigation during prosecution and pre-trial investigation in the protection of minors involved in litigation, and provides professional services in psychological counseling, legal aid, assistance to the disabled, voluntary services and social participation.

4.3   The participation of the trade union in social governance

As an important social pillar of the state's political power, trade unions serve as a bridge connecting the Party, the government and workers and the public. Taking as its major tasks representing and serving workers, trade unions play a uniquely advantageous role in balancing the interests of all parties, harmonizing labor-capital relations, safeguarding workers' rights and interests, and providing assistance to those in need.

4.3.1   The development and status quo of trade unions

4.3.1.1   The historical evolution of trade unions

The Chinese trade union is a people's organization of the working class led by the Communist Party of China. It serves as a bridge between the CPC and the government and the working class, and represents and safeguards workers' interests.

Created and led by the CPC, trade unions have always been closely involved in the revolution of the Chinese people and thus developed rapidly. Established in August 1921 in Shanghai, the Secretariat of the Chinese Labor Organization was the early leading organ of the CPC that openly led the trade union movement. In May 1922, at the First National Labor Conference held in Guangzhou, the CPC decided to establish a national trade union. And, the Second National Labor Conference, held in May 1925, established the All-China Federation of Trade Unions and passed the Constitution of the All-China Federation of Trade Unions. After the founding of the PRC in 1949, the working class entered the political arena, and trade unions became an important social pillar for the maintenance of state power, ushering in a new era in which the Chinese working class and working people became the masters of their own, thus achieving the first historic transformation in history. In June 1950, the Central People's Government promulgated the first Trade Union Law of the People's Republic of China. In May 1953, the Seventh National Congress of the All-China Federation of Trade Unions specified for the first time in its constitution that trade unions are "mass organizations established by the working class out of their own will" and formulated the working policy that is "production-centered and production-life-education integrated". In this period, trade unions, leading the working class, played a significantly indispensable role in the campaign to consolidate people's power and restore national economy.

The Ninth National Congress of the All-China Federation of Trade Unions, was held in October 1978, commencing the second historic transformation of Chinese trade unions. At the conference, Deng Xiaoping pointed out that the new historical task of the Chinese working class and trade union movement was to promote reform, build the "Four Modernizations"[1] and carry out a new Long March; trade unions must "win workers' trust and speak and work for them". The 10th National Congress of the All-China Federation of Trade Unions was held in October 1983, and the congress adopted new guidelines for trade union work, preparing the trade union for its active participation in reform and creating a new situation in trade union work. Since then, China's trade unions have carried out a series of pioneering work centered on two aspects: giving better play to the role of trade unions in the reform and the reform of trade unions. In October 1993, the 12th National Congress of the All-China Federation of Trade Unions emphasized that trade unions should better express and defend workers' specific interests while safeguarding people's overall interests, and dutifully fulfilling obligations of trade unions.

In the 21st century, the CPC has put forward the definite goal of building a moderately prosperous society in all aspects. Chinese trade unions have made many contributions in uniting and mobilizing workers to play the role of the main force in building a moderately prosperous society in an all-round way and striving to usher in a new stage of trade union work in the new century. After the 14th National Congress of the All-China Federation of Trade Unions, the new leadership of the All-China Federation of Trade Unions put forward the working policy of "organizing and effectively safeguarding rights", clarified the basic tasks, work priorities and main approaches for trade union work in the new century and new requirements for trade unions and trade union officials in the process of building a harmonious society and coordinating labor relations.

4.3.1.2   The nature and functions of trade unions

(1) *The nature of trade unions*

Article 2 of the Trade Union Law of the People's Republic of China stipulates: "trade unions are people's organizations established by the working class out of their own will". "The All-China Federation of Trade Unions and its subordinate organizations represent workers' interests and safeguard their legitimate rights and interests in

---

[1] This means integrating the development of industrialization, informatization, urbanization and agricultural modernization.

accordance with the law". Article 4 stipulates: "Trade unions must abide by and uphold the Constitution, take the Constitution as the fundamental guideline for their activities, take economic development as central task, adhere keep to the socialist path of socialism, uphold people's democratic dictatorship, and the leadership of the Communist Party of China, follow the guidance of Marxism-Leninism, Mao Zedong Thought and Deng Xiaoping Theory, and adhere to the policy of the reform and opening up, and carry out their work independently and in accordance with their constitution."

Chinese trade unions are characterized by the unity of political principles and public orientation. Its political principles are reflected in the trade union as an organization truly for the working class; it takes the working class as its class base; it is led by the CPC. This is the choice of history, the choice of the times, but also the choice of the majority of workers, as well as its fine tradition, and more importantly its most distinctive characteristics. The distinctive public characteristics of the trade union show that its source of vitality and vigor comes from the majority of workers, and that "trade unions must closely contact workers, listen to and reflect their opinions and demands, care for their lives, help them solve their difficulties, and serve them wholeheartedly".

(2) *The functions of trade unions*

Marx once said, "To fight for and protect the interests of the working class is the purpose for which trade unions arise and operate". The Trade Union Law of the People's Republic of China and the Constitution of the All-China Federation of Trade Unions have made clear provisions on the functions of the trade unions, which can be summarized as four aspects, namely, maintenance, construction, participation, and education.

Maintenance function. The trade union takes it as its basic duty to protect workers' legitimate rights and interests. This is the most important and basic function of China's trade union, as well as its basis.

In the process of developing the socialist market economy, Chinese trade unions, while safeguarding workers' political rights, protect their labor rights and material and cultural interests, participate in coordinating labor relations and regulating social conflicts, and strive to promote economic development and long-term social stability.

Construction function. Trade unions mobilize and organize the majority of workers to actively participate in economic construction and strive to complete production and work. At the same time, they actively cooperate with the Party committee and the government, carry out various forms of activities, and guide workers to take the initiative to contribute to the construction of the motherland and social prosperity, and to reform and promote the development of enterprises.

Participation function. Trade unions organize workers to participate in democratic decision-making, management and supervision of their own units through workers' congresses or other forms in accordance with the law. They represent and organize workers to participate in the management of state and social affairs, participate in the democratic management of enterprises, institutions and agencies, establish consultation systems, protect workers' legitimate rights and interests, and mobilize their enthusiasm.

Education function. Trade unions help workers to continuously improve their ethical and moral standards and scientific and cultural quality, and build an ideal, moral, educated and disciplined workforce.

4.3.2 The significance of trade unions' participation in social governance

Trade unions, under the leadership of the CPC, are influential, appealing and widely covering the Party and government organs, enterprises and institutions, and involving various industries. Trade unions have an edge in participating in social governance, and playing an important role in reflecting the interests and demands of workers, safeguarding the legitimate rights and interests of workers, helping and assisting workers in difficulties and disadvantaged groups, coordinating labor-management relations and resolving social conflicts.

4.3.2.1 Trade unions have advantages to participate in social governance

As a people's organization of the working class under the leadership of the CPC, trade unions are characterized by a sound organizational system, extensive contact with the public, familiarity with the situation at the primary level and understanding of the wishes of the people, etc. Characterized by a deep public base and perfect organizational network, trade unions give full play to their roles in social governance innovation. As of June 2013, Chinese trade union members totaled 280 million, and migrant workers' members totaled 109 million; 2.753 million grassroots trade union organizations nationwide came into being, covering 6.378 million grassroots organizations. As the largest trade union organization in the world, the Chinese trade unions have basically formed an organizational network with most wide coverage. Most grassroots trade unions work at the forefront of building harmonious labor relations, gaining a good foundation for their participation in social governance.

4.3.2.2　It is the ardent expectation of the workers for trade unions to participate in social governance

The fundamental purpose of social governance is to address the people's most immediate concerns, which is the basic duty of trade unions. With the deepening of the comprehensive reform and the gradual adjustment of the social interest patterns, workers' interest demands diversified, with higher expectations for trade unions to represent them in expressing their demands and defending their legitimate rights and interests.

Trade unions assist the Party and the government in taking the initiative to protect workers' legitimate rights and interests in employment, income distribution, social security, safety and health, etc., and promoting governmental departments to effectively address workers' immediate interests, especially for those in need, which is conducive to maximizing public interests in social governance.

Meanwhile, trade unions shall represent and organize workers to participate in social governance in an orderly manner, while maintaining, realizing and developing workers' fundamental interests.

4.3.2.3　The participation of trade unions in social governance is conducive to harmonious labor relations

Building harmonious labor relations is an important element in strengthening and innovating social governance, maintaining social order and promoting social harmony. Trade unions participate in social governance with the support of the Party and the government, promote harmonious and stable labor relations, maximize harmonious factors and minimize disharmonious factors, which is a strong guarantee for the goals of social governance.

At present, China is in a period of prominent social contradictions, with increasing social unstable factors concomitant with social transformation, especially the contradictions in labor relations, which increases the cost of social administration, and weakens the authority and credibility of the Party and the government. Therefore, it is urgent to improve the mechanism to protect workers' rights and interests, give full play to the role of trade unions' role as bridge and link, and guide and support workers to express their demands in an orderly manner.

While participating in social governance, trade unions shall center around the fundamental and institutional issues in building harmonious labor relations, highlight key points, and act as a coordinator to effectively promote enterprise development, safeguard workers' rights and interests, and promote harmonious and stable labor relations.

4.3.2.4   Trade unions' participation in social governance is an intrinsic requirement for social governance system innovation

The innovation of the social governance system requires the transformation from the traditional single-subject management to the modern multi-subject governance, and the gradual formation of the social governance system under the leadership of Party committees and the government, based on social coordination, and public participation. Therefore, the construction of a new pattern of multi-governance and shared social governance is the inevitable choice for China's social governance system reform and innovation at this stage.

As a people's organization of the working class led by the Party, trade unions are the bridge and link between the Party and the government and the majority of workers, and have significant political, organizational and mass advantages.

The active participation of trade unions in social governance and public affairs, and the effective work of the majority of workers under the new situation in cooperation with the Party committee and the government, is an important part of the framework of social governance system of socialism with Chinese characteristics, which reflects the political advantage of the CPC and the institutional advantage of socialism, and is conducive to better playing an important synergistic role in strengthening and innovating social governance.

4.3.3   The main tasks of trade unions in social governance

4.3.3.1   Actively participating in social policy making

The effectiveness of social policies in promoting social governance depends on whether they are just and reasonable, whether they represent the interests of the majority of the social public, and whether they win the approval of the majority of the social public. Trade unions are the representatives and defenders of the interests of the majority of workers, and it is their social responsibility to participate in the formulation of social policies on behalf of workers.

Trade unions should stay close to the grassroots and the majority of workers, investigate and research, accurately grasp workers' will and interests, and propose constructive suggestions for the Party committee and the government to formulate social policies, so as to make the formulation of social policies more scientific, better reflect workers' fundamental and long-term interests, and better gain the general recognition and active support of the members of society.

Involvement in making social policies by the trade union reflects people's right in policy making. This improves the transparency and effectiveness of social policies. The trade union proposes employees' interests, demands and expectations, providing valuable information and suggestions for the Party committee and the government in implementing macro control and making social policies, and thus ensuring the feasibility of policies and regulations and the correctness of policy-making.

4.3.3.2 Proactively coordinating social interests

Coordinating the interests of members of society is an important task in social governance. With the deepening of reform and continuous development of the socialist market economy, the interests between the state, enterprises and individual employees have been further clarified. The three parties gradually evolved into different interest groups, and the imbalance of their interests has caused numerous conflicts of labor relations.

Developing a harmonious labor relation is not only major job of trade unions in safeguarding human rights, but also an important means for them to participate in social governance. To do so, trade unions must vigorously develop harmonious labor relations, actively coordinate social interests, maintain a balance between the interests of employee groups and those of other social strata, promote the balanced development of the interests of all social parties, improve the mechanisms for coordinating employees' interests, expressing their demands, mediating conflicts and protecting their rights and interests, and effectively safeguard their legitimate rights and interests.

4.3.3.3 Continuously strengthening their function of social service

The workers and office staff are both the participants and beneficiaries of social construction. It is trade unions' important task in social governance to strengthen its function of social service, better and more effectively serve workers and office staff and society. By coordinating the Party committee and the government in the management of public affairs, trade unions enhance the implementation of policies concerning workers' interests, promote employment and re-employment, strengthen vocational education and training, push forward the reform of the income distribution system and collective wage bargaining, advance the establishment of a mechanism for normal wage increases and payment guarantees for enterprises, and better meet employees' diversifying needs in education, employment, healthcare, social security and housing, etc.

In recent years, migrant workers have become a new force in China's employment market. By the end of 2016, the total number of migrant workers in China has reached

282 million. It is important for trade unions at all levels to ensure quality social services available to more migrant workers, especially in terms of labor employment, wage remuneration, social security, production safety and hardship assistance, etc.

4.3.3.4 Fulfilling responsibility for social supervision

As representatives and defenders of the interests of workers and office staff, trade unions are both participants and supervisors of social governance. They should effectively fulfill their responsibility for social supervision. On the one hand, they should carry out public supervision via workers' representatives, mobilize and organize them to extensively participate in social supervision and policy making, and supervise the implementation of social governance policies.

On the other hand, by bringing into full play the role of their sound organizations, extensive contact with employees, familiarity with grassroots and knowledge of employees' expectations, trade unions should supervise the policy implementation of social governance through hotlines for trade union rights protection and legal supervision inspectors for labor protection. As effective organizers in mobilizing employees to supervise social policies, trade unions can bring together employees' individual resources and capabilities, form group demands on the basis of their individual voices and demands, and propose motions on behalf of all the employees in government decision-making and legislative hearings.

4.3.3.5 Arousing workers' awareness of participation

An important element in strengthening and innovating social administration is to cultivate and enhance the civic awareness of the public to participate in social and political affairs in an active, orderly and equal manner, to achieve self-governance and self-discipline, and to lay the practical foundation for building a democratic and law-based society.

Trade unions should function as "schools for workers", rally them into trade unions to the greatest extent possible, and mobilize the majority of them to participate in democratic management more actively and positively. At the same time, the unions should guide and urge those in charge of enterprises to establish the principle of interaction of management and sharing of benefits, and treat the democratic participation of employees with an open mind, so as to jointly create a culture in which employees are foundation of enterprises and enterprises are the homes to employees so as to lay a solid foundation for harmonious labor relations.

4.3.4 Approaches for trade unions to participate in social governance

When participating in social governance, trade unions focus on coordination of labor relations and services for workers, coordinating labor relations and social interests, and serving workers as well as society. Giving full play to its advantages, trade unions actively explore new approaches to social governance and constantly improve the social governance and employee job in the new era.

4.3.4.1 Strengthening the awareness of participation in social governance innovation

Awareness is the guide to action. Trade unions should exert their synergistic function in social governance innovation on the basis of its unique edges, accurate orientation, active participation, strengthened idea, and agglomerate consensus. Taking employee-centered and service-first as their working ethics, trade unions should constantly innovate their means of work and improve their work efficiency.

In the new era, trade unions at all levels should take workers' satisfaction as their fundamental concern in social governance, take worker service as a basic, regular and fundamental work in achieving workers' social rights and interests and promoting social governance innovation. Trade union officials should be considerate enough to solve problems for workers, in such a way that workers will really take trade unions as their home and officials as their most trustworthy "family members".

4.3.4.2 Strengthening institutional guaranttee for participation in social governance innovation

To ensure their function and position in social administration and innovation, trade unions at all levels must establish scientific, systematic and operable rules. Trade unions shall improve their mechanism, clarify their rights and obligations, set up platforms for participation in social governance and innovation, and explore the assessment system in social governance work. The joint meeting system shall be enhanced to further strengthen the collaboration between trade unions and the Party committee and government departments, thus forming an interactive mechanism to ensure trade unions' participation in social administration and innovation.

4.3.4.3 Improving the operation mechanism for participation in social governance innovation

In participating in the social governance innovation, trade unions are to improve mechanisms, make good use of opportunities and social resources, and strive to form a socialized trade unions work pattern "led by the Party and the government, supported by administrations, operated by trade unions and participated by all". Trade unions should establish sound mechanisms for coordinating interests, give full play to the role of joint meetings to safeguard staff's legitimate rights and interests, strengthen communication and consultation, and effectively solve problems in labor relations.

Trade unions should improve their mechanism for demand expression, and provide a platform for members to fully express their interests in a legitimate and rational way. They should also innovate the mechanism for resolving conflicts, popularize the legal consultation system at the primary level, the collaboration system of legal aid and the legal aid socialization mechanism, develop staff and volunteers for legal aid, guide staff to safeguard their rights and interests by legal means, and improve the efficiency of legal aid.

4.3.4.4 Safeguarding staff's legitimate rights and interests in accordance with the law

By participating in innovation in social governance, trade unions at all levels should actively work for staff's interests when making policies, strengthen the role of representatives of people's congress and members of the National Committee of the CPPCC in the deliberation and administration of state affairs, extensively touch people from various social sectors, and advance a sound system for labor legislation and law enforcement.

Trade unions should improve the democratic management system with the workers' congress as the basic elements, promote transparency in factory affairs, and protect workers' rights of knowledge, participation, expression and supervision. Unions should implement the labor contract system and collective contract system in accordance with the law, accelerate and strengthen the construction of labor standard system, promote collective wage bargaining, and solve problems concerning staff's immediate interests such as wages, social security and public services.

4.3.4.5 Delivering practical services for staff

In the near future, trade unions will focus on providing diversified services for staff and their families. They will strengthen employment services, actively carry out micro-credit loans and enhance employment and re-employment. They will also assist workers from non-public economic sectors, self-employed people and migrant employees in social insurance, and promote a regular adjustment mechanism for basic pensions.

Trade unions will improve services for young migrant employees, and effectively safeguard their rights and interests. They will promote the implementation of dispatched employees' legitimate rights and interests, such as equal pay for equal work, democratic management and welfare. They will oversee relevant departments to strictly regulate labour subcontracting. At the same time, trade unions are to protect and safeguard the special rights and interests of special staff, such as females and the disabled, etc. For example, the All-China Federation of Trade Unions has launched "Care Action" for female employees in 31 provinces across China, designating March as the "Care Action" month.

4.3.4.6 Enhancing the overall caliber of the workforce

Trade unions should guide staff in continuing the fine tradition of the working class to take the overall situation into consideration. Unions should advance the building of their publicity platform and staff's culture and sports platform, promote advanced corporate culture and staff culture, carry out enjoyable, colourful and creative cultural activities, so as to attract and unite and staff, continuously meeting staff's spiritual and cultural needs.

Trade unions will actively respond to the new trend of media and make full use of new media platforms such as Weibo and WeChat, so as to extensively elevate staff's ideals and beliefs and further cultivate and observe core socialist values.

Unions should implement the project to improve staff's quality and improve the mechanism for their growth and success. For example, since 2013, Guangdong Federation of Trade Unions has launched "Ten Million Employees Training Initiative", with an annual investment of at least RMB10 million. In 2015, trade unions at all levels in Guangdong Province invested more than RMB120 million. They created Guangdong Employees' Education Network, innovated staff training models and enriched staff services, thus implementing staff's rights of further study and development.

4.3.5 "Longgang Exploration" by trade unions to address labour disputes

With many enterprises and a large workforce in Longgang District of Shenzhen, labor disputes are prone to occur, which have become one of the main factors affecting social harmony and stability. By the end of 2016, there have been nearly 400,000 commercial entities, nearly 4 million people, over 90% of whom were migrant workers. Therefore, trade unions faced many challenges, such as dependence on others, weak foundation, inadequate human and material resources, and insufficient capacity. It's demanding to safeguard staff's legitimate interests and rights in accordance with laws.

4.3.5.1 Devising sound top-level design for source management

In recent years, Trade Unions in Longgang District has taken the initiative to explore the basic laws and effective approaches for trade union work in market economy in the new era: launching a "one-stop" comprehensive service hall for staff, formulating opinions on further strengthening the standardized democratic election of enterprise trade unions, and setting up a federation of social organizations to serve staff.

In 2008, the Union proposed the opinions on giving further play to the role of the trade unions in building harmonious labor relations. In 2010, Longgang District Committee of the CPC issued documents on measures to speed up the transformation of the economic development mode and to build harmonious labor relations. In 2014, Longgang District Committee of the CPC formulated documents of "1+6" on strengthening and improving the work of trade unions. Longgang District has taken a new approach in playing the role of a "pivotal" social organization, guiding staff to express their demands in accordance with law, and establishing a new mechanism for managing labor disputes.

4.3.5.2 Taking a new approach to social governance participation at the root

Understanding the "essence" of source governance, Longgang District is adopting a fresh approach to the rule of law. It involves exploring innovative mechanisms to protect rights, like reporting unpaid wages, and bolstering new entities such as professional vice presidents within trade unions. This initiative also entails integrating new resources like pivotal trade unions and social workers, and fostering collaborative engagement between Party committees and various departments at all levels. This comprehensive strategy aims to streamline access to rights protection and services for the staff.

So far, Longgang District Committee of the CPC has made six plans, such as the Opinions of Longgang District on Strengthening and Improving Trade Unions' Work and the Work Plan of Longgang District on Trade Union's Participation in the Early Warning and Disposal of Labor Disputes, etc. These provisions have clarified the six aspects of trade union's work in participating in early warning and handling labor disputes, promoting collective wage bargaining in enterprises, promoting the democratic construction of enterprises, democratic management, improving staff's quality, and giving play to the role of "hub-type" social organizations. Longgang District Committee of the CPC has focused on promoting the construction of service-oriented, innovative and rights-safeguarding trade unions, such as guiding staff to express their demands according to law and participating in managing labor disputes at the source.

4.3.5.3 Exploring new mechanisms for participation in governance at the root

In response to the prominent problems in recent years, such as the increasingly fierce conflicts of interests between employers and employees and labor disputes,

Longgang District has continued to open up channels to protect staff's rights, such as reporting wage arrears and lawyers joining in enterprises, and has implemented a system of monthly reporting of staff's wages, so as to nip labor conflicts in the bud.

By setting up a WeChat platform, opening the reporting function through WeChat and Internet, and setting up a "12351" staff service hotline, the general district trade union has gradually formed a "five-sphere integrated" reporting system of labor relations information: Internet, WeChat, QQ group, chairman's mailbox and "12351" hotline. To promote exploration and innovation at the primary level, the Bantian Sub-districts of Longgang District has formulated the "Trade Union Information Officer Incentives for Hidden Dangers" for trade union, and the Zhangbei Community Trade Union of Longcheng Sub-districts has set up the promotion association for source management of labor disputes.

4.3.5.4 Strengthening participation in governance at the root

Longgang District has a workforce of more than 2 million, but there exists a serious shortage of trade union officials in the communities, Sub-districts and districts, making it difficult to meet the needs of industrial upgrading and building harmonious labor relations in Longgang. For this reason, Longgang District has, on the one hand, increased its efforts on extending trade unions to communities and enterprises, forming "three-dimensional" trade unions at four levels of sub-districts, streets, communities and enterprises. On the other hand, Longgang District has appointed more officials for primary trade unions from all walks of life, adopting an operation mode of specialization, institutionalization, socialization, contractualization and professionalization. The district has recruited full-time trade union officials, appointing them to be vice-presidents in communities with over 5,000 staff. This changed the dilemma faced by the primary-level trade unions in communities and enterprises, that is "shortage of hands, inability to work, and reluctance to work".

At the same time, Longgang District trade unions constantly strengthen the quality of their professional vice-presidents, visit factories to investigate possible labor conflicts, promote collective wage bargaining, defend staff's legitimate rights and interests, and mediate labor conflicts timely. Therefore, the union has become the "new strength" to serve staff.

4.3.5.5 Integrating new resources for participation in governance at the root

How can trade unions, with limited resources, play the role of "hub-type" social organizations, gather social organizations serving staff and integrate social resources so as to better serve staff? On August 8, 2013, the Social Organization Federation for Serving Staff in Longgang District, the first district-level hub-type social organization in Shenzhen was officially established. The federation is equipped with workshops for psychological care, assistance for staff, right protection, entrepreneurship and employment, and incubation of "hub-type" social organizations. These workshops are endowed with multi-functions like creativity development, knowledge acquisition, entertainment, friendship building, emotion outlet, etc.

Functioning as a bridge and link, the federation has integrated useful social resources and effectively realized "resource matching". At present, it has gathered 34 social organizations serving staff, cultivated and incubated 15 social organizations, and established the city's first community-level promotion association for source management of labor disputes. In addition, Longgang District has also developed work injury visiting model of "trade union plus social worker", in which trade union officials and full-time social workers jointly visit those injured at their posts. In this way, professional social work resources are integrated to serve staff.

4.4   Participation of All-China Women's Federation in social governance

As an important people's organization, the All-China Women's Federation is the bridge and link between the Party and the government and women. In the new era, the Women's Federation accelerates the improvement of its own capacity, gives full play to its own advantages and takes the initiative to participate in social governance. This is a new topic for the Women's Federation in the context of promoting the modernization of the national governance system and capabilities.

4.4.1   The current development of the Women's Federation

4.4.1.1   The history of the Women's Federation

During the battles against feudalism of the May Fourth Movement, women's movements cultivated a large number of female social activists with high capability. They played a remarkable role in the liberation of Chinese women and the struggle for gender equality, and laid the historical foundation for the Women's Federation.

In July 1922, the Second National Congress of the CPC decided to set up the Women's Ministry in the Central Committee of the CPC. Later, various women's organizations came into being, such as the Women's Working Committee, the Women's Ministry, and the Women's Life Improvement Commission.

On March 24, 1949, the First National Congress of Chinese Women was held and the All-China Democratic Women's Federation was formally established, thus a national leading organ for the Chinese women's movement. The establishment of Women's Federation, which aimed to lay a broad base of women for the new China, satisfied the Party's need to found a new China.

Known as the All-China Democratic Women's Federation before, the All-China Women's Federation changed its name to the Women's Federation of the People's Republic of China at the Third National Congress in 1957 and has used this name ever since. In September 1978, the fourth Chinese Women's National Congress was held, marking the beginning of the reconstruction of Women's Federation. The federation was officially named All-China Women's Federation. Whether from its origin and leadership composition, or from foundation and method, Women's Federation has been closely linked with the CPC from very beginning. Under the leadership of the Party, focusing on the Party's central tasks, it has played the role of a bridge and link between the Party and women.

The establishment of the socialist market economy system and the readjustment of the national interest pattern harmed some women's rights and interests to some extent. Women were eager to defend their legitimate rights and interests via organizations. In 1988, the sixth National Congress of Chinese Women proposed the basic function of Women's Federation: "representing and safeguarding women's interests and promoting gender equality". In the 1990s, with women's awareness of subject and the degree of organization rising, various women's organizations sprang up like mushrooms, whose objects, tasks and scope of the work of Women's Federation continued to expand. In the 21st century, various new women's organizations are emerging, and the needs of different groups of women are becoming more diversified and complicated. And the Party's mode of governance and leadership is undergoing deeper changes, from an omnipotent government to a government with limited liability. These changes and challenges led to further adjustments and adaptations for Women's Federation's functions.

4.4.1.2   The nature and functions of the Women's Federation

(1) *The nature of the Women's Federation*

As a social organization established for further liberation by the women from all ethnic groups and all walks of life under the leadership of the CPC, Women's Federation serves as a bridge and link between the Party and the government and women. The Constitution of the All-China Women's Federation specifies that the Women's Federation works as "the social pillar of state power", is an important force in state governance, and an important organization in advancing the modernization of China's governance capacity and system. It assists the government in maintaining social stability, improving social relations and keeping social order. Under the leadership of the Party, the Women's Federation unites women of all ethnicities and from all walks of life to actively participate in national undertakings, aims to fight for and protect women's and children's rights and interests, and achieve their development and gender equality. The Women's Federation, with its widespread representation, not only works as an important social pillar of state power, but also functions as a link between the Party, the government and women's groups. Since its establishment, Women's Federation has taken it as its belief and basic function to promote women's liberation and development, to give full play to the role of spokesperson for women's groups and to lead women to strive for gender equality, and has worked independently in strict compliance with the Constitution of the People's Republic of China, the Constitution of the All-China Women's Federation.

(2) *The functions of the Women's Federation*

Since the reform and opening up, as the nature of the Women's Federation changes, its functions have also fundamentally changed. The socialist market economy provides impetus for women's organizations, so that they function better as social and people's organizations.

The first is its representation function—the most basic one for Women's Federation. The federation represents women in democratic management and supervision of social affairs, conducts in-depth investigations and studies focusing on issues such as women's employment, land rights and interests, participation in political events and protection of women's rights and interests, and involves in discussions on women's policies which provides scientific basis for the decision-making of the Party and the government. The second is the participation function. The Women's Federation actively mobilizes women to participate in the construction of our nation and promote economic boost and social advancement. The third is the education function, aiming to improve women's overall quality. The Women's Federation carries out rich and diverse educational activities to improve women's ideological and cultural awareness. The fourth is the service function. Women's Federation insists on protecting women's and children's rights and interests, actively carries out service activities, and pushes the whole society to serve women and children. The fifth is the association function. In enhancing understanding and friendship with women and women's organizations from all over the world, Women's Federation actively unites women from other political parties, the Federation of Industry and Commerce, Hong Kong SAR., Macao SAR., Taiwan region and overseas.

4.4.2   The significance of the participation of Women's Federation in social governance

As an organization for women from all walks of life in China, the Women's Federation is the link and bridge between the Party and the government to women, and is also the main channel of the Party and the government to carry out women's work. The active participation of Women's Federation in social governance, representing and safeguarding women and children's rights and interests, is of great significance in promoting the cause of women and children and strengthening the construction of a harmonious society.

4.4.2.1   Women's Federation can better serve the nation

The Women's Federation plays the role of communication and coordination between the government and women, naturally forming a connection with them. To satisfy requirements by the Party and government to further strengthen social governance and enhance the mass work under the new situation, Women's Federation is responsible for and capable of constructing an innovative system of social governance, opening up channels for women to express themselves, actively undertaking the government's functions in line with women's needs, and putting into practice doing actual deeds for women. Therefore, the participation of Women's Federation in social governance will not only better strengthen and improve the Party's mass work, but also promote women's broad participation in democratic politics, and make new contributions to stable development of the society.

4.4.2.2   It can further promote women's development

It is the historical mission of the Women's Federation to promote women's development. In the Chinese context, active participation by Women's Federation in social governance is an important measure to promote women's development in line with the times. While participating in social governance, women's federations at all levels have been able to express their interests more effectively on behalf of women, integrate social resources and help disadvantaged women by making full use of Party and government resources, social resources and giving full play to the advantages of the organizational network. This becomes useful supplements to public welfare undertakings, and enables women to get equal opportunities and enjoy fruits of development. This is also of great significance in thoroughly implementing the basic state policy of gender equality, improving women's political and social status, promoting the reform and innovation of Women's Federation, and achieving women's development.

4.4.2.3 It will better transform

With the deepening of the market economy reform in social transformation, Women's Federation strives to change their traditional ways of thinking and work, and takes the initiative to innovate their own services and ways of work, shifting their service focus from carrying out activities to participating in social governance and providing public services. The Women's Federation always keeps pace with social development and the transformation of government functions, and takes the initiative to achieve its own development.

4.4.2.4 It will promote social harmony and stability

Under the new situation, the role of Women's Federation should be given full play in coordinating the interests of different entities, promoting social justice and maintaining social stability. This is a practical requirement both for maintaining long-term social stability and building a moderately prosperous society, and for strengthening the Party's governing capacity and building a harmonious socialist society. At the same time, the construction of a harmonious society also provides a theoretical foundation as well as a broad working platform for Women's Federation, with both opportunities and challenges.

4.4.3 The main tasks of the Women's Federation in social governance

The Women's Federation has its own special political, organizational, work and coordination advantages in social governance innovation. It performs important functions in representing and safeguarding women's rights and interests, promoting gender equality, strengthening social services and improving women's ability and quality, and undertakes important tasks in serving the overall situation, the grassroots and women.

4.4.3.1 Effectively safeguarding women's and children's rights and interests

As an organization representing women's interests, the Women's Federation must always stand for women and strengthen Women's work and social work.

Firstly, the Women's Federation should represent women's rights and interests and improve the effectiveness of rights protection. In the new era, the Women's Federation should actively participate in making regulations and policies involving women and children's interests, bring the ideas of safeguarding women's rights and interests into policies and legislation, and constantly strengthen the legal protection of women and children's interests.

Secondly, the Women's Federation should timely reflect women's new needs, expand new areas to protect women's rights and interests, understand the women's diversified needs at the primary level, and constantly improve the effectiveness of its work. At the same time, the Women's Federation should actively explore new forms to protect women's rights, vigorously foster social public welfare institutions like legal services in protecting women's rights and mutual assistance cooperatives, and tap into women's potential for self-protection and mutual assistance.

Finally, the Women's Federations at all levels should speak for women, make up for the government's insufficiencies in public services, give full play to their roles of service, communication, coordination and supervision, safeguard their legitimate interests and promote causes concerning women and children.

For example, the Women's Federation of Panjin City, Liaoning Province, integrates judicial resources and connects the women's rights protection hotline with the legal aid center "12348" hotline based on the "12338" public service hotline for the women's rights protection, forming a "five-sphere integrated" public welfare service of legal consultation, dispute mediation, psychological counseling, parenting education and marriage guidance.

4.4.3.2 Helping vulnerable groups

It is a major task and immutable goal for the Women's Federation to participate in social governance and public services by focusing on people's wellbeing and actively assisting the Party committee and government in addressing issues matter most to women and children. The Women's Federation promotes women's entrepreneurship and employment through various means, such as the use of government's favorable policies, and vigorously carries out activities to help vulnerable groups. In recent years, the All-China Women's Federation has shown great concern about people's livelihood and helped vulnerable women. It launched the "Water Cellar for Mothers" project, the campaign to care for left-behind migrant children, "Spring Buds Project", "Poverty Relief Project for Mothers", and the campaign to eliminate anemia in infants and children. For example, in 1989, the China Children and Teenagers' Fund initiated the "Spring Buds Project", a public welfare project to help girls in poor areas return to school. So far, the project has sponsored 3.45 million girls and donated to build 1,489 spring buds schools.

4.4.3.3   Cultivating women's awareness of participation

The Women's Federation is responsible for uniting, leading, and serving women. By forming a social support system for women's work, the Women's Federations at all levels build communication platforms for women from all walks of life and women's social organizations to participate equally in social and public affairs, allowing those representative and influential women to participate in women's work together, and promoting integration between women's organizations of various types and levels. Giving full play to the role of various women's social organizations, the Women's Federation should focus on the initiative of women volunteers and social workers, enhance their recognition of its work, promote women's awareness of participation and volunteerism, and form a mutual benefit and win-win cooperation model and a joint participation in social governance. The Women's Federation of Dongcheng District of Beijing has taken various measures to promote the construction of the "two new" (new economic organizations and new social organizations) organizations, and has extended the Women's Federation to stair-door courtyards, setting up 592 functional women's groups of various kinds linked by interests and expertise, public welfare services and cultural and sports activities. Many groups have come into being, such as "the Neighbourhood Cooperative" in Jiaodaokou Sub-district, "Sunshine Mutual Aid Bank" in Qianmen Sub-district, and "the Giving Tree" in Yongdingmenwai Sub-district.

4.4.3.4   Expanding the scope of public service

It is an important part of the Women's Federation's work to better meet the women and children's immediate interests. In recent years, women's federations at all levels actively participate in social services, continuously increase public service projects for women and children groups, seize the opportunity of the transformation of government functions, give full play to their own advantages, and actively undertake the service provided by the government. They take the initiative to undertake service projects related to women and children transferred by government departments, effectively play the advantageous function of participating in public services, and multiply the channels for resources collection. The Women's Federations at all levels actively explore operation mode of project-based and brand, create branded public service products through employment skills training, household service and women's vocational training, improve the scientific management mechanism, establish a project undertaking and financial guarantee mechanism, strive for regular government or social investment, and continue to carry out project to achieve mutual benefit and win-win results. Jilin Women's Federation launched the "Jilin Internet Sisters" e-commerce training project in 2013, aiming to provide free training for women who are willing to start their own businesses in e-commerce. So far, only in the Jilin Women's Vocational Education Guidance Center, which is the training base of the "Jilin Internet Sisters" e-commerce project, 8,166 "Jilin Internet Sisters" have been trained free of charge and 4,399 online shops have been incubated.

4.4.4 Approaches for the Women's Federation in social governance

In the new era, the Women's Federation should actively expand the space and areas of participation in social governance, proactively undertake the transferred functions of the government-oriented by society, market and projects, effectively explore new ways to participate in social governance, earnestly represent and safeguard women's and children's interests, and continuously improve its ability to serve women in social governance innovation.

4.4.4.1 Locating itself in social governance

It is the major task and immutable goal of the Women's Federation in social governance and public services to better represent and safeguard women's interests, and the Federation must always do well in providing services for society, public welfare and routine work concerning the vital interests of women and children.

As a group organization, the Women's Federation functions twofold in social governance: the function of a link and of providing service. Firstly, the Women's Federation should link the Party and the government with women, and give full play to its role of an intermediary in social coordination and communication. The Women's Federation should give full play to the important role of women in political life, such as actively organizing and promoting women's participation in democratic management and democratic supervision, and promoting gender equality. Secondly, the function of providing service. The Women's Federation should actively provide service for women and children, actively assist the Party committees and the government in addressing issues that concern women and children, focus on women's immediate interests, serve women, unite people and promote stability.

4.4.4.2 Integrating and mobilizing all types of social resources

The important ways for the Women's Federation to give full play to its work advantages and serve women and children are to participate in social coordination, properly cooperate with government functional departments and other community organizations, realize joint governance through labor division, and fulfill the important task of social governance and public services.

Firstly, relying on resources of the Party and governments. As an organization under the leadership of the Party committee and the government, The Women's Federation has the edge of superior political resources, which should be utilized to serve women.

Secondly, making full use of the resources of the Women's Federation. The Women's Federation has established a close relationship of mutual trust and reliance with women from all walks of life. It can attract people to join its work by mobilizing, organizing and making use of the valuable resources, thus forming a joint force in social governance and public services.

Thirdly, mobilizing social resources. Faced with emergence of women's groups, the Women's Federation needs to consider how to integrate the strengths of various emerging women's organizations, unite women with itself, strengthen the work guidance to horizontal network on the basis of vertical organization system, making itself an effective working force in its work.

For example, a community-based social organization named "Warm-Hearted Helpers" was set up by 13 retired elderly women from the Dongcheng District of Beijing in July 2014, encouraging volunteers and community residents to provide daily care services for empty-nest elderly women, elderly who lost their only child, and elderly without family in the community, such as offering emotional comfort, accompanying them to see doctors.

These social organizations have not only extended the work of the Women's Federation, solved the contradiction between downward shifting of work and the insufficient manpower of primary-level organizations, but also identified the position for the Women's Federation in social governance.

4.4.4.3 Improving the service efficiency of the Women's Federation

What's most important for the Women's Federation in social governance is to provide good services, improve service efficiency and fully meet the practical needs of women and children.

Firstly, enhancing the service efficiency. The Women's Federation should effectively represent and safeguard the legitimate rights and interests of women and children, strive to improve the development environment for women and children, pool efforts to do practical jobs, do good deeds, solve difficulties for women and children, and innovate its work.

Secondly, expanding service coverage. The Women's Federation should increase its participation at source and promote the government to fully consider women's interests when making and enforcing laws and regulations. The Women's Federation should work in a socialized model, boost the government to provide public services through practical projects that serve the wellbeing and development of women and children, so as to continuously improve the popularization, socialization and specialization of its work.

Thirdly, extending its service coverage. The Women's Federation should cultivate its capacity of self-governance and expand its service outreach and participation by means of innovating organization structure, building a network of extensive contacts and supporting the development of women's organizations, thus enhancing its social self-governance.

4.4.4.4 Reinforcing personnel cultivation in the Women's Federation

The caliber of the officials and staff of the Women's Federation directly affects its efficiency in social governance. It should attach importance to the education and training of its officials, thus creating a highly qualified team of officials and staff who can answer the call of the times, so as to meet the needs of social governance and public services.

Firstly, enhancing the participation awareness of officials of the Women's Federation in social governance and improving their ability to design, mobilize and organize social governance projects.

Secondly, carrying out targeted education and training. The Women's Federation should strengthen professional ethics together with professional competence, enhance the all-round professional training of its officials, organize studying modern concepts and methods about social administration and public services, and continuously improve its professional social services through various specialized training networks, so as to extensively apply the concepts and methods of social work to the work of women and children and better utilize its capacity to serve women and children.

4.4.5 Experiment of building a "hub-type" Women's Federation in Pudong, Shanghai

Social participation and people's support are essential for innovating social governance, and energizing construction at the primary level. Therefore, a large number of active social organizations are needed to undertake social affairs.

In recent years, the Women's Federation of Pudong New Area in Shanghai has actively explored the socialized operation mechanism of group work, identifying itself as a "hub-type" organization. Oriented by the needs of women, children, and families through service projects, the federation gathers social forces, expands service functions, opens up channels of appeal, and has carried out significant practices, especially in the incubation, cultivation, guidance, and support of women's social organizations.

4.4.5.1   Attaching importance to the incubation of social organizations

The Women's Federation of Pudong New Area has been transformed into a "hub-type" organization since 2007. Guided by the needs of women, children and families and based on service project cooperation, the federation promotes and cooperates with social organizations serving women, children and families. At the same time, the federation attracts and gathers professional social workers, women volunteers, experts, scholars and other talents, forming a joint force to serve women, children and families, serving more than 2.2 million people online and offline.

In order to attract and serve around 170,000 female talents in Zhangjiang Park, the Women's Federation of Pudong New Area has created the first "Women's Home" named "Zhangjiang O2O (Online to Offline) Home of Beauty" in Pudong New Area. Some major activities have been held by "Zhangjiang O2O Home of Beauty", such as parent-child fellowship, lecture for keeping fitness and activity for making friends, etc. Through online and offline platforms, more than 50 offline activities have served more than 16,000 people, uniting white-collar women with the Federation's service.

At the same time, the Women's Federation of Pudong New Area focuses on searching "bellwethers". It purposefully identifies, unites and cultivates a group of leading figures who are enthusiastic about public welfare, highly capable and influential among women.

In order to achieve good communication with women representatives, executive committees of Women's Federation, women's groups and social organizations, the Women's Federation of Pudong New Area has established a "Salon for Leading Figures of Social Organization" by means of regularly holding brainstorming seminars for group leaders, difficult case analyses, information release conferences, and so on.

4.4.5.2   Building a project-based operating model

Most of the social organizations incubated and nurtured by the Women's Federation of Pudong New Area are born out of basic demand of the primary level and thrive for projects. From the emergence of women's social organizations to their growth and maturity, the Women's Federation of Pudong New Area has offered not only the "soil" but also the "fuel".

The exploration of Management by Projects by the Women's Federation of Pudong New Area in 2007 experienced two phases of development: The first phase is from 2007 to 2011, focusing on internal MBP. Officials from the Women's Federation of Pudong New Area served as project leaders. Then project-based operation was extended to the Women's Federations at the primary level in 2008, mobilizing the executive committee of Women's Federation and women's representatives to participate in the project; and in 2009, women's social organizations registered in the Women's Federation of Pudong New Area applied for and undertook women's work projects. Thus the MBP of women's work gradually became clear, with a large number of non-staffed women workers standing out. The second phase lasts from 2011 to the present, when the MBP has been shifted from in-system to outside the system. Since 2011, the "Family Service Projects for Women and Children in Pudong New Area" is launched every October to the whole society for advices, and social demand surveys and social force mobilization are extensively carried out, thus the role of the Women's Federation of Pudong New Area transforming from "project manager" to "project supervisor".

In this process, the Women's Federation of Pudong New Area, on the one hand, has provided one-stop guidance for women's social organizations entrusted on Pudong Public Welfare Promotion Association, helped the project team land in the community through activity monitoring, stage evaluation, individual consultation, and course guidance, etc. And the Association guides social organizations to achieve their own sustainable development with document preparation, plan execution, activity implementation, resource integration, team operation and vision planning. On the other hand, in line with actual demands by women, children, and families, the Women's Federation of Pudong New Area highlights the gender perspective and the characteristics of "womanness" in the project design, thus making the development of social organizations match the functions of the Women's Federation, the demands by service recipients and the expected social benefits of the project.

4.4.5.3 Creating brand-name projects for featured services

The Women's Federation of Pudong New Area cultivates social organizations in the project-based philosophy, guiding each women's social organization to cultivate their special brands according to their own advantageous resources, social needs and projects developed. When these social organizations develop, they are guided towards specialization and socialization.

In order to meet the diversified and plural needs of women and women's groups in the new context, the Women's Federation of Pudong New Area has intentionally gathered many professional social organizations to provide "many-to-many" services for women, children and families, covering legal services, anti-domestic violence, parent-child education, care for special families, community parenting schools, quality and ability improvement, traditional Chinese medicine health care, rehabilitation of intensive illnesses, mental health, care for retired "March 8th Red-banner Pacesetter"[1], care for special groups and friendship building among young people.

At present, the Women's Federation of Pudong New Area has a total of 206 projects rooted in communities, creating a series of Women's Federation brands with wide coverage, high quality, good implementation and many praises, such as "Happy Families—Heart Station", "Intimate Sisters", "Women's Farming Brand", "Women's Happiness of Power Academy", etc.

4.4.5.4   Advancing Management by Projects to Women's Federations at the primary level

In order to deepen and expand the Management by Projects of family services for women and children, the Women's Federation of Pudong New Area has taken it as its key part to promote the MBP from the District Women's Federation to women's federation at primary level, gradually influencing and benefiting sub-districts, towns and villages.

In this process, Pudong New Area trained the officials of women's federations at two levels to supervise projects, thus Women's Federation shifting from project implementer to supervisor.

In addition, the Women's Federation of Pudong New Area in Shanghai pays great attention to investment, constantly improving the mechanism for women's federations at district, sub-districts and town levels to purchase services from social forces. And incorporating the costs into the budget through government purchase of services, implementing contractual management and introducing third-party evaluation.

According to statistics, in 2017, Women's Federation of Pudong New Area planned to invest 87.5% of the total expenditure in 27 projects at the district level and 36 projects at sub-districts and town levels, all of which were carried out in "Family

---

[1] "March 8th Red-banner Pacesetter" refers to an honorific title for women who have extraordinary achievements and outstanding contributions in the construction of socialist material and spiritual civilization on all fronts in China.

Centers" in sub-districts and towns and "Women's Family" in villages, covering single-parent families, low-income families, white-collar women, rural women, elderly women living alone, women and children with intellectual disabilities, families bereft of their only child, disabled elderly women, myopic and obese children, and parents of school students, etc.

Chapter 5
Participation of Social Organizations in Social Governance

The social governance is characterized by multiple governing actors, democratic consultation, acting according to law, and people-centered.[1] Social organizations are one of the important actors in social governance. They, along with the government, market organizations, and members of society, participate in social affairs, and strive for the sound operation of the society and the maximal public interests. Among them, social organizations have played an important role in mobilizing social resources, providing diversified and personalized public and social services, and participating in social affairs management. After 40 years of the reform and opening up, Chinese social organizations have experienced four stages of development: rise of academic organizations (1978–1991), overall stagnation (1992–2001), stable development with private non-enterprise units, associations and chambers of commerce and other emergent social organizations as the mainstream (2002–2012), an overall growth of social organizations (2013 to the present).[2] The swift transformations in society, along with the emergence of new opportunities and challenges, have sparked significant growth in social organizations. This growth is evident in terms of their numbers, scope, and roles, and it has played a crucial role in enhancing social governance.

5.1 The definition, types, and current situation of social organizations

5.1.1 The definition of social organizations

5.1.1.1 The concept of social organizations

Social organization is a new concept first raised on the Sixth Plenary Session of

---

[1] Gong Weibin, "Social Governance is an Upgraded Version of Social Management", *Theoretical Horizons*, 2014 (1).

[2] Wang Ming et al., *Social Organizations and Social Governance*, Beijing: Social Sciences Academic Press (China), 2014, p. 4.

the 16th CPC Central Committee. It generalizes internationally accepted terms such as non-governmental organizations, non-profit organizations, third or independent departments, tax-free organizations, civic organizations, voluntary organizations, autonomous organizations, intermediary organizations, etc. (hereinafter referred to as "social organizations"). The proposal of "social organization" is intended to highlight its social characteristics in function and attribute.[1] Unlike the bureaucratic relationship in government organizations or the material interest relationship in economic organizations, the fundamental feature of social organizations is society, which reflects the relationship between people. In social organizations, citizens form a variety of groups by enjoying and exercising their right to associate. Through organized efforts, they pursue common objectives and, based on this foundation, work towards maximizing societal benefits.[2] In addition, unlike other terms which highlight certain characteristics, such as the implicit awareness of the relationship between government and the people in civic organizations, the emphasis of non-profit organizations on the connotation of business, the concept of "social organizations" is a more comprehensive, inclusive and flexible, which comprehensively shows they are social, non-profit, non-governmental, independent, voluntary and public.

5.1.1.2   The definition of social organizations

There are broad and narrow definitions of social organizations. According to Professor Lester M. Salamon, social organizations share five basic characteristics: formal, private, non-profit-distributing, self-governing and voluntary. These organizations operate outside the government mechanism; are not primarily engaged in business, do not distribute profits among board members or "owners"; are self-managed and membership is voluntary.[3] In a broad sense, social organizations may have some of the characteristics in the above definitions, mainly including social groups, private non-enterprise units, foundations, intermediary agencies, people's organizations, public institutions, social enterprises, neighborhood committees and village committees.

The narrow sense of social organization is what this chapter will focus on. Based on the list of the scope of "social organizations" in the Sixth Plenary Session of the 16th CPC Central Committee, combined with the actual situation of the development of

---

[1] Gong Weibin, *Social Management and Social Construction*, Beijing: National School of Administration Press, 2011, p. 64.

[2] Zhang Haijun, "The Concept of Social Organisation and Its Importance", *China Social Organisation*, 2012 (12).

[3] Lester M. Salamon, S. Wojciech Sokolowski et al., *Global Civil Society: Dimensions of the Nonprofit Sector*, Chinese Edition, translated by Chen Yimei et al., Beijing: Peking University Press, 2007, p. 2.

social organizations, this chapter considers social organizations in a narrow sense mainly include society groups, private non-enterprise units, foundations, intermediary agencies,[1] and various grassroots self-governing organizations, such as urban and rural community grassroots organizations and other unregistered organizations, etc.

5.1.2   Types of social organizations

The classification of social organizations is a widely discussed issue, but there is no unified international or national standard. The International Classification of Non-profit Organizations (ICNPO), proposed by the research group of Salamon and Anheier in 1996, is the earliest specific classification system for social organizations. According to activity fields and scope, activity modes, activity objects and beneficiaries, this system divides social organizations into 12 categories, including cultural and entertainment organizations, education and research organizations, health organizations and social services organizations, and further subdivides them into 27 subcategories.[2] In addition, according to the nature of the activities, The National Taxonomy of Exempt Entities (NTEE) formulated by the National Center for Charitable Statistics divides them into 25 categories, such as education, health, mental healthcare, etc.[3]

Chinese government departments and scholars also put forward a variety of classification methods. According to the nature and purpose of the organization, the government divides the social organizations into three categories: associations, private non-enterprise units, and foundations. By the activity fields, the Ministry of Civil Affairs proposed a new classification system for the annual inspection of social organizations at the end of 2006, which increased the number of associations and private non-enterprise units from 9 to 14. Including technology and research, ecological environment, education, health, social services, culture, sports, law, industrial and commercial services, religion, agricultural and rural development, professions and practitioners, international and foreign-related organizations and others, According to the standard of administrative degree and whether registered in the Civil Affairs Department, some scholars divide social

---

[1] The Sixth Plenary Session of the 16th CPC Central Committee, Decision on Several Major Issues Concerning the Construction of a Harmonious Socialist Society.

[2] Lester M. Salamon, Helmut K. Anheier, The International Classification of Nonprofit Organizations: ICNPO-Revision 1, 1996, Soviet Phys. - Cryst. (English Transl.), 2015, 8 (1): 14-25.

[3] Julian Wolpert, "Applying the National Taxonomy of Exempt Entities: Geographical Profiles", *VOLUNTAS: International Journal of Voluntary and Nonprofit Organizations*, Kluwer Academic Publisher.

organizations into registered associations and private non-enterprise units, unregistered private non-enterprise units, eight major people's organizations, other quasi-governmental organizations, and grassroots organizations.[1] In terms of legal status, it can be divided into corporate body and non-corporate body. In terms of the purpose of the activity, it can be divided into public welfare groups and mutual benefit groups. In terms of the needs of administration, it can be divided into people's organizations, autonomous organizations, industry organizations, academic organizations, community organizations, other kinds of non-governmental organizations and public welfare foundations. According to the strength of government and profit-making, it can be divided into social organizations with strong government and non-profit (similar to "quasi-government departments"), social organizations with strong government and profit-making (mainly operating public institutions), social organizations with strong non-government and profit-making (mainly private non-enterprise units), social organizations with strong non-government and non-profit (mainly diversified grassroots rights protection organizations).[2] The broad social organizations can be classified into people's organizations, organizations exempted from registration, village committees, and neighborhood committees, non-governmental organizations (NGO), public institutions, and unregistered organizations. Among them, NGOs are further divided into mutual benefit organizations (economic mutual benefit organizations, social mutual benefit organizations) and public welfare organizations (membership public welfare organizations, non-member public welfare organizations).[3]

5.1.3   The development of social organizations

5.1.3.1   Policy support for social organization development

The rapid development of social organizations is inseparable from the government's policy support. The development of social organizations has been gradually incorporated into the national strategic plan since the end of the 20th century. The 15th CPC National Congress clearly put forward that we should "foster and strengthen social intermediary organizations". The Fourth Plenary Session of the 16th CPC Central Committee further

---

[1] He Jianyu, Wang Shaoguang, "Chinese-Style Revolution of Associations: A Quantitative Description of the Panorama of Associations", in Gao Bingzhong, Yuan Ruijun, *Blue Book on Civil Society Development in China*, Beijing: Peking University Press, 2008.

[2] Kang Xiaoguang, Lu Xianying and Han Heng, "State-Society Relations in the Age of Reform: Administrative Absorption of Society", in Wang Ming, *Emerging Civil Society in China, 1978-2008*, Beijing: Social Sciences Academic Press (China), 2008.

[3] Cheng Yue, Ma Qingyu, "An Analysis of the Classification Methods of NGOs", *CASS Journal of Political Science*, 2008(3).

requested the non-governmental organizations to function, namely to give full play to the social, industry and intermediary organizations in providing services, reflecting demands and regulating behaviors, to cooperatively manage and serve the society. The Sixth Plenary Session of the 16th CPC Central Committee put forward the concept of "social organization" for the first time, and systematically elaborated on developing social organizations and enhancing social service function. The 12th Five-year Plan proposes strengthening the construction of social organizations, attaches equal importance to cultivation and development, management and supervision, promotes the healthy and orderly development of social organizations, and gives full play to their functions of providing services, reflecting demands and standardizing behaviors.

The 18th CPC National Congress has incorporated the construction of social organizations into the construction of social management system, "We should focus on establishing a socialist system of social management with Chinese characteristics" and "quicken the pace of building a system of modern social organizations in which functions of the government are separated from those of social organizations, rights and responsibilities are clearly established, and social organizations exercise self-governance in accordance with the law". The Third Plenary Session of the 18th CPC Central Committee, for the first time integrated the development of social organizations with the innovation of social governance, proposed "innovating social governance", "improving social governance methods, and stimulating the vitality of social organizations", and encouraged social organizations to participate in the field of social governance in their unique way, a symbol that the government is no longer the sole actor of social governance. The Fourth Plenary Session of the 18th CPC Central Committee further strengthened the legal construction of social organizations, called for "strengthening legislation on social organizations", and played a positive role of social organizations in legislative consultation, law popularization, and observance of the law, and construction of a society based on the rule of law.

Meanwhile, Chinese government has issued a series of laws, regulations, and specific systems to promote and regulate the development of social organizations in recent years. In September 2013, the State Council promulgated the Guidelines on the Government's Purchase of Services from Non-Governmental Forces to establish and improve the mechanism of government's purchase of services from non-governmental forces. In November 2014, the State Council issued Guiding Opinions on Promoting the Sound Development of the Cause of Charities to further improve the management and supervision of charitable organizations, stimulate their vitality, and promote their orderly development. In May 2015, the Ministry of Civil Affairs issued the Guidelines on the Establishment of a Third-Party Evaluation Mechanism for Social Organizations, which defined the general idea, basic principles, policy measures, and organizational leadership of establishing a third-party evaluation mechanism for social organizations, improving the comprehensive supervision system for social organizations. In July 2015, the General Office of the CPC Central Committee and the General Office of the State Council issued the Framework Plan for the De-Affiliation of Administrative Agencies from Industry Associations and Chambers of Commerce, suggesting de-affiliation in five aspects: institutions, personnel, functions, finance, Party development, and foreign affairs. In April 2016, the 20th session of the Standing Committee of the 12th National People's Congress voted through the Law of the People's Republic of China on the Administration of Activities of Overseas Non-Governmental Organizations within the Territory of China, the first legislation for overseas non-governmental organizations in China. It provides a code of conduct for overseas non-governmental organizations to follow in activities in China. In July 2016, eight departments, including the Publicity Department of the Communist Party of China, the Central Civilization Office, and the Ministry of Civil Affairs, jointly issued Opinions on Supporting and Developing Voluntary Organizations, offering specific guides to encourage their legal registration, internal governance and fund management, laying a policy foundation for their development. In August, Opinions of the General Office of the CPC Central Committee and the General Office of the State Council on Reforming the Social Organization Administration System and Promoting the Sound and Orderly Development of Social Organizations was issued, which put forward specific requirements in improving the development policy of social organizations, conducting close examination on registration of social organizations in accordance with the law, exercising strict management and supervision, and strengthening the self-building of social organizations.

In September 2016, China formally put into effect the Charity Law of the People's Republic of China, an essential and comprehensive law for the development of the charity system. It sets out clear provisions on significant issues such as charitable activities, charitable organizations, charitable donations, and charitable trusts. Among them, the direct registration of charitable organizations, tax incentives, the release of public offering qualifications, and other provisions provide a legal basis for social organizations to break through the dual management system and enjoy charitable tax incentives, and provide new impetus for social organizations to play a better role of public welfare and charity. At the same time, to support the official implementation of

Charity Law of the People's Republic of China, China has issued Measures for the Accreditation of Charitable Organizations, Measures for the Administration of Charitable Organizations' Fundraising from the Public, Provisions on the Annual Expenditures for Conducting Charitable Activities and Administration Expenses of Charitable Organizations, Measures for the Administration of Public Fundraising Platform Services. In addition, Regulation on the Administration of the Registration of Social Organizations, Regulation on Foundation Administration, and Interim Regulations on Registration Administration of Private Non-Enterprise Units are being revised.

The governance innovation of local social organizations is also developing rapidly. Many provinces and cities have issued policies to promote the social organization registration system reform, carried out or tried out direct registration of social organizations, and further extended the registration authority of non-public foundations and non-local chambers of Commerce.

5.1.3.2 The quantity and structure of social organizations in China

Since 2002, China's social organizations have entered a period of stable development. The number of social organizations rose from 244,000 in 2002 to 498,000 in 2012, [1] as shown in Table 5–1. In 2013, as the country began to comprehensively deepen its reform, social organizations entered a period of growth, the number reached 547,000, an increase of 9.6% compared with the previous year. From 2013 to 2016, social organizations continued to grow, with an average annual growth rate of about 8.8%. By the end of 2016, China had 699,000 social organizations registered in civil affairs departments, [2] increasingly becoming an important social force and participant of social governance.

Table 5–1   Changes in the number of social organizations
in China from 2006 to 2016

Indicator	2006	2007	2008	2009	2010	2011	2012	2013	2014	2015	2016
Social organizations (10,000)	35.4	38.7	41.3	43.0	44.5	46.1	49.8	54.7	60.6	66.2	69.9
Social groups (10,000)	19.2	21.2	23.0	23.9	24.5	25.5	27.1	28.9	31.0	32.9	33.5
Foundation (10,000)	1,144	1,340	1,597	1,843	2,200	2,614	3,029	3,549	4,117	4,784	5,523
Private non-enterprises (10,000)	16.1	17.4	18.2	19.0	19.8	20. 4	22. 5	25. 5	29. 2	32.9	35.9

---

[1] Wang Ming, *Introduction to Social Organizations*, Beijing: China Society Publishing House, 2010, p. 87.
[2] The data in this section comes from the Ministry of Civil Affairs, Statistical Bulletin on the Development of Social Services, http://www.mca.gov.cn/.

In recent years, the structure of various social organizations in China has been basically stable. According to *Statistical Report of the People's Republic of China on the Development of Social Services in 2015* released by the Ministry of Civil Affairs, the top three social organizations are: 62,000 for agriculture and rural development, 48,000 for social services, and 37,000 for industrial and commercial services followed by culture, sports, occupation and employment, science and technology research, etc. In the category of private non-enterprise units, the top three social organizations are 183,000 in education, 24,000 in health, and 49,000 in social services. Based on the academic researchers in 2008 and 2013,[1] by adding the number of associations and private non-enterprise units in 2015, it showed that the distribution of social organizations was as follows: 193,000 (29.3%) for education, 97,000 (14.7%) for social services, 62,000 (9.4%) for agriculture and rural development, 50,000 (7.6%) for culture, 40,000 (6%) for industrial and commercial services, 37,000 (5.6%) for sports, 34,000 (5.2%) for health, 33,000 (5%) for science and technology research. The percentage of occupational and professional organizations, ecological environment, law, religion, international and other foreign-related organizations was all under 5%. Compared with the statistical data in 2008 and 2013, the distribution of social organizations in China was still relatively concentrated, and different types of social organizations continued to develop steadily, with no significant changes in their percentages.

At the same time, social organizations are still insufficient in numbers and imbalanced in structure. In terms of the number of social organizations, China had 5.1 social organizations per 10,000 people in 2016, far behind that of developed countries. In terms of structure, there are inadequate social welfare organizations in China. These organizations are oriented toward the general public and meet the needs of social interests, while mutual organizations mainly meet the internal needs of the organization. International experience suggests that a reasonable structure of social organizations should include more than two-thirds of public interest organizations. At present, they only account for about half of the total. In addition, according to the statistics in recent years released by the Statistical Communique on Social Services of the Ministry of Civil Affairs, compared with educational social organizations, social service organizations account for a relatively small percentage. Social organizations are also more focused on

---

[1] Ge Daoshun "The Development of Social Organizations in China: From Social Subjects to National Consciousness", *Jiangsu Social Sciences*, 2011 (3); Gong Weibin, Gong Chunming, *Socialist Social Governance System with Chinese Characteristics*, Beijing: Economic & Management Publishing House, 2016, pp. 172-173.

education and training, daily services, cultural and sports activities, and other fields at the neighborhood or community level. There is still much room for the development of social welfare and charity organizations and urban and rural community service organizations.

5.1.3.3   The status quo of social organizations

China has initially established a social organization system covering all urban and rural areas, involving all sectors of the national economy and all fields of social life, with complete categories, multiple levels, wide coverage and strong functions. It plays an increasingly important role in developing public welfare undertakings, providing public services, and enhancing international communication and cooperation.[1]

Social organizations support public welfare and charity undertakings. The ability of social organizations to mobilize social resources has been continuously strengthening. By the end of 2015, China's social organizations had received donations of RMB61.03 billion, of which public and non-public foundations had received donations of RMB43.93 billion. Social organizations actively participate in poverty alleviation, helping the elderly, helping the disabled, disaster relief, education funding, and other public welfare and charity undertakings through various ways such as donation funds and project guidance.

Social organizations shall develop social welfare undertakings. Social organizations have become important providers and participants of social services such as elderly care, mental health, children, the disabled, and social assistance. Taking the accommodation service as an example, in 2015, 31,000 social service institutions provided 3.932 million beds, housing 2.316 million people. Of these institutions 12,000 are social organizations, accounting for 38.7% of the total.

Social organizations provide public services. As one of the main bodies of governance, social organizations have undertaken part of the public service transferred by the government, especially playing an important role in community management and public service. In recent years, through the purchase of public services and other means, the government has vigorously supported the development of community social organizations, providing cultural and educational services to community residents, coordinating community relations, and providing support for vulnerable groups.

---

[1] Zhao Boyan, "Research on the Role of Social Organizations in Promoting Harmonious Social Development", *Theory and Modernization*, 2012 (3).

Social organizations can enhance international exchanges and cooperation. The influence of China's social organizations in the world keeps increasing. Taking social organizations in the field of disaster management as an example, in recent years, the China Foundation for Poverty Alleviation (now China Foundation for Rural Development) and The Amity Foundation has successively participated in international projects such as disaster assistance in the Philippines, the United States, and Haiti. In 2013, on behalf of Chinese Red Cross International Emergency Response Team, the Blue Sky Rescue and 999 Rescue participated in the rescue of a severe typhoon disaster in the Philippines. In the Nepal Earthquake happened on April 25, 2015, seven foundations and more than 20 private rescue teams participated in the rescue operation, including the whole process of emergency rescue, transitional resettlement, and post-disaster reconstruction.

5.2　The role of social organization in social governance

5.2.1　The necessity of social organizations' participation in social governance

In China, social governance refers to the governance activities of public affairs under the leadership of the ruling party, led by government organizations, incorporating social organizations and other governance actors. Social governance is a process that "focuses on realizing and safeguarding the rights of the people, gives play to the role of multiple governance actors, improves social welfare, ensures and improves people's wellbeing, defuses social contradictions, promotes social fairness, and promotes orderly and harmonious social development in response to social problems in national governance".[1]

Social organizations' participation in social governance effectively makes up for the government's deficiencies caused by rigid institutions and administrative systems as governance carriers. Social organizations are large in numbers, diverse in categories, great in flexibility, and prominent in humanization, which, just like capillaries, can provide individualized, diversified, and humanized services for members of society, especially the underprivileged groups.[2]

---

[1] Jiang Xiaoping, "Social Governance System Innovation in the Process of Modernization of National Governance", *Chinese Public Administration*, 2014 (1).

[2] Zhao Xiaoping, Tao Chuanjin, *Community Governance: Dilemmas and Solution in the Transformation of the Patterns,* Beijing: Social Sciences Academic Press (China), 2012, p. 11.

Social organization is an important factor of social governance, playing the role of managing and serving social members and providing public services. It also functions as a supervisor for the government while carrying out self-management and self-restraint. At the same time, social organizations unite the isolated and scattered social individuals and form a social middle zone connecting the nation and the individuals. Besides, it cultivates its members' concept of independence, awareness of self-governance and sense of responsibility by making independent organizational rules, performing internal mobilization and management, and strengthening the communication, cooperation, and consultation between members and between the organizations. It also serves as an important platform for expressing public interests, maintaining social stability and providing social services through self-creation, self-management, and self-service. Modern social governance needs not only top-down administration but also self-management of social organizations and other social self-governing forces. The complementary integration of the two makes social governance both orderly and dynamic, offering both common services for the whole society and individualized services for specific groups.

5.2.2   The role of social organizations in social governance

5.2.2.1   Mobilization of social resources

Social governance is a major subject facing China, which requires both the active participation of all sectors of society and great long-term capital investment. The government is an important and responsible entity of social governance whose administrative and financial support is the main source of human and financial resources. At the same time, to solve the complicated problems in China's social transformation, it needs the support of social resources, for government investment is far from enough. Social organizations have a strong ability to mobilize social resources by widely pooling financial and human resources, and investing them into social public services, community management, and other social governance fields. In particular, foundations are charitable property trusts formed on the basis of donations. Through public fundraising, fund operation, and public welfare support, they can effectively integrate a large number of social resources and put them into social welfare undertakings.

Since the 5 · 12 Wenchuan Earthquake, the donations received by the government and social organizations have increased sharply. In 2008, the total amount of donations reached the highest level in history, totaling RMB 76.4 billion, about 5.7 times that of 2007, including RMB49.88 billion by the Ministry of Civil Affairs and RMB7.73 billion by various social organizations registered in the Ministry of Civil Affairs. It is worth noting that since 2010, the amount of donations received by social organizations has increased significantly, and the amount of donations raised by social organizations has greatly surpassed that of government departments, becoming an important entity of receiving donations of social welfare. Changes in the amount of social donations received by China's Civil Affairs Departments and Social Organizations from 2010 to 2015 see Table 5–2 for the specific data.[1]

Table 5–2   Changes in the amount of social donations received by China's Civil Affairs Departments and Social Organizations from 2010 to 2015

Unit: RMB100 million

Indicators	2010	2011	2012	2013	2014	2015
Acceptance of social donations by the civil administration	193.7	101.4	108.0	107.6	79.6	44.2
Acceptance of social donations by social organizations	417.0	393.6	470.8	458.8	524.9	610.3
Total	601.7	495.0	578. 8	566.4	604.4	654. 5

In terms of human resources, volunteers are more enthusiastic than ever before. Substantive progress has been made in institutionalizing voluntary services in China. By the end of 2015, China had achieved full coverage of volunteer service organizations in 31 provinces, autonomous regions and municipalities, covering more than 100 million volunteers.[2] Supported by the Volunteer Cloud technology, the China Volunteer Service Federation has set up a national volunteer service information system. So far, 26 provinces, autonomous regions and municipalities, and 71 prefecture-level cities (districts) have been connected to the system, with more than 28.25 million real-name registered volunteers.[3]

A case in study is the mobilization of social resources in the Lushan Earthquake. After the Lushan Earthquake, social organizations quickly started to mobilize resources and provided support for disaster governance. At the first moment of disaster, social

---

[1] The data in this section comes from the Ministry of Civil Affairs, Statistical Bulletin on the Development of Social Services, http: //www.mca.gov.cn/.

[2] Wang Kai, "China's Voluntary Service Organizations Achieve Full Coverage and Number of Volunteers Exceeds One Hundred Million", *People's Daily Online*, http: //ccn.people.com.cn/n1/2015/1218/c366510-27947063.html, Dec.18, 2015.

[3] Summary of the Work of the Chinese Federation of Voluntary Services in 2016, Official website of the Chinese Federation of Voluntary Services, http://www.cvf.org.cn/show/6292.html, Jan. 24, 2017.

organizations were actively involved in rescue and fundraising and used the collected funds at different stages for emergency relief, transitional settlement, post-quake reconstruction. For example, One Foundation responded quickly in just half an hour after the earthquake. After launching the emergency response mechanism, it soon began emergency search and rescue transfer and material distribution, and appealed for donations from the public. By the end of March 2017, One Foundation had received RMB390 million in donations and use it for emergency relief and material assistance, as well as disaster relief projects for schools and communities. The foundation has spent about RMB260 million, accounting for 67.94% of the total donations. A total of 56 spending projects of Lushan Earthquake were set up, including the construction of 8 quake-resistant schools, 20 disaster-prevention sports fields, 14 rural kindergartens, 358 earthquake-resistant steel-structured houses for farmers, 12 community disaster relief centers, and emergency training and drills for rural community volunteer rescue teams, contributing greatly to the restoration of production and life of the people and emergency response capacity in quake-stricken areas.[1]

Meanwhile, social organizations in disaster-stricken area took action quickly, launched the establishment of network platforms for social organizations, sharing information and coordinating efforts, and effectively guiding the volunteers and organizations. On April 20, 2013, the day of the Lushan Earthquake, a number of social organizations jointly established 4·20 Joint Relief Action of Chengdu Social Welfare Organizations by April 28, 2013, a total of 68 members and partner organizations had joined the action. In addition, there were platforms such as 4·20 China Nonprofit Network for Disaster Risk Response initiated by the Red Cross Society of China and the Narada Foundation, as well as the China NGO Center for Disaster Risk Reduction jointly initiated by the China Youth Development Foundation, the China Foundation for Poverty Alleviation and other foundations. While mobilizing non-governmental rescue teams and volunteers to participate in disaster relief, the social organization network platform also provided logistical support, skill training, and project support to coordinate non-governmental rescue forces and avoid disorderly disaster relief.

5.2.2.2   Social service provider

Social organizations' participation in social services is an essential part of transforming government functions, promoting cooperation between government and

---

[1] Report on the Fourth Anniversary of the One Foundation Lushan Earthquake, One Foundation official website, http://www.onefoundation.cn/Uploads/201704/58f5c16b6dd99.pdf.

society, and fostering new types of social governance actors. At present, insufficient supply of public services cannot meet the diversified demands for public services. It is impossible for the government to directly manage all social affairs. Some of the functions and responsibilities of public welfare and service have to be transferred to other social actors to relieve the conflict between supply and demand and encourage more diversified participation. At the same time, social organizations are non-profit and voluntary, which can give full play to their unique advantages in the field of social services, such as further stimulating citizen participation and collaboration, enhancing social trust, and fostering public spirit and sense of social responsibility.

China's social organizations assume more and more social service responsibilities and the ways of participating in social service are becoming increasingly diversified.

China takes community social organizations as the carrier to provide grassroots social services. In recent years, China's community social organizations have developed rapidly, covering a number of community public services such as elderly care, medical care, education, rights and interests' protection, especially playing an irreplaceable role in aiding the underprivileged groups and developing public welfare social services, and becoming an important participant in community governance. In Hangzhou, there were more than 7,000 community social organizations by the end of 2010, and most of the communities had more than 10 community social organizations, many of which stood out to be prominent, such as On Other Side of Water Mutual-aid Association in Shangcheng District, the Peacemaker Association in Xiacheng District, Love Community Health Service Center in Xiaoshan District and "Spark" Home Care Service Center in Yuhang District, and so on.[1]

Chinese government purchases social organization services. The central government has allocated special funds since 2012 to encourage social organizations to participate in social services. In 2017, RMB190 million was budgeted to fund 480 projects, covering the elderly care, child care, helping the disabled, social work services, capacity-building and personnel training.[2] At present, all projects work well. The Disabled Club in Tongxin County, Wuzhong City of Ningxia Hui Autonomous Region, for example with the support of the fund, has carried out supportive employment activities such as rehabilitation lessons, training and on-the-spot entrepreneurship

---

[1] Lang Xiaobo, Yu Yunfeng, "Participation of Social Organisations in Public Services: Organizational Advantages and Path Choices", *Journal of the Party School of CPC Hangzhou*, 2011(5).

[2] The 2017 Implementation Programme of the Central Financial Support for Social Organisations' Participation in Social Service Projects.

guidance for the disabled, so as to improve their survival ability, labor skills and social adaptability, and provide more employment opportunities for the disabled, known as "helping people to help themselves." Meanwhile, many local governments are showing their support by purchasing the services from the social organizations. Of all the Top Ten Social Welfare Community Organizations in Nanjing in 2015, more than half of them are those of elderly and child care, which can operate the projects purchased by the governments. Since its founding in 2003, Kind Elderly Care Center in Gulou District has been operating in the mode that the government purchases the service the organization offers. The government has paid for more than RMB4 million for the service purchase. The seniors the center takes care of have risen to 1,600 from 100, comprehensive services are provided such as senior care, health care, teaching and entertainment.

5.2.2.3　Prevention and settlements of social conflicts

At present, China is still in a time when radical social transformation, social conflicts keep emerging and becoming more and more complicated. The mode of "disputes settlement by government alone" can no longer meet the social needs. It is one of the main missions of social governance to innovate the system of effectively preventing and resolving social conflicts. At present, a system for the prevention and resolution of social conflicts is taking shape, with government departments taking the leading role and the social forces as the participants. Social organizations can tolerate and reconcile diversified social demands and values, which can, prevent the ineffectiveness and disorder of individual interest expression, and ease the conflicts between different groups. Some social organizations have become one of the institutional platforms for the expression of the people's interests, participating in dispute resolution in labor, medical care, community, and other fields, providing interest expression channels and communication feedback mechanisms for different social strata and interest groups, especially the underprivileged groups.

Let us take the social organizations that protect workers' rights as an example. The rapid economic development leads to the rapid rise of labor disputes, which has become one of the prominent social conflicts in China. With the improvement of the consciousness of rights and interests of the workers, some social organizations, for example, have emerged with the purpose of safeguarding workers' rights.

Beijing Workers' Home, full name Beijing Workers' Home Cultural Development Center, located in Picun Community, Jinzhan Town, Chaoyang District, is a social welfare organization established by migrant workers themselves, committed to protection of migrant workers' rights and interests concerning social, cultural and educational needs as well as the promotion and improvement of their wellbeing. In October 2009, the Beijing Workers' Home Labor Union was established, which incorporated rights protection into daily basis and helped them in an organized way. For example, the odds of success are much greater if the labor union, on behalf of the workers negotiates with those in arrears with the wages for their unpaid salary.[1]

In addition to the service of safeguarding rights and interests, the trade union also provides the workers in Picun Community with various kinds of cultural education and training, daily cultural and recreational activities, and rights and interests assistance services, mainly including library, cinema, literature and art group, Unions' Day, unions' activities, mutual benefit shop, culture and art museum, community activity center and so on. All these make a platform for workers to read, study, communicate with each other and obtain legal aid, enrich their education and cultural life and establish a solid social support network for them.

Little Bird Mutual Assistance Hotline is a public welfare organization specialized in providing legal services to safeguard the legitimate rights and interests of migrant workers. It has 27 full-time and part-time staff, 585 lawyer volunteers, and 5,092 ordinary volunteers, offering services in the cities such as Beijing, Shenzhen, Shenyang, Shanghai, and Chongqing. While providing legal consultation for workers, Little Bird Mutual Assistance Hotline solves labor disputes through mediation and non-litigation way so as to minimize the gap between enterprises and workers and promote harmonious labor relations. By the end of 2016, Little Bird Mutual Assistance Hotline had helped workers ask back more than RMB297 million of their unpaid wages, directly benefiting 170,000 workers and indirectly benefiting more than 300,000 workers.[2]

The role of social organizations in the protection of labor rights and interests is mainly reflected in representation of the labor interests, such as communication with enterprises through organized and institutionalized channels, adopting diversified ways such as judicial proceedings, resorting to the media and civil mediation. This, therefore, has prevented and resolved a large number of labor disputes by dissolving the conflicts at the grassroots level, conducive to the establishment of harmonious labor relations. At

---

[1] Zhao Boyan, *Research on the Role of Social Organisations in Public Conflict Governance*, Tianjin: Nankai University, 2012.

[2] Website of the Little Bird Mutual Assistance Hotline Organisation, http://www.xiaoxiaoniao.org.cn/Item/Show.asp?id=1746&m=1.

the same time, social organizations have improved the situation of workers and to some degree changed the unequal labor-management relations to some extent.

5.2.2.4   Promotion of social self-governance

Society is the middle zone between the state and the private, and a bridge between the state and the members of society. Social self-governance is the self-management and self-service of the members in the society. By taking part in social affairs together, the consciousness of the actor can be stimulated, social responsibility enhanced, and governance ability improved. Social self-governance is the self-management and self-service of the members of society. Joint participation in social affairs can stimulate actor consciousness of the participants, raise their sense of social responsibility, and improve governance ability. Social organizations, acting as the organizers of scattered individuals in the society, provide platforms for the members to participate in the management of social affairs in various fields such as public welfare undertakings and grassroots construction, and become the carriers that promote the social of the society by cooperating with the government.

Industry associations and members of the chamber of commerce organizations, for example, can play a role of self-discipline in their own industries. In Anhui Province, 17 municipal-level insurance associations have promoted orderly competitions among the members by formulating more than 10 regulations, and service standards by setting up self-regulatory committees and self-regulatory inspection teams and by improving the arbitration mechanism of insurance contract disputes.

At the same time, social organizations also play a unique role of self-discipline and self-governance in the development of primary-level bodies. Social organizations in the Yuancheng District of Heyuan City in Guangdong Province, for example, participated in the management of the floating population. In order to promote the self-organization and self-management of the floating population management, Yuancheng District takes the Rental House Owners Association and the Floating Population Mutual Aid Association as the carrier to perform service management of the floating population among them, Rental House Owners Association organizes its members to research the management of the floating population and rental services, providing assistance to the government in formulating the planning of the housing rental, the business regulations, and the code of self-discipline, which may best protect the legitimate rights and interests of both the owners and tenants, mediate the rental disputes, and can also provide services of rental information, employment information. The scattered owners regard the association as a platform for rental information, price negotiation and dispute resolution, bringing a harmonious neighborhood.[1] The Floating Population Mutual Aid Association, namely composed of the floating population, strengthens the ties between the members through various activities, and provides them with the service as assistance, dispute mediation, training, and employment. At the same time, the association provides a sound expression channel for the floating population. These expressions, after collected and openly discussed, will be summarized as effective policy suggestions submitted to the government, a rather systemized self-organized democratic procedure. In another case, for example, there is a two-hour gap of home time between the other migrant workers and their children. After public discussion, it was suggested that, with the help of the volunteers and professional teachers, a "New Hakka 16:30 Classes" be set up in the communities where the migrant workers gather to provide nursing services for the children. In the end, the local government approved the service application in the form of service purchase.[2]

5.3 The mechanism and challenge of social organizations' participation in social governance

5.3.1 The mechanism of social organizations' participation in social governance

In the context of promoting the modernization of national governance system and capacity, social organizations are playing an increasingly important role in social governance, and their participation mechanism is well worth an in-depth discussion. At present, the institutional basis, main development directions, and leading development mode of social organizations participating in social governance have been taking shape.

5.3.1.1 Institutional basis: the legal and policy environment under the reform

In recent years, institutional room for the development and expansion of social organizations has been provided as China accelerates the introduction of series of laws and policies to support the participation of social organizations in social governance.

In terms of promoting the reform of the registration system of social organizations

---

[1] Wang Wei, Zhang Wenzhong, "Reform Attempts and Laws of Social Organisations' Integration into the Service Management System of the Floating Population: Practices in Yuancheng District, Heyuan City, Guangdong Province", *Lingnan Journal*, 2012(6).

[2] "Floating Population Management in Yuancheng District, Heyuan City", *People's Daily Online*, 2014 Innovative Social Governance Theme, http://leaders.people.com.cn/n/2014/0709/c382918-25259484.html.

and supporting the development of community social organizations, the Third Plenary Session of the 18th CPC Central Committee clearly stated that the focus should be on cultivating and prioritizing the development of social organizations in the fields of industry associations and chambers of commerce, science and technology, social welfare and charity, and urban and rural community service. These organizations can directly apply for registration and establishment in accordance with the law. By September 2014, a total of 27 provinces, autonomous regions, and municipalities had carried out or tried out the direct registration of social organizations. The Opinions of the General Office of the CPC Central Committee and the General Office of the State Council on Reforming the Social Organization Administration System and Promoting the Sound and Orderly Development of Social Organizations issued in 2016 pointed out that, we should steadily promote the direct registration of social organizations, public welfare and charitable social organizations that provide services for poverty alleviation, poverty relief, support for the elderly, orphans, the sick, and the disabled, disaster relief, medical assistance and student assistance shall directly apply to the civil affairs department for registration in accordance with the law. China should vigorously foster and develop community-based social organizations, encourage the community social organizations in urban and rural communities that provide services for the people, elderly care, public welfare and charity, harmony, cultural, recreational and technical services in agriculture, measures should be taken to lower the threshold of access to support and encourage the development of these organizations.

In terms of the government's purchase of social organization services, Guidelines on the Government's Purchase of Services from Non-Governmental Forces issued in 2013 pointed out that the government should gradually increase its purchase of services from social forces in such basic public services as education, employment, social security, medical and health care, housing security, culture and sports, and disability services. In 2016, the Opinions on Supporting and Developing Voluntary Organizations mentioned that voluntary service organizations should be greatly supported with more investment in the fields of poverty alleviation, poverty relief, elderly assistance, orphan assistance, sickness relief, disability assistance, disaster relief, medical assistance, and education assistance, and to increase financial funds' support for the operation and management of voluntary services.

At the same time, the Charity Law promulgated in 2016 has a number of provisions on the direct registration of charitable organizations and the opening up of public fundraising qualifications, which provides a good space for promoting social governance innovation at the social level, including fund-raising and donation at the community level, and community-level charitable organizations.[1] At present in Shanghai, Shandong, Jiangxi, Qingdao, and other places, the registration system of the social organizations at the community level is introduced on the trial basis. To be more exact these organizations still without corporate capacity are registered at the county (district, city) civil administration departments, and supervised at the sub-district (township) level.

5.3.1.2 The main development direction: sharing some functions of government management

As the traditional top-down management mode of the government can hardly meet the diversified and multi-level social needs of social members, it is necessary for other actors to share some of government management functions through function transfer, government entrustment, or service purchase. According to the 13th Five-Year Plan for Promoting Equal Basic Public Services, the government will no longer directly undertake services that can be purchased, but rather taken over by the qualified and reputable social organizations, institutions and enterprises. At the same time, social organizations have unique advantages in performing social service functions transferred from the government. The social organizations, with the characteristics such as public welfare, equality, and closeness to the people, make themselves more likely to gain a sense of identity and belonging.

The transfer of some functions of government management provides the social organizations with an opportunity for the rapid development. At present, the governments at all levels in China strongly support social service-oriented social organizations. In 2016, for example, Shanghai, to further promote the participation of social organizations in social governance, took community social organizations as the focus for support. mainly including social organizations such as daily services, public welfare and charity, cultural and recreational activities, and mediation service in the communities.

Meanwhile, the government's purchase of services from social organizations, an important way of support, greatly promotes the development of social organizations. In December 2012, the government issued Guidelines on the Purchase of Social Services. At the same time, the local governments at Guangdong, Beijing, and other places also established special funds to purchase public service projects from the social

---

[1] Wang Ming, "How China's Charity Law is Reshaping Social Governance", Mar. 9, 2016, http://news.youth.cn/gn/201603/t20160309_7725145.htm.

organizations. Since then, it has become a common practice for governments at all levels to purchase social services from social organizations, establishing a new cooperation mechanism between the government and social organizations. As social organizations themselves are powerful enough, they need the support of government, whose preferential policy in the purchase of social services may guide the development of social organizations. Of all the services, community services and management services are one of the key purchases, including assistance to the elderly, and the disabled, social assistance, migrant population management, conflict mediation, public welfare services, etc., a guide for social organizations to become producers and suppliers of social service products, and to develop to the full in social governance.

5.3.1.3   Leading mode of development: giving play to the leading role of Party organizations

In recent years, progress has been made in strengthen the Party in social organizations. While further consolidating the ruling foundation of the Party, strengthen the Party in social organizations provides resources for social organizations to better develop and participate in social governance. Under the pattern of multiple social interests, it is difficult for a single actor to solve complex social problems. Only under the leadership of the Party organizations, with the cooperative participation of the Party and social organizations, can the complicated problems be effectively solved. In 2015, the Opinions on Strengthening the Party Development Work of Social Organizations (Trial) clearly stipulated that Party organizations in social organizations play a key political role in social organizations, and one of their basic duties is to guide and support social organizations to participate in social governance, provide public services, and assume social responsibilities in an orderly manner.

The work of strengthen the Party guides social organizations to go forward on the right track and strengthen their service functions so as to provide better services to the government and the people. For example, in recent years, the Party Committee of Guangzhou Lawyers Association, with more than 100 members, mainly Party members, called on its members to participate in the settlement of disputes over compensation for housing demolition and relocation. They have provided legal public services for more than 3,500 families of demolition and relocation and handled 28 cases of disputes.

With the Party development, social organizations are functioning better in participating in community-level social governance. Compared with social organizations, Party organizations are more trustable and acceptable among the residents. Strengthen the

Party in social organizations can help social organizations more quickly gain the recognition of residents and gain a foothold. At the same time, driven by the work of strengthen Party, some social organizations and Party organizations have joined the local framework of Party development, becoming one of the participants in democratic decision-making and democratic consultation participating in primary-level social affairs in an all-round and multi-layered way.

5.3.2 Obstacles and challenges for social organizations to participate in social governance

With the continuous development of China's economy and society, social organizations have further expanded their development space and played an increasingly important role in innovating social governance and promoting social undertakings. At the same time, the ability of social organizations to participate in social governance has not been fully brought into play, and there are still some obstacles and challenges.

5.3.2.1 Spatial barriers of social structure

Before the reform and opening up, China implemented a highly centralized planned economy system, and the "omnipotent government" controlled the society. The government was the dominating social management actor all the way from the top to the bottom, providing a very limited space for social organizations. After the reform and opening up, China has been transformed from a planned economy to a market one. With the disintegration of the institutionalized system and the People's Commune system, the unified social management system of the government was gradually loosened, and social forces began to be involved in the management of affairs.

In recent years, in a new stage of historical development, the government has further transferred its functions, increased the efforts of streamlining administration and delegating powers, and handed over part of the responsibilities in administrative approval to social organizations in the way of socialized service and self-regulation of an industry. With the increasing room for development and growing vitality, more social organizations are involved in the field of social governance. Despite the unprecedented progress, the government still has such problems as underdevelopment of social organizations and overcommitment of the government's responsibilities for social affairs. Besides being overburdened, these problems also limit the room for social organizations to participate in social governance and kill their vitality. At present, because the boundary between the government and society is not clear enough, a large number of social resources are still in the hands of the government, leading to a strong administrative dependency of some social organizations in terms of funds, projects, policy support and other aspects, which restricts the independent development of social organizations.

5.3.2.2   Barriers of institutional space

In terms of policies and regulations, till now, there is no specific basic law for social organizations in China, and no comprehensive and systematic regulation for the establishment, status, functions, property attributes, and relevant rights and obligations of social organizations. Besides, the law-making concerning the participation of social organizations in social governance also falls behind. In the existing laws and regulations, there are more procedural provisions on the registration, supervision, and management of social organizations than operational provisions on the fostering, support, and cooperation between government and social organizations. The imperfection of policies and regulations brings a certain degree of fuzziness to the development of social organizations, which affects the effectiveness of their participation in social governance.

In the management of social organizations, China still takes the system of dual management in registration and management. Since 2013 although the government has implemented the reform of the management system that intends to promote the direct registration system for social organizations in such fields as industry associations and chambers of commerce, science and technology, public welfare and charity, and urban and rural community service, the effects still remain to be further observed. For example, the unclear definition of the four types of social organizations for direct registration brings the uncertainty because whether social organizations can register directly depends, to a great extent, on the attitude of local governments and registration authorities. In addition, the dual management system for social organizations excluded from the scope of direct registration makes some competent authorities take a cautious attitude in order to avoid any risks in case, which makes it difficult for some social organizations under planning win support. At the same time, due to the high threshold in terms of capital, number of people, places, and other aspects, a large number of social organizations cannot meet the requirements of official registration. According to an empirical study, the number of officially registered social organizations only accounts for about 10% of its actual number.[1] The current system is not conducive to the standardized management and guidance of these social organizations, nor is it conducive

---

[1] Wang Ping, "Breaking the Paradox of Actual and Contingent of the Legal Status of Social Organisations in China", *People's Tribune*, 2016(25).

to their development and growth.

The supervision system of social organizations is not yet complete. The existing policies and regulations lack definite and detailed provisions for the supervision of social organizations. The supervision functions are scattered among registration authorities, administration departments, and functional authorities, without an inter-department coordination mechanism. Besides, there are other problems such as simple means of supervision and law enforcement, lack of information transparency and lack of social participation. With the implementation of the direct registration system, the corresponding regulatory system and the allocation of regulatory resources have not been established accordingly, and the registration administration agencies are inadequate in terms of the number of personnel, professionalism, and capacity. In addition, it is worth noting that there is a lack of supervision and loopholes for emerging social organizations, such as the booming network societies and WeChat societies.

The government needs to further strengthen the construction of supporting systems such as purchasing social organization services and preferential policy of finance and tax. For example, the government doesn't have a definite rule that are included in the purchase of social service of social organizations. In practice, what is included in the purchase projects varies from place to place with great arbitrariness, and the social services catalog for purchase does not have a systematic mechanism for public participation. The existing fiscal and tax policies do not have enough e support for social organizations, with very limited coverage of preferential financial assistance to the social organizations.

5.3.2.3 Inadequate capacity building of social organizations

From the perspective of the internal construction of social organizations, some are underdeveloped, with a low degree of specialization, limited human resources, capital resources, and project resources. They are so highly dependent on the government, that "the social dysfunctions" often occur in the process of purchasing social services when very few social organizations are able to undertake the functions transferred by the government. In Anhui Province, for example, of all the 22,356 social organizations fewer than 28% have the experience of undertaking the public services transferred by the government by way of directional entrusts or project funding. This shows there is much room for social organizations to undertake the transferred government functions.[1]

---

[1] Zhao Han, "Social Organisations' Ability to Undertake the Transfer of Government Functions Urgently Needs to be Improved", *CPPCC Daily*, Apr. 20, 2011.

Some social organizations do not operate internally in a regular way, such as in sound organizational structure, rules and regulations, supervision and constraint mechanism, etc. Besides, the function of the board of directors and the board of supervisors is often a mere formality. At the same time, there is a lack of incentive and accountability mechanisms for the management of social organizations.

5.3.2.4   Inadequate social participation

There is a need for greater participation of the social members in the process of social organizations in the grassroots governance. First of all, social members have a low degree of recognition and lack of understanding of the basic nature, development concept, operation mode, organizational culture and other aspects of social organizations. Especially in grassroots social governance, they mistake social organizations for the recreational teams or quasi-governmental organizations in the communities. As something new, they tend to take a cautious attitude toward the formal social organizations.

At the same time, effective participation of social organizations in social governance also requires a greater number of social members with strong subjectivity and self-governance, which is also a prerequisite for the development and growth of social organizations. In reality, it is still a long way to go for members of society. Although China already has a considerable number of volunteers, there are more administrative management than exercising initiatives and self-governance in the management of these organizations. There are rather few volunteers in real work as some are just passive in participation, though there seems a larger number of registrations. It is one of the important issues as to how to promote the active participation of members of the community. "As citizens, each of us needs to possess a range of capabilities that enable us to consciously serve the public interest, thereby safeguarding the freedom of our community and ultimately ensuring the strength of the community and our own individual freedoms."[1]

5.4   Development and management of social organizations

Due to the immature development of social organizations at the present stage, restricted by many factors such as social space, institutional system, government

---

[1] Quentin Skinner, "The Paradoxes of Political Liberty", in Xu Jilin, *Republics, Communities and Citizens*, Nanjing: Jiangsu People's Publishing House, 2004.

supervision and management, and self-capacity building, their participation in social governance is far from satisfactory. To better promote the participation of social organizations in social governance, their regulated development is the foundation.

The development of China's social organizations is to improve the ability of social organizations, reform and optimize their systems: they become the working actors in social governance and their rise in capacity o shall be reflected in the increase of the number, their scientific structure of social organizations, their specialization and professionalism, and the steady growth of charitable donations, so as to realize that social organizations can truly become the important actors in social governance; a complete institutional system of social organizations shall be established, including a complete system of laws and regulations s, a service management system, and a series of support policies so as to create a fair and regular institutional environment suitable for their development; a modern social organization system featuring that "functions of the government are separated from those of social organizations, rights and responsibilities are clearly established, and social organizations exercise self-governance in accordance with the law" shall be formed. The government fully delegates power to social organizations, establishes their role of governance actors, clarifies the boundaries, responsibilities, and powers between the government and social organizations, and realizes their self-management and operation under the guidance of law.

In order to achieve the above goals, the development of social organizations in the future should focus on the following aspects.

5.4.1 More room for the participation of social organizations

The dominating position of the government causes the underdevelopment in the social field and the inequality between the state and society. In order to realize the harmonious co-governance by the state and society, the government needs to strengthen the top-level design and leave adequate space for social organizations to participate in social governance.

China will speed up the transformation of government functions. Further, the transformation of ideas involves the law-based management of social organizations, respect for their dominant position an open mind towards their development and functions. The boundary between the government and society should be clearly drawn. The work that can be undertaken by social organizations, the social services that are suitable for social organizations to provide, and the matters that social organizations can solve through self-discipline should be transferred to social organizations.[1] A list of the government's powers in the social field and a list of guidelines for social organizations to provide social services should be drawn up to clarify the scope of the powers and responsibilities of the government and social organizations and form a scientific system of rational division of labor and mutual support.

China promotes the separation of government and society. On the basis of promoting the decoupling of industry associations and chambers of commerce from administrative organs, we should gradually realize the de-administration of all social organizations and decoupling from the government in terms of institutions, personnel, assets, etc. It is necessary to explore a pattern of multiple associations in one industry and introduce the competition mechanism of social organizations.

China is exploring a classified reform of public institutions. As the public institutions have always been monopolizing traditional social services, it is necessary to break its monopoly and introduce the external competitors to make room for the development of other social service actors as social organizations. For example, in the "incremental reform" and "stock reform", no more new public institutions should be set up for new social services, and the procedures and supervision mechanisms for the participation of social organizations should be clarified. In existing public institutions, we will gradually separate administration from institutions, management from operation and reduce their privileges in assessment and permission on qualification, professional qualification, and professional title assessment, allowing equal participation from social organizations and other social service entities.

5.4.2 Improvement of the policies and regulations of social organizations

China has issued the Charity Law of the People's Republic of China and the Law of the People's Republic of China on Administration of Activities of Overseas Non-Governmental Organizations within the Territory of China and is speeding up the revision of the Regulations on the Administration of the Registration of Social Organizations, Regulations on Foundation Administration and Interim Provisional Regulations on the Registration Administration of Private Non-enterprise Units to create a more relaxing and better regulatory environment for social organizations. For example, in the Regulations on the Administration of the Registration of Social Organizations (Draft

---

[1] Liao Hong, Xu Yun, "Operational Frameworks: How Chinese Social Organizations Engage in Social Governance", *Environmental Protection*, 2014(23).

Amendment), it is stipulated that four types of social organizations can be registered directly, that "One Industry and One Association" is restricted only for national-wide social organizations, that social organizations can regulate and discipline themselves, and that credit constraints on social organizations are strengthened.

At the same time, due to the lack of clear definition of on the status and nature, role and function, rights and obligations of social organizations in China, it is very necessary to strengthen the legislation of social organizations and formulate a basic and guiding law as soon as possible. "While specialized laws and regulations in various key areas are undoubtedly important, their hierarchical differences and diverse supervisory authorities often lead to varying priorities and difficulties in establishing effective interconnection and internal coherence among them. This can result in an incomplete legal framework."[1] Legislation on social organizations will help to regulate the behavior of social organizations, clarify the boundaries and responsibilities between the government, social organizations, and enterprises, establish the boundary of property rights and code of conduct of social organizations, protect the legitimate rights and interests of social organizations and their members, and form a standardized and unified legal and regulatory framework for the management of social organizations.

5.4.3 Innovation on the management system of social organizations

Since the 18th CPC National Congress, there has been a consistent national policy aimed at lowering the barriers to entry for social organizations and facilitating their direct registration. However, the direct registration of social organizations still needs to be clarified in practice. What should be done next is to accelerate the establishment of the legal system and related supporting systems for the direct registration of social organizations and clarify the classification criteria, registration scope and procedures for the direct registration so that there are rules to follow. At the same time, their registration requirement, such as the capital and number of staff, can be lowered to include more social organizations into the system.

The regulatory system is to be enhanced. First, after the further opening up to the social organizations, the pre-management has to give away to the post-management as the traditional management is no longer applicable. At the same time, the goal of supervision and administration of social organizations are to regulate their behavior, protect their public property, and prevent their abuse of economic and political power.

---

[1] Yu Chenyang, "Drafting of 'Social Organisation Law' Needs to be 'Fast-Tracked'", *Legal Daily*, Aug. 30, 2016.

As these possible negative behaviors only occur after their establishment, it is essential to shift the focus of the supervision to the post-management after the establishment of social organizations. Second, as to the problems of decentralized functions in different regulatory departments, it is necessary to explore the mechanism of joint supervision by different departments, and to gather the forces of civil administration, taxation, industry and commerce, finance and other parties. Third, in an era of internet, it is possible to explore a mode of network supervision. On the one hand, we should accelerate the information disclosure of social organizations and try to build a national system of social organizations and various regulatory platforms. On the other hand, we should conduct in-depth research on the management of new social organizations, such as network societies and WeChat societies, and accelerate the formulation of relevant laws and regulations. The fourth is the introduction of social supervision. With the increase in the number of social organizations, it is difficult to comprehensively supervise multi-level and multi-type social organizations only by relying solely on governments. Therefore, it is necessary to introduce social forces and public opinion. For example, a third-party evaluation mechanism for the performance and credit evaluation of social organizations can introduced to give play to the management and constraint role of independent professional intermediaries on social organizations so that social supervision and administrative supervision can be integrated.

The construction of the support system. For example, in terms of the government's purchase of social organization services, we need to clarify the scope and procedure of the government's purchase of social services as earliest possible, study and formulate a "catalog of the government's transfer of social service functions" and a "catalog of the government's purchase of social services", to regulate the services purchased by local governments. In addition, it is necessary to support the social organizations in way of finance and project resources, and expand the coverage of government purchase service. It is also necessary to adopt a competitive mechanism and establish a standardized evaluation process to ensure the equal participation of social organizations in government purchase services.

5.4.4   Self-improvement of social organizations

Enhancing the ability of social organizations will help them truly have independence and self-governance and can provide more standardized, more professional, and higher-quality social services.

Their capacity is to be improved. The dilemma of social organizational ability does not only reflect their lack of external resources but also their weak organizational construction. To improve the capacity of social organizations, first of all, we can provide sustainable external resource support for social organizations by increasing government investment and project support. At the same time, social organizations should also strengthen their ability to mobilize resources. For example, by fully investigating social needs and the preferences of independent actors such as the government, enterprises, and foundations, high-quality service projects, they can build high-quality brands to attract the inflow of resources. Secondly, they should develop the professional ability of members through organizational practice and the evaluation mechanism in learning, training, and evaluation. Social organizations should strengthen their professionalism and specialism by introducing professionals with professional knowledge and high-level talents. At the same time, we can give full play to the role of experts to provide intellectual support for the development of social organizations by establishing a stable database of experts for research and consultation.

The social organizations toned to improve their internal governance mechanism. First of all, they should establish and improve their governance structure so that they can realize self-governance and become independent legal entities. Social organizations should give full play to the functions of the members assembly, the board of directors, the board of supervisors, and the secretariat to establish a mechanism of checks and balances between departments of decision-making, supervision, and enforcement to enhance the independence and self-governance of the organization, and improve the internal supervision and restraint mechanism. Secondly, the incentive mechanism in social organizations should be further enhanced. For example, we should improve the social and political status of social organizations. Shenzhen, Wenzhou, Anhui and other provinces and cities have increased the percentage and number of representatives of social organizations in Party deputies, deputies to people's congresses, and members of CPPCC committees, and provide political incentives to talents of social organizations and channels to express their interest.

5.4.5 Cultivating the sense of participation of social members

Public awareness on social organizations should be raised. On the one hand, social organizations need to give prominence to the publicity about their own organizations, especially in the form of new media. The social governance projects they participate in and the achievements they have made should be greatly publicized so that more people can know what social organizations are and what they have done. On the other hand, strengthening CPC organizational development in social organizations is an opportunity, with the help of the resources of the regional Party organizations, to be immersed in the people. For example, in social governance at the grassroots level, lack of trust in social organizations makes it difficult for them to work. Social organizations can enhance their brands and popularity in serving the people by strengthening the contact and cooperation with the local sub-district and community-level CPC organization, by making use of their administrative resources and mass base to help themselves get involved in community services.

Besides raising understanding of the social organizations, we should cultivate social members' awareness to take the initiative in social affairs, and improve their capacity of self-management, self-service and self-supervision, which is the essence for prosperity and development of social organizations. In the next step, the government needs to leave more space for social development. The government has long undertaken almost all the responsibilities of social affairs, leading to people's dependence on it, skepticism about their own ability and role, and thus depriving them of their opportunities. Therefore, it is necessary to further enhance multi-actor participation in social governance and hand over to the society some functions that have overburdened the government. In addition, it is also necessary to establish incentive and guarantee mechanisms to encourage social members' participation and protect their rights and interests. For example, volunteers who participate in social welfare activities and their organizations should be awarded with honors. Besides, volunteers should be allowed to ask for leave to participate in voluntary activities during working hours and be subsidized for their work.

Chapter 6
The Governance of Urban Community

Since the reform and opening up, significant changes have taken place in China's urban-rural relations, and the urbanization process has been dramatically accelerated. In 2017, China's urbanization rate increased from 17.92% in 1978 to 58.52%. The driving force of urbanization comes from three aspects. The first is for steady rise of population in the cities; the second is the urbanization of rural areas in the suburbs; the third is that many farmers migrate to the cities for work, business or settlement. The acceleration of urbanization is the result of the socialist market economy, and it in turn promotes the further development of the market economy. And in this process, great changes have taken place in the urban economic and social structure, which makes the traditional social governance mode difficult to adapt to the ever-changing cities. Since the 1980s, the government and people at the primary level have been exploring new urban governance modes. The transformation of the urban social governance mode in China is mainly reflected in the development and change of the urban community governance mode.

6.1 The rise and course of urban community governance

6.1.1 The connotation of urban community

The term "*shequ*" originates from the English word "community", denoting individuals sharing common interests within a specific locale. Over time, "community" has solidified in meaning, encompassing two key facets: social interaction and geographic location. Thus, a community embodies both aspects, signifying individuals with shared social bonds residing in a particular area. Community is the essential and basic component of a society while society consists of individuals, families, communities and social organizations at different levels and features, such as individual, family, community, and social organizations. So community refers to the collection of people in a particular area who interact with each other, who share the similar sense of belonging and similar sense of identity.

Chinese urban communities always refer to the administrative scope of urban neighborhood committees. The Chinese city falls into several administrative levels, such as municipality directly under the central government, sub-provincial city, the provincial capital, prefecture-level city, county-level city, and so on. Geographically, there are cities in developed coastal areas, as well as the cities in central and western regions. Cities at different administrative levels and areas vary significantly in population, resource acquisition capabilities, and economic development. So does the social governance within cities. Urban government management structure falls into two categories: cities with districts and cities without districts. Cities with districts usually involve three levels of government and four levels of administration, i.e., municipal Government, district government, sub-district office (government-dispatched administrative agency), neighborhood committee. Usually, no matter how big its population is, the county-level city doesn't have districts; in its place are several towns. The town where county government is located usually has the largest population, the most developed economy, and the most complicated social affairs, which include neighborhood committees and involve two levels of government and three levels of administration.

In the time of planned economy, most people in the cities worked and lived in different work units, which serves as the main governance actors and the carriers of the governance. A small part without work units was included in the governance system of the sub-district offices and neighborhood committees. At that time, the urban social governance was characterized by work units plus sub-district offices and neighborhood committees, with the former as the dominating actors. Under such system, people who came from the same places were familiar with each other. The work units, sub-district offices or neighborhood committees, which controlled most of the work and living resources, exercised strong control over the residents, while the residents strongly relied on them and were frequently interactive with each other. The urban social governance system, with the third-level governments and second-level governments, as the dominating position, with the work units as the main actors and the sub-districts and neighborhoods as a complement, met the needs and the characteristics of the planned economy.

6.1.2   The service of urban community

After the reform and opening up, with the disintegration of the work unit system, the transformation of government functions, the establishment of the modern enterprise system, and the development of urbanization, the urban social governance system has undergone significant changes. In the process of this drastic change, urban community began to gain great attention. Urban community governance in China started with community services, community construction, and community development.

In the early 1980s, the Ministry of Civil Affairs put forward the idea of "social welfare being managed by society", an alternative to "social welfare being managed by work units". And the role of sub-districts and neighborhood committees became more and more prominent. Since the 1980s, the sub-district offices have taken on dozens of responsibilities, such as urban management, community services, economic development, welfare, social security, culture, education and health, family planning, judicial mediation, and people's wellbeing. In 1984, at the first conference of civil affairs held in Zhangzhou City, Fujian Province, the Ministry of Civil Affairs further clarified the guiding philosophy of "society-based welfare". It was also proposed that social welfare should be transferred from a single, closed, state-run system to a system co-run by the state, collectives, and individuals. Furthermore, social welfare should be open to multiple channels, various levels, and multiple forms. In 1985, the Ministry of Civil Affairs summarized and promoted the experience of Shanghai, i.e. coordinated welfare service network at the levels of city, district, subdistrict and neighborhood committees so that urban social welfare services could reach out to society and community. In September 1987, the Ministry of Civil Affairs held the "National Seminar on Urban Community Service" in Wuhan, where the experiences of 20 large, medium, and small cities, such as Wuhan, Shanghai, Beijing, Tianjin, and Changzhou were exchanged community services were decided to spread in cities to explore a social service system with Chinese characteristics, involving the spirit of mutual assistance among the people and flexible and diversified forms of social services to provide social welfare for residents, especially those in need.

With the encouragement of national policies, community services were promoted in cities across the country. Many urban communities such as Wuhan, Shanghai, Tianjin, Chongqing, Changzhou, and Yiyang established community service coordination organizations with a management mechanism of clear responsibilities and smooth operation. Plans for community services, relevant policies and regulations were also formulated, and community service teams were established. A large number of community service facilities were built, with different features for service of different people such as the disabled, children, and teenagers, and people with special difficulties.

All this was greatly welcomed by the general public.

In September 1989, the Ministry of Civil Affairs held a national conference on community service work in Hangzhou, which summarized and promoted the experience of community service throughout the country and developed some guiding ideas for further development of this work, demanding that the community service should have more macro-guides including planning and law-making, that it must rely both on government and society, especially more support from all society and that it must take the social effect as its end and economic benefit as its means so as to achieve the way that the social service supports the community service.

In December 1989, the National People's Congress adopted the Organic Law of Urban Residents Committee of the People's Republic of China, which clearly stipulated that "the neighborhood committees shall be responsible for the development of more community services for the convenience of the people", a legal guarantee for community service to spread to the communities at the primary level. Several local municipal and district administrations had integrated community services into governmental agendas and target management systems, aiming to foster their consistent and sustainable growth. By the end of 1993, nationally, over 80% of urban areas were equipped with community service facilities, totaling 112,000 establishments. These encompassed 24,000 facilities tailored for the elderly, 9,000 for the disabled, 16,000 for the underprivileged, and 63,000 comprehensive service centers and other amenities geared towards public convenience.[1]

6.1.3   The construction of urban communities

The widespread development and deepening of community services promoted the development of various forms of community work, which came to be accepted by the public. Nevertheless, numerous non-community service elements, such as public security and community culture, were also incorporated, leading to a divergence from the intended scope of community service. Consequently, the essence of community service was compromised and did not fully align with its intended purpose. In 1991, academic theorists and governmental departments put forward the community construction as a new concept by borrowing the concept of "community development" from foreign countries and combining it with the actual situation in China, expanding

---

[1] Zhao Chenxin, *Urban Community Building and China's Political Development*, Beijing: The Contemporary World Press, 2001, p. 60.

and replacing the original concept of community service.

After the concept of community construction was put forward, the Ministry of Civil Affairs specially issued the Notice on Gathering Views on the Community Construction, asking for opinions and suggestions from the whole country on community construction. Then the Hebei District of Tianjin and Xiacheng District of Hangzhou were chosen as the pilot districts for community construction.

Shanghai played a leading role in the promotion of urban community construction in China. After the development of Pudong, Shanghai underwent a new round of great development. With the large-scale construction and rapid development of the city, its management became more challenging and complicated. The original urban management system of "two-level government and three-level administration (referring to the municipal, district, and sub-district levels)" involved so-called "compartmentalization". Sub-district offices in the front line of urban grassroots management were limited in power of management. For them many urban management problems were often "visible and tangible, but unmanageable" while for the functional departments of the governments these problems were "manageable, yet invisible", a phenomenon that "those who know the problems are unable to manage them and those who can manage them cannot reach them". Under such circumstances, in 1995, Shanghai proposed new ways in exploring urban management under socialist market economy and selected 10 streets for a comprehensive reform pilot. In 1995, the Shanghai Municipal Committee of the Communist Party of China organized an extensive research on community management and construction of grassroots political power. On the basis of this research, the Shanghai Municipal Party Committee and Municipal Government established "two-level government and three-level administration" system as the general guideline as the urban management system reform. In 1996, it was systematically proposed that primary-level bodies, with communities as the foundation, are essential for strengthening Party development, enhancing spiritual civilization, consolidating grassroots strength, improving urban management, maintaining social stability, and raising the quality of life. The goal of community construction and management by the year 2000 was put forward. To achieve this goal, the Shanghai Municipal Party Committee and Municipal Government decided to take a series of measures to solve the major problems in the management system, law enforcement team, staffing, financial guarantee, and facilities construction so as to provide the necessary material support for community construction and management. In 1997, the Standing Committee of Shanghai Municipal People's Congress passed the Regulations of Shanghai Sub-district Offices. Since then, more than 10 related supporting policies were issued, focusing on clarifying their respective management duties of the municipality, districts, and sub-districts so as to promote community construction, and the establishment and improvement of management system.

The practice and experience of community construction in Shanghai exerted great influences on the whole country. Many cities have begun to explore the establishment of a new system "two-level government, three-level administration, and four-level implementation". For example, in June 1996, Shijiazhuang Municipal Party Committee and Municipal Government formulated the Opinions on Further Strengthening Community Work. It clearly proposed the establishment of a new system of "The two-level government (the municipal-level and district-level governments), the three-level administration (the municipal-level, district-level and sub-district level governments), and the four-level implementation (the municipal-level, district-level, sub-district level and community-level governments)", so as to clarify the relationship between the municipality, districts, and sub-districts, enhance the functions of communities, vigorously carry out community building, and promote the all-round development of community economy and social undertakings.

After several years of theoretical and practical exploration, the concept of urban community building came to be accepted and recognized by people. In July 1998, according to the new round of State Council institutional reform plan, the State Council approved the Ministry of Civil Affairs to establish the Department of Grassroots Governance and Community Development, building upon the former Department of Grassroots Governance Development. The new department also assumes the responsibility of the community service originally under the Social Welfare Department, indicating that community development became a special administrative function of the government.

After the establishment of the Department of Primary-level Power Construction and Community Governance, it immediately started experiment of the community construction. In March 1999, the Ministry of Civil Affairs held a symposium on experiment of community construction in Nanjing, suggesting that 11 urban districts be included as Pilot Zone of Urban Community Construction. In the first half of 1999, the

Ministry of Civil Affairs listed Xicheng District of Beijing, Luwan District of Shanghai, Jiangbei District of Chongqing, Gulou District of Nanjing, Xiacheng District of Hangzhou, Shinan District and Sifang District of Qingdao, Chang'an District of Shijiazhuang, Zhendong District of Haikou,[1] Shenhe District of Shenyang and Hexi District of Tianjin as Pilot Zone of Urban Community Construction. From October to December of the same year, other districts—Xuanwu District of Nanjing, Heping District of Shenyang, Xishi District of Hefei,[2] Heping District of Tianjin, Nangang District and Daoli District of Harbin, Xihu District of Benxi, Xincheng District of Xi'an, Yuanhui District of Luohe, Kaiyuan District of Xiamen,[3] Karamay District of Karamay of Xinjiang, Chaoyang District of Changchun, Lixia District of Jinan, Foshan and Jianghan District of Wuhan—added to the list. Till then, experimental zone reached 26. Some provinces such as Liaoning and Hubei decided their own experimental zones of community construction.[4] These experimental zones brought a lot of experience in large-scale urban community construction and produced great constructive effects.

In August 1999, the Ministry of Civil Affairs held a national symposium on the Experimental Zone of Urban Community Construction in Hangzhou, putting forward three levels of community construction. The first level was to establish a community construction management system and operation mechanism geared to the socialist market economy and explore the establishment of new communities. The service and management functions of the subdistrict offices and neighborhood committees were to be completed to promote the community-based work of the subdistrict offices and the neighborhood committees and socialization of community work. The second level was to build a civilized community with a beautiful environment, good public security, a convenient life, and harmonious interpersonal relationships on the basis of strengthening community functions. The third level was to expand democracy at the grassroots level and implement democratic election, democratic decision-making, democratic management,

---

[1] In October 2002, the State Council officially approved Hainan Province's administrative restructuring plan to abolish Haikou City's Zhendong District and establish Meilan District under the jurisdiction of Haikou City.

[2] Renamed as Shushan District in March, 2002.

[3] In April 2003, the former Kaiyuan District, Siming District and Gulangyu District were administratively amalgamated to constitute the newly established Siming District.

[4] Tang Zhongxin, *An Overview of Urban Community Building in China*, Tianjin: Tianjin People's Publishing House, 2000, p. 68.

and democratic supervision of neighborhood committees. The "four democracies" helped realize the self-management, self-education, self-service, and self-supervision of the residents in the communities.

In November 2000, the General Office of the CPC Central Committee forwarded the Opinions of the Ministry of Civil Affairs on Promoting the Construction of Urban Communities in the Whole Country (hereinafter referred to as the Opinions), put forward after summarizing the over one-year pilot experience of 26 experimental zones in community construction. The Opinions clearly defined the connotation of community and community construction, pointing out that "community refers to community in which people gather and live in a particular area for social life. At present, the scope of an urban community generally refers to the area in the charge of the neighborhood committee after the reform of community system"; community construction refers to the process during which, under the leadership of the Party and the government, by relying on community strength, utilizing community resources, the community function has been strengthened, problems in the community solved, the politics, economy, culture and environment are healthily and harmoniously developed and the quality of life of the members in the community keeps improving. The Opinions put forward the principles of urban community construction as follows: (1) people-centered, serving residents; (2) resource sharing and co-residing; (3) unified responsibilities and rights and scientific management; (4) democracy expansion and residents' self-governance; (5) progressive development geared to local conditions. The Opinions planned major tasks of urban community construction, mainly as follows. Firstly, expanding community services. It was required that in large and medium-sized cities the focus was the construction and management of community service centers in the districts, sub-district offices, and community service stations in neighborhood committees. Community service mainly involves social assistance and welfare services for the elderly, children, the disabled, the underprivileged, and special care recipient, convenient and beneficial services for community residents, socialized services for the institutions in the community, reemployment services for laid-off workers, and socialized services for social security. Secondly, medical service in community. It mainly involves the construction of community clinics and medical services such as disease prevention, medical treatment, health care, rehabilitation, health education and family planning so as to facilitate people for medical treatment and steady improvement of the health conditions of community residents. Thirdly, prosperity of the community culture. The community cultural undertakings shall be encouraged by constantly improving public cultural facilities to strengthen ideological and cultural education. Fourthly, improvement of the community environment. It is required that the community environment be greatly improved by purifying, greening and beautifying the community. Fifthly, community security. A comprehensive management network of social security shall be established to improve the crime prevention system of social security, and implement policy of grassroots crime prevention. Activities about laws such as regular grassroots legal education and legal consultation, civil mediation, employment, assistance and education of released prisoners and those released from reeducation through labor and the management of the floating population. The Opinions was a sign that the basic ideas of promoting urban community construction in China were formed, an indication that the urban community construction was now in a stage of comprehensive promotion.

The Ministry of Civil Affairs decided to carry out demonstration activities of urban community construction in order to further stimulate the enthusiasm of the construction from the local governments, summarize and popularize the practical exploration experience of urban community constructions across the country, and further promote the continuous development of urban community construction in the whole country. In July 2001, the Ministry of Civil Affairs issued the Guiding Outline for National Model Community Construction (hereinafter referred to as the Outline). The release of the Outline marked the official launch of the national campaign for model urban community construction. The Outline listed the objectives, tasks, working principles, and requirements of the campaign and stipulated the scope, acceptance, and confirmation procedures of model units. According to the Outline from 2001, all provinces, autonomous regions, and municipalities directly under the Central government should select large and medium-sized cities with a certain working foundation as model units for community construction in an organized, planned, and progressive manner. By 2005, the community construction of municipalities directly under the central government, provincial capitals, and cities under separate state planning would meet the requirements of the Opinions. The main tasks of model units were (1) to reform the urban grassroots management system, transform government functions, clarify community responsibilities, rights, and relations, and establish community management system and operation mechanism geared to the socialist market economy; (2) to strengthen the construction of community organizations and teams, expand community management functions, regulate the community management, improve construction systems, and establish a community organization system and working mechanism of self-management, self-education, self-service and self-supervision through democratic election, democratic decision-making, democratic management and democratic supervision in the community; (3) with community service as the core, to develop community medical service, enrich the community culture, beautify the community environment, work for better community security, complete community functions, constantly enrich community construction; (4) to comprehensively raise the awareness of the self-government and ability of the neighborhood committees and the residents in the community, mobilize and rely on the people in an effort to build a number of new modern communities with regular management, complete services, beautiful environment, good security, convenient life and harmonious interpersonal relationships. By August 2012, a large number of advanced models of community construction emerged across China, among which 27 model cities of national community construction and 148 model districts were entitled by the Ministry of Civil Affairs.[1] The campaign, of the "Model City of Community Construction" and "Model District of Community Construction" set the examples and improved the system and mechanism, staff, service guarantee conditions, community organizations and other aspects of urban community construction. The Fourth Plenary Session of the 16th CPC Central Committee put forward that the community construction should be integrated into the construction of a harmonious society. In October 2008, the Ministry of Civil Affairs formulated the National Guiding Standards for Construction of Harmonious Model Communities (for Trial Implementation). In October 2009, the National Conference of Harmonious Community Construction was held to commend the model communities. In November of the same year, the Ministry of Civil Affairs issued the Opinions on Further Promoting the Construction of Harmonious Communities, which marked the successful concluding of promotion for model community construction.

In the process of promoting urban community construction, people came to realize that neighborhood committees were the core link of organization construction and played a vital role in the effectiveness of community construction. However, with the urban construction and development, neighborhood committees found themselves hard to adapt to the new situation in many aspects. Therefore, in 2010, the General Office of the CPC Central Committee and the General Office of the State Council issued the Opinions on Strengthening and Improving the Construction of Urban Neighborhood Committees. The opinions pointed out that since the state decided to carry out urban

[1] Li Xueju, "Grasping the Foundations, Solving Key Issues and Continuing to Take Urban Community Building Deeper", *China Civil Affairs*, 2002 (10).

community construction in 2000, urban community neighborhood committees had played an irreplaceable role in serving the residents, in urban management, in strengthening the ties between the Party and the people, and in maintaining social stability. However, as new and profound changes were taking place at the urban grassroots level, the social management tasks undertaken by neighborhood committees were becoming more arduous, with maintaining social stability in a prominent position, and more demands from the community's residents. However, many problems still remained to be solved in the neighborhood committees to keep pace with such changes, such as incomplete organization, unsatisfactory working relationships, not well-educated staff, weak service facilities, and shortage of working funds, and so on. All these proved to be in the way of role of the neighborhood communities and community construction. The opinions put forward the basic principles, objectives, and tasks of strengthening and improving the work of neighborhood committees in urban communities, further clarifying their main responsibilities. It also required constant improvement of the organizational system of neighborhood committees, expansion of their staff, more self-governance under the leadership of urban community Party organizations, improvement of their service facilities, clarification of the relationship between neighborhood committees and related organizations, and stronger the leadership over the construction of neighborhood committees. Although the opinions were issued in the form of strengthening and improving the work of neighborhood committees, its essence was to take it as a breakthrough in the construction of urban communities so as to comprehensively improve the urban community construction in China.

In the process of the urban community construction led by civil affairs departments, community service remained one of the important missions and an important goal of community construction. In April 2006, Opinions on Strengthening and Improving the Community Service by the State Council was issued. In May 2007, the National Development and Reform Commission and the Ministry of Civil Affairs issued the Development Plan for Community Service System During the 11th Five-Year Plan. In December 2011, the General Office of the State Council issued the Community Service System Construction Plan (2011-2015).

6.1.4 Urban community governance

Since the 1990s, foreign governance theories came to be known by Chinese scholars, and gained good popularity and wide application. Since the reform and opening up, after Chinese government introduced two leading concepts: community service and community construction other relevant concepts such as community work, community management, and community governance also came along, which were often applied alternately with concepts such as community service and social construction. The concept of community governance often contains the content of community service and community construction, which, evolving on the basis of community service and community, construction, is much richer in connotations and more developed in system. It has both service and management, government and diversified social actors, and rule by law and rule by virtue. In October 2013, the Third Plenary Session of the 18th CPC Central Committee proposed to "promote the modernization of the national governance system and governance capacity". The word "governance" spread quickly and was widely valued by people. Community construction naturally developed into community governance, becoming one of the major tasks for the Party and the government to promote social governance. While continuing to carry out urban community service and community construction, the country turned to a wider and more modern urban community governance, exploring and innovating in more aspects such as ideology, system and mechanism, methods, resource guarantee and organizational system. To regulate and further promote community governance, in July 2017, the General Office of the CPC Central Committee and the General Office of the State Council issued Opinions on Strengthening and Improving Urban and Rural Community Governance by the CPC Central Committee and the State Council. The opinions pointed out that urban and rural communities are the basic units of social governance. Urban and rural community governance is closely related to the implementation of the major policies of the Party and the state, the vital interests of residents, and the harmony and stability of urban and rural grassroots. The opinions made arrangements in the aspects as establishing the urban and rural community governance system, continuously improving the urban and rural community governance, efforts in strengthening the weak links of urban and rural community governance, and strengthening organizational guarantee. The goal was, till 2020, to basically form an urban and rural community governance system led by grassroots Party organizations and grassroots governments, improve the urban and rural community governance system, significantly improve the governance capacity, and effectively guarantee the public services, public management and public safety of urban and rural communities. In another five or ten years, a developed urban and rural community governance system would be established. and the governance capacity would be fully promoted so as to provide stronger support for consolidating the ruling foundation of the Party and the grassroots political power, and to lay a solid foundation for promoting the modernization of the national governance system and governance capacity. The opinions emphasized the principles of upholding the Party's leadership, serving residents, and governance according to law and coordination of urban and rural areas. The opinions pointed out that as an important development of the theory and practice of community construction in China since the reform and opening up and, it clarifies the direction and key tasks of reform and development and gets rid of some misunderstandings and improper practices, a general guideline for urban community governance in the new era.

6.2   The effectiveness and experience of urban community governance in China

6.2.1   The effectiveness of urban community governance

After more than 40 years of exploration and practice, China's urban community governance has achieved remarkable results, which can better adapt to the new situation of urban community development and change, meet the growing diversified needs of residents, promote the community harmony and stability, and lay a good community foundation for social governance.

Firstly, it brings great conveniences to the residents. In the practice of community governance in various places, people-centered and service-first philosophy has always been advocated. First, the services for residents have been given prominence, especially in facilitating the community, and service improvement. Services such as community housekeeping service centers, government service centers, "16:30 Classes", caring service for the seniors, the young, and the disabled have been established. Second, investment has been increased in resources, such as convenience shops and "love supermarkets" in the community. Recreational centers for the residents have also been built to provide a public platform for community residents. There are public rooms in most residential quarters as required for community residents to study, entertain, and even hold weddings and funerals. In recent years, Beijing has strengthened the construction of a "quarter-hour community service circle"[1] and made great progress and achievements. By

---

[1] It refers to a concept where community residents can access convenient, fast and comfortable services within a 15-minute walk. This includes basic public services provided by the government, voluntary mutual assistance services provided by social organizations and individuals, as well as convenient services provided by the market to benefit the community.

the end of 2017, a total of 1,452 "quarter-hour community service circles" had been built in Beijing, covering 2,706 communities, with a coverage rate of 87.5%.

Secondly, the community environment has been greatly improved. The community environment mainly refers to the facilities and conditions, the order of placing articles, and the cleanliness of public places in the community. With the joint efforts of sub-district offices, town governments, the neighborhood committees, property companies, owners' committees, and residents, the roads in most communities have been well-planned and repaved. the facilities for exercises and children have been built and installed in public places; environmental sanitation has been well maintained, and community greening, lighting, and beautification projects have been continuously followed up. As the communities in urban village traditional communities in the old districts, districts with both local residents—migrant population on the edge of the city are underdeveloped in community governance, local grassroots governments and community organizations have attached greater importance to the construction of these areas. They have made remarkable achievements. For example, the provisional liability registration with phased remediation, the urban village environment and fought against the illegal construction. Innovative governance mode has been introduced to renovate the old residential quarters, maintain the roads, street lamps, parking spaces, and other public facilities, and improve the greening and cleaning.[1]

Thirdly, the community culture has been enriched. In a sense, community culture is also a part of the community environment, known as soft environment. As community culture is an integrated part of the public community service system, enriching community culture has always been the key task of community service, community construction, and community governance. Many communities have set up libraries, reading rooms, and cultural rooms and organized various cultural and recreational activities, such as chess and card competitions, and square dance training. Community education has been greatly developed by innovating the carrier and form of community education and learning, making use of community intellectual resources and hardware facilities. Lectures such as about calligraphy, laws, health knowledge, domestic service and internet application, etc. The construction of learning community was to, meet the needs of people's growing spiritual culture and physical fitness, to develop people's sense of community identity and belonging, and to and guide residents to be actively

---

[1] Li Yingsheng, Yang Jing and Xu Xiangwen, "Exploration of Social Governance Innovation in Urban Old Community: Taking Sub-Districts P of Beijing as an Example", *Journal of Renmin University of China*, 2017 (1).

involved in the community activities.

Fourthly, the community order has been maintained. The governments across the country have established and improved the mechanism for the community residents to express their interests. In some places, a joint community system has been explored by including Party Congress representatives, NPC deputies, and CPPCC members into the community sessions. The system of direct contact with the people by Party members and officials has been improved to guide the people to express their interests rationally and legally. The mediation mechanism for disputes has been established by following the from Zhejiang's "Fengqiao Mode" to peacefully settle the disputes and construct a peaceful community so that "the minor disputes are resolved at village level, major ones at the town level without being transferred to the upper-level government", and strive to achieve "disputes solvable, peace maintainable and service available". Since the 18th CPC National Congress, some places have begun to establish psychological counseling mechanisms by relying on social work service agencies and other professional social organizations. The safety of the residents has been guaranteed by promoting the construction of safe communities, spreading digital management for a matrix of urban communities with the support of community comprehensive management centers, constructing the network of community security, and improving the community policing strategies. This has effectively improved the comprehensive administration of community security, and prevented and cracked down the organized crime groups.

Fifthly, it has laid the foundation for governance. The practical exploration of community governance has not only accumulated experience and laid a foundation for promoting wider and deeper social governance and but also has provided sources for the theoretical development of community governance and social governance. In the exploration and practice of community governance for more than 40 years, first, the organizational system of community governance has been continuously improved. The community governance organization system includes community Party organizations, community self-governing organizations, property companies, owners' committees, various social organizations, and institutions in the community, among which the community Party organizations play a leading role in the community organization system, an organizational guarantee and an important support for strengthening and innovating community governance. Community self-governing organizations and various social organizations constitute the major organizational forms and supports of community governance. In the construction of community organization systems, two orientations always go along with each other, namely, "building community-level governance" orientation and "fostering community-level governance" orientation. The two have been interacting with each other. The goal of community political power construction is to strengthen the management of grassroots society by transferring the attention to the primary levels, while in the process of grassroots social development, community residents can acquire more new resources, acquisition channels and interest expression mechanism. In these two processes, develop two different actors which compete against and cooperate with each other. The governance mode has been transformed from the single actor management mode—"sub-district office and neighborhood committee system" to the new "co-governance" mode in which the community has both governance and self-governance, competition and cooperation.[1] Second, working methods have been constantly improved. The principle of people-centered management according to law with multiple strategies has been implemented. The source governance and pluralistic governance have been given prominence to give full play to the role of civil mediation, judicial mediation, administrative mediation, etc., and integrate management into service and implement humanized and flexible management by means of ideology and morality, residents' conventions, autonomous articles of association, communication and education, etc. Professional social work methods are introduced to public services and mediation and settlements of social conflicts and disputes. Legal education and the activities of bringing the law to communities have been carried out by giving full play to the role of those related to law, such as police officers, judges, prosecutors, lawyers, notaries, and grassroots legal service workers, so that the community's ability to handle affairs according to law and manage a community ruled by law has been enhanced. IT application has been introduced to community governance. Information-based management and digital management for a matrix of urban communities have been explored. Problems and conflicts in the community can be discovered and solved by building smart communities, digital communities, and community information platforms. After the 18th CPC National Congress, the intelligence, specialization, refinement, and rule of law in community governance have been further improved.

6.2.2   The experience of urban community governance in China

The achievements of community governance practice benefit from the reform and innovation of local officials and the people under the promotion of national policies and

---

[1] Yan Zhilan, Deng Weizhi, "Analysis of Challenges and Path Innovation of Urban Community Governance in China", The *Journal of Shanghai Administrative Institute*, 2014(4).

in combination with the actual situation. In this process, some valuable experiences have been formed as follows.

Firstly, both management and service have been integrated. Community governance needs not only management but also good service, with management achieved in service and service improved in management. On the one hand, the community governance forces must be enhanced. The information technology is applied to personnel, and material technological preparation for innovation in social conflicts. Service and management for key places and priority population are given prominence to, and the digital management for a matrix of urban communities is promoted. On the other hand, providing and improving basic public services for community residents is regarded as the prerequisite and important means of innovative governance. All localities have increased investment in social services and established community residents' service centers and convenience service centers so that communities have money to do practical things for the people and some people to solve difficult problems for the people. Many places began to build public welfare information service facilities such as community information kiosks and community information service terminals, promoted the construction of comprehensive information platforms for community public services, promoted applications with unique ID numbers, one-stop services, availability of online service, and strengthen the model of one-stop community service.

Secondly, it is necessary to coordinate people's wellbeing and democracy. Local communities try their best to help community residents address issues concerning people's wellbeing, such as living services, old-age care and child care. However, most places have limited financial resources, so it is necessary to prioritize and solve them step by step. Some public affairs involving community governance, such as environmental governance and public welfare activities, need to respect the wishes of the community masses, listen to their opinions, and make democratic and scientific decisions. In some places, democracy is combined with people's wellbeing, democracy is used to promote people's wellbeing, residents are allowed to participate in discussions on people's wellbeing and community public affairs, and the people are mobilized to offer suggestions. People's participation in the decision-making of people's wellbeing and community affairs is a process of concentrating people's wisdom and optimizing decision-making and ensuring that people's wellbeing and community affairs are understood and supported by the people. In July 2015, the General Office of the CPC Central Committee and the General Office of the State Council issued the Opinions on Strengthening Urban-Rural Community Consultation, which called for the development of grassroots democracy, the smooth flow of democratic channels, the development of various forms of grassroots consultation, and the promotion of institutionalization, standardization and proceduralization of urban-rural community consultation.

Thirdly, it is necessary to make overall plans for the rule of virtue and the rule of law. Since the 21st century, in the practice of community governance innovation, all localities have made efforts to promote governance according to law, regulate and restrain the behavior of public officials by law, and protect the legitimate rights and interests of the people. In order to strengthen the legal education for ordinary people, including community residents, educate the people to abide by laws and regulations, fulfill their civic obligations, be law-abiding citizens, and guide the people to safeguard their rights and interests according to law, express their interest demands in an orderly manner according to law, and participate in public affairs. At the same time, we should attach importance to the important role of ideology and morality in community governance, advocate a new civilization among community residents, select "civilized households" and "good deeds", set a moral example, guide community residents to form correct concepts of right and wrong, good and evil, beauty and ugliness, and cultivate a social mentality of self-esteem, self-confidence, rationality, peace and positive progress.

Fourthly, it is essential to make overall plans for safeguarding rights and maintaining stability. With the opening and progress of society, more and more leading officials deeply realize that safeguarding the legitimate rights and interests of the people is fundamental to achieving long-term social stability. In the innovation of community governance, all localities start with respecting and safeguarding the people's right to know, participate, express and supervise, actively explore and open up channels for expressing residents' demands, smooth the mechanism of reflecting public opinion, and give full play to the important role of grassroots mass autonomous organizations and various social organizations in safeguarding residents' rights and interests. The maintenance and realization of residents' legal rights is an important guarantee to promote community harmony and stability and also an important guarantee to stimulate community vitality and promote community development and progress.

Fifthly, making overall plans for Party and government leadership and social participation. In the final analysis, community governance is the service, regulation, monitoring, and management of community needs and community relations by various social subjects, including the government. Therefore, community governance not only needs to strengthen and improve the social management of the government but also to expand and improve the social participation of various social subjects outside the government. In many places, the street office system and street residence system have been reformed, residents' self-governance has been expanded, and social organizations have been cultivated and strengthened so that they can bear some community governance responsibilities transferred by the government. Since the 18th CPC National Congress, while building a multi-party community governance system, all localities have generally strengthened community-level Party development and further strengthened the leading core role of the Party in community governance.

Sixthly, making overall plans for system reform and method innovation. A certain governance system determines the scope and range of governance methods, while appropriate governance methods can enlarge the positive role of a scientific and reasonable governance system. All localities strive to straighten out the relationship between street and residence, set up community workstations, reduce the administrative intervention of streets on residents' autonomous organizations, reduce the administrative burden of community neighborhood committees, and strengthen residents' self-governance. Encourage and support neighborhood committees to establish an access system for community matters according to the list of community work matters so as to reduce burdens and increase efficiency for community mass autonomous organizations. Implement the "Internet + Community" action, adopt the basic information of community governance by modern scientific and technological means, and use new media such as community forums, microblogs, WeChat and mobile clients to guide community residents to keep close daily contacts, participate in public affairs, carry out consultation activities, organize neighborhood mutual assistance, and explore the grid-based community governance model.

6.3 The problems and solutions of urban community governance in China

6.3.1 The problems of community governance in China

Although China's community governance has been actively explored in practice, achieved good results, and accumulated a lot of valuable experience, there are still many problems compared with the ever-changing and growing needs of urban and rural residents.

Firstly, the community scope is vague. Community refers to the community of social life composed of people living in a certain geographical area. The scope of the urban community generally refers to the area under the jurisdiction of neighborhood committees whose scale has been adjusted after the reform of the community system.[1] Therefore, urban communities are generally highly isomorphic with residents' committees, and people often call residents' committees "community residents' committees". According to the Organic Law of the Residents Committee of the People's Republic of China, which was implemented on January 1, 1990, residents' committees are generally set up in the range of 100-700 households according to the living conditions of residents and the principle of facilitating residents' self-governance, generally including several residential quarters with similar geographical locations. With the rise of the concept of community and the replacement of the concept of residents' committees, the scope of community has been continuously adjusted and expanded. At the end of the 1990s, in the process of exploring the ideas of urban community construction, Tianjin, Nanjing, Qingdao, Shenyang, Wuhan, Xi'an, Harbin, and other cities positioned the community scale in the areas naturally formed by urban grassroots units. Generally, according to the scale of 1,000-2,000 households, the jurisdiction of residents' committees is adjusted.[2] With the development of urbanization and the increase of migrants, the number of households and populations managed by urban community residents' committees is increasing, especially in Type-I big city, megacity, super-large city. The actual population under the jurisdiction of community residents' committees is generally tens of thousands, and the existing community workforce is difficult to complete the heavy task of community governance.

Secondly, community residents' participation is insufficient. Generally, the elderly are the main groups participating in community governance, while young people are less involved. Various surveys show that most of the elderly who participate in community governance receive welfare, and community participation is more manifested as a recessive exchange relationship: a prerequisite for the elderly to participate in community affairs is to give them priority to various community welfare. Young and middle-aged residents lack interest in community activities and are unwilling to participate in elections or other community activities. All kinds of community problems are more about looking for property and solving them through market-oriented channels, and this solution is often

---

[1] It refers to Opinions of the Ministry of Civil Affairs on Promoting the Construction of Urban Community in the Whole Country.

[2] Wei Liqun, *Contemporary Chinese Social Events (1978-2015)*, Vol. 3, Beijing: The Commercial Press, Sino-Culture Press, 2018, p. 249.

more efficient than the community.[1]

Thirdly, there are too many administrative tasks. Community committees are called autonomous organizations, but they are still treated as their "legs" and subordinate bodies by the higher administrative organs. Especially with the reform of the grassroots governance system, the adjustment and merger of the internal institutions of street offices, and the expansion of the scope of the community, the workload of the community has increased greatly, taking on a lot of work that is unable to do or should not do. Communities are overloaded with many tasks, summarized as "Six Manys": many evaluations, many institutions, many studies, many meetings, many reports, and many statistics. Some communities have as many as 260 assessment items; some communities have more than 80 additional organizational titles, and some communities need to do more than 250 kinds of accounts, seriously squeezing the space of community organizations' self-governance. Community residents' committees have to handle community-wide public affairs and public welfare, mediate civil disputes, assist in maintaining social security, develop public undertakings and various cooperative economies, and assist the grassroots government in completing public service matters, including undertaking a large number of task for strengthening the Party, discipline inspection and supervision, press and publicity work, undertaking building economy, commercial character streets, commercial model communities, social units, energy saving and emission reduction, and inspection of construction sites and storefront renovation sites, and inspection and maintenance of urban flood control facilities. Faced with the current complex and diverse community governance situation, the quality and level of competence of the residents' committee as a grassroots autonomous organization is also somewhat overwhelming. In terms of the personnel composition of the residents' committees, most of them are laid off and retired, farmers of relocated households, etc. Many families are in financial difficulties, and their professionalism is weak. Except for a few places such as Shanghai, most places have poor career promotion channels for the personnel of community residents' committees, especially for some young and middle-aged backbone of community residents' committees, which affects their work motivation, initiative and creativity.

Fourthly, the interaction between the government and the community is not smooth. The reason why the community takes up a large number of administrative affairs is that

---

[1] Chen Peng, "Innovations in Community Governance Reform Since the 18th CPC National Congress", in Gong Weibin, *Report on Social Institutional Reform in China, No 6 (2018),* Beijing: Social Sciences Academic Press (China), 2018, p. 66.

there is a single main body of community governance. Although the community is positioned as an autonomous organization, more often than not, the government sings a "one-man show" and does not encourage, support, or even suppress the development of social organizations, and community autonomous organizations and other social organizations are underdeveloped and not vigorous enough. The establishment of a cohesive community governance framework proves challenging to attain. Even if there are a small number of public service and hobby social organizations in the community, their channels of participation in community governance are very limited. The grassroots government is not good at guiding and supporting social organizations to participate in community governance by means of purchasing services. Very often, urban community governance is still government-controlled, with strong administrative power and weak community self-governance and social organizations, making it difficult for the government and the community to interact with each other in a positive way.

Fifthly, the lack of community services and management resources became worse. Now, in many urban grassroots social governance systems and resource allocation, there is a "top-heavy" phenomenon. The author found in a large southern city research, from the sub-district office to the district (which may form a real sense of the community) a total of four levels, namely the sub-district office, community work stations, community committees and district units, and other different levels. A large number of people, financial and material resources are held at the upper level, "a needle below a thousand threads above", and the work has to be done by the community, but the community is not provided with the corresponding resource guarantee. Some administrative departments control the resources in their own hands, while the work has to be done, and the responsibility has to be borne by the community. Many departments operating under specific titles within the community have expanded their functions to encompass additional administrative tasks. However, this expansion often occurs without corresponding financial support, leaving them burdened with additional responsibilities without adequate funding guarantees. The higher functional departments of law enforcement work are also assigned to the community, but the community does not have such power, equipment, and personnel.

Sixthly, community policies and evaluation criteria are not sufficiently targeted. Different types of communities vary greatly due to their geographical environment, infrastructure, demographic structure, social needs, and resource endowment. Generally speaking, community types in large cities are more complex and diverse. In Beijing, there are old neighborhoods, unit compounds, ordinary commercial housing communities, high-end residential communities, affordable housing communities, low-cost housing communities, shantytown renovation communities, relocation and resettlement housing communities, urban village communities, concentrated residential areas for landless farmers, communities with migrant populations, concentrated residential areas for ethnic minority groups, and foreigner communities. Since the commercialization of housing began in the mid-1990s, the living conditions of residents have been significantly improved, and the urban landscape has changed dramatically. However, there are many problems and challenges in the governance of commercial housing communities. First, many commercial housing communities face aging infrastructure and inadequate public facilities, which require financial support for maintenance. Theoretically, commercial housing communities have a public maintenance fund, but how to use the fund is a problem. Second, the problem of disputes over the rights and interests of the common ownership part of commercial housing communities. Now, most commercial housing communities do not set up owners' committees, and the exercise of the community owners' common property rights is restricted, belonging to the owners of common property rights of public service rooms, parking spaces, and underground space property management; the majority of owners cannot monitor; they do not mention the disposal of revenue. For example, most of the residents of old neighborhoods are disadvantaged, while most of the residents of high-end commercial housing communities are politically, economically, and culturally successful, and the governance requirements and capabilities of these two types of communities are very different. Now, the vast majority of cities do not categorize the requirements and assessment of different types of community governance performance; instead of requiring localization and categorization, they use a ruler to measure the effectiveness of different types of community governance, which is difficult to achieve the purpose of stimulating the advanced and spurring the backward.

Seventhly, in 2011, the General Office of the State Council issued the Notice on Community Service System Building Programme (2011-2015) (hereinafter referred to as the Notice). The Notice proposed to develop multi-level and diversified community services, improved the network of community service facilities, strengthened the construction of community service personnel, and promoted the innovation of community service system and mechanism. The Notice also proposed to focus on the construction projects of community public service facilities, community service talents, and community service information construction. Substantive progress has been achieved in infrastructure upgrading and service delivery capacity enhancement of urban communities during the current planning cycle. However, in contrast, there is very little interaction among community residents. Residents of the same building do not know each other, do not interact, and interpersonal relationships within the community are indifferent. People are accustomed to focusing on their own affairs and not caring about others. As a result, the development of social relationships and the accumulation of social capital lag behind. Community culture and spirit are insufficiently cultivated, and residents' sense of identity, belonging, and participation in the community is low, leading to weak community cohesion.

Eighthly, relevant policies and regulations are not strong enough. Although China's community governance has received unprecedented attention since the 18th CPC National Congress, ushering in a peak period of legislation and the issuance of various relevant policy documents, there are still some issues, such as gaps in the basic legal system. For example, the Organic Law on Urban Residents' Councils has been in place for nearly 30 years but has not been revised, seriously lagging behind actual conditions and failing to meet the needs of community governance. As a new self-governance organization, the owners' committee lacks a dedicated organic law to regulate and protect it. Due to the lack of legal personality for owners' committees, some communities that have established these committees face a series of problems, such as operational difficulties, issues with renewal, and problems with filing. Some sub-districts and communities are insufficiently aware of the owners' committees, supervising and guiding them in a formal way, or even adopting an avoidance or laissez-faire attitude to avoid causing trouble.[1] As a new sector, property management requires further improvement in relevant policies and regulations. Social workers and community workers, who are a vital professional team for community governance, also lack special laws at the national level to protect them.

6.3.2   The reflection on the innovation of urban community governance in China

There are many issues in China's urban community governance, not only due to the lingering old administrative control mindset but also because of the insufficient power of community self-governance and limited participation channels. However, the main challenge lies in the lack of a clear understanding of the laws and characteristics of urban community governance in the context of open, mobile, and commercialized housing, which has led to the inability to find effective community governance method. During

---

[1] Chen Peng, "Innovations in Community Governance Reform Since the 18th CPC National Congress", in Gong Weibin, *Report on Social Institutional Reform in China, No 6 (2018),* Beijing: Social Sciences Academic Press (China), 2018, pp. 67, 69.

the planned economy, cities monopolized resources through the "institutionalization" and used administrative control to achieve the purpose of social governance. In the process of industrialization, marketization and urbanization, the heterogeneity of the modern urban community governance model has increased greatly and must be transformed and innovated. In the future, Party committees and governments at all levels should suit to China's national conditions, especially the stage characteristics and specific conditions of local development, draw on useful experiences at home and abroad, adhere to people-centered philosophy, emancipate the mind, encourage innovation, and explore the path of urban community governance with Chinese characteristics.

Firstly, we must strengthen the community-level Party. Party leadership is the essential feature of the socialist system with Chinese characteristics and the greatest advantage of socialism with Chinese characteristics. Urban community governance must adhere to the leadership of the Party to ensure that community governance is aligned with the correct political direction. To strengthen the construction of Party organizations, fully implement the system of responsibility for Party development improve the long-term mechanism of strengthening the Party, and ensure that the work of Party development is put into practice. We should innovate the methods of strengthening the Party, enhance the cohesion and fighting power of community-level Party organizations, play the leading role of Party organizations at the primary level, build an organizational platform for all kinds of organizations to participate in community governance, and embody the core and leading role of Party organizations. The work of community-level Party organizations should be established on the basis of a two-way commitment and two-way supervision coordination mechanism led by the community-level Party organizations and involving the Party organizations of the working bodies in the district, and clearly stipulate the responsibilities of the Party organizations in the joint work of community Party organizations. The Party organizations of the units in the district educate and guide the Party members of their units to actively participate in community activities under the guidance of the community-level Party organizations and jointly promote the work of strengthening the Party. Develop a joint meeting system for community-level Party development, establish a regular communication mechanism between Party organizations, and jointly study and solve problems arising from the work of community-level Party development.

Secondly, the community governance system should be innovated. First, the functions of the sub-district office should be accurately positioned, the internal structure of the sub-district office should be reasonably set, the relationship between the sub-district office and relevant departments should be handled, and the relationship between the sub-district office and various organizations in the community should be handled. The public service and social management functions of sub-district offices should be strengthened, their economic functions should be reduced or completely abolished, their coordination functions should be further developed, and a grassroots governance system with accurate positioning, clear authority and responsibility, decentralized resources and services, standardized behavior, strong coordination and efficient operation should be built to provide strong administrative guarantee and a relaxed environment for community residents' self-governance. Second, we should increase the efforts to de-administrate community committees and return them to their original functions so that they can return to their original position as grassroots mass self-governance organizations. Of course, self-governance is not separate from the leadership and administrative guidance of the Party, but to maintain its relative independence and self-governance, balance between being responsible to the superordinate and being responsible for subordinates, taking into account the administrative and mass. Third, we should innovate the carriers and ways for residents to participate in community governance and broaden the channels for community residents to participate in community governance. Finally, we should also actively cultivate and develop community social organizations to strengthen the power of community governance.

Thirdly, the government should strengthen the construction of community talent teams. Community governance requires a group of officials and talent teams that are enthusiastic about community affairs and have the energy and ability to serve community residents. First, we should strengthen the construction of community workers. Community work mainly refers to the staff of community Party committees, community neighborhood committees, and community work service stations, which are also commonly referred to as community officials. They undertake important tasks and play an important role in community governance. However, the working conditions and abilities of community workers are not quite commensurate with the role they play, and there are problems such as unclear role orientation, lack of work awareness, unreasonable age, gender and knowledge structure, low salary, awkward social status, serious staff turnover, lack of professionalism, and lack of incentive guarantee and training mechanism. Therefore, it is necessary to improve the selection and use mechanism of community workers, clarify the scope of duties of community workers, improve the personnel treatment, and establish a sound incentive guarantee and training mechanism.[1]

---

[1] Wang Yan, "Current Situation and Countermeasures of Community Staffs' Team Building", *Modern Business Trade Industry*, 2017(14).

Second, it is necessary to strengthen the construction of professional community social work teams. Due to the diversification, individualization, and advanced demand of community residents' services, the traditional community service management model has made it difficult to meet the new requirements. It is imperative to provide high-quality community services and management by using the professional, vocational, standardized, and humanized approach of the social worker team. Since 2006, the state has started to consciously promote the construction of social worker teams and professional social workers in the community, which has achieved certain results. However, the overall situation is not satisfactory. The total number of social workers is still relatively small and inexperienced, and there is no corresponding working platform for professional social workers in the community, and the brain drain is serious. Therefore, it is necessary to further innovate the institutional mechanism of community social work and improve the development environment; further broaden the professional service platform of community work and enhance the service effectiveness; further promote community work services in a classified manner and improve the level of refined services.[1] Finally, we should pay attention to the role of retired senior officials, labor models, Party members, teachers, legal workers and other social veterans.

Fourthly, the government must improve the supply capacity of community services. The government should increase the efforts of community public service system construction, improve community service institutions, compile a directory of community public service guidance, increase resource investment and protection, do a good job in labor and employment, social security, health, education, social services, housing security, culture and sports, public safety, public legal services, mediation and arbitration and other public service matters, and improve the capacity and level of community medical and health services. Strengthen the construction of community informatization and improve the level of community informatization. Through tax incentives, site support, supporting funds, service guarantees, etc., guide and support the participation of various market players and various social organizations in community services to provide diverse resources and services for community governance. Communities should explore establishing a mechanism for the comprehensive use of community public space, rational planning, and construction of self-service facilities for culture, sports, commerce, logistics, and so on.

---

[1] Sun Ying, Wu Jun, "Ten Years of Exploration on Community Work", *China Civil Affairs*, 2016(23).

Fifthly, the government should promote the rule of law in community governance. First, on the basis of revising and improving existing laws, we should speed up the legislative work on community governance, clarify the connotation and scope of community, make provisions on the tasks, institutional mechanisms and resource guarantees of community governance, clearly define the legal status and mutual relationship of different subjects of community governance, and establish a sound legal system of community governance. The legal status of other forms of community self-governance organizations, such as community members' congresses, community consultation and deliberation councils, and community management committees, should be clarified as soon as possible. The legal protection of many aspects and aspects of work, such as community public services, community environmental management, community health service management, community cultural construction, community education, community dispute settlement, community construction funding guarantee, and community workers' team building should be strengthened. Second, we should improve the authority and binding nature of laws related to community governance. Now, many laws related to community governance are still mainly manifested as departmental regulations and local laws and regulations, which are not of high legal rank and authoritative enough. Many laws and regulations are only advocacy and declaratory soft laws, lacking in compulsion and discipline, resulting in some laws and regulations not being truly and effectively implemented.

Sixthly, it is important to cultivate community awareness among residents. Community awareness refers to the psychological state of community residents' perception, identification, and participation in the community. It is the sense of belonging and identification of community residents with the community they belong to, including five aspects of community emotional identity, degree of community participation, community satisfaction, trust and dedication, and attitude toward community development. Community awareness is the software in community governance, which is of great significance for improving community relations and promoting community harmony, expanding community organizations and forming governance synergy, enhancing community capital, and promoting institutional transformation. [1] In strengthening community public services, expanding residents' participation, and developing community democracy, we should integrate the education and guidance of community consciousness and cultivate residents' sense of home and

---

[1] Wang Chuhui, Zhu Yanlong, "Community Identity and Its Governance Implications: Empirical Perspectives from H & Y Communities in Tianjin", *Sociological Review of China*, 2015(1).

community. By carrying out activities that are diverse, rich in content, vivid and interesting, and healthy and beneficial, we can enhance the attractiveness and appeal of community participation, thus stimulating community residents' motivation to participate in community governance, cultivating and enhancing their emotions toward the community, establishing a sense of community ownership, laying the foundation for community residents' self-service, self-management, and democratic consultation to resolve community affairs and cultivate modern citizenship, and providing community governance.

Seventhly, the government should adhere to local conditions and classification of policy. Community governance should not only follow the common laws, adhere to universal principles, strengthen policy planning and top-level design, but also adhere to local conditions, specific analysis of specific problems, and specific solutions. Some communities have more prominent environmental improvement problems, some communities have a heavier administrative burden, some communities are lack of resources, some communities have dilapidated infrastructure, some communities have a lot of contradictions in property management, some communities have poor people-friendly services, some communities lack public activity venues, and so on, so we need to find the right problem and provide right solutions. Especially for the current urban community composition of China's increasingly diverse and complex reality, the implementation of the classification of governance, the formation of differentiated governance measures: the governance of commercial housing communities should focus on the shift from "stranger community" to "new acquaintance community". The key is to make use of the original neighborhood relationship, recreate the community self-governance organization mechanism, increase the investment and guarantee of community utilities, and improve the level of community public service guarantee; the key to governance of urban government-subsidized housing communities is to prevent the gathering of disadvantaged people, which may lead to new poverty and new social problems; the key to governance of the urban village community is the community environment and security governance; in the community with a large migrant population should be put on the protection of equality, community integration, and community environmental governance.[1]

---

[1] Chen Peng, "Innovations in Community Governance Reform Since the 18th CPC National Congress", in Gong Weibin, *Report on Social Institutional Reform in China, No 6 (2018)*, Beijing: Social Sciences Academic Press (China), 2018, pp. 69-70.

Chapter 7
Rural Social Governance

Rural social governance is the most fundamental link of innovation, with an urgency of time and continuity in historical context. In China's rural areas, the development of different regions varies greatly in economy, society, and culture, so does the social governance. However, there are different practical experiences in rural areas among developed areas, underdeveloped areas and areas with large ethnic minority populations after the reform and opening up.

7.1 The backdrop of social governance in rural China

7.1.1 Further diverse demands promoted by market economy

After the concept of socialist market economy system was put forward and its relevant theory have been established before being put into practice, the egalitarian, known in China as "eating from a big pot", was eliminated, thus greatly stimulating the enthusiasm of workers during the reform and opening up for more than 40 years. The incomes of farmers have been greatly increased and their living standards have also been improved with the rapid development of economy. At the same time, with the profound change in the ideas of the farmers brought about by market-oriented economy and political democracy, their awareness of economy and society has been heightened and widely embodied in their daily life and practices. In particular, they have a strong wish to participate in state affairs and to voice their demands on democratic election, public infrastructure construction and land acquisition and demolition. However, compared with other groups of the society, the farmers have a sense of "relative deprivation" caused by the negative aspects of the market economy, such as the widening gap between the rich and the poor and the increasing conflict of interests. Therefore, there is an urgent need for farmers to exercise their democratic rights to handle public affairs rather than just waiting to accept the decisions.

Amid that, the traditional values and motives of farmers have been transformed greatly, which eventually boosts diverse demands of interest and further intensifies the social atomization[1] and disintegration of traditional communities. In the traditional rural areas, villagers adhere to a highly similar value system and act in unison, where the fine tradition of mutual help naturally grows. This close human bond has a positive effect on organizing production, resolving social conflicts and maintaining village stability. However, farmers become more utilitarian in the incomplete market economy and tend to be cold towards village affairs, but uncompromising about their own personal interests. As the bond of rural social relations has been greatly undermined, social morality and virtues have been fond memories. What is contradictory to the rapid growth of their interest is these disadvantages such as the impeded channels for expressing farmers' demands and the existing channels with insufficient humanistic care and low communication efficiency, which further intensify the contradictions between farmers and farmers, and those between farmers and grassroots governments, which may bring the uncertainties in rural society. Therefore, it is the historical background for the requirement of rural social governance innovations that the market economy boost farmers' diverse demands. [2]

7.1.2 Rural transformation accelerated by scientific and technological progress

Since the reform and opening up, great breakthroughs and constant innovations in science and technology have also exerted a great and far-reaching influence on the rural society, mainly reflected in the following aspects:

First, it has greatly improved the efficiency of farmers in production. In the past, when production mainly relied on manpower or animal power, whatever efforts the farmers have made, they could hardly improve their efficiency and income. Nowadays, the wide application of modern agricultural machinery such as tractors and harvesters has greatly improved production efficiency, which raises their incomes, increases their entertainment time and improves their quality of life. Second, it has transformed farmers' worldview and values. Benefiting from the policies such as "home appliances going to the countryside", every family has TV and everyone has mobile phone in most rural

---

[1] It refers to scattered, unorganized farmers.

[2] Zhang Hongxia, "Rural Cultural Change and Social Governance Mechanism Innovation", *Guihai Tribune*, 2014(5).

areas. As more and more information channels became available in rural areas, farmers greatly transform their worldview and values in the process of acquiring information outside village, and in turn greatly change their expectations and cognition of their life. The sense of independence, individual consciousness, and awareness of protecting their rights and upholding the rule of law from outside the village has also taken root in farmers' minds, especially in globalization process. Therefore, they no longer solve problems based only on their own past experiences or entrenched rules of the village.

It is also noticed that some negative effects have been brought by technological advances to rural social governance. While it can provide farmers with additional entertainment, such as playing chess or poker on their cellphones or browsing sites of interest, it also greatly diminishes face-to-face interaction among villagers. Some young and middle-aged farmers are increasingly indifferent to public affairs in rural areas, which definitely reduces their participation rural public governance. Besides, the rural social governance will also be influenced as the deceptive information on the internet, which the farmers may not tell because of their educational background, may be misled into violating the law and regulations.

7.1.3   Outflow of rural elites led by urbanization

With the promotion of the reform and opening up and the market economy, more farmers are flooding into cities for work or business, an important way to improve their wellbeing and increase income. However, such urbanization has also led to brain drain in rural areas and "hollowing-out" of villages.

Due to the impact of industrialization, urbanization, and market development, the traditional rural civilization has given away to modern urban civilization, which challenges the traditional values and village rules. After a large number of young and smart elites follow the progress of modern urban civilization, the elderly, women, children, and the disabled are left behind in rural villages, which causes a common phenomenon, known as "hollow village".

For young adults or elites who have been working in cities for many years, it is their priority to stay in city while countryside is just an option when they can hardly survive in the cities. Therefore, it is difficult for them to participate in the decision-making on village public affairs. On the contrary, the disadvantaged groups known as the "386199 troops"[1], who are unable to participate in and make decision, however, are

---

[1] "386199 troops" refer to women, children and the elderly community.

the major targets for village governance. Efforts focused on attracting elites to return villages are the key task of innovative governance for many villages, because there is the shortage of talent in social governance due to urbanization as well as due to brain drain, aging population or even the illiteracy of elderly officials.

7.1.4 Rapid growth of rural social organizations

China's grassroots social organizations have developed rapidly since 2006.[1] The two factors—external environment and internal demands, altogether contributed to the development of rural social organizations. First, the disintegration of the People's Communes left enough room for governance in rural society. On the one hand, the withdrawal of the government caused the short supply of social services and public products. On the other hand, the growth of the market economy promoted the rapid demands. All these leave great room for the participation of the non-governmental organizations. Second, farmers are more likely to rely on themselves or join in their own social organizations to participate in public activities after they gradually develop an awareness of rights, law and the sense of citizenship, then increasingly hope to achieve self-regulatory, self-education and self-service.

The rural social organizations, which play an irreplaceable role in rural public governance, rely on villagers themselves for development. First, these organizations can adopt more flexible methods to meet farmers' diverse demands for interests. As farmers know better about their own social environment, principles of relationship and the code of the behaviors; they can settle public affairs by their down-to-earth approach. Second, they can better represent the interests of farmers. Since it is hard for atomized individual farmers to form strong synergy for handling conflicts of interest, the support and reliance of the organizations make it more efficient for farmers to regulate and organize the channels to express their interests and more operable to satisfy their demands that are collected and refined by organizations. Third, they can coordinate the relationship between villagers and resolve social conflicts at the earliest possible. This does not only prevent the conflicts before they start but also provides a platform to communicate and settle the conflicts in case they occur. Fourth, they can spread positive social energy to educate and guide villagers. The villagers can participate in active and healthy recreational and sports activities organized by rural cultural organizations rather than

---

[1] Gong Chunming, "The Realistic Picture of Grassroots Social Organizations and the Concept of Development", *Journal of Guangxi Minzu University (Philosophy and Social Science Edition)*, 2015(4).

falling into bad habits such as gambling.[1] Therefore, a happier and healthier lifestyle bring the villagers benefit the villagers both physically and mentally, and brings social harmony and stability.

7.1.5   The outdated traditional mode

If the reform and opening up are taken as the dividing line, China's rural social governance model can be roughly divided into the "integration of government administration and commune management" during the period of people's commune and the "township administration and village governance" after the reform and opening up. In the planned economy, the state power was highly centralized and their authorities went directly to the rural areas, The government pooled the rural social resources to serve the country's socialist construction by integrated leadership. In such specific historical stage, the mode of "integration of government administration and commune management" created the material and capital needed for the industrialization. The integrated management and control brought the stability of rural society. However, shortcomings in this mode were obvious. When the centralized government tried to take on all the responsibilities in of rural affairs, expense of administrative management had always been greatly high. Besides, the direct intervention of state power greatly damaged the ability of rural society in self-management, self-regulation, self-service and self-development, resulting in the stagnation of social mobility and the lack of social vitality and creativity. Moreover, the obvious deficiency was that the egalitarianism discouraged the farmers from putting in their efforts in work. the quantity and quality of the work were subject to the personal character of the individuals. The enactment of the Organic Law of the Villagers, Committees of the People's Republic of China in 1987 marked the legal confirmation of the "township administration and village governance" mode. The working mode of "going through the motions" in the planned economy gave away to the farmers' passion for production and vitality of the rural economy, which effectively promoted the progress of rural socialist construction. This working mode, however, began to show its limitations that neither "township administration" nor "village governance" could meet many of the planned functions.

What the central government had intended when establishing township governments was to its direct interference in rural society and to further grant farmers

---

[1] Zhou Xiaohua, "Operational Mechanisms of Rural Civil Organizations in Grassroots Governance: An Evidence-Based Approach from China's Rural Revitalization Practices", *Journal of Anhui Agricultural Sciences*, 2012(33).

more self-governance in production and initiatives. It turned out that when the township governments within the administrative system and the villagers' committees outside the administrative system represent different interests, where the power of the former is bestowed by the state power while that of the latter is endogenous in the rural society itself. the two sides may not effectively coordinate their interests.

As the lowest level of state power in China, township institutions function as the link between the central government and the villages, where their work was oriented to rural social members. However, excessive, deficient and improper exercise of their power was not uncommon due to the complexity of rural social problems, the deficiency of the current system and the vague boundaries of the powers and responsibilities of the township governments. At the same time, township governments are often overburdened with a series of mandatory tasks from higher-level governments, such as infrastructure construction, land requisition and demolition and are underbudgeted for such missions.

To some extent, "self-governance" in villagers' committees sometimes does not match reality in practice. On the one hand, as villagers' committee members have a direct influence on the implementation of the policies of township governments the villagers' committee election, to a large extent, is subject to the likes or dislikes of the township government. Over time, the villagers' committee are becoming "subordinates" or even appendages of township governments, village committees have gradually lost their independence and lost their voices in negotiation with township-level governments. On the other hand, due to deficiency of the system, the newly-elected village leaders, who tend to be an egomaniac can hardly represent the interests of the people. What's worse, the existing system isn't effective enough to restrain such behaviors. After the reform of rural taxes and fees, the traditional political ecology of rural society has undergone great changes the deficiency of the "township administration and village governance" is obvious. Under such circumstances, village officials tend to be indolent of their duties, while atomized farmers are losing their interests in taking participation in village affairs under the influence of the market economy. For a long time, there is an urgent need for a new governance mode to keep pace with the development of rural society to avoid a lack of management in rural social governance.

It is in such a context that the rural areas all over the country are actively exploring ways and means of social governance that meet the characteristics of local economic and social development, forming a distinctive style of rural social governance.

7.2 Rural social governance in developed areas

The rapid transformation of society has brought great changes to rural society and its internal and external environment, and further promoted its shift of the governance mode from control to management and then to governance. Comparatively speaking, the developed regions were the first to realize the conversion in both concept and practice. Therefore, rural social governance in developed areas has also gone great changes from traditional mode to a modern one by accepting new ideas and constant innovation in practice. and achieved certain success. Though with great success, there are still some problems in the process of exploration and practice.

7.2.1 Status quo and problems

7.2.1.1 Status quo

(1) *Constant innovation of the social governance mode*

There is no specific definition about developed and underdeveloped areas. Generally, the regions above the national average level are called developed areas, typically along the southeast coastal region, and vice versa, mainly in central and western China. Since the 21st century, the social governance in developed areas has been under constant innovation, as their developed economy provides a solid material foundation and financial guarantee for the innovation of rural governance. With a high degree of economic openness, these areas have more interactions both in economy and ideas with outside world, providing them with more chances to learn the modes of advanced governance around the world, which can be localized for practical use. Therefore, the diversified positive factors have contributed to the innovation of rural governance modes in developed areas. Furthermore, some seemingly unfavorable factors, such as the complexity of the rural affairs, become a trigger for innovation and improvement instead. For example, e-government is the first to be implemented in developed regions partly because of the progress of science and technology and more importantly because of a governance mode that can improve efficiency, optimize accuracy and improve service is urgently needed due to heavy and complex public affairs.

(2) *Remarkably successful government procurement of public services from nongovernmental sectors*

The grassroots administrations in rural areas in developed areas have successfully carried out the government procurement of public services from nongovernmental sectors, covering elderly services, medical and health services, education services, community services, training services, employment services, family planning services, and various professional social services.

For example, the subsidy for home-based senior care services has been fully incorporated into the government budgets in 2004 by the Shanghai Municipal Government, and the system of "government procurement of public services from nongovernmental sectors" has been established. The "six public services of small projects" have been implemented in the new rural construction in Songjiang District, Shanghai, so as to improve the basic supply of public services in rural communities by providing villagers with convenient, fast, high-quality and inexpensive public services enjoyed by urban residents. The so-called "six public services of small projects" known as small supermarket, small theater, small medicine box, small school, small window, and small traffic. The "six public services of small projects" specifically means that the farmers can enjoy convenient services as shopping, recreation, health care, education, government service and transportation by just staying in the village, which has greatly improved rural public services after its implementation. In this process, contract leasing, public-private partnerships, user payment and subsidy system have become the public services of frequent purchase for governments.[1]

(3) *High motivation of social organizations in participating in rural affairs*

A large number of specialized farmer cooperatives and other social organizations have emerged due to the rapid growth of the rural economy in developed areas. Generally speaking, farmer cooperatives in the developed areas, widely involved farmers' economic lives, provided specialized technical guidance, sold agricultural materials to farmers at or below the market price and bought products in a unified manner. Agricultural structure with local characteristics has been established in some developed areas thanks to farmer cooperatives, which has greatly promoted the economic development of rural communities, and further laid a solid economic foundation for governance. For example, nationally known vegetable planting industry in Shouguang, Shandong Province, has established farmer cooperatives which further encourage the growth of the local vegetable industry. In this process, a working positive feedback mechanism has been formed.

In addition, the senior citizen associations organized by seniors themselves play a

---

[1] Zheng Weidong, "A Preliminary Study on Government Purchase of Public Services in Rural Communities-Centering on Songjiang District, Shanghai", *Journal of China Agricultural University (Social Sciences Edition)*, 2011(4).

vital role in their life among some developed areas. For example, in most rural areas of Zhejiang, fixed places and appropriate financial support are provided for senior citizens to gather for activities such as tea, chatting, chess, etc. which, to some extent, satisfies the daily spiritual and cultural needs of the elderly in rural areas and improves their quality of life.

(4) *Enterprises are gradually becoming the mainstay of innovation*

Developed areas are the "incubation bases" for enterprises in China, especially for small and medium-sized enterprises and private enterprises, which are large in quantity and intensive in distribution. The practices have proved that local enterprises have played a more and more important role in the rural social governance in developed areas. In other words, rural economic development and public services are increasingly benefiting from the advanced governance, innovative management or specialized production and operation of enterprises. In terms of economy, the enterprises have provided more channels for farmers to increase their income by the upgrading local industrial and employment structures. Rural infrastructure construction has also been transformed and improved with the development of enterprises.

In terms of politics, corporate executives often have great influence on political and business, and apply their experience and skills in corporate governance to local government affairs. At the same time, people in developed areas with more enterprises tend to have greater passion to participate in public affairs. For example, some traditional industries were moved to the rural areas in northern Guangdong when the "double transfer" strategy of enterprises was implemented in Guangdong Province in 2008, which developed an important force in rural social governance by establishing a three-subject social structure i.e. government-enterprise-farmer(employees) structure.[1]

(5) *Rise of opinion leaders*

Generally speaking, opinion leaders in developed areas, falling into four categories according to their growth experience, are beginning to play their roles in rural governance. (i) The management personnel during the planned economy period. They have already had the ability of industry and commerce or administrative management, have accumulated enough human and material resources for future development, and have seized the opportunities in the market economy with their insights. (ii) The skilled craftsmen with practical skills. They generally have mastered one or more irreplaceable production skills

---

[1] Ke Fenghua, Zhang Zhaohua, "The Effect of Industrial Transfer Enterprises' Participation in Rural Governance and Its Path Construction", *Journal of Shanxi Agricultural University (Social Science Edition)*, 2016(6).

and are reputable and acceptable in social networks. (iii) The smart wealthy villagers a wide social network. Such villagers can lead other people to become rich while accumulating their own wealth. (iv) Introduced talents like college graduates working as village officials. They tend to be better educated and quick-minded. Their constructive suggestions for village public activities often bring vitality to the rural development.

Opinion leaders in developed rural regions are generally economically successful in their respective fields, reputable and popular. The local government appreciates such rural talents by providing them with policy support. These opinion leaders, on their way to the positions of rural governance, or even being leading official, can contribute to rural areas while achieving their personal ambitions.[1]

7.2.1.2 Problems

As the rapid economic development in developed areas has brought great changes in all areas of society, the rural social governance, with some new features, has evolved into a multiple-factor and collaborative governance. In this process, government, social organizations, enterprises and opinion leaders all take their own shares. However, some problems still remain to be solved.

(1) *The blurred boundaries of government power*

As the economy and society in developed areas are more complex, more factors should be taken into consideration in the process of governance. the working system of the government still needs as the governing philosophy falls behind the social transition. Therefore, it is common that the boundaries of rural grassroots government are blurred in exercising its power in developed areas.

First, excessive governance. For example, the government interferes too much in social organizations and civil organizations in the name of guiding work, and even directly intervenes in the internal operation and management of rural social organizations, limiting their capacity of self-organization and self-management. It may be, to some degree, beneficial for the work of the government. It, however, may discourage the social organizations from participating in governance.

Second, improper governance. This refers to the phenomenon where higher-level government entities intervene in the functions of lower-level governments, resulting in blurred responsibilities between different departments at the same level and leading to inefficiencies in governance.

---

[1] Wang Jinhong, "Self-governance for Villagers and the Development of Rural Governance Model in Guangdong", *China Rural Survey*, 2004(1).

Third, lack of governance. It means that the public services that should have been provided by the government failed to be put into use. For example, the construction of transportation and water conservancy facilities cannot satisfy the increasingly growing need of production and life, and the construction of cultural and educational sites cannot meet the spiritual and cultural needs of the villagers. [1]

(2) *"Matthew Effect" in allocation of resources*

With abundant project resources, rural economy is well-developed in developed areas. However, the monopoly of the resources by a few village elites causes the "Matthew effect". Then farmers can be simply divided into advantaged farmers and disadvantaged farmers according to their capacity in production and management. With extensive social network resources and political and economic strength beyond the average level, advantaged farmers can play a dominant role in market competition. Their economic power will be further strengthened by making use of the financial resources and investment, which may win them better say in public affairs.

On the contrary, it is not easy for disadvantaged farmers to be favored by market and government because the farmers are less competitive in the process of unequal resource allocation, because their operations cannot adapt to changes in the market and the contracts between farmers and markets are weak. The information on projects and resources in community have been monopolized by a very small number of people, and so have the reward of the resources. This definitely widens the gap between the rich and the poor. Although resources are not scarce in developed areas on the whole, the idea that "inequality is more threatening than poverty" may not tolerate such a gap, which could be reflected in the frequent mass disturbance.[2]

(3) *The confusion of the identity of social organizations*

The dilemma of social organizations in their identity is caused by many factors. Externally, as the government still has misunderstandings about rural social organizations, a controlled management is generally adopted. Specifically speaking, the incomplete institutions system greatly restricts the development of rural social organizations in the time of rapid social transformation. While it hopes that rural social organizations can participate in village affairs to make full use of their advantages of contact with the people the government still harbors a sense of distrust in them. For

---

[1] Ma Qingyu, "An Explanation of the System of Government Functions in China", *Journal of Chinese Academy of Governance*, 2003(5).

[2] Xing Chengju, Li Xiaoyun, "A Study of Elite Capture and Deviation from the Objectives of Financial Poverty Alleviation Programs", *Chinese Public Administration*, 2013(9).

example, some officials belittle social organizations, believing they just play a very limited role. Others are holding uncooperative or even opposing attitude as they are worried that the authority of the government in governance will be threatened if the social organizations are growing too strong.

Some developed areas may have broken the rules and regulations due to lack of effective supervision and clear definition. For example, some charitable organizations raise money by illegal means for personal gain in the name of charity, turning the underprivileged the victims, seriously hurting grassroots people. In addition, some cults, under the disguise of religion, spread rumors and even mislead people into committing crimes, bringing great hidden hazards to society. Unable to recognize rumors, some farmers joined the cults and even commit people suicide as they believe in the heresies. Such extreme cases so seriously undermine the trust of the government and farmers in social organizations that some well-operated social groups lose the opportunities to participate in governance under this prejudice.[1]

(4) *Hidden hazard of population*

While migrants have made various contributions to the urban and rural construction in developed regions after the reform and opening up, they also bring serious challenges to the governance of local communities. the latest data released by the sixth national census shows that the registered floating population in Zhejiang Province has reached as much as 22 million, and the number of floating population from other provinces was as great as 11.82 million, accounting for more than 1/5 of the resident population, most of whom worked in township industrial parks.

However, these migrants are difficult to integrate themselves into the local community due to the cultural gap, their low education background, or the xenophobia of local villagers. It is local enterprise elites who have acquired the largest share of the profits from the rapid development of economy in developed regions, while the migrant workers who work harder than anyone else may be discontent with meager wages. In addition, if their basic needs such as labor rights protection, children's education, and medical treatment are not met, some may even go to extremes for their personal interests. It has undoubtedly increased the difficulty of social governance and constituted hidden hazards to social stability.[2]

---

[1] Xu Wanqiang, Deng Xiaowei and Zhu Zhe, "Research on the Development Dilemmas and Paths of Rural Social Organizations Under the Perspective of Social Management Innovation", *Social Science in Guangxi*, 2012(6).

[2] Lu Kerong, "Zhejiang's Experience and Model of Social Management Innovation by Rural Social Organizations in Collaboration with Grassroots Government", *Journal of Wuhan University of Science and Technology*, 2013(6).

(5) *The construction of spiritual culture*

Previous news reports and empirical studies have shown that farmers in developed areas, with a greater market awareness, tend to be more concerned with their own income and judge others in economic terms. Moreover, there is a wide income gap in rural areas in developed areas, which may lead to a sense of discontent or jealousy in the local farmers themselves. The rich farmers are likely to have greater say in their social network. They tend to have a sense of personal achievement and superiority even when interacting with those well-educated.

While a large amount of investment in developed areas has been put into the cultural construction such as advanced public cultural, sports and entertainment facilities and places, government's later publicity and findings are not consistent. The monotonous cultural activities can hardly attract farmers. Generally speaking, and the damaged cultural facilities, which remain unrepaired in time or unused for a long time, not only occupy the public space but also are sheer waste of investment. This has prevented the farmers from cultivating their public awareness such as consultation and cooperation among farmers and observance of public morality, and farmers' enthusiasm to participate in public affairs, a discouragement to the village governance.[1]

7.2.2 Exploration and practice

7.2.2.1 The mode of "strategic decoupling of political and economic engagements" in Nanhai District, Foshan City, Guangdong Province

The mode of "strategic decoupling of political and economic engagements" refers to separation of self-governance and social management at the political level from collective economic management at the economic level. Practice has proved that the "strategic decoupling of political and economic engagements" model has strengthened the stability of rural economic order and social management. In the Pearl River Delta where rural industry is well developed and migrant workers has outnumbered the local residents, the village has great industrial income and other financial sources from property rental. It is also common that a single person grabs the powers of multiple responsibilities, which may give rise to dictatorial leadership and corruption. Nanhai District, Foshan City, Guangdong Province, after realizing the deficiency caused the blurred boundaries between the administration and economic management, successfully

---

[1] Guan Ruihua, "Study on the Construction of Rural Spiritual Culture in the Perspective of Harmonious Society", *Social Sciences Review*, 2011(10).

carried out the pilot governance mode known as the "strategic decoupling of political and economic engagements". At the end of 2010, Nanhai District formally established the Social Work Committee and the Office of Collective Economic Management, and formulated documents as Opinions on Deepening Comprehensive Reform of Rural Institutions, the main practices being as follows.

(1) *Clarification of the boundaries of governance actors*

The "five separations" were carried out in the following five aspects: voter qualifications, organizational functions, official management, statutory segregation of accounting entities and asset portfolios, and deliberation and decision-making. "Separation of voter qualifications" means that the leadership of the Party organization is elected by Party members, the village committee leadership by all villagers, and the leadership of the economic organizations by shareholders. "Separation of organizational functions" means that the Party organization is responsible for Party affairs, Party administration, services and supervision, the villagers self-governance organization for rural social public affairs, and the economic administration for village economic operation and management. "Separation of official management" means that officials of the Party organization, officials of the village committee and leaders of the economic organization are independent of each other. "Statutory segregation of accounting entities and asset portfolios" means that the non-business assets belong to the villagers' self-governance organization and the ownership of village land belong to the collective economic organizations. "Separation of deliberation and decision-making" means that the Party organizations, villagers' self-governance organization and collective economic organization discuss the affairs and make decisions within their own scope according to the regulations and regular procedure.

(2) *Government as the core in rural governance*

As the number of all rural Party members in Nanhai District accounts for over 70% of the total in the district, all rural Party branches have been incorporated into community general Party branches and Party branches in the rural economic organizations have been established so that the Party organizations can effectively supervise the economic activities in villages. In addition, experience and lessons are often summarized and analyzed and joint meeting system, democratic evaluation system and other systems have also been established and improved in village activities. Since the implementation of the "strategic decoupling of political and economic engagements", more than 400 university students have been trained as village officials, over 100 volunteer teams have been formed and dozens of Party member offices have been established to participate in innovative village governance in Nanhai District. It has been proved the establishment of the government leadership can improve the efficiency among multi-governance actors and prevent the state of "no-leader" in village-level self-governance or economic activities.

(3) *Construction of rural communities*

The Nanhai District is one of the most developed areas in Guangdong province where the traditional "villagers self-governance" system is no longer applicable. Therefore, Nanhai District began to take the initiative to transform urban villages into residential quarters from January 2011. Up to RMB350,000 per year have been subsidized govern to each neighborhood committee to cover the insufficient budget. An extra RMB60,000 has been paid to each community official to encourage their work in the grassroots communities. What is more humanistic is that the migrants are included in the system of public service so that they have a better sense of well-being.

(4) *Improvement of the villagers' council system*

Meetings for villagers are held at regular intervals to encourage villagers and to express their views and suggestions on community governance and economic activities. On this public platform, villagers who harbor complaints can discuss village affairs in a rational manner and the two conflicting sides can negotiate with mutual respect under the coordination of village leaders. It supplements the inadequate grassroots democracy, ensuring the villagers' right of self-management and self-organization. Such a system encourages villagers to participate in social governance, and helps the government have a better understanding about village affairs, effectively preventing the grassroots conflicts.

(5) *Introduction of social governance actors*

Though in dominating position, the government also introduces social organizations and charitable organizations into rural governance with institutional support. Contrary to the cautious attitude in other places, the Nanhai District government boldly helps develop social organizations, guides them to participate in voluntary services, and assists them in service specialization and service diversification. In Nanhai District, there are 244 social work stations, 5 non-government professional social work organizations and 646 social organizations. They are playing their own unique role in social governance among all aspects of village life including health care, voluntary services and sports development. [1]

---

[1] Li Xiaoyan, Yue Jinglun, "Beyond Local Corporatism: The Example of Separation of Government and Economy Reform in District N", *Academic Research*, 2015(7).

7.2.2.2   Innovative practice in Dalian Village, Dongyang City, Zhejiang Province

Dalian Village, an administrative village in the Nanshi Street, Dongyang City, Zhejiang Province, formed by merging seven natural villages, takes furniture industry as its pillar, and more than 300 enterprises and 200 stores have earned a fame as rural market. However, many governance problems go hand in hand with its rapid economic development, such as unfair distribution of the village profits and frequent conflicts between participants of different interests. Based on the situations in the village, a governance mode known as "self-governance in group affairs" was established, which solved the tricky problems caused by the merging of the villages, such as community integration, villagers' self-governance and service supply. Groups to administer village affairs have been established based on the system of "self-governance in group affairs".

The seven natural villages became seven groups, with a leader and other members as representatives including 191 Party members and eight Party branch members at the village-level Party branch. Each group was responsible for the its own management of services about production and life and gave feedback to the Dalian Village Committee. The group leaders were entitled to the major decision-making of the village committee. It has been proved that the village group has played a key role in public affairs management and collective economy development.

A supervision committee is also set up to restrain and supervise group members, ensuring the fairness and transparency of the group affairs. The deputy secretary of Party branch serves as the chairman of the supervisory committee of the village, with 6 additional members of the Supervisory Committee deployed to ensure each natural village is allocated one oversight commissioner. The village supervisory member is also the leader of the group supervisory committee, which involves other two members from the group and takes the responsibilities of carrying out group policies, reviewing the process of organization affairs execution and confirming the financial revenue and expenditure, ensuring the transparency of village affairs.[1]

7.3   Rural social governance in underdeveloped areas

The rural social governance in underdeveloped areas, compared with that in developed areas, is falling behind in both ideas and reality. Fortunately, there is some progress in the rural social governance in underdeveloped areas in recent years.

---

[1] Yang Liangcheng, Lu Kerong, "Research on the Predicament of Suburban Rural Community Governance and System Innovation", *Fujian Tribune*, 2015(3).

7.3.1   Status quo and problems

7.3.1.1   Status quo

(1) *Introduction of new governance philosophy*

As the economic base determines the superstructure, besides economy, the underdeveloped areas also fall behind in science and technology, education, and governance philosophy.

The rural social governance started rather late in underdeveloped areas. However, their potential is now released thanks to their rich natural resources and ecological environment after the implementation of the national strategies such as the large-scale development of the western region, Northeast Revitalization and the Rise of the Central China. Many reforms have also been made in rural governance. Particularly after many delegates in the underdeveloped areas are sent each year for advanced experiences in social charity, social welfare in developed areas some governance modes have been successfully established based on situations and practice.

(2) *Leading role of the grassroots government*

The government plays a greater role in rural social governance in underdeveloped areas, as the government has to take many responsibilities that the enterprises and social organizations do in developed areas.

First, grassroots governments in underdeveloped areas have played an important role in infrastructure construction. The poor transportation and roads in many villages used to prevent the villagers from participating in production and exchange with the outside world. In recent years, infrastructure construction such as paved roads, street lights or public restrooms has been carried out in many villages, which have greatly improved the environment in rural areas and promoted the development of economy. Second, the government also guides rural villages to develop education and to preserve traditional rural culture and organizes healthy activities for the villagers to meet their intellectual and cultural needs. The government-oriented rural governance has achieved obvious success including fast improvement of farmers' living standards and comprehensive promotion of public undertakings.

(3) *The important role of the clan organizations*

Traditionally clan culture used to be very important in maintaining the stability and unity of local society. However, it was strongly hit by successive wars during the early half of the 20th century. Clan activities had been restricted in the 30 years since the founding of the People's Republic of China. However, structure bound by blood and land had never been dismantled, clan culture acquired the chance to come back to life with the upward shift of state power and the weakening of government's direct control over rural society after the reform and opening up. Nowadays, clan culture has already been revived in underdeveloped areas, especially provinces where clan culture has taken root such as Jiangxi, Hunan, Hubei. For example, clan organizations have been established and ancestral halls have been built in many natural villages of Jiangxi Province. Some clan activities, such as electing clan leaders, revising family genealogy, formulating family rules, and worshiping ancestors, are carried out from time to time.

Nowadays, in underdeveloped areas, especially in rural areas with strong clan culture, clan organizations still play important roles in three aspects: Firstly, clan power has forcefully exerted influence of checks and balances on the grassroots political power, village Party branches and village committees. Clan organizations, natively grown and on behalf of the interests and demands of villagers, could play the role of mediation to guarantee villagers' interests when there is any interest conflict. Secondly, clan organizations have contributed some to the liberation of productive forces in rural areas. Members in clan organizations can help each other because of their tight and stable bond of blood, which may have an influence on acquiring more sources of family income. Finally, clan organizations also play the role of education. For example, the clan council usually would hold a banquet in the ancestral hall to celebrate and award teenagers who are admitted to university and also raise funds as scholarships or tuition for these college students in order to spread the values or traditional virtues in their clan. The clan members gradually attach importance to education, which would have an influence on the long-term development of rural areas. The clan will formulate rules to regulate and restrain illegal and criminal activities in accordance with the law for ensuring the public order in village. [1]

(4) *Introduction of external resources*

A large number of NGOs have been growing rapidly in China, especially in developed areas highly open to the outside world, due to the market economy and the rise of global associations. Some of these NGOs began to redirect their work to the poverty alleviation in the undeveloped rural areas. External organizations are also engaged in poverty alleviation in terms of culture and education in order to improve the diversity of the rural culture and education in underdeveloped areas. It is worth noting that a lot of fresh blood has been introduced into underdeveloped areas by NGOs outside

---

[1] Yu Lei, "Functional Analysis of Clan Organization Revival in the Process of Rural Modernization", *Journal of Chifeng University*, 2012 (10).

the village which excel in high-quality organizational members, professional scientific research and education capabilities, high-performance emergency response mechanisms and village governance philosophy. The support for villages by external organizations is mainly reflected in the following aspects:

First, the local agricultural production potential has been fully stimulated with the help of external agricultural organizations. Even with rich natural resources, the development of the villages in underdeveloped areas has been hindered due to their lack of scientific planning and farming caused by their poor educational background and non-professional production experience. The external agriculture organization, however, can guide and help local villagers to choose whatever crops are suitable for local natural environment and improve planting techniques, trying to maximize the incomes of the farmers. For example, Jiayi Women's Development Center, Shaanxi Province, mainly helps women develop distinctive circular agriculture in a cooperative way and organizes them to carry out ecological agriculture activities such as raising chickens, sheep, and cattle, and planting vegetables to improve the output, quality and product sale.

Second, the help of the external chambers of commerce in attracting investment in underdeveloped areas. The external chambers of commerce would make use of their own social resources and bring them to the undeveloped areas in order to broaden the sales market. Through a mutual benefit process, they do not only drive the economic development in underdeveloped areas, but also promote their own growth as well. For example, the Zhejiang Chamber of Commerce, after realizing the importance of the favorable location of Xinjiang decided to move into it to promote the sales of the products from Zhejiang enterprises. Nowadays, the blooming private enterprises from Zhejiang bring Xinjiang farmers more employment opportunities.

Third, more participation of external social service organizations in poverty alleviation. With the help of advanced service philosophy and capabilities, external organizations have provided various public welfare services such as career planning, skill training, legal services, health care, cultural education, sports and so on based on the diversified needs in rural poverty-stricken areas. As a result, villagers can gradually get rid of misunderstanding in their life and be open to the changes of the village in all aspects. For example, 147 social organizations in Shaanxi Province had been added to the "project database" targeting poverty alleviation, with a total investment of RMB130 million.[1]

---

[1] Wan Jun, Lin Yangfuyun, "One hundred and fourty-seven Social Organizations in the Province Added to the Project Database Targeting Poverty Alleviation", *Shaanxi Daily*, May 24, 2017.

(5) *Role of village talents in governance*

Village talents generally are advantaged in economic and social resources, and reputable in rural areas. Some of them have mastered unique skills in production. Some are large-scale grain producers, others smart businessmen and others respectable scholars. They all contribute to good governance in the countryside. Good governance means the multi-actors can take bottom-up participation in public affairs. In fact, the new farming and cultivating techniques introduced by those talents will soon be spread and followed, either intentionally or unintentionally driving the development of economy in rural community. Village cultural talents have inherited traditional culture, promoted the development of local culture, rallied the people's support, enhanced people's cultural self-confidence and maintained the "etiquette" order of the village to a certain extent through the renewal of genealogy and excavation of traditional folk customs. Village political talents have played a great important role in promoting good governance in rural areas. Some of them handle interest disputes in a legal and rational way, which may set an example for people to strive for their rights and interests according to the rules and laws, preventing the unexpected mass incidents and helping maintain social stability. It is through bottom-up actions of the multi-actors that a comprehensive village development in its economy, politics and culture has been achieved, thus bringing the rural community gradually moving towards good governance.

7.3.1.2 Problems

(1) *Conventional management concepts*

Under the shadow of feudal autocracy for thousands of years, the mindset of superiority of being officials of judging one's social worth solely by one's official status has long been deeply imprinted in people's minds; the "official rank standard" is more ingrained in underdeveloped areas. In rural areas, many officials working in local communities have misunderstandings about villagers' autonomous organizations and naturally believe that they are the only and absolute governors while villagers are just governed targets and village committees are merely the subordinates of township governments. So, in practice, they always tend to give official orders or interfere in their daily affairs, severely impeding the self-organization and self-management rights of villagers' committees. Correspondingly, villagers' committees and villagers are also shackled by stereotyped ideas. Villagers' committees tend to wait for orders from township departments rather than taking the initiative to deal with the village's public affairs. The villagers with economic and social resources take it for granted that village governance is just "the business of officials", and what they are more concerned about is whether they could lead a decent life. The villagers with few resources regard themselves as inferior to "officials", so that they do not have the confidence to participate in governance. Even when some of them want to have special issues solved or their voice heard, they quickly dismiss their ideas, believing that "It doesn't work to resort to the officials at all" because of their inaction. In underdeveloped areas, as conventional management concepts lead to a vicious circle in rural governance, it is difficult to form a diversified governance structure, and rural governance remains stagnant.[1]

(2) *The challenge of clan forces against the authority of the government*

In undeveloped areas, while we must admit the clan forces contribute to the sense of belonging of the villagers' emotional belonging, the improvement of village harmony, and the inheritances of traditional cultures, we also need to recognize their negative influences in village governance.

For instance, in some villages, the members of the villagers' committee have long been dominated by a small number of powerful clans from extended families, and so have the decision-making power of village public affairs, reducing villagers self-governance to a mere formality. Backed by the powerful background, some clans challenge the authority of the grassroots governments by suppressing other villagers for their own benefit, refusing the cooperation in decisions of the villagers' committees, and interfering in the performance of official duties by grassroots officials.

(3) *The underdevelopment of native non-governmental organizations*

In underdeveloped rural areas, social organizations are small in scale and number, lagging behind other areas. Preliminary statistics indicate that in the 12 underdeveloped provinces in the central and western regions, social organizations comprise 25% of the total nationwide, social groups make up 30%, private non-enterprise units contribute 20%, and funds represent 18%. However, the slow development of social organizations hampers the establishment of a collaboratively governed environment by diverse governance actors, limiting governance coverage across all areas and aspects.

The underdevelopment of rural social organizations in underdeveloped areas is mainly reflected in the following two aspects.

---

[1] Zhou Renbiao, "On the Path to Improving Rural Grassroots Self-Governance", *Socialism Stidies*, 2009(3).

First, the small number, small scale, and few categories of registered social organizations. Statistics show that, in underdeveloped rural areas, only 1/3 of social organizations have been registered, and their registered funds, mainly about RMB20,000-RMB30,000, are far from enough for operations. However, most social organizations are cooperative organizations in the agricultural field, like agricultural associations, and agricultural cooperatives, etc. Very few social organizations play the role in protecting the legitimate rights and interests of villagers, participating in and providing rural social services, and enriching the spiritual and cultural life of villagers.

Second, inadequate operation mechanism and structure. Social organizations in underdeveloped areas are not professional in operation and not scientific in planning of finance, human resources, supervision, performance appraisal, etc. The settlement of village issues is often arbitrary and subject to the personal will. For example, the organization members usually properly handle the affairs of villagers who are economically tied with them and ignore the interests of villagers with few resources.[1]

(4) *The insufficient supply of funds for rural construction*

The biggest difference between developed areas and underdeveloped areas lies in "money". The lack of funds in the underdeveloped rural areas makes them fall far behind the developed rural areas in agricultural technology, financial resources, regular governance and diversification of governance actors. Especially in the underdeveloped rural areas, there is still much room for improvement in infrastructure. Although considerable achievements have been made under national support and many policies that can effectively improve the living conditions of villagers, such as paved roads, street lamps, etc., a series of problems have been exposed in construction and maintenance, including poor quality, high cost, inadequate supporting facilities, broken capital chain, and so on.

The grassroots governments and villagers' committees are helpless with such problems caused by lack of funds. The construction of large infrastructure requires a lot of humans, material, and financial resources, while, generally, the state allocates a certain amount of funds to villages as annually planned, which can hardly meet the village's urgent needs. Under such circumstances, some villages adopt the wait-and-see policy. When funds come, construction begins, when funds break, construction stops. This prolonged constructions often wastes more materials and money. Some other

---

[1] Chen Peng, Wang Hongwei, "Institutional Synergy Between Village-Based Civil Groups and Rural Emergency Governance Systems", *Chongqing Social Sciences*, 2013(4).

villagers' committees choose the "deficit administration", by asking the villagers to invest with their money and human resources, which adds a lot of extra economic burden to the villagers who are not rich enough in undeveloped areas.

(5) *Brain drain's influence on long-term rural development*

In underdeveloped areas, the underprivileged economy and low income force many youths to go out to work, leaving the old people and women behind. The structure of left-behind people has changed saliently in recent years. A survey in rural areas of Jiangxi Province indicates that rural left-behind people are mainly composed of the old because most women work in cities with their husbands, with their children going to schools nearby in cities. The Yimen Chen Natural Settlement Cluster in Jiujiang City, Jiangxi Province, maintains a minimum 2.03-kilometer separation buffer from its designated administrative village jurisdiction. There are only three old people left behind, all over 60 years old; it can be expected that the village would vanish with the passing away of the three elderly people. The villages are in such a decline that it's difficult for them to carry out the basic production activities and festive celebrations in the villages. After visiting many rural areas in less developed regions, we have found that many leaders of villagers' committees are older than usual and indolent at performing their duties. So, the generally low quality of village officials makes village governance inefficient.

7.3.2 Exploration and practice

7.3.2.1 The participation by the Villagers' Council in village governance in Wangjia Village, Futian Town, Jiangxi Province

Located in the Qingyuan District of Ji'an City, Futian Town was rated as one of the "Famous China Historical and Cultural Towns" by the Ministry of Housing and Urban-Rural Development and the National Cultural Heritage Administration in 2010. The Futian Village Committee govern three natural villages: Wangjia Village, Wenjia Village, and Jiangcheng Village, among which, Wangjia Village is the richest and largest. Wangjia Village boasts its 10,000 *mu* (about 667 hectare) of mountain forest. Established in 2003 and endowed with such rich natural resources, the village council of Wangjia Village has enough room to give its full play and has accumulated a lot of governance experience in the process of handling the village affairs. Some experiences are to be recommended:

(1) *Clear division of roles among members*

In Wangjia Village, the basic structure of the family council is not complicated. Although it consists of only eight members the council involves six positions, including president, vice president, accountant, cashier, custodian, and two council members. The president, as the core of the council, shoulders the full responsibilities such as making plans, organizing work, leading the team, and reception; the vice president, being second only to the president in responsibility, who often shares the part of the responsibilities for the president, generally exercise the president's responsibility to provide work guidance, suggestion and supervision for all members; the accountant is responsible for managing all the affairs of accounting; the cashier is mainly responsible for cash receipt and payment, cash deposit and withdrawal, travel reimbursement and other money management works; the custodian is responsible for properly preserving and controlling the quantity and quality of public goods in Wangjia Village; the two council members have no special functions, but follow the principle of "go wherever there is need", aiding the above members to complete their work.

(2) *Wide range of services*

In Wangjia Village, the relationship in Wang's family is close and clear; Wang's family is strictly divided into five branches. Most of the clansmen can tell their blood ties in relation to other villagers, and the relationship between villagers is relatively harmonious. The village council is composed of members of Wang's family. When they serve the village, they also serve their relatives and friends, so the council participates in the public affairs of the village almost without any reserve due to their constantly rising sense of achievement and sense of being masters in serving the village. Researchers found that the council has played an irreplaceable role in all aspects of public life, such as managing public assets, building roads and water conservancy facilities, participating in ancient village reconstruction, carrying out family activities, contacting family clans, revising genealogies, assisting the village committee and mediating conflicts and disputes among villagers.

(3) *Scientific operation mechanism*

The operation mechanism of the villagers' council of Wangjia Village resembles a villagers' committee but quite different. It shares the same workplace, conference room with, villagers' committee of Futian Village. When there comes information from the villagers' committee in daily work, the members of the council will work with the villagers' committee. When communicating with villagers, the council will give full play to its advantages as a family council. In village governance operations, the council leverages kinship-based governance advantages through close community connections that enhance policy implementation efficacy, while strategically balancing lineage interests with collective welfare. This operational paradigm fundamentally stems from members' embeddedness in local kinship networks—council representatives being nominated by lineage branches through transparent clan-endorsed selection processes, a mechanism surpassing standard Village Committees in procedural legitimacy.

The family council of Wangjia Village is not only an assistant of the villagers' committee but also owns a great degree of self-governance. For instance, the council can directly manage 10,000 *mu* (about 667 hectares) of mountain forest. In terms of decision-making mechanism, small village affairs are directly decided by the members responsible, but other members have the right to know and make suggestions. The important issues are decided by voting of all members with the rule of majority. The operating funds, coming from the rich natural resources in the village, are managed by the accountant and the cashier separately. One manages the money, and the other the accounts, which ensures the transparency of the funds by mutual supervision. Undoubtedly, transparency highlights the family council of Wangjia Village in the overseeing and control mechanisms. In terms of incentive mechanism, council members enjoy equal pay with the villagers' committee members, and the incentive mainly comes from the decision-making power in village affairs and the potential benefits deriving from it.

The questionnaire on villagers' recognition of the family council of Wangjia Village has further confirmed the efficiency of the services from the council. In July 2016, we distributed 90 questionnaires in Wangjia Village and retrieved 81 valid ones, with an effective recovery rate of 90%. The statistical results showed that 78.25% of the villagers were satisfied with the work of the council; the council not only played its due role in leadership and organization but also indirectly increased the satisfaction and happiness of the villagers. The family council serves as a model of rural governance and provides valuable experience in underdeveloped areas.

7.3.2.2　The reconstruction exploration by Sanbao Village in Wuxi County of Chongqing Municipality

With its harsh natural environment and severely underdeveloped economy, Wuxi County in Chongqing is one of the most remote and underdeveloped areas in China. Located in the heart of Wuxi County, Sanbao Village has been plagued by many practical problems, such as poor life of villagers, serious brain drain, lack of construction funds, rural hollowing, and so on. However, this situation has changed since 2007. The new leadership of the village took drastic measures to rebuild the village instead of ignoring its decline. The village started its reform mainly from four aspects.

(1) *Conflict settlement: establishment of mediation group*

Conflicts and disputes inevitably occur during the work and life of the farmers. In Sanbao Village, these conflicts, if not handle in time, may lead to rising grudges between the conflicting sides. Some may even escalate into violence, seriously affecting the stability of the village. The new village officials, after realizing the potential risks that may caused by such small disputes decided to set up the mediating group involving many reputable elites including older Party members, retired senior officials, rural teachers, rich villagers and scholars, mainly responsible for dispute investigation, facts disclosure, public evaluation and results announcement. Besides, they also hold lectures, regularly inviting to experts share with the villagers their experiences and the knowledge, such as ideas for getting rich and relevant laws.

(2) *Virtues publicity: record of good deeds*

During the time of the planned economy in Sanbao Village, there was a tradition of solidarity and mutual assistance among villagers, which has faded somewhat after the reform and opening up. Therefore, to regain this fine tradition, good deeds were recorded in a book and were publicized in various forms on various occasions. In addition, some villagers' autonomous organizations, such as the "mutual funds" and "five households joint defense system", were set up for teamwork and resource sharing.

(3) *Democratic supervision: disclosure of village affairs*

In the past, the village affairs of Sanbao Village had also been disclosed in the village affairs board, but only to a limited extent with some insignificant contents. However, villagers felt greatly dissatisfied because they could hardly know about the core rural issues, especially about village funds. After the new leading group took office, the villagers' committee changed its role from an operator to a supervisor. In the form of "official account" recording, the disclosure of village affairs was implemented boldly, and the villagers were encouraged to elect some reputable representatives to manage the accounts, which shall be used to keep each account and have them disclosed regularly and publicly for mutual supervision.

(4) *Integrated development: juxtaposition of economy, culture and ecology*

In Sanbo Village, the per capita income greatly exceeded the county average after their reform. In the Spring Festival of 2009, the Sanbao Village Party branch secretary declared that they should not only pursue development in economy and transportation but also preserve the ecology, traditional culture, and fine virtues left by the ancestors. Shortly after that, many clubs, such as the Basketball Association and Tai Chi Association, were organized in the village one after another to encourage the villagers to go out of their houses for more recreational activities. Furthermore, the villagers' committee was innovative in sanitation and law popularization.

From 2007 to 2009, the reconstruction of Sanbao Village in all aspects achieved great effect. The old village now is booming with vitality: conflicts have given away to harmony. Good deeds rather than complaints are more on people's lips. Moreover, the attitude of the people towards villagers' committee officials has also changed from one of resistance to one of sincere admiration and gratitude. Today, Sanbao Village continues to pursue "good governance".[1]

7.4 Rural social governance in areas with large ethnic minority populations

7.4.1 Current situation and problems

7.4.1.1 Current situation

(1) *Improvement in stability under the guarantee of preferential policies*

In areas with large ethnic minority populations of China, harsh natural conditions, coupled with poor infrastructure constructions. In order to promote coordinated development nationwide and prevent the "Matthew effect", the country has implemented preferential policies in rural areas with large ethnic minority populations so as to narrow or bridge the gap between rural areas with large ethnic minority populations and those in developed areas in terms of social governance and economy.

The preferential policy is mainly implemented in the following aspects: First, the preferential policy in investments. Local governments harness the rich natural resources of areas with large ethnic minority populations by investing in key projects, such as hydropower stations, wind power, or mineral resources. Second, the preferential policy in finance. In areas with large ethnic minority populations, without much economic strength, this policy allows key projects to be funded by loans with state subsidies in interest and the loans to be repaid with the return of the projects. Third, preferential policy in horizontal collaboration, namely, integrating the abundant financial resources of developed areas with the rich natural resources of areas with large ethnic minority populations for a win-win outcome. Fourth, special funds. For instance, special funds

---

[1] Yuan Jinhui, "Anomie and Reconstruction of Rural Social Governance in Underdeveloped Areas: A Case Study of Sanbao Village", *Journal of the Party School of the Central Committee of the C.P.C. (National Academy of Governance)*, 2011(2).

for education were set up to subsidize ethnic primary schools, which effectively eased the financial pressure on local governments.[1]

(2) *Comprehensive rural governance led by the governments*

Compared with ordinary rural areas, the natural and social environment in areas with large ethnic minority populations is more complex, and factors should be taken into consideration by governments in rural social governance. Grassroots governments in areas with large ethnic minority populations always play the role of "forerunner" in many aspects of rural governance.

In terms of development funds, the grassroots governments in areas with large ethnic minority populations always keep up with national preferential policies while researching to obtain real and detailed data within the villages. Whenever there is any chance, they would apply for national fund to build their village. In terms of village planning, grassroots governments usually can consider local natural and social environments and design rural development plans based on local conditions. For instance, in villages rich in mineral resources, the governments will actively support the development of industrial and mining enterprises, or in villages rich in tourism resources, the governments will develop tourism to overcome "bottlenecks" in land, manpower and other resources. No matter what is chosen, the local people will benefit from it, promoting the development of the village. In terms of cultural construction, grassroots governments have made many practical measures to support the preservation and development of national cultures. For instance, some governments have established online information platforms, hired cultural celebrities to teach national traditional skills, and applied for intangible cultural heritages. In terms of marketization, by combining national culture development with marketization operation, some governments have helped organize performance teams and cultural companies, which can not only popularize and protect traditional national cultures, but also train national technical and management talents, as well as can increase farmers' incomes.[2]

(3) *Role of the religion*

Religious groups have always been a tradition in village governance, especially village charities. For example, religious groups make effective use of their social

---

[1] Liu Zonglin, Zeng Shaohua, "A Discussion of Policy Inclination and Institutional Innovation in Areas with Large Ethnic Minority Populations", *Heilongjiang National Series*, 1994(4).

[2] Tang Huhao, "Reform and Innovation: The Role of Grassroots Government Functions in the Process of Urbanization Construction", *Journal of Hubei Minzu University (Philosophy and Social Sciences)*, 2016(6).

resources in rural revitalization or devote themselves to the cause of education in areas with large ethnic minority populations. Religious believers believe that doing more good deeds in this life will benefit the afterlife. Their passion for charity is reflected in efficiency in public causes.

(4) *Pioneering spirit of ethnic elites*

Academically, ethnic elites generally fall into four categories, namely, political, economic, intellectual, and cultural elites.[1] They all play a leading role in their respective fields.

Ethnic political elites include government officials who participate in village political affairs, leaders of villagers' autonomous organizations, or religious leaders who participate in political affairs. With outstanding political accomplishment and personal capability, they come up with forward-looking, feasible, and constructive suggestions for their villages and play an important role in the ultimate decision-making function. Their long time's village service has won them great popularity in village and has helped develop unique viewpoints and ingenious ways for the solution of village conflicts, the coordination of relations among people of all ethnic groups, and the guarantee of stable and harmonious development in areas with large ethnic minority populations. Ethnic economic elites are usually businessmen with quick minds and rich social resources. They put the unique resources in areas with large ethnic minority populations into the market so as to increase their income, also contributing greatly to the village. The main contribution of ethnic intellectual elites lies in improving the education in areas with large ethnic minority populations. Compared with other places, people in areas with large ethnic minority populations are not well educated, and particularly, many grassroots officials are also well-educated, some even cannot read and write, which may have seriously hindered rural public affairs. By imparting knowledge and specific technologies to others, intellectual elites have trained high-quality successors to the countryside so that the short supply of rural talents has been largely mitigated. Ethnic cultural elites play a role in the inheritance of national traditional culture. Some of them compile the popularization manual of folk culture, some deliver cultural lectures in schools, some set up folk cultural groups, and some bid for the World Heritage List. All of them are doing their best to show their admirable pioneering spirit.

---

[1] Yang Kunfei, "Ethnic Elites, Social Capital, and Mobilization Capacity: The Organizational Logic of Ethnic Group Events", *Guangxi Ethnic Studies*, 2016(4).

7.4.1.2 Problems

(1) *Policy support: a temporary effect*

The preferential policies may just help the villagers get through temporary problems rather than bring the sustainable development of villages. Therefore, once the external assistance stops, the village may "return what it used be". What is worse, some villagers, being too dependent on the support of the country or other social organizations, may lose the morale to walk out of their e predicaments with their own efforts. Whenever any problem arises, they first turn to the governments for resources instead of their own efforts. In the long run, the idea of "relying solely on support" would be a potential blight for future development.

(2) *Incomplete law and regulation system*

In areas with large ethnic minority populations, things are more complicated because of their uniqueness in beliefs. While the impact of the market economy after the reform and opening up has brought great changes to the openness, competitiveness, ethnic relations, and conceptions in areas with large ethnic minority populations, the existing ethnic laws and regulations with their inherent limitations, can hardly meet the needs of rapid political and economic development and sometimes people cannot find the right laws and regulations when dealing with the problems. This is often reflected in the following ways.

First, the limited number of laws and regulations and the lack of operability. Most current laws and regulations are too general and abstract without detailed provisions for some frequent specific cases in villages. For instance, some of them are vague in description, and some are too flexible. In areas with large ethnic minority populations, laws concerning economic development and traditional culture preservation are far from enough to cover every aspect of rural society.

Second, the blind spots in legal supervision mechanism. Due to the incomplete law enforcement supervision mechanism and some grassroots officials ignorant of legal concept, some departments, in the process of law enforcement, are arbitrary in practice, losing the trust and respect of the villagers, which ultimately prevents the rural governance.

Third, inadequate publicity of laws and regulations. Popularization of law in areas with large ethnic minority populations was difficult due to inaccessible geographical environments, poor education background, and diverse languages, coupled with short supply of funds and outdated means for publicity, the officials and the public in areas with large ethnic minority populations do not understand the significance of governing the country according to law and constructing a socialist country ruled by law.[1]

(3) *Complicated religious factors in in governance*

While religions have made positive contributions to promoting ethnic unity and social stability, they also have added to the difficulty of rural social governance in areas with large ethnic minority populations due to their negative influence.

In areas with large ethnic minority populations, religions vary greatly in doctrines and beliefs which used to cause disputes, conflicts or even wars in the history. Some religions have also split into different denominations, which caused conflicts of succession of religious rights, doctrinal disputes, and power struggles; these conflicts remain unsolved because of the unresolved historical issues. The differences between different religions or intra-differences of a same religion may give birth to small arguments, which, if not carefully handled, may escalate into bigger conflicts or even large-scale incidents.[2]

7.4.2   Exploration and practice

In areas with large ethnic minority populations, the factors of dealing with rural affairs are often different from those in other areas, and the ways, behaviors, and habits of officials and the people directly affect the rural governance. Under special governance environments, many innovative governance modes with ingenious ways and clear goals have been explored in areas with large ethnic minority populations.

7.4.2.1   Community governance mode in Kangding County[3], Sichuan Province

In order to improve community governance and explore a new and harmonious mode of community governance, the Kangding County Government of Sichuan Province launched a pilot activity known as "community participation under the guidance of government" in 2013 so as to achieve three goals: first, to explore a new village-level governance mode; second, to improve the pertinence and effectiveness of rural community work; third, to train a group of capable community workers with a very good sense of service.

After a detailed analysis of the specific conditions of each township and village, selected six administrative villages were selected as the pilot mode and measures such as the

---

[1] Anargul, Argen. "Strengthening the Construction of Ethnic Legal System and Developing Socialist Ethnic Relations", *Journal of Yili Prefecture Communist Party Institute*, 2006 (1).

[2] Gao Chengjun, *Rights Protection and Ethnic Identity: A Perspective on Civil Rights Protection in Areas with Large Ethnic Minority Populations of Northwest China*, Lanzhou: Northwest Normal University, 2008.

[3] Upgraded to a city in 2015.

transformation of the management mode of projects for improving people's wellbeing, the improvement of tourism service in villages, and the improvement of community public health conditions were carried. The specific implementation steps are as follows.

(1) *Consensus on decisions within the leadership*

To ensure the smooth development of the later work, the leadership of the county Party committee and the county government, after many meetings and discussions about any possible details of the activities, and finally reached an agreement on the schedule and the plan of the pilot activities.

(2) *Establishment of working teams*

Due to the heavy workload and shortage of hands, the county Party committee and the county government decided to select the team members from township staff to establish the Kangding County Participatory Community Capacity Building Pilot Office, responsible for the organization and implementation of the whole plan.

(3) *Confirmation of pilot villages*

Within Kangding County, there are Tibetan plateau areas in high altitude and ordinary farming areas. After taking many factors into consideration, three villages in high-altitude pastoral areas and three in low-altitude farming areas were chosen so as to compare the differences under the same model in different governance environments.

(4) *Personnel training*

The county Party committee and the county government decided to train the working team through lectures and other activities, and exercised their ability by pushing them into the practical work in the communities.

(5) *Establishment of a platform for the public opinions*

The public know best about the issues they want to deal with urgently, and the platform is established for them to freely express their interests and demands. The people put forward the urgent problems that need to be addressed, and the working team work out plans for solutions.

(6) *Evaluation of the work*

To prevent "going too far if the work goes wrong" and evaluate their work, the leadership carefully designed evaluation indicators so that the people could evaluate the quality of the pilot activities, and suggest what to be improved.[1]

Finally, Kangding County achieved the expected goal of the pilot activity of

---

[1] Han Wei, "Innovative Pathway Design for Rural Community Governance Optimization Improvement", *Rural Economy*, 2014(11).

"community participation under the guidance of the government", the people were effectively stimulated to participate in the public affairs of the village, which increased the satisfaction and trust of the people to grassroots officials.

7.4.2.2 The way out of poverty alleviation in Jinzhu She Ethnic Township, Le'an County, Fuzhou City, Jiangxi Province

Located in the southernmost part of Le'an County, the former Zhenxing County, Central Soviet District, Jinzhu She Ethnic Township is one of the eight ethnic minority townships in Jiangxi Province and the only one in Fuzhou City. With a total area of 248 square kilometers, the township boasts 330,000 *mu* (about 220 square kilometers) of mountain and forest areas, 10 villages' committees, and a total population of 12,563, of which 4,045 are the She people. Due to the long-term limitation of natural conditions, geographical environment, population quality, and many other factors, its economy of the township lagged behind seriously, and from the 12th Five-year Plan to the 13th Five-year Plan, there were always five poor villages. The underdeveloped economy prevented their rural governance. Therefore, for Jinzhu Township, its priority to achieve effective governance was poverty alleviation. After a long time research, the Party Committee and the government of Jinzhu Township decided to explore a comprehensive mode of poverty alleviation in line with the local reality by benchmarking the eight indicators for poverty alleviation formulated by Jiangxi Province and making full use of the township's rich natural resources and tourism resources. After the economic development, various undertakings in the township took on a new look, and rural governance was steadily advanced. Jinzhu Township mainly achieves its goal of poverty alleviation through nine projects as follows.

(1) *Industrial poverty alleviation projects by promoting distinctive farming and husbandry*

Jinzhu Township, boasts many advantageous resources including alpine beef, spotted pig, Mao-Tai leek, rice-field fish, spring fish, indocalamus leaves, dried bamboo shoots and so on. According to local conditions, the government actively promoted the rural strategy of "one village, one product" in poor villages. The government also encouraged and guided enterprises and large-scale agricultural producers to develop industries with special characteristics so that the underprivileged households could be hired, get higher income, and get out of poverty.

Photovoltaic poverty alleviation project. Five hundred and sixty-six underprivileged households in the township have been covered by the photovoltaic industry project, from household photovoltaic power stations and village-level photovoltaic power stations.

Rural poverty alleviation tourism. The tourism is developed based on the culture of the She ethnic group and integrates the Jinzhu Waterfall, the most famous site in the township, and entertainment. Twenty poor people were hired in the scenic spot. With the introduction of farm stay, sightseeing and picking, and health resorts, the disadvantaged villagers benefit a lot by having more opportunities to increase their income.

Beneficial e-commerce to the underprivileged. Keeping up with the pace of the times, the township government integrated "Internet Plus" into poverty alleviation to promote e-commerce poverty alleviation project. E-commerce platforms such as ULE Shopping and Rural Taobao have been introduced, and their supporting facilities such as village-level service points have been set up. More than 20 rural e-business personnel have been trained. Local governments have broadened sales channels by promoting online sales of local specialty agricultural products.

Investment return for poverty alleviation. By investing RMB400,000 into six poverty alleviation bases of characteristic industries, the government encouraged industrial cooperatives to employ the underprivileged take in their investment, 30% of the profits go to underprivileged.

(2) *Project of poverty alleviation through employment*

For those underprivileged who have the ability to work but without any skills, special training such as techniques of carp in paddy field and high yield technology of Phyllostachys pubescens forest were carried out. Those rich villagers were encouraged to lead the underprivileged farmers to work outside, and migrant workers were supported to return home and start businesses to lead the employment and income growth of the underprivileged people. Through training programs such as the "Dewdrop Project" and "Red Azalea Program", more than 140 people have been trained yearly, and the average annual labor income of underprivileged people has increased by more than 15%.

(3) *The project of poverty alleviation through relocation*

On the premise of fully respecting the wishes of the people, the township government promoted poverty-alleviation relocation and guided the underprivileged to move into new communities in counties, small towns, and central villages, involving them in the planning of urbanization and industry zone construction. The government set up two centralized relocation sites (namely Longlin New Village and Jinshengyuan New Village) in areas with convenient transportation, adequate environment capacity, and balanced soil and water resources. The underprivileged villagers were encouraged to move into Houfa Industrial Park to settle down and work.

(4) *The project of poverty alleviation through ecological protection*

The government has striven to apply for many major ecological projects such as turning marginal farmland into forests, closing mountains for afforestation, and public welfare forests, benefiting the underprivileged people both financially and ecologically. With the ecological compensation and ecological protection project funds, the government was able to employ 28 underprivileged people as ecological protection personnel, such as forest rangers whose annual income increased by RMB8,000 to RMB12,000.

(5) *The project of poverty alleviation through education*

We should conscientiously implement the related policies of the state, province, and city to ensure the school-age children of underprivileged families will not drop out of school because of poverty.

(6) *The project of poverty alleviation through social security*

We should provide as much as social securities to those underprivileged people such as the five-guarantee household and low-income households band those who have lost their ability to work. The social securities for the extremely underprivileged, such as old people, juveniles, and severely disabled people from underprivileged families, should be improved, and their basic livelihood ensured.

(7) *The project of poverty alleviation through healthcare*

For the villagers who fall into poverty because of illness or disability the township government has expanded the coverage of the serious illness relief system for the rural underprivileged and reduce the economic burden of their families by formulating preferential policies and improving the new rural cooperative healthcare system.

(8) *The project of poverty alleviation through infrastructure construction*

The township government has made every effort to win the support from above for the construction of transportation networks in counties and townships. Paved were all roads in towns, villages, and natural villages with more than 20 households. The government implemented the project of poverty alleviation through water conservancy construction, carried out improvement project of drinking water, and enhanced the construction, management, and maintenance of the water conservancy project, especially the "last kilometer" project of agricultural irrigation. The government implemented the rural power grid renovation and upgrading project, and accelerated the rural power infrastructure renovation and upgrading. It also improved the rural informatization construction, strengthened the information infrastructure construction in rural and remote areas, and provided the compensation mechanism for rural telecommunications service, to improve the internet service of poor villages.

(9) *The project of poverty alleviation through the reconstruction of old houses*

The township government conducted comprehensive and thorough investigations of the houses of the underprivileged households and carried out reconstruction projects for their dilapidated buildings. For those who cannot afford the reconstruction of the houses, the government has explored different solutions, such as loan interest subsidies and turnkey after centralized construction.

Under the government's guidance and concerted efforts of all the people, the township's work of villages' poverty alleviation has made remarkable achievements. In 2016, with a per capita income of RMB4,620, Jinzhu Village, took the lead in poverty alleviation while other villages followed. In this township, by the beginning of 2017, 2,879 underprivileged people had walked out of the poverty, and poverty had dropped by 20.3 percentage points. On the whole, Jinzhu Township is committed to poverty alleviation not only for getting rid of poverty but also involving all aspects of rural governance. With the growth of people's economic income and living standards and the overall improvement of rural public utilities, village governance is heading in the right direction.

Chapter 8
Network Social Governance

8.1 Background and connotation of network social governance

8.1.1 Background and significance of network social governance

In this day and age, a new round of sci-tech revolution has swept the globe, and as a result, big data, cloud computing, mobile Internet of Things, artificial intelligence, and blockchain have been integrated into economy and society in an unprecedented breadth and depth. This revolution is profoundly changing modes of production and ways of life, exerting increasingly significant influence on national and social governance.

An all-inclusive network society has taken shape in China, encompassing every aspect of society such as social practices, politics, economy, and culture. The new media which are digital, interactive, prompt, personalized and globalized have given birth to a virtual world, which is adsorbing more and more individuals, agencies and organizations. According to The 38th Statistical Report on China's Internet Development, as of June 2016, the number of Internet users has reached 710 million, with a population coverage of 51.7%. When so many people are using the Internet, social conflicts as the result of current-stage development have found their way into the virtual world and loom magnified. Actually, the more the social structures and interest patterns undergo profound changes, the more frequently social conflicts will occur in the real world. Nonetheless, the number of Internet users still has potential to grow—especially from marginalized groups, such as rural residents, under-age persons and senior citizens. Under these circumstances, the conflicts in the virtual world will be more complex and unpredictable.[1]

Since the 18th CPC National Congress held in November 2012, General Secretary Xi Jinping has expounded the importance of cyberspace governance on many important

---

[1] Yu Shui, Song Ruijuan, "The Logic of Virtual Society Disorder in the New Media Environment under the Framework of Meta-Governance", *Academic Exploration*, 2017(2).

occasions, putting forward the major proposition of "building a community with a shared future in cyberspace" from a strategic perspective. The three subsequent world Internet conferences provided a direction for network globalization and social governance. The first one, held in November 2014 in Wuzhen, Jiaxing, Zhejiang Province, took "an interconnected cyberspace shared and governed by all" as its theme. Xi remarked in his message of congratulations, meanwhile, the development of the Internet has posed new challenges to national sovereignty, security and development interests, which requires the international community to meet urgently and seriously and pursue common governance and win-win outcome. Network society is an area where national sovereignty matters most. There are about 200 countries in the world, each having its own geographical boundary. As an important component of national sovereignty, the Internet also has national boundary and access rights, which should not be trespassed or manipulated by foreign countries. Thereupon, it is an obviously important issue to safeguard the sovereignty and information security of the network society.

In December 2015, in Xi Jinping keynote speech at the Second World Internet Conference, Xi spoke, "Greater efforts should be made to strengthen ethical standards and civilized behavior in cyberspace. We should give full play to the role of moral teachings in guiding the use of the Internet, to make sure that the best accomplishments of human civilization will nourish the growth of cyberspace and help rehabilitate the cyber ecology." In November 2016, at the opening ceremony of the Third World Internet Conference, Xi Jinping delivered a speech via video, pointing out that the development of the Internet knows no national or sectoral boundaries and that the sound use, development and governance of the Internet thus calls for closer international cooperation and joint efforts to build a community of common future in cyberspace. Actually, China's initiatives have played a positive role in strengthening global cyberspace governance. [1] In short, these three conferences expounded the importance of network governance from three aspects—cyber sovereignty, cyber ecological civilization, and international cyber cooperation.

Furthermore, the shaping and development of the network society does not just concern cyberspace; it has exerted immense influence on the structure of the whole real society and corresponding governance system as well. The realization of the goal set by

---

[1] Xiong Guangqing, "The CPC's Exploration on the Governance of Internet Society since the 18th National Congress", *Theory and Reform*, 2017(2).

the Third Plenary Session of the 18th CPC Central Committee—constructing a modernized national governance system—is inseparable from the successful governance of the network society. The governance of the virtual society and that of the real society constitute a complete national governance system.[1] At present, whether the network social governance is successful or not has become an important indicator of national governance capabilities and the status quo. Therefore, effective network governance is of great significance to China's stable and steady economic and social development.

8.1.1.1 Providing a clear channel for public opinions to get through or for citizens to participate in the discussion and management of state affairs

In this era of mass media, online communication enables public opinions to spread more conveniently and effectively. Through Sina Weibo, WeChat and other blog platforms, information circulates faster and faster. By resorting to online channels, citizens acquire opportunities to express their appeals and participate in the discussion and management of state affairs. The Internet has become a powerful distribution center for public opinion, where people become more concerned about national politics. Therefore, the Internet has not only cultivated netizens' sense of democracy and improved their capability to participate in the discussion and management of state affairs, but also promoted the resolution of social problems to a certain extent. However, some improper public opinions could also incur network social conflicts which would be brought into reality. Therefore, it is necessary to guide online public opinions. In this guidance effort, legal, administrative and other means should work together to ensure that the Internet is manageable and controllable. Then, a clean and clear cyber environment will ensue.

8.1.1.2 Offering citizens a desirable communication platform to make anonymous and guileless utterances

The Internet has served as a cross-domain digital platform for human beings. People can access or exit, as they like; be real-time online and make instantaneous interaction. They are no longer geographically confined. This is a new activity space that can be extended across regional boundaries and in which netizens from different places can be synchronously present. In other words, by virtue of the Internet, people around the world can not only spread, exchange and share all kinds of information, knowledge and opinions, but also get united in the process of communication and

---

[1] Cheng Lin, "Strengthening Network Social Governance to Create a Civilized Network Environment", *Journal of People's Public Security University of China* (*Social Sciences Edition*), 2014 (3).

interaction. Then, powerful forces are likely to emerge to influence and change individuals, groups and even society. What's more, netizens have come to practice and enjoy such values and norms as self-governance, equality, diversity, inclusiveness, interactivity, and sharing, which will penetrate into different fields and aspects of offline social life.[1] A vigorous network society is rising rapidly. The institutional structure of the whole society, including online and offline worlds, is undergoing profound changes.

8.1.1.3 Promoting effective interactions between the government and the public

Supported by IT, the Internet has cut off some levels in the bottom-up communication hierarchy in economic, political and social fields. The multi-level communication mode between the government and the public has gradually been dissolved and communication costs reduced. The information revolution, which "has given birth to a new politics of trust whose transparency is increasingly becoming an asset of power", has constantly promoted political restructuring and helped actualize public interests. Take Sina Weibo — a microblog platform — as an example. "Effectively employed, it will undoubtedly help alleviate social pressures, ease social conflicts and promote sound communication between the governing Party and citizens."[2]

8.1.1.4 Responding readily to public concerns and thus contributing to social consensus

At the end of March 2016, it was reported that Shenzhen had begun to implement the most stringent "ban on motorcycles and restriction on electric bicycles", which triggered public resentment. Then, WeChat public platform of Shenzhen Traffic Police Authority Release and microblog account of Shenzhen Traffic Police made an announcement to invite media across China and representatives from all walks of life to attend a press conference and a focus group. On April 4, 2016, the WeChat public platform of Shenzhen Traffic Police Authority Release responded to public concerns by declaring to extend the "transition period" before this policy was implemented. On April 5, the Shenzhen Traffic Police sponsored the focus group as scheduled, whose participants included representatives from associations of industries such as express delivery and logistics, as well as the NPC deputies and CPPCC members. The purpose of the focus group was to discuss the ban and hear voices from all sides. The meeting

---

[1] Chang Jinfang, *An Introduction to Network Philosophy: The Transformation of Human Existence in the Network Age*, Guangzhou: Guangdong People's Publishing House, 2005.

[2] Duan Gang, "Research on Network Social Governance Becomes a Hot Spot", *Social Sciences Weekly*, Jul. 2, 2015.

addressed the questions and doubts from the public. Since then, public resentment subsided so that the policy continued to be enforced. Let's take another example. Rumors related to the G20 Summit were spread on the Internet before it was held in September 2016 in Hangzhou. The local government made investigations and cleared them up one by one as soon as possible. In this way, public doubts were resolved, the summit preparation went smoothly, information transparency was achieved, and the residents' stable life was not disturbed.[1]

8.1.1.5   Helping supervise public power

Since the 18th CPC National Congress, the situation of combating corruption and building a clean government has remained severe. In terms of the Party's self-improvement, extensive and powerful network supervision can effectively improve its self-purification ability. Network supervision works especially well in the We-Media era, when public opinions about anti-corruption on Sina Weibo, WeChat and other blog platforms and online forums spread in more liberal, individualized and diversified ways, and are known by more people. Through the Internet, many corruption cases have been disclosed. These cases attracted attention and thus brought about huge effects on our society. Therefore, in the times of information, network supervision is a more effective and powerful way to fight corruption.

8.1.2   Definitions of network social governance

Some scholars defined virtual society or network society as follows. According to He Mingsheng, society is an embodiment of all kinds of connections and associations generated by people's mutual influence within a certain period of time; the virtual society created by netizens' interactions, is an embodiment of all kinds of connections and associations between people in the virtual space.[2]

Wang Lin and Liu Junling held that the virtual society and the real society are essentially the same in nature, with the differences just in space and in outcomes of interactions to some extent. In the real society, people's life is in a relatively static field, and they directly interact with each other on a one-on-one basis, while on the Internet people indirectly interact in a multifold way: human—machine—human. The virtual society which exists on the basis of the virtual network, with netizens as central points

---

[1] Liu Pengfei, "The Law of Public Opinion Guidance Based on Cases in Recent Years", *News and Writing*, 2017(3).

[2] He Mingsheng, "The Conceptual Positioning and Core Issues of Virtual Social Governance", *Journal of Hunan Normal University*, 2014 (6).

and the generation and transmission of information as the goal, gives birth to some virtual social relations.[1] Interactivity is highlighted there.

Jin Wulun proposed that virtual society, also known as cyber society, is a virtual space in which Internet users are connected with each other through computers or other remote communications terminals to interact with one another, and share and exchange information. He reckoned that the virtual society is a kind of sub-society. Feng Binyuan held that, in some sense, virtual society is an extension of the real society. However, due to its sub-social feature, virtual society has unique attributes, obviously different from those of the real society.[2]

There are also different definitions of network social governance. Li Yi referred to it as one form of social governance practice that involves the Internet and the network society and was implemented through collaborative efforts of multiple actors and social forces such as the government, enterprises, social organizations, and individuals; it draws on and adheres to the values, institutional designs, structures and means of modern social governance; its purpose is to enable the online social life to operate properly and the online groups to maintain order, thus promoting the healthy and sustainable development of online social civilization. Network social governance focuses on the virtual social community. It can be also expressed as "the governance of the Internet society", or more accurately as "the social governance of the Internet society".[3]

Xiong Guangqing considered the network social governance as a form of social governance that took the network society as the object and that is implemented by social forces such as the government, enterprises, social organizations and citizens based on the values, institutional designs and other means of governance. Three things should be noted in this definition: Firstly, the object of governance is the network society. The concept of governance provides a good perspective on how to deal with the problems in the network society, and this concept is consistent with the ever-changing network society. Secondly, there are multiple actors of governance—the government, enterprises, social organizations, and citizens. All netizens there can become the governance actors. Thirdly, the concept of governance is different from conventional ideas of ruling and management. For example, the management and the managed in the virtual world enjoy

---

[1] Wang Lin, Liu Junling, "Virtual Society Administration by the Government: New Challenges and Countermeasures", *Journal of Chengdu Administration Institute*, 2017 (1).

[2] Yang Xin, "The Characteristics of Virtual Society and Its Management", *Journal of Social Work*, 2012 (1).

[3] Li Yi, "A Research on the Target Orientation and Action Principles of Social Governance of the Internet Society", *Zhejiang Social Sciences*, 2014 (12).

equal status to some extent, and they can switch roles. In other words, fellowship and negotiation matter most out there.[1]

Network social governance is a practice implemented for the virtual society. In actual operation, it requires effective participation of the government, enterprises, social organizations and individuals. To ensure its safe and healthy development, we should resort to legal, ethical and administrative means and give full play to the power of collaborative work, to regulate and coordinate all kinds of rights and interests, and to ease and resolve conflicts.

8.2 Characteristics and governing principles of the network society

8.2.1 Characteristics of the network society

Apparently, network society is a world of countless linked computer terminals, but actually in terms of space and interactional field, it is inhabited by people as users and workers. Originally created for political, military and technological purposes, it has gradually evolved into a liberal interactive space with cultural, social, private features. Actually, it has become a unique "real" social field based on IT development, signifying a new form of space, a new form of society, for people to colonize and communicate with one another. Network society is the extension as well as high simulation of the real society, but by no means a mere copy. Though closely and inextricably connected with the real society, it has its own features.[2] To conduct good administration, we must follow the basic laws of the network society. Compared with the conventional society, the network society has the following features.

8.2.1.1 Virtuality

As we know, netizens' gender, age, habits and other information can be fictitious,[3] and the scope and space of online activities are nonmaterial. When they engage in activities, they depend on symbols or numbers as intermediaries. At the same time, not

---

[1] Xiong Guangqing, "Cyberspace Governance Architecture and National Political Security Framework in Contemporary China", *Social Scientist*, 2015(12).

[2] Peng Mei, Xia Yan, "Network Society and Legal Construction under the Perspective of Globalization", *Academic Forum*, 2010 (5).

[3] Liu Na, "Research on Governance Measures of Network Society in the Internet Era", *Heilongjiang Science and Technology Information*, 2017 (4).

limited by time and space, they can be unreserved within the bounds of legal provisions. Furthermore, the topics dealt with online are also virtual: people can be as imaginative as possible when communicating by WeChat and Sina Weibo.

8.2.1.2 Liberty

The network offers an open field for users to shuttle through and do whatever they like via computers and servers. For instance, they can hunt jobs, do shopping and take exams anytime and anywhere. They can also engage in activities which they are interested in, and choose to stay with or away from those individuals or groups that make them feel uncomfortable. In other words, they just follow their own mind, disregarding the social hierarchy that must be observed in real life.

8.2.1.3 Interactivity

One of the important features of a mature and well-developed virtual society is that people exerts effects and influences on one another through interaction. Since there are no limits to time and space, members can engage in real-time, all-round, multi-directional, and unrestricted interactions—which are unattainable in real life—through information dissemination, opinion expression, and emotional exchange. To put it another way, many of the interactions among Internet users are synchronic, nonlinear, and one-to-many. Compared with real-life communication, the contents shared on the Internet are richer and more colorful, and the modes of life are more dynamic, which satisfy, to a large extent, the psychology of those who are not satisfied with real-life communication.[1]

8.2.1.4 Membership diversity

With the rapid technological advancement, the Internet has become the world's largest and most complex library or database—a collection of all kinds of information from all around the world, and an open information system which is constantly being updated. Anyone with some basics in computer science and Internet browsing can access the virtual world, anytime and anywhere, to retrieve the information needed or offer opinions. The Internet is where people, regardless of age, race, nationality, religious belief and social status, are gathered from different countries and regions, hence an immense community; the Internet is also where people can follow their own mind, visiting their preferred cyberspaces and taking up their interested topics for

---

[1] Wang Lin, Liu Junling, "Virtual Society Administration by the Government: New Challenges and Countermeasures", *Journal of Chengdu Administration Institute*, 2017 (1).

communication. In other words, the network society is readily receptive, whose threshold for membership is rather low.

8.2.1.5   Anonymity

The network society, which is intangible in nature, embodies itself in images, sounds, and electronic texts. In front of the Internet user is a symbolic world of virtual space and time. The complexity and uncertainty of transmission technology make it difficult for one user to know for sure the identity of another. For net users can conceal their true identities by creating multiple fake identities through a variety of technical means. In other words, in the network society, people can keep true information about themselves private. So anonymity is one of the important features of cyberspace; to the person seated at another terminal, you are just an interlocutor without identity, or a nobody whose identity means nothing to him or her.[1]

8.2.1.6   Decentralization and flat structure

The network society is unstratified and features a flat structure. All communicators enjoy equal status, which is different from the conventional social relationship between the leading and the led. The operation of the Internet relies on effective communications and interactions rather than on dictations and orders from one network user to others. The insurmountable social hierarchy and privileges in the real society are tremendously challenged on the network.

The network society is dynamic and decentralized, in which many nodes exist and none of them takes a central position. Netizens can aptly communicate with one another in this flat structure where there are no overriding authorities. It's apt to say that everything is centered around, yet nothing truly takes center stage there.

Decentralization and the flat structure of the network society make it necessary for us to change our governance style from domination to communication, from closed-mindedness to open-mindedness, and from unidirectional dictation to multidirectional interaction. Only in this way can online governance be effective, can public opinions be received properly, and can problems and conflicts be better resolved.[2]

8.2.1.7   Globalization with no sense of time zones

As a global platform for information flow and social interaction, the network society has transcended geographical and cultural boundaries and time zones. Individuals from different regions are enabled to conduct direct dialogues and

---

[1] Yang Xin, "The Characteristics of Virtual Society and Its Management", *Journal of Social Work*, 2012 (1).
[2] Ibid.

communications. In the past, cultural exchanges between countries were constrained by conventional media and channels. However, in the network society, information transmission is not hindered by geographical distance. No matter how far the actual distance is, sending and receiving information happen at almost the same time, with the time gap hardly perceived. Anyone can access any corner in the world by a click of the mouse, which is exactly what globalization means.[1] This new mode of space use has broken through all kinds of tangible and intangible boundaries between countries and between regions, turning the world into a "global village".

8.2.2 Fundamental principles on network social governance

8.2.2.1 Collaboration of multiple actors

The Third Plenary Session of the 18th CPC Central Committee pointed out that the overall goal of continuing the reform to a deeper level is to develop the socialist system with Chinese characteristics, and modernize our national governance system and capacity. In the light of political development in the human society, the transformation from politics to management then to governance (including the change from social management to social governance), is not a play of words, but a renewal in thoughts and values.

Specifically, politics distinguishes between rule and governance in five aspects. Firstly, the power subjects are different. Rule implies a unitary subject, namely, the government or other public authority, while governance involves diverse subjects, including the government, enterprises, social organizations, and autonomous community bodies. Secondly, the power natures are different. Rule is coercive while governance is typically negotiatory. Thirdly, the power sources are different. Rule gains power from coercive national laws, while governance from noncoercive contracts as well as national laws. Fourthly, power runs in different directions. In the case of rule, power runs top down, while in the case of governance, power can run top-down, but more often than not, it runs horizontally. Fifthly, the covered ranges are different. Rule only covers what the government power reaches, while governance covers the whole public domain—the range of the latter is much broader than that of the former.[2]

---

[1] Peng Mei, Xia Yan, "Network Society and Legal Construction under the Perspective of Globalization", *Academic Forum*, 2010 (5).

[2] Yu Keping, "Promoting the Modernization of National Governance System and Governance Capacity", *Frontline*, Feb. 27, 2014.

The proposal that national governance system and governance capacity should be updated has been made to engage the government, social organizations and every citizen in the management of state affairs and public affairs. To achieve the updating of this kind, the government and the society, or the authorities and the populace, should attach importance to "consultation, cooperation, coordination and collaboration".[1] Such governance conception and approach also apply to the network society; that is to say, the rigid conventional conception of control should be left behind and the principle of collaboration adhered to. Collaboration means that, under the basic network social standards and regulations, autonomous and diverse governance actors, including the government, social organizations, enterprises and citizens' network communities, can jointly maintain the network public order through interactions.

8.2.2.2   All-people engagement

As a public realm which features liberty, interactivity and actor diversity, the Internet provides a platform for citizens to express opinions and exchange ideas freely. At the same time, it practices public values such as equality, fairness, and justice. Therefore, as the main participants of network social governance, netizens should play an active role in maintaining social order. Everyone should strictly follow the network's social norms and take responsibility for their own words and deeds. A consensus can be reached that the network society is for all and by all. Only in this way, effective governance can be achieved.

8.2.2.3   Incorporation of reality into virtuality

To incorporate reality into virtuality is to consider both the particularity of the network society and the advantages and mechanisms of the social governance system in reality. For example, what behaviors will infringe on the rights and interests of others and endanger public safety should be clearly defined, and related regulations should be introduced. What behaviors can merely be punished within the virtual world, and what behaviors must be taken into the real world—they must be demarcated. And detailed regulations are necessary for online penalty and offline penalty. In other words, a complete restraint system is to be established that can be implemented online and extended to the real world.[2]

---

[1] Ren Weide, "Achieving Coordinated Governance between the State and Society", *Inner Mongolia Daily*, Nov.19, 2013.

[2] He Zhe, "Key Theoretical Issues and Governance Strategies of Network Social Governance", *Theory and Reform*, 2013 (3).

8.2.2.4 Putting the network under the rule of law

The Fourth Plenary Session of the 18th CPC Central Committee proposed advancing law-based governance across all fields of endeavor. The overall goal of this mode of governance is to build a socialist legal system with Chinese characteristics and eventually a socialist country ruled by law. The network society has its own characteristics, which cause great difficulties in governance. People depend on the Internet because they take for granted its sound and stable operation. Once technical problems or management accidents occur, consequences are unpredictable and remedies can be hard to figure out. For instance, the system of network infrastructure may be vulnerable to viruses and hacker attacks; the features of easy access, anonymity, and interactivity make it difficult to verify the authenticity of some information. Worse still, when some false and harmful information circulates and is exaggerated, the "effect of sheep flock" is likely to occur. That is to say, netizens get panicked, mass incidents may follow up, and social stability is threatened.

Adherence to law is the essential principle by which to regulate netizens' behavior and to administer the network. Some agreed-on basic values, a set of behavior norms, and a system of network social laws—these three things determine the effectiveness of the network governance. Therefore, the law that can nourish the network society should keep being ameliorated, and the concept of law-based governance should be well understood. Meanwhile, both "soft law" and "hard law" should be depended on to safeguard national security, public interests, social harmony and stability.

8.3 New challenges for network social governance

With the increasing popularity of the Internet in China, more and more citizens join the ranks of netizens. The network has penetrated into every corner of national economy and social life, forming a brand-new virtual society. However, network is a double-edged sword, bringing convenience and freedom, and also new problems such as infringement, fraud, threats, pornography, rumors, improper ideology, and information security risks, etc. Meanwhile, the concepts and modes of conventional governance are facing new challenges, such as lack of legal guarantees, absence of collaboration between multiple governance actors, want of multi-skilled professional talents, and inadequacy in international cooperation.[1]

---

[1] Guo Yongzhen, "Exploring the Path to a Legalized Network Society from the Perspective of Marxism", *The World & Chongqing*, 2016 (12).

8.3.1 Dramatic rise in network crimes

As a virtual extension of the real society, the network society brings us convenience and benefits. However, the incidence of illegal activities online is constantly rising, largely hindering the sustainable development of the network society. Illegal activities can take the following forms. Firstly, rampant fraud. With more and more people using the mobile Internet, cyber frauds occur increasingly frequently. In 2015, the number of rogue programs detected in China exceeded 1.45 million, up 52% year on year. Scammers not only use those programs as "offensive weapons", but also make some scenario-based fraud strategies, resulting in great difficulties for netizens to protect themselves.[1] Secondly, anarchy. For example, to seek profits, "big shots", posters, and the ghostwriters cooperate like on an assembly line: the posters fabricate false information by which the "big shots" expand their influences, and the ghostwriters spread negative messages to slander the rivals. In addition, some people even use the network to defraud, gamble, and spread pornography, superstitions, rumors and so on. According to Report on Chinese Netizen Information Security of 2012 and 2013, 38.2% and 36.3%, respectively, out of the total Internet users received "Internet phishing messages". Among these false messages, "fake websites" accounted for 17.6% and 22% respectively, and privacy leakages 7.1% and 13.4% respectively.[2] Therefore, cybercrime also accounts for an important part in the governance of the online society.

8.3.2 Frequent occurrence of Internet mass incidents

China is now in a period of social transformation, which leads to frequent conflicts. When some underprivileged groups of people express their appeals or vent their dissatisfaction through the Internet, subtle differences in individual behaviors may lead to significant changes in collective behaviors, which may transform ordinary public incidents into public emergencies. Once public emergencies break out, they will exert extensive impact on the society, giving rise to chain reactions, and producing instant effects, butterfly effects, and global effects.[3] If improperly handled, they are likely to result in major mass incidents, involving casualties and property losses. In recent years,

---

[1] Yu Shui, Song Ruijuan, "The Logic of Virtual Society Disorder in the New Media Environment under the Framework of Meta-Governance", *Academic Exploration*, 2017(2).

[2] Wang Lin, Liu Junling, "Virtual Society Administration by the Government: New Challenges and Countermeasures", *Journal of Chengdu Administration Institute*, 2017 (1).

[3] Li Leiming, "Strengthening and Innovating Network Social Governance", *Ningbo Daily*, Jul. 8, 2014.

public opinions have been raging like storms in virtual society. The outbreak of almost every crisis is closely related to the Internet.

8.3.3   Network security risks

The problems of computer viruses, hackers, spams, system loopholes, cyber thefts, and false online information are becoming increasingly serious around the world. Immature technology makes it easy for hackers to steal private information, which does harm to state security. According to the statistics released by China National Computer Network Emergency Response Technical Team (CNCERT), in 2015, China had more than 120,000 cyber incidents, up 125.9% year-on-year.[1] Computer viruses and hacker attacks have been posing great threats to IT-dependent industries such as banking, transportation, medical services and telecommunications. In addition, cyber espionage, loopholes in network devices, and inadequate security mechanisms also jeopardize national security.

8.3.4   Mainstream ideological security undermined

Nowadays, the Internet has become an important channel for Western countries to drain their ideologies into China. Developed Western powers, depending on capital and advanced technology, have conducted network penetration into China's political, economic, cultural, military and diplomatic fields, in an attempt to seek cyberspace and cultural hegemony. The network has even become a vital tool for international terrorists to conduct evil activities in China. For instance, some of them, especially the United States, constantly propagandize their values, in an attempt to interfere in other countries' internal and foreign affairs. Also, some people attack China's political institutions and cultural attachments by publishing false information on the Internet, to create panics and thus threaten China's national security and social stability.[2] Furthermore, some countries, under the camouflage of "free mass culture", spread a large quantity of negative information on the Internet which is replete with pornography, violence, superstition, etc. Such things are especially targeted at Chinese youth, whose mentality and values are possibly significantly impacted, which may seriously threaten China's mainstream ideology.

---

[1] Yu Shui, Song Ruijuan, "The Logic of Virtual Society Disorder in the New Media Environment under the Framework of Meta-Governance", *Academic Exploration*, 2017(2).
[2] Ibid.

8.3.5　Lack of diverse approaches to network social governance

Since the network society is interwoven, interactive and cross-domain and has diverse administrators, the unified and rigid traditional administration has failed to meet the needs of its governance. For example, "blocking" is the major approach to traditional management, which involves post-deleting or account-locking once a government department discovers radical remarks in the post. However, such management will undoubtedly result in netizens' distrust in the Internet, and even lead to confrontation between the government and the public. It will make things worse if it is taken as the basic management measure to deal with risks. Besides, the network is a flat structure with multiple centers; that is to say, there is no absolute authority. Diverse governance actors, particularly social organizations and individual citizens, crave for power sharing. Each actor, who enjoys equal status in communication and interaction, expects optimal allocation and sharing of network resources so that multiple cultures and values can coexist and coordinate with one another. However, at the present stage, the network social governance is still dominated by the government. Participation of both social organizations and general public in the governance is far from enough. Consequently, resource sharing and collaboration in governance are yet to be achieved.

8.3.6　Absence of legal protection for network social governance

As the Internet has been incorporated into every aspect of economy and society, significant changes have taken place in how people communicate and how they live their lives. Meanwhile, hackers apply new technology to disrupt the network, stealing national or personal information, or committing cyber fraud or network monitoring—all these things show that due legal guarantees are absent in China's network social governance. In response to these problems, China has strengthened legislation on the development and governance of cyberspace in recent years and has issued hundreds of regulations. For instance, The Cybersecurity Law of the People's Republic of China, promulgated in November 2016 and implemented on June 1, 2017, has become the general law to ensure cybersecurity. However, there are some problems concerning the laws and regulations and the law-makers. Some laws and regulations are not specific enough, or impractical; there are cases to which no law or regulation can be applied. The departments that make the laws are not authoritative enough in the government hierarchy; most of the laws they make are for the management of their own departments, and are not consistent with other laws made by other departments. Consequently, when it comes to conviction of lawbreakers, electronic evidence is usually found to be insufficient and further evidence is beyond reach. What's more, as cybercrimes tend to be cross-domain, it is difficult to decide into whose jurisdictions they fall. And there are cases which find themselves in a vacuum free from laws or regulations and thus get by unpunished. Then, there is the problem of law enforcement. When illegal conducts cannot be properly characterized by law, and when detailed operation rules and effective supervision mechanism are lacking, law enforcement tends to get bogged down. Furthermore, public power abuse still exists, which used to be violent law enforcement and now takes the form of ubiquitous information and privacy control. Once public officials take advantage of their power unconstrainedly, no one in the network society can get by safe and sound.[1] Still, gaps exist between China's laws on network social governance and the relevant international regulations. In other words, China's laws fail to be consistent with international regulations.

8.3.7 Lack of moral self-discipline in network social governance actors

Anonymity, virtuality and decentralization of the network society easily cause the failure of the function of moral norms and the occurrence of network anomie. Firstly, some Internet and telecom operators have an inadequate sense of law and social responsibility. Illegal operations are frequently detected on their websites. Their anomie in behavior and a lack of regulations to guide their behavior have undermined public trust in network communication. Secondly, some network users deliberately exaggerate social problems to mislead public opinions. To achieve this purpose, they send spams, spread rumors, and develop viruses. All of these things dramatically threaten the harmony and stability of the network society. Thirdly, netizens, as a whole, have a low level of network ethics and a lack of self-disciplining sense. They disregard social responsibilities and constraints. In fact, people's deep-rooted bad habits tend to rise to the surface in a field free from mandatory "heteronomy"; they behave as they like: speak vulgar language, act against civility, refuse to follow ethical codes, etc. Moreover, some netizens do not register with their real names, nor do they use them; instead, they have virtual names (one person under several names sometimes)—factors that make it difficult to manage and supervise online behaviors. When judicial organs are trying to

---

[1] Guo Yongzhen, "Exploring the Path to a Legalized Network Society from the Perspective of Marxism", *The World & Chongqing*, 2016 (12).

crack down on cybercrimes, they find that the cost is high while clues are elusive.[1]

8.3.8   Want of multi-skilled governance talents

In recent years, cybercrimes have become further emboldened in China. Most of the criminals are intelligent and skilled in Internet application. They find cyber defects and loopholes, and then attack network systems, steal or tamper with confidential information. When this happens in the core areas of political, economic, and military systems that are crucial to national economic lifeline and national defense security, huge losses will occur. At present, although the Chinese government, NGOs and the public have their respective edges in network social governance, problems still exist. For instance, network supervisors and judicial personnel tend to confine themselves to their own professional fields; that is, the former have little knowledge of the latter's field, and vice versa. Consequently, some cybercrimes get away undetected or unpunished. Therefore, the participation of the government, social organizations and the public in network social governance is not sufficient, especially when cybercrimes involve high technology. With the development of the Internet, the shortage of multi-skilled talents (armed with both IT and legal knowledge) stands out as a severe problem in the effective prevention and handling of cybercrimes.[2]

8.3.9   Insufficient international cooperation on network social governance

At present, as the Internet is increasingly globalized or internationalized, developed and developing countries should cooperate more extensively in online social governance. However, since the international situation is complex in nature and keeps changing, and since every country puts their own interests in the first place, effective joint efforts are difficult to take for network governance. On the one hand, the developed countries, especially the United States, take advantage of their advanced hard and software technologies to export the so-called "freedom, equality and human rights" to those emerging network powers. On the other hand, the most important thing for countries to govern the Internet is to balance ideology, network sovereignty, and network liberty. As all sovereign countries aim to safeguard their own interests, it is difficult to achieve international cooperation in the network field in a short time.

---

[1] Cheng Lin, "Strengthening Network Social Governance to Create a Civilized Network Environment", *Journal of People's Public Security University of China (Social Sciences Edition)*, 2014 (3).

[2] Guo Yongzhen, "Exploring the Path to a Legalized Network Society from the Perspective of Marxism", *The World & Chongqing*, 2016 (12).

8.4   Direction for network social governance

On October 9, 2016, the Political Bureau of the CPC Central Committee held the 36th group study session to discuss the national cyber development strategy. General Secretary Xi Jinping pointed out that with the development of the Internet, especially that of the mobile Internet, social governance mode is shifting from one-way management to two-way interaction, from offline management to online-offline integration, from government's exclusive supervision to a governance style that attaches importance to collaboration between the government and social forces. This is a clear manifestation of applying the idea of governance to network society.[1] At the same time, General Secretary Xi Jinping also stressed that we need to accelerate and strengthen the security and defense capacity, to improve social governance through the network information technology, to amplify China's voices on the international stage and rule-making power over cyberspace, and to make unremitting efforts towards the goal of building a cyberspace power.[2] This provides a general direction and action guide for China's governance of network society.

8.4.1   Guidance on online public opinion

The Internet has become a distribution center of ideological and cultural information and the main battlefield for ideologies. Therefore, correct guidance of network public opinion becomes the prerequisite and foundation for successful network social governance. Then, how to guide online public opinion? First, we should form a unified, coordinated, responsive and efficient team, which respects objective facts and whose members have their respective duties and can give guidance in a timely manner. Second, the websites of governments at all levels should play the leadership function in applying new network technology and releasing authoritative and positive-energy information. In addition, the government can strengthen network supervision by taking rewarding and punishment measures, to ensure clean and clear cyberspaces. Third, once an online public opinion crisis occurs, the government should make prompt and truthful reports. Only by respecting the audience's right to get informed, can the government alleviate their dissatisfaction and thus avoid online uproar and panic. Meanwhile, there

---

[1] Xiong Guangqing, "The CPC's Exploration on the Governance of Internet Society since the 18th National Congress", *Theory and Reform*, 2017(2).

[2] Ibid.

should be follow-up stories and insightful elucidations; only in this way, can negative media speculation be avoided, and netizens' sense of social responsibility be enhanced.[1]

At the same time, we must constantly guide online public opinions, practice the core socialist values, uphold our mainstream ideology, and meet people's intellectual or cultural needs. Firstly, we should create online channels to give direct guidance, or provide explanations, or hold dialogues, thus helping netizens recognize public opinion objects and distinguish right from wrong. Only then can the government keep track of the current ideological orientation and take efforts to keep netizens' ideology on the right track. Only then a sound atmosphere of socialist public opinion culture can be created. Secondly, we should steer the theme of online ideology by vigorously spreading truths and fine traditional virtues. But importance should be attached to the art of steering. For instance, communication should be conducted in a friendly manner. As a matter of fact, when the governments at different levels are playing the guidance role, they are applying the Party's various policies and governance concepts to network information services, and thus stabilizing the order of network public opinions and consolidating our mainstream ideology. In fact, if the Internet should not be used to engage in intellectual and cultural activities of the socialist ideology which are salubrious, interesting and rich in content and popular with the general public, it would be taken over by other ideologies.

8.4.2   Innovation in network social governance

Network social governance is an important part of Chinese social governance. As it plays a significant role in maintaining social stability, we should constantly improve our governance competencies and levels, and update our notions of governance. For this purpose, first of all, the actors should make good sense of the new patterns or features of network social development. Negative attitudes like cyber phobia, hostility and contempt should give way to positive ones like cyber affinity, guidance and application.[2] Secondly, we should abandon the traditional method and the closed-minded, one-way administration mode. The practices of traditional method are no other than freezing up opinion channels. Of course, harmful online opinions should not be ignored, otherwise the network social order will be affected. Thirdly, government departments at all levels should take up their

---

[1] Yan Weiqing, Weng Licheng, "Cyberspace Social Ontology: Theoretical Foundations and Governance Paradigms in Virtual Communities", *Journal of Guangdong Institute of Public Administration*, 2013(5).

[2] Ran Lian, "Virtual Social Governance Innovation: Connotation, Challenges and Path", *Journal of Intelligence,* 2017 (2).

own responsibility and open direct channels for public opinions to get through, such as open forums, government affairs micro-blogs, and government affairs communities, to ensure people's rights to engage, to know and to have a say. In the face of crises, we should challenge them and resolve them. Finally, it is necessary to bear in mind that there are multiple governance actors: government departments, computer suppliers, NGOs, and netizens—they have to negotiate and cooperate with one another to resolve conflicts and disputes, and at the same time practice self-discipline and self-governance as far as possible in the network society.

8.4.3   Actor diversity in network social governance with Chinese Characteristics

As a new form of society, the cyberspace is virtual and has multiple centers and multiple nodes. Its governance objects are diversified and operation modes are complicated. We should coordinate the strengths of all netizens, and at the same time, define their rights and obligations. The purpose is to form a resource-sharing network social governance system, in which social consensus is maximized and the multiple governance actors can cooperate well.[1] Firstly, governments at all levels should play their roles well as policymakers, supervisors and arbitrators to achieve good governance effect. More channels should be created for social organizations and the public to engage in the governance. The functions of self-healing and self-purification should be enhanced to reduce the cost. Secondly, the government should establish a good "partnership" with social organizations and individual citizens. Online social organizations are important elements in the endeavor of good governance of network society. We should see to it that they operate within the bounds of the law, and on this ground, they are encouraged to manifest their vitality to the greatest extent, and then coordination is conducted among different organizations. In other words, a new form of partnership is to be established between the government and network social organizations based on the present framework of network social governance. At the same time, we should allow network social organizations to give full play to their role of governance. For instance, industrial associations and organizations can use more technical means than other governance actors, to directly administer the network with higher efficiency. Thirdly, individual engagement is the key to the good governance of online society. So it is necessary to cultivate netizens' civic awareness and cyber-ethics, which can help regulate their behavior and speech. As subjects of the network society, netizens should also be

---

[1] Li Leiming, "Strengthening and Innovating Network Social Governance." *Ningbo Daily*, Jul. 8, 2014.

encouraged to engage in social governance through some efficient and convenient platforms. In addition, the rights and obligations of multiple governance actors should be clearly defined to promote effective collaboration.[1]

8.4.4   Laws and regulations on network social governance

The Fourth Plenary Session of the 18th CPC Central Committee proposed boosting legislation concerning the virtual world to keep online behavior in the track of law. Legislatures at all levels should have their respective top-level designs, and, accordingly, introduce new laws, make amendments to established laws, abolish outdated laws, and provide interpretations to keep up with cyber IT progress. Only in this way, can the Internet be managed on the basis of legal codes. Then, law-breakers, either individuals or organizations, must take up their legal liability. To put it another way, the implementation of statutes is a sure guarantee for the Party's leadership over ideology.[2] Meanwhile, we should refer to the legislative experience of foreign countries, especially the legislative and practice experience of the United States on industrial and public interest standards and the EU legislative experience on network information security. Only in this way, can we promote cooperation and consistency between Chinese cyberspace governance laws and regulations and international cyberspace governance laws and regulations. Depending on foreign and domestic laws and regulations, we can make contributions to the establishment of an international cyber law system.[3]

8.4.5   Self-discipline of participants in the network society

It is urgent for China to conduct moral and ethical construction in network society. Moral and ethical principles can help regulate and restrain the behaviors of netizens, enterprises and industrial associations. Or rather, they can help them cultivate a strong sense of self-discipline, thus improving cyberspace environment and guaranteeing its vitality.

Internet self-discipline involves industrial and individual self-discipline. Industrial self-discipline means both the supervision from an affiliated industrial association or

---

[1] Liu Na, "Research on Governance Measures of Network Society in the Internet Era", *Heilongjiang Science and Technology Information*, 2017 (4).

[2] Shi Yanliu, "Realization and Strategic Transformation of Ideological Leadership of the Communist Party of China over the Virtual Society from the Perspective of Governance", *Truth Seeking*, 2016 (9).

[3] Ran Lian, "Virtual Social Governance Innovation: Connotation, Challenges and Path", *Journal of Intelligence*, 2017 (2).

organization, and the self-supervision of the online company itself. Individual self-discipline requires netizens to be "prudent even when alone", careful not to trespass the legal and ethical bottom lines, and to stand on guard against bad practices. However, Internet self-discipline cannot do without the supervision of the general public. So mutual discipline is needed between the public and the network.[1]

The cultivation of the Internet's moral self-discipline means that its members should have a strong sense of social responsibility. Online enterprises should effectively practice industrial ethics, and regulate and standardize their production activities. In other words, on the App service chain, service providers must oversee computer rooms, network access points, and network platforms, to ensure cybersecurity and keep unhealthy information away. Besides, corporate internal management should be strengthened—online business operation and cooperation should be procedure-based. Only in this way, can our sense of self-protection and our capabilities to resist malicious attack be enhanced, and eventually, can a virtual society of fair play be established.[2]

Netizens should observe ethical norms and build a sense of self-disciplining. On the one hand, we should have a strong sense of social responsibility, confining our own activities within the legal bounds, and cherishing the values of respect, moderation, integrity, salubrity and safety. On the other hand, the governmental watchdog departments should establish a set of ethical norms based on the psychology and habits of network users in China, for the Chinese netizens to follow and discipline themselves. In addition, we should attach great importance to cybersecurity education, vigorously disseminating public ethics and network ethics through a variety of mainstream media, and resolutely cracking down on rumormongers and illegal operators. What's more, we should practice the online real-name registration system, thus creating a salubrious network culture which seeks truth, goodness and beauty.

8.4.6 Cultivation of multi-skilled talents in network social governance

General Secretary Xi Jinping once remarked, "To build China into a cyber power we should pool all our resources of talent and train them to become a powerful force with political integrity, top-flight expertise and fine conduct. 'It is easy to muster a 1,000-

---

[1] Tang Huimin, Fan Hesheng, "The Construction of Cyberspace Rules and Soft Law Governance", *Study and Practice*, 2017 (3).

[2] Ran Lian, "Virtual Social Governance Innovation: Connotation, Challenges and Path", *Journal of Intelligence*, 2017 (2).

man army, but hard to find a capable general.' We should train globally renowned scientists, leading Internet sci-tech figures, outstanding engineers and high-level innovation teams."[1] This shows that the CPC Central Committee with Xi Jinping at the core attaches great importance to cultivating network sci-tech talents. Thereupon, with the growing influence of the network society on the real society, China should not only cultivate a large number of high-tech talents who are proficient at network technology, but also train network social governance talents who are both specialists in IT and universalists in many other fields.[2]

Firstly, we should make full use of higher education institutions to cultivate multi-skilled, innovative, competent talents who are not only capable of researching and developing network technology and applications (including network construction and maintenance, software development and programming, information security and maintenance, etc.), but are also good at applying the rule of law to the network social governance. Then, we can effectively defend ourselves against negative impact from the network, and thus maintain national cybersecurity. Secondly, in-service network technicians should have regular and targeted legal publicity education and training, so that they can develop and apply core network technologies within the bounds of law and stop high-tech crimes opportunely and efficiently in the virtual world. Finally, legal practitioners should receive training in computer science and network technology, so that they can find the causes of online crimes and determine the nature of particular cases. Their jobs can help ameliorate the network society legislation. In short, network social governance requires specialist skills. Only by turning out a large number of network social governance talents proficient in both computer science and law, can China constantly improve national network governance level and governance competence.[3]

8.4.7   Establishment of a sound system for international governance cooperation

In recent years, network information has been flowing freely from country to country. As the online boundaries are growing increasingly ambiguous, national sovereignty is sometimes disturbed. Therefore, it is urgent for every country to cooperate with each other for effective governance of the network society. On December

---

[1] Xi Jinping, *The Governance of China*, Vol. Ⅰ, Beijing: Foreign Languages Press, 2018.
[2] Guo Yongzhen, "Exploring the Path to a Legalized Network Society from the Perspective of Marxism", *The World & Chongqing*, 2016 (12).
[3] Ibid.

16, 2015, General Secretary Xi Jinping delivered a speech at the Second World Internet Conference, in which he proposed four Internet governance principles (respect for cyber sovereignty, maintenance of peace and security, promotion of openness and cooperation, and good order) and five points in the endeavor of building a community of shared future in cyberspace. Obviously, respect for network sovereignty is fundamental for countries to cooperate in building a sound system of international Internet governance.

We need to practice collaboration across the globe in the network social governance, for which multiparty participation is a prerequisite. National governments, international social organizations (such as some international cybercrime supervision associations), NGOs, industrial and commercial enterprises and citizens—all these players should conduct both extensive and intensive communication and cooperation with one another, establish a multi-level and long-term cooperation mechanism by way of dialogue and negotiation, and formulate global cyberspace governance rules, so that the online society can operate in a salubrious and orderly manner. Besides, a sound assistance mechanism in international law enforcement and administration of justice for cybercrimes should be established. Then cyber security can be better guaranteed and the combat against cybercrimes can be more effective. What's more, a technical exchange platform is required, so that countries can learn from each other in terms of advanced Internet technology, and jointly contain IT abuse, cyber monitoring and hacker attacks. In this way, transnational cybercrimes and cyber terrorism can be tackled forcefully.

Chapter 9
The Establishment and Development of Modern Emergency Management System

Social governance encompasses both routine practices and emergency responses. As the world continues to modernize, human society faces greater risks. Like other countries, China is exploring new models and approaches to daily routines and emergency responses in social governance, to establish a modern emergency management system with Chinese characteristics.

Emergency management is the all-round and full-process management of emergencies (including natural disasters, accidents and disasters, public health emergencies, and social security incidents), covering emergency prevention and preparedness, monitoring and early warning, emergency response and relief, and recovery and reconstruction. Emergency management and regular social governance are two sides of the same coin. On the one hand, people live and work in a normal state. On the other hand, they may be subject to emergencies. Therefore, both routine governance and emergency management are necessary. Emergency management and human activities are intertwined and changes with time. China is a country of high hazard vulnerability. In combating against natural and man-made disasters, we have accumulated rich experience and fostered a unique model of disaster prevention. However, most of the traditional emergency management in China responded passively instead of ahead of the disasters. The current department-based management has flaws in that each department is responsible for a single disaster. As a result, there is inadequate comprehensive management and difficulties in coordination between departments albeit relatively smooth vertical management within a department. Relying on single experience, China lacks comprehensive, systematic, and in-depth research and a law-based, well-conceived, and sensible system for emergency administration.

China did not deploy and promote emergency governance in a systematic, law-based, and scientific way until 2003 when it won the fight against SARS. An emergency response system has been built in the 11th and 12th Five-year Plan, and a Chinese-style modern emergency response system with "One Plan and Three Systems" as its core has been put in place and is steadily moving forward.[1] It has contributed to preventing and controlling China's major emergency and safeguarding public security for China's reform and opening up, and modernization.

9.1 The start of China's modern emergency management system

9.1.1 The sudden outbreak of SARS

From the end of 2002 to the spring of 2003, a sudden SARS epidemic raged across China, severely threatening people's health and lives, taking a grave toll on the reform and opening up and modernization, and the social life in some areas. According to the statistics released by the World Health Organization (WHO) on April 21, 2004, a total of 8,096 cases were confirmed and 774 people died from 29 countries and regions from November 2002 to July 2003. China had a total of 7,429 cases, and 685 deaths (accounting for 91.8 % and 88.5 % of the global cases respectively) with the mortality rate of 9.2%. Other countries had a total of 667 confirmed cases and 89 deaths with the mortality being 13.3%. The Chinese mainland claimed 5,327 confirmed cases and 349 deaths, raising the mortality to 6.6%. Most cases were from Beijing, Guangdong, Shanxi, Inner Mongolia, Hebei, and Tianjin. Beijing and Guangdong reported 4,033 cases, accounting for 75.7% of the total cases in Chinese mainland.

The SARS epidemic broke out unexpectedly and spread rapidly, taking a grave toll on the socio-economic activities like tourism, air traffic services, food services, and foreign exchanges. As some of China's outbound activities were affected, some international conferences and events originally scheduled to be held in China were

---

[1] As a late starter, who embarked on modern emergency management in 2004, China is updating and deepening its understanding of the basic emergency management concepts and theories. For example, the two pairs of concepts in this book, "public emergency" and "emergency", "emergency response system" and "emergency management system", though different in references, deliver the same meaning. Prior to 2007, "public emergency" was used in national plans on emergency response. After the Emergency Response Law of the People's Republic of China was promulgated, "public emergency" was amended to "emergency". In the establishment and planning of emergency response system of the 11th, 12th and 13th Five-year Plan, "emergency response system" was widely used, while the academic circles normally adopt "emergency management system".

postponed or even cancelled, gravely damaging China's international image. SARS is a perplexing disease which has not been fully recognized by human. It is the first major global public health crisis for the 21st century and also a daunting challenge in terms of state social emergency governance.

9.1.2   Practice and enlightenment in the fight against SARS

After a brief period of ignorance, disorder and confusion, the CPC Central Committee took a stock of the situation, made crucial decisions and adopted a series of effective countermeasures in April 2003 as they recognized the dire damage that SARS had caused and might cause further. Local Party committees and governments at all levels were in the front line of fully implementing the decisions and plans made by the CPC Central Committee. The Chinese government took immediate actions to prevent and control group infection and the whole society was set in motion to join the people's war against SARS. Since mid-May 2003, the daily confirmed cases and tolls decreased significantly, the number of cured patients spiraled upwards. The epidemic was under control. On May 23, 2003, the WHO announced in Geneva that it had decided to cancel travel warnings to the Hong Kong SAR and Guangdong Province, in which the SARS epidemic was considered under control. Since the beginning of June 2003, daily confirmed cases had significantly decreased to zero or less than ten. On June 24, 2003, the WHO announced to withdraw the tourism warning of Beijing and remove Beijing from the list of SARS-affected areas. This indicated that China controlled the pandemic, making initial progress in fighting against SARS and reducing the losses caused by the epidemic. China owed its fast victory in the battle to the strong leadership of the CPC Central Committee who adopted both old practices and pioneering new methods. Two aspects have deeply impressed people.

9.1.2.1   Timely epidemic information release

At the beginning of the SARS epidemic, hearsay, speculations and even rumors spread far and wide due to the unclear causes, high infection rate and daunting mortality. The whole society was plunged into panic, anxiety and shock, causing panic buying of daily necessities, food and medicines, aggravating the social chaos. Some doubted whether the government could control the epidemic and hospital treat and cure the patients. The CPC Central Committee and the State Council soon realized the importance and urgency to disclose information, and decided to make information transparent. This helped the government regain the initiative in public opinions. From

April 20, 2003, the State Council required the health department to hold a press conference timely and disclose the latest information about the epidemic to the public every day. From April 26, 2003 to June 26, 2003, CCTV (China Central Television) broadcast live the Daily Epidemic Report of the health department at 4 p.m. every day. From early April to June 24, 2003, 67 press conferences were held by the health department. Epidemic-related information was open to the public on time and their right to know was safeguarded. The Chinese government won the trust of its people at home and abroad. As their panic and anxiety were well eased, people became rational to the epidemic, and willing to help and support the government.

9.1.2.2 Epidemic control depending on science and technology, laws, and the public

"Three Depends", namely depending on science and technology, laws, and the public, is the main approach with which we combated SARS and also the valuable experience we have learned. First, the Regulation on Responses to Public Health Emergencies were formulated immediately. The State Council merely took roughly 20 days including motion and promulgation to announce the regulations, the shortest time in the Chinese history. The promulgation marks that China's public health emergency response has embarked on the track of the rule of law. Second, we strengthened scientific research on disease diagnosis, treatment, and epidemic prevention. On the basis of summing up the treatment experience in Guangdong and other places, health authorities revised and supplemented relevant treatment standards, and took effective measures such as the combined use of traditional Chinese medicine and Western medicine for better efficacy. At the same time, we set up a joint research group consisting of experts in health, education, science and technology, and military systems to research SARS etiology. A SARS laboratory research network was built up to enable researchers to exchange research results, samples, and experimental information, and to concentrate on finding the etiology and pathogen. We carried out the research and production of SARS vaccines, therapeutic drugs and rapid temperature detection equipment. We strengthened exchanges and cooperation with WHO and other international organizations. A contact mechanism for SARS prevention and control was set up with Hong Kong SAR and Macao SAR. We fully listened to the opinions of experts from all walks of life to make decisions more scientific. Third, we established a joint prevention and control mechanism. SARS spread rapidly across different regions and cities, in which the large population flow increased the risk of epidemic spread. As each region is administered independently, traditional management approaches based on local leadership, and resource integration could not effectively respond to the new changes brought by SARS epidemic. Such being the case, the CPC Central Committee decided to set up a joint working group to take charge of SARS prevention and control of the Party and government organs, armed forces, group organizations and public institutions based in Beijing. The central government asked to implement joint prevention and control, requiring Beijing, Tianjin, Hebei and Inner Mongolia to inform each other of the epidemic situation, learn, support and help each other, and coordinate joint prevention and control. Fourth, we implemented localized management and group prevention and treatment in key areas and groups; especially rural areas, migrant workers, and college students based on primary-level communities, units, and school to prevent the spread caused by the flow of population. In the rural areas with weak public health foundation, a group prevention and control system of "self-prevention by people, villages and towns" was formed.

After the successful fight against SARS, the CPC Central Committee and the State Council summed up what they had learned. First, the health emergency must be comprehensively strengthened. The epidemic has exposed deficiencies in managing major public health emergencies. The outstanding issues include the absence of a uniform system of emergency command, an ineffective emergency plan to respond to public health events, a deficient information reporting network for major infectious diseases, and the need for strengthening and upgrading emergent medical treatment capacity and disease prevention and control systems. The deficiencies and problems lead to the failure of timely and effective response to public health emergency, contributing to the spread of epidemic. Learning from the bitter experience, China initiated the building of the national public health emergency system. According to the decisions and plans by the central government, China's public health emergency systems consist of the following main respects: the command system of public health emergency, the system of disease prevention and control, the medical treatment system, and the system of health law enforcement supervision. Second, to promote the top-level design of the emergency system. After the phased winning in the battle over SARS in 2003, China based on the health emergency work and adopted a top-level strategy by incorporating emergency response in the public health field into the comprehensive emergency system centered on "One Plan and Three Systems". It has laid a sound foundation for China's modern emergency system development.

9.1.3 The full start of building a modern emergency management system

In October 2003, the Third Plenary Session of the 16th CPC Central Committee adopted the Decision of the Central Committee of the Communist Party of China on Some Issues Concerning the Improvement of the Socialist Market Economy, making a clarion call to "establish sound mechanisms for emergency response and improve the government's ability to respond to emergencies and risks". In 2004, the State Council decided to make it a top priority to improve emergency plans, establish a sound emergency response mechanism, and improve the government's capacity for addressing emergencies.

At the start of 2004, Hua Jianmin, the then State Councilor and Secretary General of the State Council, held a working meeting, attended by leading officials of the departments of the State Council, on formulating and revising emergency plans. This is the first special meeting on emergency management held by the State Council. Hua Jianmin systematically specified the formulation and revision of the emergency plan, and the development of emergency system, mechanisms and legal systems. He pointed out that this formidable work required a lot of arduous efforts with institutional development as the foundation. The key was to formulate and improve the plan for public emergency, and work hard to establish a sound emergency mechanism and law system. Later in the same year, in Zhengzhou and Tianjin, he presided over the working conferences on making emergency preparation plans for partial provinces and metropolitans, further elaborating the formulation and improvement of public emergency plans, the establishment of a sound management system, mechanism and legal system for responding to public emergency, and the dialectical relationship between "One Plan" and "Three Systems".

On March 14, 2005, the Third Session of the 10th National People's Congress reviewed and adopted the Report of the Work of the Government 2005, which wrote "we have formulated the overall emergency plan for national emergency, as well as 105 special and departmental emergency plans for response to natural disasters, accidents and disasters, public health and social security. Provinces (autonomous regions and municipalities directly under the central government) have also completed the preparation of the overall emergency plan at the provincial level". The report fully affirmed the achievements made by the governments at all levels in emergency management in the previous year, showing that the government attached great importance to emergency management. On July 22, 2005, the first national emergency management conference was held in Beijing. Then Premier Wen Jiabao, made an important speech, stressing that governments at all levels should focus on "One Plan and Three Systems" and comprehensively strengthen emergency management. In

October 2005, the Fifth Plenary Session of the 16th CPC Central Committee adopted the Proposal on Formulating the 11th Five-Year Plan for National Economic and Social Development, calling for establishing a sound social early warning system and a mechanism for emergency relief and social mobilization, and improving the ability to control emergencies.

On March 15, 2006, the Fourth Session of the 10th National People's Congress approved the Outline of the 11th Five-Year Plan for the National Economic and Social Development of the People's Republic of China. In the chapter of "Strengthening Public Security", specific arrangements were made to strengthen the capacity for disaster prevention and mitigation, improve workplace safety, ensure food and medicine safety, maintain national security and social stability, and enhance building the emergency response system. In June 2006, the State Council issued the Opinions on Comprehensively Strengthening Emergency Management. On July 7, 2006, Hua Jianmin made an important speech at the second National Conference on Emergency Management in Beijing. On September 23, 2006, he attended the meeting on emergency management and plan preparation of central enterprises in Nanjing and addressed an important speech.

In October 2006, the Sixth Plenary Session of the 16th CPC Central Committee approved the Decision on Major Issues concerning Building a Harmonious Socialist Society (hereinafter referred to as the Decision), which proposed a complete schedule for "One Plan and Three Systems" for the first time. The Decision proposed to improve the emergency management systems to effectively respond to various risks, establish a sound localized emergency management system with category-based management, different levels of responsibility, and tiered arrangements, forming an emergency management mechanism with unified leadership, nimble response, orderly coordination and efficient operation, so as to respond to natural disasters, accidents and disasters, public health events and social security events, and improve the ability of emergency management and risk resilience. In the light of the principle of paying equal attention to prevention and emergency response, and combining the routine management with emergency response, we should establish a unified and efficient emergency information platform and professional emergency rescue teams, improve the emergency plan system, refine relevant laws and regulations, raise public awareness, expand public participation, and improve their ability of self-rescue. That is how China realizes the coordinated movement of social early warning, social mobilization, rapid response and emergency response.

On May 19, 2007, Hua Jianmin made an important speech at the National Grassroots Emergency Management Forum held in Zhuji, Zhejiang Province. In July 2007, the General Office of the State Council issued Opinions on Strengthening Emergency Management at the Primary Level. On August 30, 2007, the 29th Session of the Standing Committee of the 10th National People's Congress adopted the Emergency Response Law of the People's Republic of China. This is a general law for strengthening China's emergency management and a fundamental law for emergency prevention and response. It serves as legal protection for the government to practice the law, prevent and respond to emergency in scientific approaches.

From 2003 to 2007, China witnessed a rapid development of its emergency management with a clear development trajectory in a step-by-step manner. The emergency management forged ahead in an orderly and comprehensive way. The year of 2003 represented a year for China to sum up the experience and lessons of SARS, and it was the first year for China to embark on developing its emergency management. The year of 2004 can be called the year of compiling national emergency plan. The year of 2005 saw China's implementation of emergency plan. The year of 2006 witnessed China's further promotion of "One Plan and Three Systems" and emergency management going into enterprises. In 2007, China promoted the emergency management system and saw emergency management going into the grassroots level.

9.2 The development of emergency management system in the 11th Five-Year Plan period

9.2.1 Issue and implementation of the special development plan in the 11th Five-Year Plan

On December 31, 2006, the State Council issued National Emergency Management System Plan During the 11th Five-Year Plan Period (hereinafter referred to as the Plan). The Plan is divided into six chapters: preface, emergency system, guiding principles, development concepts and objectives, overall planning and main tasks, key projects, and policies and measures. It is China's first all-round comprehensive national special plan for emergency management. It is a programmatic paper guiding the establishment of China's emergency response system during the 11th Five-year Plan period.

9.2.1.1   The basic orientation of the Plan

Following the requirements of category-based management, different levels of responsibility, linear and local leadership combined, and localization, the Plan implemented fully the deployment of emergency response system in the 11th Five-year Plan. On the basis of keeping the existing division of responsibilities and classified management pattern among the departments, the Plan, supported by corresponding special plans, specified the targets and tasks of the emergency system development. We must make full use of and integrate idle resources including emergency response information, work teams, devices and supplies in all regions and industries. We need to make it a priority to strengthen the weak links and solve common problems across the board, and improve the comprehensive capacity for preventing and responding to extraordinarily serious public emergencies. The National Overall Plan for Public Emergency, its special plans and departmental plans clarify and standardize the responsibilities, procedures and operation mechanisms for emergency prevention and response. While the tasks and projects clarified in the Plan laid a foundation for the implementation of all kinds of emergency plans at different levels.

9.2.1.2   The guiding principles of the Plan

Guided by Deng Xiaoping Theory and the Theory of Three Represents[1], we must put in place the scientific outlook on development, adhere to the people-centered philosophy, emphasize both emergency prevention and response, combine routine measures with abnormal ones, coordinate overall planning and key development, and focus on short-term tasks and long-term goals. We should play full use of science and technology, and potential sources, and ensure more projects to settle, strengthen the weak links and solve common problems on extremely severe public emergency. We should strengthen public awareness, social participation, comprehensive ability to control public emergencies as we seek to protect people's lives and property, maintain social stability, and promote the comprehensive, coordinated and sustainable development of economy and society and build a harmonious socialist society.

9.2.1.3   The principles of the Plan

By effectively using potential resources, sharing resources, specifying tasks and dividing responsibility, we should make full use of existing resources, tap potentials,

---

[1] It refers to represent the development trend of China's advanced productive forces, represent the orientation of China's advanced culture, represent the fundamental interests of the overwhelming majority of the Chinese people. The principal proponent is Jiang Zemin. —*Tr.*

strengthen integration, improve efficiency and avoid redundant projects; give full play to the role of policy guidance, introduce market-based mechanism, and mobilize all parties to participate in establishing the emergency system. Government management should be coordinated with social participation to improve the socialization of emergency management.

9.2.1.4 The objectives of the Plan

On the basis of the 11th Five-year Plan and the Opinions of the State Council on Strengthening Emergency Management in an All-Round Way, the Plan specified the overall goal for establishing the system of national emergency response in the 11th Five-year Plan period. That is to form a mechanism for public emergency response with unified leadership, relevant structure, nimble response, efficient operation and powerful guarantee by 2010, to strengthen the capacity for public emergency response, public emergency prevention and preparation, monitoring and early warning, emergency disposal, recovery and reconstruction, and emergency support, to significantly improve the overall capability for emergency governance, and to reduce the number of extremely severe and major public emergencies and decrease the fatality and property losses. To realize the goal, the Plan put forward 20 detailed indicators as the classified targets. Among them, the indicator in natural disaster focused on the ability of monitoring and early warning and disaster relief. The indicator in accidents and disasters stressed the effect of prevention and rescue. The indicator in public health events targeted the ability of early detection and emergency response. The indicator in social security events aimed at comprehensive prevention and control.

9.2.1.5 The primary tasks and key projects of the Plan

The Plan stressed ten aspects, including monitoring and early warning, information and command, emergency response teams, material supplies, emergency transport, communication support, recovery and reconstruction, scientific and technological support, training and drill, and emergency management demonstration. It coordinated the overall planning and concrete tasks of the emergency response system in the 11th Five-year Plan period. Through full consideration and utilization of the existing resources, general requirements as well as specific tasks were specified for relevant departments and local authorities. After full discussion and overall consideration, the Plan selected 10 key projects, each of which was directly corresponding to or closely related to the construction objectives and main tasks of the emergency system. They were profoundly significant in that they all affected the overall picture of China's emergency management work.

9.2.2   Achievements in the 11th Five-Year Plan period

With considerable attention by the CPC Central Committee and the State Council, governments at all levels and related departments remained committed to the people-oriented approach, equal importance to prevention and disposal, and integration of regular and emergent management. The Plan for the Development of National Public Emergency Response System in the 11th Five-Year Plan period was implemented in full around the improvement of the capacity for emergency control. Government authorities intensified their efforts to set up the emergency plan, the system, mechanism and laws of emergency response, with remarkable achievements made in our thematic education initiative on emergency response. In Summary, it is "Improvements in Eight Capacities" as follows.

9.2.2.1   A package of systems was established

Governments at all levels set up leading emergency management institutions and administrative bodies with considerable efforts made by related government authorities in different regions following clear division of responsibilities and personnel allocations. A primary emergency response system should incorporate unified leadership, integrated coordination, category-based management, tiered responsibility, and localized governance. Emergency committees were set up in 24 provinces (autonomous regions and municipalities). Seven provinces (autonomous regions) defined leading emergency management bodies. All provinces (autonomous regions and municipalities) established emergency management offices. Some local authorities strengthened the emergency management system in the reform of government institutions. More than 96% of the prefecture-level cities in China and over 80% of the county-level governments founded emergency management agencies.

9.2.2.2   A package of mechanisms was improved

First, we established a sound mechanism for risk screening, monitoring and early warning. The emergency platform led by the State Council was established. The comprehensive capability for the monitoring and early warning of disasters related to meteorology, earthquake, health, hydrology, geology, and forest fire prevention was improved. Gas monitoring system was established in high-gas mines, coal and gas outburst and low-gas mines. A 100% network direct reporting rate was achieved of public health emergencies and infectious diseases in disease prevention and control institutions at all levels. A food safety information network was completed in over 300 cities in China.

Second, a sound emergency response mechanism was established. Departments in safety, civil affairs, public health, environmental protection, transportation, water conservancy, agriculture, safety regulation, seismology and meteorology established a mechanism for information sharing and coordinated emergency response. A joint mechanism for coordinating regional response was set up in the Pan-Pearl River Delta, Shanghai-Jiangsu-Zhejiang, Jiangsu-Anhui-Shandong-Henan, the three northeast provinces (Liaoning, Jilin and Heilongjiang), the Yellow Sea and Bohai Sea, and the six central provinces (Shanxi, Henan, Anhui, Hubei, Jiangxi and Hunan) was established. The Ministry of Foreign Affairs, the Ministry of Public Security, the Ministry of Transportation, the Ministry of Commerce, the Ministry of civil affairs, China Earthquake Administration and other departments and units established a well-conceived mechanism for foreign-related emergency prevention and response.

Third, a sound mechanism for post-disaster restoration and reconstruction was set up. In response to major and extraordinarily serious disasters and other emergencies, China promptly released a series of policies on disaster relief and support, compensation, solatium, subsidies and pensions, and resettlement in accordance with the law. Plans for restoration and reconstruction were formulated in a timely manner, and relevant policies and measures to resume production, life and social order were introduced. Less than two months after the earthquake in Yushu County, Qinghai Province, the State Council issued the Overall Plan for Post-Disaster Restoration and Reconstruction of Yushu, carrying out the post-disaster reconstruction at the fastest speed.

9.2.2.3 A set of plans was improved

First, we intensified our efforts to draw up plans. An overall plan for national emergency response, a special emergency plan and a departmental emergency plan were established. More than 2.4 million emergency plans at all levels were formulated, providing action guidance for all kinds of major emergencies. All provincial and prefectural governments and more than 90% of the governments at county-level compiled the overall emergency plan. All kinds of emergency plans at different levels basically covered common emergencies, of which the plans for workplace safety covered all high-risk industries, playing an important role in responding to emergencies.

Second, the plan management and drill were strengthened. A dynamic management system of plan preparation, reporting, drill, assessment and revision was formulated to continuously make the plan more targeted, feasible and practical. In accordance with the requirements of the Emergency Response Law of the People's Republic of China, local governments carried out more than 1.54 million emergency drills at different levels in flood control and emergency rescue, earthquake rescue, fire and rescue, chemical leakage prevention, environmental pollution control, response to public health events, maritime rescue, extensive blackout response, emergency communication security, anti-terrorism and nuclear accidents. More than 180 million people participated in the drill, playing a positive role in plan inspection, team training, mechanism running-in, and raising public awareness.

9.2.2.4 A set of laws and regulations was promulgated

On November 1, 2007, the Emergency Response Law was officially put in place, marking that China managed its emergencies in a law-based and well-conceived manner. More than 70 laws and regulations concerning natural disasters, workplace safety, public health and social security were formulated or revised. We formulated or revised the Regulation on the Defense against Meteorological Disasters, Regulation on the Implementation of the Food Safety Law of the People's Republic of China, and other relevant laws and regulations for the departments and central authorities. Local governments, in Beijing, Liaoning, Hunan, Guangdong, Shandong and other places issued local laws and regulations to implement the response law.

9.2.2.5 A powerful rescue team was formed

First, we built up specialized emergency rescue teams. Governments at all levels and their relevant departments expanded the specialized emergency rescue teams for public security firefighting, earthquake rescue, flood fighting and emergency rescue, forest fire fighting, maritime and land search and rescue, emergency communication, road access, emergency transportation, railway rescue, electric power repair, mine rescue, hazardous chemicals disposal, medical treatment, health and epidemic prevention and nuclear accident disposal.

Second, we established rescue teams for comprehensive emergency response. Based on departments of public security and fire prevention and control, comprehensive emergency rescue teams were set up in 31 provinces (autonomous regions and municipalities), all prefectural cities and 90% of counties.

Third, we strongly support full-time and part-time rescue teams and volunteer teams. All levels of governments promoted enterprises and institutions to establish full-time and part-time rescue teams undertaking the assistance of emergency rescue. The departments in civil affairs, transportation, earthquake administration and other sectors, along with the Central Committee of the Communist Youth League, and the Red Cross, etc. devoted themselves to the building of emergency volunteer team with nearly ten million registered volunteers.

Fourth, we promoted the military rescue team to be incorporated into the national emergency team system. The army established eight emergency teams in flood relief and emergency rescue, earthquake rescue, traffic emergency rescue, maritime emergency search and rescue, emergency communication support, medical and epidemic prevention rescue, nuclear and biochemical emergency rescue, and air emergency transportation services. The armed police established a professional emergency rescue team for hydropower and transportation, and further strengthened the building of specialized emergency rescue teams for anti-terrorism, anti-hijacking and earthquake disasters.

Fifth, the expert teams were further developed. The State Council and most provinces (autonomous regions and municipalities) formed expert groups to provide decision-making suggestions for emergency management.

9.2.2.6 A vision was reinforced

Taking the opportunity of implementing the Emergency Response Law, Party schools, administrative colleges and other training institutions at all levels listed emergency management as a compulsory training course, and held more than 400,000 emergency management training sessions at different levels, further enhancing the government awareness of timely and proper emergency response, and strengthening the awareness and understanding of "human life is of vital importance".

9.2.2.7 An awareness was cultivated

Public safety knowledge was incorporated into the national education system. The responsibility of workplace safety was further clarified, and the safety knowledge and emergency skills training for employees was widely carried out. May 12 was set as the National Day for Disaster Prevention and Mitigation, aiming to promote the popularization and education of emergency management into enterprises, communities, rural areas and families. More than 3 million diverse activities were organized, and more than 20 billion copies of popularization and education materials were distributed, benefiting more than 7 billion personnel times. As a result, the public awareness of disaster prevention and risk avoidance, and the ability of self-help and mutual rescue were significantly improved.

9.2.2.8   A set of capabilities were improved

First, the capacity for ensuring emergency supplies and funds was improved. All regions and related departments strengthened emergency material reserves and specialized rescue devices for flood control and drought relief, earthquake prevention and disaster mitigation, major epidemic response and medical treatment. A reserve network for emergency supplies at national, provincial, municipal and county levels was established. The variety and quantity of relief supplies were increased significantly compared with the early period of the 11th Five-year Plan.

Second, the infrastructure for disaster relief was improved. In early 2008, after extensive low temperature, rain, snow and freezing occurred in southern China, the safety standards of power, road, communication and other infrastructure were raised. After the Wenchuan Earthquake on May 12, 2008, the seismic fortification level in schools, hospitals and other densely populated places across the country were raised. The flood control projects of the Yangtze River and Yellow River etc. and coastal dams were consolidated. More than 100,000 emergency shelters were built in administrative divisions above the county level. Emergency shelters were set up in provincial capitals and large and medium-sized cities.

Third, the capacity for supporting major engineering projects in emergency management was improved. Ten key projects were implemented, including the national emergency platform system, the early warning information release system, the national land search and rescue base, the national nuclear & biochemical emergency rescue base, the national air emergency transportation service base, the national emergency material support system, the national public emergency satellite communication network, the national emergency management personnel training base, and so on. They played an important role in responding to major emergencies.

Thanks to the "Improvements in Eight Capacities" mentioned above, China's ability to prevent and control emergencies was significantly improved. China has withstood severe tests of all kinds of major emergencies, and successfully coped with natural disasters such as low temperature, freezing rain and snow in southern China, the mega earthquake in Wenchuan, the intensive earthquake in Yushu, the mountain torrent and debris flow in Zhouqu, Gansu Province. We successfully carried out rescue operations in Wangjialing coal mine, prevented and controlled the H1N1 influenza, highly pathogenic avian influenza and other public health incidents, minimizing casualty and property loss caused by the incidents, and maintaining social harmony and stability.

9.2.3　Weak links in the emergency system development

Although remarkable achievements were made in the development of China's emergency management system during the 11th Five-year Plan period, China's emergency response system still shows many weak links when benchmarked against the needs of the people, the new changes in China's modernization drive and the capacity of developed countries.

First, the overall capacity for emergency management was weak. The system, mechanism and plan for community-level emergency management needed to be improved. The overall emergency capacity was weak. The development of emergency management in communities, villages, schools, enterprises and other grassroots organizations and institutions was unbalanced. The grassroots officials and technical personnel lacked systematic emergency capacity training. Some infrastructures such as bridges, tunnels, embankments, reservoirs lifeline projects were weak in face of disasters. The infrastructure for disaster prevention and mitigation in urban and rural areas was poorly developed, especially in rural areas. The ability to rapidly assess and recover losses was yet to be strengthened. More studies and research on the occurrence and forecasting of major natural disasters and public health incidents were yet to be deepened. The timeliness, accuracy and coverage of early warning information release needed to be further improved. The system of standardized emergency management required further improvements. Generally, the ability to prevent and mitigate disasters with the power of science and technology was low.

Second, the ability of emergency response coordination and inter-connectivity needed to be strengthened. The coordinated ability of emergency management and the functions of emergency command system needed to be improved. The mechanism for close coordination between regions, departments, sections, and between the armed force and local authorities was insufficient. The joint training and drill for different types of emergency teams was insufficient, making it difficult to quickly form joint force in emergency response, and to properly integrate various disaster relief elements. Due to different standards of emergency communication and information system among relevant departments, it was difficult to fully share information resources.

Third, emergency rescue can be more professional. The number and types of professional rescue equipment were far from enough, large-scale and special professional equipment was insufficient, and the basic conditions of training and drill needed significant improvement. Nuclear and biochemical emergency rescue, marine oil spill emergency response, anti-terrorism and emergency response teams needed further development. The professional means and ability to quickly gain and transmit on-site information were insufficient. The emergency supply reserves were limited in types and quantity and with a poorly-designed layout. The system for comprehensive information dynamic management and resource sharing management of all kinds of emergency materials needed to be improved. The capacity for fast transporting bulk emergency materials and large equipment was still gravely insufficient. The comprehensive coordination mechanism of multiple transportation modes needed to be improved.

Fourth, social participation in emergency management needed to be intensified. The public's participation in emergency management was not well-organized or standardized enough. Professional volunteers are in shortage. The culture of public safety of participation by whole society was not yet formed. The publicity and education of knowledge about emergency response needed to be strengthened. Emergency training and drill involving volunteers and the public needed to be further standardized and strengthened. The mechanism for emergency social mobilization and the disaster insurance needed to be improved. The government policies and systems that encourage enterprises to participate in the development of emergency industry remained to be improved.

9.3   The development of emergency management system in the 12th Five–Year Plan period

9.3.1   The issue and implementation of the special development plan in the 12th Five-Year Plan period

By summarizing the achievements and shortcomings of China's emergency system development during the 11th Five-year Plan period, and analyzing the trend of China's economic and social development and the characteristics of emergencies in the next five years, the State Council continued to support the preparation of special plans for the emergency system. In August 2012, the General Office of the State Council issued The 12th Five-Year Plan for the Development of the National Emergency Response System (hereinafter referred to as the 12th Five-year Plan). This was the second five-year special plan for emergency system. It continued with the structure of the 11th Five-year Plan, including five parts: status quo, guiding concept, basic principles and goals, main tasks, key projects, relevant policies and safeguard measures. The 12th Five-year Plan inherited the achievements made in the 11th Five-year Plan. It was a plan that forged ahead by sustainable innovation and upgrading.

Unlike the 11th Five-year Plan, the 12th Five-year Plan prioritized strengthening emergency management foundation and the improvement of the ability to cope with major emergencies in terms of guiding concept, devoting to intensifying weak links and solving common problems, and quickening the establishment of a national emergency system with unified leadership, well-conceived structure, nimble response, powerful guarantee and efficient operation. It pursued to improve the nation's comprehensive ability to cope with the complex and changeable public security situations to minimize the casualties and hazards, and advance sustainable development of economy and society in an all-round and coordinated fashion.

The 12th Five-year Plan followed the principle of overall planning, focusing on key points, scientific layout, comprehensive planning, device upgrading, government responsibility, social coordination, category- and tier-based principle and solid foundation. China worked to strengthen the weak links of the emergency system and the priority development capacity, by focusing on emergency prevention and preparedness, improving the capacity for emergency prevention and response and solving the prominent problems such as weak foundation and insufficient coordination and connectivity of primary-level community. We effectively made full use and tap the potential of the military reserve resources and local resources to realize sharing. We promoted the integration of information, personnel, equipment, supplies from various regions and industries, improved the capacity for comprehensive emergency response, and avoided redundant construction projects. By refining the pattern of emergency management, we made sure that governments at all levels fulfill their responsibilities so as to realize the integration of government, society and individuals. We followed policy guidance, introduced market-based mechanism, mobilized all parties to participate in the emergency system construction, and expanded social participation in emergency management. Governments at all levels and relevant departments were given due tasks in a reasonable and power-based manner and performed their duties and responsibilities.

The 12th Five-year Plan, like the 11th Five-year Plan, set both overall and specific goals. The overall goal stipulated that by 2015, the national emergency response system would be further improved. The basic capacity of emergency management such as major infrastructure disaster resistance and urban-rural disaster prevention and mitigation would be significantly enhanced. The comprehensive emergency response capacity such as emergency prevention and preparedness, monitoring and early warning, emergency response, recovery and reconstruction and emergency support would be significantly strengthened. The security of lives and property of the people would be fully guaranteed. The categorized objectives encompass four key dimensions: foundational emergency management capabilities, monitoring and early warning capacities, emergency rescue competencies, and emergency support systems, comprising 23 specific targets in total.

Centering on the overall goals and specific objectives, the 12th Five-year Plan deployed the project construction from 10 respects: the development of the capacity for basic emergency management, monitoring and early warning, information and command system, rescue team, support security, emergency transportation and communication security, emergency recovery, technological and industrial support, training and drill, and publicity and education, etc.

9.3.2   Achievements in the development of emergency management system during the 12th Five-Year Plan period

During the 12th Five-year Plan period, China made notable progress in the construction of China's emergency response system and significantly improved its comprehensive ability to prevent and respond to emergencies, mainly in the following aspects.

In terms of emergency management system, first, we improved the disaster relief and emergency response mechanism with central leadership, local command, tier-based responsibility and mutual coordination. After Lushan Earthquake on April 20, 2013, instead of taking direct command as they used to do, the CPC Central Committee and the State Council leaders fully respected local officials' opinions and practices, and minimized the intervention in specific job. They set an example for leading officials at all levels to assume their own responsibilities, reasonably divide their work, and support each other. That was how they followed the principle of localized management. Second, we established a post-disaster recovery and reconstruction mechanism under the overall leadership of the central government, with local governments as the main bodies and the extensive participation of the people in the disaster areas. On the basis of the experiences and lessons of the reconstruction after the earthquakes in Wenchuan and Yushu, and following instructions by the General Secretary Xi Jinping, relevant departments of the central government, Sichuan Province, Ya'an City and the local people took the lead in finding a new road for disaster recovery and reconstruction by soliciting public opinions and sharing governance. The CPC Central Committee and the

State Council no longer made promises and fully dominated post-disaster reconstruction. Instead, they took concerted efforts to mobilize local governments, leading officials and the public in disaster areas while fulfilling the macro leadership and support. Third, we established a safety production responsibility system with the same responsibilities for the Party and government, one position with two responsibilities, joint management and holding those responsible accountable. In terms of workplace safety, we constantly summed up the practical experience of local and grassroots institutions, attentively listened to the opinions of government and enterprise leaders, and further improved the accountability system for workplace safety, endeavoring to make the Party committee and the government undertook the same responsibilities. Fourth, more than 5.5 million emergency plans were formulated and revised, upgrading the emergency management system.

In terms of monitoring and early warning, the capacity for emergency prevention was significantly enhanced. First, the National Early Warning Center based on China Meteorological Administration was officially put into operation on February 26, 2015. The center provides an authoritative and unified release channel for the State Council to release early warning information. The center sets up a comprehensive early warning information release platform at national, provincial, municipal and county levels, and is able to receive, process and timely release early warning information of natural disasters, accidents and disasters, public health incidents and social security incidents. It is also connected other early warning information release platforms for meteorological, marine, and geological disasters. In the future, it will promote the unified access to early warning information release in relevant ministries and commissions. The China National Emergency Broadcasting based at the China National Radio (CNR), was established to publicize public safety knowledge and undertake disaster early warning and emergency rescue. Second, the projects for natural disaster prevention and mitigation, and hidden danger screening and control were carried out. Third, the system for internet public opinions, emergency monitoring and early warning was set up.

In terms of emergency rescue and support, the rescue teams continued to be improved and their ability was rapidly strengthened. First, 99% of the county-level governments set up comprehensive emergency rescue teams with support from fire and rescue departments. Second, the armed police were incorporated into the national emergency response system. Third, national nuclear emergency rescue teams, national health emergency rescue teams, national mine rescue teams and national emergency surveying and mapping support teams were formed. Fourth, a national emergency platform system was established.

In terms of scientific, technological and industrial support, the capability for technical equipment and scientific research was strengthened. First, AG600 large amphibious aircraft for fire-fighting/water rescue, mobile bio-safety three-level laboratory, and major multi-functional demolition-rescue integrated emergency facilities were successfully invented. Second, the national emergency industry demonstration base was built up. Emergency industry provides special products and services for emergency prevention and preparedness, monitoring and early warning, disposal and rescue. Over the years, China saw the rise and rapid development of its emergency industry which contributed greatly to China's response to emergencies. However, the industry system remained to be improved, the market demands remained insufficient and the development of key technologies and equipment remained slow. To promote the healthy and rapid development of emergency industry, the General Office of the State Council issued the Opinions on Accelerating the Development of Emergency Industry in December 2014. At the same time, the Ministry of Industry and Information Technology, the National Development and Reform Commission and the Ministry of Science and Technology carried out the application and evaluation of national emergency industry demonstration bases for the first time. In 2015, the Fengtai Park of Zhongguancun Science and Technology Park, the Huai'an Industrial Park of Hebei Province, the Yantai Economic and Technological Development Zone, the Hefei High-tech Industrial Development Zone, the Suizhou National Economic and Technological Development Zone, the Guiyang National Economic and Technological Development Zone, and China Hisense Innovation Industrial Park, were approved as the first seven national emergency industry demonstration bases. Third, a number of social organizations such as the China Society of Emergency Management and China Safety Industry Association were established. In September 2014, with the support of the Emergency Response Office of the State Council and with the approval of the Ministry of Civil Affairs, the China Society of Emergency Management was established based on the National Academy of Governance. China Society of Emergency Management is a national, academic and nonprofit corporate social organization composed of voluntary experts, scholars, practitioners and relevant professional institutions, enterprises and institutions, non-governmental organizations engaging in theoretical research, teaching and training and consulting services of emergency management at home and abroad. It is committed to the development and application of modern emergency management to improve the ability of the whole society to prevent and respond to all kinds of emergencies. The establishment of China Society of Emergency Management set up an exchange platform for the theoretical and practical workers engaged in emergency management.

In terms of grassroots capacity, public awareness of disaster prevention and risk avoidance were further enhanced. First, comprehensive disaster reduction demonstration communities, safety demonstration communities, comprehensive health emergency demonstration areas and other grassroots demonstration projects were promoted. Second, the national emergency new media platform was established. Third, the science popularization and education, and emergency drills were widely carried out.

China plays an increasingly important role in international and regional emergency response. First, China participated in international emergency rescue and humanitarian emergency assistance, successfully organized and implemented large-scale evacuation of Chinese nationals from Libya, assisted West African countries in fighting against Ebola hemorrhagic fever (EBHF), and consoled the families of victims of Malaysia Airlines MH370 airliner. Second, China made full use of the frameworks and mechanisms of Shanghai Cooperation Organization (SCO), Asia-Pacific Economic Cooperation (APEC) and ASEAN Regional Forum to continuously deepen international exchanges and cooperation in emergency management. China's political and organizational advantages in dealing with major disasters had widely endorsed by the international community.

Compared with the figures in the period of the 11th Five-year Plan, the number of deaths and missing persons, and direct economic losses caused by natural disasters went down by 92.6% and 21.8% respectively. Workplace safety accidents and deaths decreased by 30.9% and 25% respectively. Public health incidents and reported cases declined by 48.5% and 68.1% respectively. Mass incidents dropped by 25.9%. Under the strong leadership of the CPC Central Committee and the State Council, China succeeded in responding to earthquake disasters in Lushan of Sichuan, Ludian of Yunnan, Minxian and Zhangxian of Gansu, the floods in the Songhua River and the Heilong River basins in Northeast China, the capsizing of the "Oriental Star" passenger ship, and the leakage and explosion of Sinopec Donghuang oil pipeline on November 22, 2013 in Qingdao, the fire and explosion at a dangerous goods warehouse in the Tianjin Port on August 12, 2015, and the landslide accident in the muck receiving yard of Guangming New District in Shenzhen on December 12, 2015. China prevented and controlled the outbreak of acute infectious diseases such as H5N1 avian influenza, H7N9 avian influenza, Middle East respiratory syndrome (MERS), Ebola hemorrhagic fever and plague. As a result, the emergency system stood the test and was improved.

9.3.3 Weak links in the development of emergency management system

China's emergency management system has made impressive achievements in the past few years after the fight against SARS and the key promotion during the 11th Five-year Plan and the 12th Five-year Plan. The framework of modern emergency management system with Chinese characteristics has been basically formed. The emergency capacity in key areas has been steadily improved. The public awareness of disaster prevention and mitigation, and the emergency response capacity are also growing. However, facing the grave and complex public security context, China's emergency management system still faces many challenges.

First, post-disposal outweighs preparation, the screening and management of potential risks are not in place, the standard system of laws and regulations remains to be improved, the information resource sharing is not sufficient, the policy guarantee measures need improvement, and the basic ability of emergency management requires to be strengthened.

Second, the rescue equipment and core competence of the emergency specialists remain to be improved, and the professional and regional distribution structure is unbalanced. A considerable China's emergency rescue teams are established on the basis of large state-owned enterprises. With a dip in economic revenue in all kinds of enterprises, China is facing problems in building emergency rescue teams, such as large debts, insufficient devices and weak core competence, the unbalanced professional and regional distribution structure, backward technology, and low emergency support ability.

Third, the emergency supply reserve is structurally unreasonable, the efficiency for rapid transportation and distribution remains to be raised, the mechanism for resource sharing and emergency requisition compensation needs to be improved. The release and dissemination of emergency information is insufficient. Scientific and technological innovation in public security is weakly founded. The commercialization of technology remains low. The market potential of emergency industry is not transformed into actual demands. The emergency support ability needs to be further improved.

Fourth, China has entered a new stage for urban development. We face more pressure on building an emergency management system that suits urban safety security. Rapid urbanization has brought 656 cities and 20,515 towns by the end of 2015, 463 and 18,342 more than those in 1978 respectively. In 2015, the urbanization rate stood at 56.1%, urban population increased rapidly, with permanent residents being 770 million, 3.5 times more than that in 1978, which was 170 million. The annual average population growth was 16 million. The urban built-up area increased from 7,438 square kilometers in 1981 to 51,948 square kilometers in 2015, a 6-fold increase, with the annual average increase of 1,309 square kilometers. From 1981 to 2015, the popularization rate of urban water use increased from 53.7% to 97.7% and gas coverage from 11.6% to 95.3%, sewage treatment rate from 3.8% to 91%, urban central heating area from less than 20 million square meters to 6.42 billion square meters, per capita road area from less than 2 square meters to 15.6 square meters. As cities sprawl, the urban system is becoming more and more complex and vulnerable, and common and unusual urban security risks increase. The risks faced by cities, especially big cities, are increasing. The occurrence of single city security problem often leads to a series of secondary and derivative security problems, resulting in huge casualties and accidents, property losses and adverse social impacts.

Fifth, the grassroots emergency response capacity is low. Public participation in emergency management social organizations is low. The public safety awareness and self-help and mutual rescue ability are generally weak. The social collaborative response mechanism needs further improvement.

Sixth, with the implementation of the Belt and Road Initiative (BRI) and the establishment of the new pattern for all-round opening up, there are more demands for protecting the safety of our overseas citizens and institutions, the emergency system needs to be expanded, and our ability to participate in international emergency response remains to be improved.

The issues present in China's emergency management system building during the 12th Five-year Plan period persist as challenges that need to be addressed in the current emergency management system. These problems reflect the current situation and level of China's emergency management system, including the problems proposed in the planning but not well solved. There are also some new changes and problems with the development of China's modernization and the deepening of its opening up. Some problems cannot be completely solved through one or two five-year plans, but be overcome with sustained efforts. Therefore, the building of modern emergency management system is an ongoing cause.

9.4   Thoughts on the development of emergency management system in the 13th Five-Year Plan period

As China's modernization is advancing, we should not be overly optimistic about public security as it is facing many challenges.

9.4.1   Emergency management remains to be strengthened

The fight against SARS in 2003 was a turning point in China's emergency management. Since then, China's emergency management has been developing in a standardized, legalized and relevant manner. The modern emergency management pattern has gradually formed. Over the past 20 years, we have made great achievements in our emergency management. First, the emergency plan system continues to improve. Second, the emergency management system has been sustainably upgraded. Third, the emergency management mechanism has been stronger. Fourth, the emergency laws and regulations have been improved. Fifth, the emergency support capacity has been enhanced. Sixth, the emergency management concepts have been constantly changed. The emergency management system with Chinese characteristics is being formed and improved. However, facing the increasingly complex and severe public security situation and people's new expectations and demands, China's emergency management system building still has a long way to go.

Firstly, safety awareness needs to be further strengthened. Many leading officials still fail to give due concern on emergency response, and lack awareness of potential risks and fundamental thinking. They take a chance on that there would be no risk in the region, the department, the institution and the activity. They only pay attention to normal management, overlook or even ignore emergency management, not deeming due importance to emergency management. In some places and cities, to varying degrees, priority is placed on response rather than prevention, on over ground infrastructure rather than underground infrastructure, on window dressing rather than foundation, and on immediate interests rather than long-term ones. Though there are objective, irresistible reasons for frequent occurrences of major emergencies, human factors such as the lack of vigilance, slack working attitude and the unfulfillment of the accountability are the more important reasons.

Secondly, the management plan needs further strengthening. Emergency plans are still absent for some important fields, activities and goals. Some departments and places cannot correctly position the function of emergency plans. On the one hand, emergency plan is confused with emergency planning. They do not make response plans based on the existing conditions such as teams and supplies etc., improperly emphasizing planning and foresight of the emergency plan. They do not tackle the situation according to the situation but create situation according to their own needs. On the other hand, the key links of the emergency plan are not accurate. The emergency plan should run through the whole process of emergency management, including prevention and preparation, monitoring and early warning, response and rescue, recovery and reconstruction. Rather than merely focusing on post-emergency response, we must make it a priority to standardize emergency response measures, by specifying what, how and who to do. While preparing emergency plans, most local authorities and departments lacked systemic analysis of risks, the characteristics of emergencies and the realities of current emergency resources. They failed to combine their own emergency resources with the available perimeter emergency resources. There are many prominent problems in the measures proposed in many plans, such as more single department measures, less comprehensive cooperation measures, more rear command measures and less front organization measures. Plans for emergency measures stick too much to principles, or even become ambiguous or impractical, affecting the feasibility of the plan. The connection between the plans is not strong enough, and there is a lack of overall planning, resulting in repeated, overlapping or even conflicting plans. Many organizations take the preparation of emergency plans for work to palter with the next-level inspection and shirk responsibility. After the preparation, they put them aside, neither drilling, revising or improving the plans based on the reality and new changes. [1]

Thirdly, the emergency management system and mechanism need to be further refined. The coordination between the Party and the government, between the army and the local government, between different departments and between different localities need to be further strengthened. The integration and utilization efficiency of emergency resources also need to be improved. There is a lack of standardized and scientific definition of emergency management functions among departments. Some departments

---

[1] Emergency Management Office, the General Office of the State Council, "Research Report on the Construction of National Emergency Plan System", *China Emergency Management*, 2013(1).

have similar or overlapping functions, but they are in charge of different sections, which leads to loopholes and overlapping power. Some locals or fields put the risk prevention work under the responsibility of professional emergency command organizations, while others put it under the responsibility of normal functional departments. Due to the lack of standardized regulations, the prevention work is often not in place. Local emergency management agencies are not standardized. The responsibilities and levels of emergency management offices are different. The coordination ability and roles are also different. The mechanism for emergency command and coordination is not clear and well-regulated. Most of the emergency rescue teams are dispatched by different next-level departments and sometimes they work separately. The headquarters are often not initiated until casualties occur, or even a temporary headquarter is set up, sometimes leading to lagging leadership. Public opinion monitoring and guidance mechanism remains to be improved. Social mobilization and social organization participation mechanisms need to be standardized.

Fourthly, the ability of monitoring, early warning and rapid response needs to be intensified. The ability of meteorological disaster pre-assessment and early warning is not sufficient. Earthquake prediction is still in the exploratory stage. The monitoring network for geological disasters and forest fires needs improvement. There is still a big gap compared with developed countries in disaster information acquisition and processing, remote sensing disaster reduction application and so on. The "last kilometer" and "bottleneck" problems of early warning information release have not been well solved, especially the early warning information service in rural and remote areas needs to be strengthened. The technology applied in equipment for emergency communication professional support team lags behind the development of network, mobile communication and special communication equipment is insufficient, which cannot meet the needs of emergency command in the case of routine communication failure. Professional emergency teams, especially the rescue team and equipment, are insufficient in quantity, unreasonable in layout, and lack of large and special equipment. The on-site disposal ability, especially the first-time life search and rescue ability, needs to be intensified. In the case of catastrophe, transportation, power and other important infrastructure damage, there are inadequate backup systems and circuitous routes and lines. The lack of air rescue and large equipment to quickly arrive at the scene, and that of aircraft rescue equipment in special environment affect the emergency rescue in remote areas and areas difficult to reach by conventional traffic. The type and quantity of emergency material reserve are still limited. The layout is not reasonable, and the emergency production, procurement, storage, transportation and distribution system of large emergency materials need to be improved.

Fifthly, the risk awareness and the ability of self-help and mutual help remain to be strengthened. Public safety awareness is unsatisfactory in that they lack the knowledge and skills of disaster prevention and emergency response. Many people are often at a loss in the face of emergencies. The equipment and facilities for families, communities and primary-level organizations to escape from danger and rescue themselves are not well prepared. Every year, accidents and disasters caused by improper command and operation, as well as unexpected casualties caused by people's lack of self-help knowledge in danger are not hard to find.

In addition, the legal system of emergency management needs to be further improved. The Emergency Response Law needs to be revised in many respects. At the same time, a supporting system is also wanting. Corresponding and applicable laws and regulations are still absent from the prevention and response of some emerging emergencies.

9.4.2 Overall idea of strengthening emergency management

Based on the experience of developed countries and the reality of China's emergency management, in near future, especially in the 13th Five-year Plan period, the overall idea of the development of China's emergency management should be guided by the ideas of social governance, in line with "One Plan and Three Systems", directed by comprehensive emergency, and focusing on capacity-building.

Guided by ideas of social governance. Social governance is an important means for a modern country to maintain social order, safeguard public security, stimulate social vitality and promote social harmony. Social governance sticks to the people-centered philosophy, aims to safeguard the people's dignity, protect their rights and interests and meet their needs. Social governance must be committed to systematic governance. Under the leadership of the Party committee and the government, we should encourage and support enterprises and institutions, people organizations, grassroots autonomous organizations, social organizations and individual citizens to participate in social governance. Social governance must be carried out according to the law. Problems must be solved according to the law. Social governance requires that we should adhere to comprehensive governance, through various methods to stimulate social vitality and maintain social order from multiple levels and dimensions. Social governance requires governance from the source, which means starting from the front, maintaining fairness and justice, conducting risk assessment, eliminating hidden dangers and problems in the early stage, and timely addressing risks. As abnormal social governance, emergency management also needs to follow the people-centered approach and the principles of systematic governance, source governance, law-based governance and comprehensive governance.

"One Plan and Three Systems" as the main thread. Since 2003, an important experience in promoting emergency management is to firmly grasp the main thread of "One Plan and Three Systems". "One Plan" refers to compiling emergency plan. "Three Systems" refers to the system in terms of institution, structure and law. To establish the emergency plan and strengthen the plan management is the basic and key work of emergency management. The emergency plan is a summary of the past experience on emergency management, a work plan for the current and future risk assessment and response to emergencies, an important carrier of the emergency management system, and a necessary supplement to the emergency laws and regulations. In the future, we should still take "One Plan and Three Systems" as the general starting point to deploy and promote emergency management. First of all, we should do a good job in compiling, exercising and revising the plan, and we should innovate the emergency management systems and build the emergency management legal system.

Directed toward comprehensive emergency. The general momentum of international emergency management development is (i) transferring from single incident response to comprehensive management of multiple incidents; and from single disaster reduction to comprehensive disaster reduction, the comprehensive emergency response to natural disasters, accidents and disasters, public health and social security incidents is improving; (ii) transferring from single department emergency response to multi department collaborative response; (iii) expanding from simply dealing with emergencies in one region to more fields, with more focus on cooperation, coordination, connectivity and efficiency.[1] The practical experience of China's emergency management also fully demonstrates that we must comply with the demands for developing comprehensive emergency response, and reforming the mechanism for emergency management. We must strengthen multi-party coordination, straighten out the relationship between all parties, integrate various resources, and improve response efficiency.

Focusing on capacity building. Emergency management capacity is first reflected

---

[1] Shan Chunchang, Xue Lan, *Introduction to Emergency Management: Theory and Practice*, Beijing: Higher Education Press, 2012, p. 18.

in human ability and material capacity. Human ability includes the ability of leading officials, rescue teams and ordinary people. The material capacity includes the capacity of supplies and equipment for emergency support, transportation and communication, etc. The combination of human capacity and material capacity in emergency management can be reflected through capacity of organizations, systems, grassroots organization, science and technology, etc. The "bottleneck" of China's emergency management lies in inadequate ability in response of leading officials, rescue teams and disaster victims, as well as inadequacy in material supply and transportation and communication. Such being the case, in the future, efforts should be channeled into improving leading officials' emergency decision-making and command ability, and strengthening the construction of response and rescue ability of professional and comprehensive rescue teams. At the same time, we should promote safety culture from the basic level, and improve all people's ability to avoid danger, help themselves and help others. We will vigorously develop related science and technology, upgrade emergency equipment, strengthen emergency monitoring and early warning, emergency transportation and communication support, and thus improving emergency support capacities.

We should manage emergency prevention and response. In recent years, some fields and industries have a high incidence of emergencies in environmental issues, food and drug, violence and terrorism, and foreign-related incidents. There are also some fields with high risk of emergencies, such as some important urban infrastructures. Due to poor layout and obsoletion, great risks exist in underground piping networks in big cities. In many cities, underground civil air defense works are converted into shopping malls, hotels and restaurants, with dense population and many hidden dangers in safety protection and evacuation routes. With the rapid development of Metro in big cities and huge passenger flow, how to prevent and respond to all kinds of natural and artificial emergencies is an urgent and grave issue. It is necessary to strengthen the research on the occurrence and development of emergencies in new areas, and on the prevention, early warning, and control of such emergencies. We should carry out the construction of major emergency scenarios, and study the possible causes, general evolution process, consequences, basic coping strategies and specific tasks of these major emergency scenarios to provide specific objectives for emergency preparation. These scenarios can coordinate the goal, planning and drill in emergency management.[1]

---

[1] Liu Tiemin, "Research on Scenario Planning and Construction of Major Emergencies", *China Emergency Management*, 2012(4).

We should intensify public education. Effective response to emergencies mainly depends on how the public carries out self-help and mutual help. They can learn emergency knowledge and skills from schools, society and families. Public emergency knowledge and skills can be improved through public education, knowledge teaching, skills training and emergency drills. We should strengthen the popularization of emergency knowledge and skills training, and raise the awareness and ability of risk prevention in the whole society. To strengthen school and social emergency education, we should introduce emergency education and training into the government organs, schools, communities, enterprises, rural areas and families. We should incorporate public safety knowledge into the national education system, opening different courses for early childhood education, primary and secondary education and higher education. All regions and relevant departments shall organize the compilation of emergency knowledge manuals and distribute them to communities, rural areas and other grassroots organizations. We should enhance enterprise emergency management training. We should further strictly implement pre-job and in-job education and training system for personnel working in high-risk industries and fields and strengthen intensive training on emergency management knowledge and on the ability for leading officials at all levels. We should strengthen emergency skills training and emergency drills. We should make full use of various news media to popularize emergency knowledge and plans.

Chapter 10
New Trends in Chinese Social Governance in the New Era

The 19th CPC National Congress in October 2017 made an overall plan for China's socialist modernization: "We will continue the Peaceful China initiative, strengthen and develop new forms of social governance, and ensure social harmony and stability. We must work hard to see that our country enjoys enduring peace and stability and our people live and work in contentment."[1] The congress insisted on making innovations based on our heritage, upheld the idea of integration and inclusiveness, and proposed creating a social governance pattern of collaboration, participation and common interests based on China's national conditions and the characteristics of socialist development at the present stage. It also made arrangements of crucial importance for the goal of effective social governance and good social order. It is foreseeable that under the guidance of Xi Jinping Thought on Socialism with Chinese Characteristics for a New Era and in accordance with the plan made by the 19th CPC National Congress, the modernization drive of Chinese social governance in the new era will make steady progress, and the socialist social governance system with Chinese characteristics will be further ameliorated.

10.1 Institutions and mechanisms of social governance further improved

10.1.1 Leadership of the CPC further strengthened

The leadership of the CPC is the defining feature of socialism with Chinese characteristics, and the greatest strength of this system. The 19th CPC National

---

[1] Xi Jinping, "Secure a Decisive Victory in Building a Moderately Prosperous Society in All Respects and Strive for the Great Success of Socialism with Chinese Characteristics for a New Era", a speech delivered at the 19th National Congress of the Communist Party of China on October 18, 2017.

Congress stressed that the Party exercises overall leadership over all areas of endeavor in every part of the country. The endeavor of strengthening social governance and developing new practical approaches to it must be under the leadership of the Party. The leadership of the Party and the socialist system are important guarantees and prominent advantages for the endeavor to be successful. Social organizations, non-public sector entities, and new types of communities—each and every one must strengthen their construction of Party organizations, which are the backbones of these fields. The 19th CPC National Congress pointed out that the social governance system should be improved through Party committee leadership, governmental responsibility, social coordination, public participation, and legal guarantee. In the new era when we are confronted with new situations and new tasks, it is urgent to build a social governance system engaging participation of multiple actors, among which the Party stands in the core. The reasons why the Party's leadership must be strengthened and improved are as follows. Firstly, it is a sure guarantee for our politics to be in the correct direction, and for our social governance to run in the right track of socialism with Chinese characteristics. Secondly, it is the Party committees that make overall plans and policies, regularly study and assess situations, analyze problems and find solutions, and provide support for social governance. Thirdly, it is also the Party committees that oversee the overall situation, coordinate all actors, integrate various forces and resources, and build a platform for multiple actors to participate in the handling of complicated relations so that social governance can proceed in an orderly manner. The endeavor of strengthening social governance and developing new approaches to it should be included on the agendas of Party committees and governments at all levels and in the performance assessment system of local Party and government officials. This doesn't mean that all social governance responsibilities are assumed by the Party, but that the other actors in social governance should be mobilized and depended on. The relationship between the Party and the government and that between the Party and the other actors should be properly handled, so that the governance pattern of "multiple actors around one core" will come into being.

10.1.2   The mode of coordination and integration, and openness and collaboration encouraged

In October 2016, General Secretary Xi Jinping pointed out that social governance must be one of coordination and integration, and openness and collaboration. Coordination and integration mean that rights and responsibilities are defined more clearly, then the actors within the government system can cooperate with one another more smoothly, and operators can run their businesses more efficiently. Openness and collaboration signify that all forces within and without the government system join hands in the administration of our society.

Since the interests of the general public and related social problems and conflicts usually involve several government departments and organizations, it is difficult for a single department or organization to make proper responses to public appeals. Coordination and cooperation are required between Party committees and the government, among the Party committees at different levels, among governments at different levels, among different departments, and among government departments and enterprises and institutions. Therefore, it is necessary to sort out and standardize the social governance functions of the Party and government departments, and highlight top-level designs and overall plans. For this reason, power lists will be made and an accountability practice will be introduced in the social governance realm, and then clear-cut demarcation lines will appear between powers and responsibilities, and between rewards and punishments.

As for the complaints from the public, interest disputes among people, and social dissatisfactions, they have been caused by both historical and contemporary factors, and some are justifiable while others are not; some are due to economic interests while others are ideological or psychological in nature. To resolve such issues, it is often far from enough to rely on the Party committees or the governments. Rather, it requires the engagement of relatives and friends of the party in question, the engagement of local distinguished figures, of related social organizations and other civil forces. Indeed, kinship and fellowship can help much. Besides, professional social workers can be resorted to, for their approaches are humane and compassionate. In this new era, just as social groups or social classes are becoming increasingly pluralistic, so people's needs are more and more diversified and individualized, and social interests, problems and conflicts more and more entangled. In this context, the traditional way that the Party committees and the government take charge of all does not work any longer. The 19th CPC National Congress proposed that the reform of the Party and government institutions and the system of government administration should be continued; that a comprehensive approach be adopted to the setup of the Party and government institutions; that powers should be designated properly and functions and duties be defined clearly both for the institution themselves and their internal bodies; that government functions be further transformed; and that administration be further streamlined and powers delegated. These proposals will create favorable conditions for the social governance that features coordination and integration, and openness and collaboration.

10.1.3   Infrastructure of social governance further improved

The core function of social governance is to serve and guide people. The healthy operation of society and its coordinated development and effective governance require a set of sound infrastructure, including legal codes and social norms, to ensure that institutions and mechanisms and methods and measures can play their due roles. Social credit and information systems are an important component of the infrastructure of social governance. The Fifth Plenary Session of the 18th CPC Central Committee held in October 2015 proposed that the infrastructure of social governance be strengthened through the establishment of a basic national database for demographic information and through the unification of social credit record systems and related real-name registration systems. The 13th Five-year Plan (2016-2020) offered procedures for this proposal. Firstly, after citizen ID card numbers have had their accuracy and uniqueness guaranteed, the national demographic information management system will be upgraded; the replacement of ID cards and remote application for them and registration of fingerprint information should be promoted; a system for online query of and comparison between household registration information and ID card information should be launched. Then, the integration and sharing of cross-departmental and cross-regional information will be gradually materialized. In recent years, China has worked hard to promote the ID-based trust system of "one ID for one person lifelong" and conducted the real-name registration in terms of mobile phone numbers, bank cards, the Internet accounts, mail and express delivery services; the purpose is to leave no room for fake IDs online and offline. Positive results have been made in this respect. Secondly, the establishment of the social credit system will be promoted. The Credit Law was drafted based on extensive investigation; the legislative process of regulations concerning public credit information management and unified social credit codes has been accelerated; normative documents concerning government integrity, personal credit and e-commerce honesty have been issued. Also, rules and regulations which concern government information collection, sorting, processing, saving and use, and concern integrity incentives and dishonesty punishments should be formulated by related departments in all regions. In 2014, the Social Credit System Construction and Planning Framework (2014-2020) was issued. In 2016, the Guiding Opinions on Establishing and Improving the System of Joint Incentive for Keeping Faith and Joint Punishment for Losing Faith and Accelerating the Advancement of the Development of Social Honesty, and

Opinions Accelerating the Advancement of the Development of a Credit Supervision, Warning and Punishment System of Dishonest Persons Subject to Enforcement were issued. Credit reference capabilities should be improved, and infrastructure of the credit system should be strengthened. For instance, the national credit information sharing platform should be launched online, keep being updated, be sorted in terms of contents, and be promoted.[1] All in all, transformation from a traditional society to a modern one is taking place in China. The old institutional system and social governance methods have turned out to be outdated, and unable to keep up with the times. Many essential social governance systems need to be re-assessed and updated. This is a long-term project, which cannot be accomplished overnight. However, advancing in the reform direction and laboring within the established framework, we will certainly make notable progress in Chinese social governance.

10.2 Concepts and principles of social governance further improved

10.2.1 People-centered philosophy taking root in social governance

The report delivered by Xi Jinping to the 19th CPC National Congress pointed out that people are the creators of history and the fundamental force that determines the future of the Party and the country. Therefore, we must ensure the principal status of the people, and adhere to the Party's commitment to serving the public good and exercising power in the interests of the people. We must observe the Party's fundamental purpose of wholeheartedly serving the people, and put into practice the Party's mass line in all aspects of governance. The concept of the people is concrete, not abstract. It involves persons from different fields. In other words, the people are composed of individuals from different groups and social classes. To recognize the idea of people orientation is to represent their interests, respond to their appeals, and defend their rights. In this new era, we must be more concerned about the people who are in straitened circumstances or underprivileged, and help address their difficulties in subsistence and in work, and safeguard their legitimate rights and interests. In the progress of urbanization, China's migrant population has reached 245 million, a considerable portion of whom are "semi-residents" in cities, especially in major cities. So they have more and greater difficulties

---

[1] Xu Shaosi, *Introduction to The Outline of the 13th Five-Year Plan for National Economic and Social Development of the People's Republic of China*, Beijing: People's Publishing House, 2016, pp. 396-398.

in employment, social security, housing and children's education, etc. than local full residents. From time to time, conflicts arise between them and the full residents.

When so many people migrate to work in cities, there emerge empty-nest households and three kinds of "left-behind" people (left-behind children, wives, and old people) in rural areas. In addition, vulnerable groups such as the laid-off and unemployed, children in difficult circumstances and the disabled are the major concerns in the social governance. As the saying goes, "Remedy the short slab and the wooden bucket can hold more water."

Only when the rights and interests of the people in difficulty are taken good care of, can social stability and harmony be kept. To take the people-oriented approach is to understand their most urgent concerns and most practical interests issues, including education, employment, income distribution, social security, medical care, environmental protection, and safety guarantee systems.

When dealing with these issues, we should first consider the interests of the majority in the spirit of maintaining fairness and justice. But there are cases when we must make preferential policies to support the vulnerable groups and people in difficulty. The 19th CPC National Congress proposed to develop a new model of social governance system based on collaboration, participation, and shared benefits. By definition, collaboration and participation are measures while shared benefits are the ultimate goal; collaboration is the prerequisite while participation is the guarantee; collaboration and participation, as mutual conditions for each other, work together for the ultimate goal of shared benefits. This model of social governance is the practical outcome of the people-centered philosophy.

10.2.2   Fairness and justice at the core of social governance[1]

With principal contradictions taking different forms in Chinese society, fairness and justice will become stronger and more urgent demands from people after their material and cultural demands have been satisfied. General Secretary Xi Jinping once remarked that as China develops further and the people's living standards improve, public awareness of equality and democracy, and of rights and interests has been steadily enhanced, and thus people's resentment at injustice becomes more pronounced.[2] He laid great emphasis on the core role and position of fairness and justice in social governance, insisting that injustice and inequality caused by man-made factors should be prevailed

---

[1] Wei Liqun, *New Ideas, New Practices, New Horizons in Social Governance*, Beijing: China Yanshi Press, 2017, p. 3.

[2] Xi Jinping, *The Governance of China*, Vol. I , Beijing: Foreign Languages Press, 2018, p. 107.

over through innovative institutional arrangements; that people's rights to equal participation and development ensured; equal rights, equal opportunities and fair rules for all achieved; that in consideration of the most immediate and realistic public interests, a new development mechanism built which features fairness and justice, collaboration and shared interests. In this way, economic development will be more inclusive and the general public can have access to the fruits of reform and development. He further maintained that "Judicial, procuratorial and public security officers should use the scales of fairness and the sword of justice to guarantee a fair and just society with concrete actions, and ensure access to fairness and justice for every individual."[1] In this new era, a new type of urbanization through further transformation of the household registration system will be stepped up; the barriers for rural people to settle down in cities will retreat; the difference in the rights and interests between native and non-native residents will dwindle. In short, it will be easier for migrant population to get assimilated into the new community. The implementation of the rural revitalization strategy will greatly promote the integration of urban and rural development; the relationship between urban and rural areas will take on a new look; the development gap between urban and rural areas will also be greatly narrowed. Under the principle that the Party should operate under strict discipline, to catch "tigers" as well as "flies"—to punish senior officials as well as junior ones guilty of corruption, to crack down on organized crime and local mafia, so that the social governance environment can be cleansed and public fairness and justice guaranteed. The enhancement in the reform of the judicial and law enforcement systems, the improvement in the employment and income distribution system, and the betterment of the social security system—all of them have provided institutional guarantees for the practice of fairness and justice in social governance to attain a higher level.

10.2.3 Order and vitality balanced

Social governance pursues the integration of order and vitality, with importance attached to both the maintenance of stability and order and the bringing out of social vitality. The pursuit of the integration of order and vitality is an important development of the concept of social management. For a considerable time in the past, there was the problem that tight management led to deadlock while lax management ended up in chaos. Between laxity and tightness, and between order and vitality, a balance was lacking. General Secretary Xi Jinping once pointed out that social governance is a science; that tight control leads to stagnancy while laxity to chaos; and that we have to properly

---

[1] Xi Jinping, *The Governance of China*, Vol. I , Beijing: Foreign Languages Press, 2018, p. 164.

handle the relationship between vitality and order in a dialectic manner.[1] Since the 18th CPC National Congress in November 2012, the Party committees and governments at all levels have been trying to correct the one-sided practice that the maintenance of social order was emphasized while social vitality overlooked, in order that a vibrant, harmonious, and orderly society can be created. And remarkable achievements have been made. To bring out vitality, the Party and the government have always regarded "streamlining administration, delegating powers, and improving regulation and services" as the central task in the reform of the system of review and approval by government bodies. What should not and cannot be done or cannot be done well by the government have been handed over to the market and the society. What should be done by county- and township-level governments has been delegated to them. The relationship between the government and the market, between the government and the society, between the society and the market, and between the central government and the local government should be properly handled. To create a booming market and a thriving society, the government should encourage and support people to start businesses and make innovations, so that their talent can be fully unleashed and their aspirations be attained. Specifically, we should make efforts to change the old measures of social stability maintenance—controlling, blocking, suppressing and punishing, for they are simplistic and inflexible, ruthless and relentless. Instead, we should go all out to mediate and resolve conflicts, and maintain stability in a flexible and compassionate manner. Social forces and even the whole society should be mobilized or organized to participate in the job of social stability maintenance. The Report to the 19th CPC National Congress required that the role of social organizations be leveraged and that government's efforts on the one hand and society's self-regulation and residents' self-governance on the other hand reinforce each other, so that the vitality and order of social governance can be guaranteed institutionally and organizationally.

10.3   Methods of and approaches to social governance to be more scientific

10.3.1   Legal protection further strengthened

The 19th CPC National Congress in October 2017 proposed to "improve the law-

---

[1] Publicity Department of the CPC Central Committee, *Readings from General Secretary Xi Jinping's Series of Important Speeches* (2016 Edition), Beijing: Xuexi Publishing House and People's Publishing House, 2016.

based social governance model under which Party committees exercise leadership, government assumes responsibility, non-governmental actors provide assistance, and the public gets involved. We will strengthen public participation and rule of law in social governance, and make such governance smarter and more specialized."[1] The rule of law is the best mode of social governance. Law-based social governance is an inevitable requirement and an important indicator of the modernization of social governance. Ensuring every dimension of governance is law-based is an important part of Xi Jinping Thought on Socialism with Chinese Characteristics for a New Era. Therefore, after the 19th CPC National Congress, the process of making, revising, and abolishing laws and regulations concerning social governance speeds up, and so do the formulation and improvement of related policies and institutions. Also, the revision of laws and regulations such as the Organic Law of Urban Residents Committee and the Organic Law of the Villagers Committees steps up. A legal system of social governance that makes coordinated use of national and local laws will surely be formed. While the legal system of social governance is being improved, officials at all levels should hone their ability to think and act in accordance with the law, and rely on the law to resolve conflicts and problems and promote harmony. The people must express their appeals and safeguard their rights and interests in accordance with the law. While emphasizing the rule of law, we must continue to promote the role of ethics on which conventional social governance used to depend, painting the picture with the two brushes of ethics and law. Chinese history has always attached importance to the combined role of ethics and law in social governance, for the governments in past dynasties realized that law cannot go into effect by itself. The Fourth Plenary Session of the 18th CPC Central Committee held in October 2014 pointed out that it is the requirement of good national governance and social governance that law and ethics work together. The 19th CPC National Congress proposed to make more efforts to popularize civil laws and cultivate a law-based socialist culture, which follows that citizens' understanding of the rule of law must be improved, that their conviction in law must be strengthened, and that the core socialist values must be practiced. Only in this way, can the notion that the Constitution and laws are above everything else be deep rooted in people's mind; can the idea of the rule of law be the guidance in the thinking and behavior of the whole society. The finest elements of Chinese traditional legal culture should be recognized. The big-picture view that family and country are mutually supported, the values of

---

[1] Xi Jinping, *The Governance of China,* Vol. 3, Beijing: Foreign Languages Press, 2021.

benevolence, righteousness and integrity, the idea of harmony between humanity and nature, the concept that order is produced by ethics and law working together, and the concept of justice that integrates compassion, reason and law—these finest elements of and time-honored civic virtues in Chinese traditional legal culture should all be carried forward, so that people will eventually take it for granted to maintain public order and follow good conventions.[1]

10.3.2   The role of modern technology further manifested

Different approaches can be applied to realize comprehensive social governance. One of them is modern technology, which provides tools and means for increasingly complex social governance innovation to be made. The development and progress of science and technology are both important impetus and inevitable achievement of modernization. However, modern science and technology is also a "double-edged sword", which can benefit and harm human beings and their society. The more sophisticated the modern science and technology are, the greater impact they will exert on people's work and life. Science and technology have opened unexpected spaces for mankind, creating numerous opportunities and favorable conditions for people to tap potentials unconstrainedly and in all respects, and providing convenient conditions and means to address social problems and conflicts, interest disputes, and public security. However, the rapid advancement of modern science and technology is also the root cause of many social problems and conflicts, which may put social stability at stake. Sci-tech development must guard against latent problems. The achievements of modern information technology such as the Internet, the Internet of Things, artificial intelligence, cloud computing, and big data technology are representatives of modern sci-tech development. They have brought benefits to mankind on the one hand, and caused many social problems on the other. They are also changing social governance modes, providing convenience for problems in social governance to be coped with. On October 9, 2016, in the 36th group study session of the Political Bureau of the CPC Central Committee, General Secretary Xi Jinping pointed out that with the development of the Internet, especially that of the mobile Internet, social governance mode is shifting from one-way management to two-way interaction, from offline management to online-offline integration, from government's exclusive supervision to a governance style that

---

[1] Wang Yongqing, "Intensifying the Practice of the Rule of Law", in *The Guidance Reader on the Report to the 19th CPC National Congress*, Beijing: People's Publishing House, 2017, p. 284.

attaches importance to collaboration between the government and social forces. He also asked us to develop a profound understanding of the role of the Internet in national administration and social governance. By the promotion of e-government and smart cities and through data concentration and sharing, an integrated national big data center can be built, which will embrace technology and business in a cross-level, cross-region, cross-system, cross-department, and cross-business sense. In recent years, smart cities have been emerging, which make full use of big data and cloud computing technologies to conduct social governance. Economically developed areas such as Zhejiang Province, Shanghai City and Shenzhen City have been at the forefront, while economically underdeveloped areas such as Guizhou Province are not far behind either. By planning carefully and seizing the development opportunity, Guizhou-Cloud Big Data (an industry development Co., Limited) has emerged and become a model for the entirety of China as well as the western region of China, offering good experience for social governance innovation.

10.3.3 Refinement and specialization further developed

With the continuation of urbanization and modernization, the division of labor in society is getting finer and finer; social affairs more and more complicated; people's needs more and more diversified, showing the characteristics of demassification, differentiation, and individualization. Social governance has entered an era of refinement and specialization. In 2017, China's urbanization rate exceeded 58%, with more than 800 million people working and living in cities and towns all year round. A considerable portion of urban residents lives in major cities with a population of over 1 million. Among those major cities, 30 have a population of over 8 million, and 13 over 10 million[1] — this fact brings new challenges for urban social governance. During the National People's Congress and the Chinese People's Political Consultative Conference (hereinafter referred to as "Two Sessions") held in March 2017, General Secretary Xi Jinping spoke to the delegation from Shanghai that it is a major issue to find a new path to social governance that conforms to the characteristics and operation law of a megacity and this issue concerns the development of Shanghai. Xi also stressed that smart management must be enhanced to raise urban management standards and information technologies such as the Internet and big data must play their full roles to enable urban

---

[1] "China: 30 Cities with a Population of Over 8 Million and 13 Cities with over 10 Million", *China Business News*, Aug. 11, 2017.

management to attain the level of scientization, refinement and intelligence. The prerequisite for refined governance is to recognize people's needs, grasp the nature and characteristics of social problems and conflicts, and take targeted measures rather than cure-all measures. Specialization is the prerequisite for and guarantee of refinement. They are inseparable, both contributing to sophisticated social governance. When social needs and social problems have been fully understood, professionals and professional methods should be relied on to serve people and solve problems. Along with refinement and specialization in social governance, there has emerged grid management, which is growing more and more mature. Then ever-updated social investigation and research methods will be applied in social governance, and the emerging professions such as social work will play a more important role in social governance.

10.4   The key tasks of social governance will be up-to-date

10.4.1   Promoting coordinated overall risk management and emergency response

Social governance includes two types and two links: risk management under normal conditions and emergency response under urgent conditions. For a long time, the theorists have focused on the governance of social risks in a normal state, such as how to coordinate interest relationships, how to prevent and control risks, how to solve social problems and social conflicts. There has been insufficient research and preparation as to how to deal with sudden emergencies. Departments involved don't lay due emphasis on risk management, and they often take chances on emergencies. Once problems or emergencies strike, they are at a loss, not knowing what to do. After the fight against SARS in 2003, China began to establish a modern emergency response system centered on "One Plan and Three Systems". After over ten years of development, China's emergency management undertaking has made considerable progress; the institutional mechanisms have been continuously established and improved; management has gradually become standardized, relevant, and legalized; and the ability to handle all kinds of emergencies has been significantly improved. In January 2017, the General Office of the State Council issued the 13th Five-Year Plan for the Development of the National Emergency Response System, which provided a blueprint for the construction of the national emergency response system in the new era. Following the principles of "making up shortcomings, weaving the bottom network, strengthening the core, and promoting synergy", we should strengthen capacities in the following aspects: basic emergency management, core emergency rescue, comprehensive emergency management support, social coordinated response, and foreign-related emergency response. The implementation of this plan will not only further improve the weak foundation of emergency system construction, lagging theory, and low capacity, but also further promote the extension of emergency management to the front line of risk governance, combining risk prevention and emergency response, and finally jointly improve social governance ability.

10.4.2   The status of public safety is more prominent

Public safety is an important part of social governance. Relevant laws and policies show that China's public safety mainly involves the prevention, handling, and reconstruction of four types of emergencies: natural disasters, workplace accidents, public health events, and social safety incidents. With the continual modernization of socialism with Chinese characteristics, risks are increasing, and safeguarding public safety has become increasingly urgent and important. Judging from the trend, emergencies are still prone to happen. Earthquakes, geological disasters, floods, droughts, extreme weather, oceanic disaster, forest and grassland fires, and other serious natural disasters are distributed in a wide area, causing heavy losses and difficult disaster relief. For example, in 2016, natural disasters affected nearly 190 million people, with 1,432 death tolls and 274 missing; collapse of 521 thousand houses and damage of 3.34 million houses in varying degrees. The affected area of crops was 26.22 million hectares, of which 2.9 million hectares harvested nothing with a direct economic loss of RMB503.29 billion.[1] The total number of production accidents is still too huge. Major accidents occur frequently in key industries such as road transportation, coal mining, and hazardous chemicals. Hidden dangers for some urban buildings, lifeline projects, underground pipe networks, and other infrastructures increase as time goes by. Emergency pollution incidents frequently occur due to production accidents, pollutant discharge, or natural disasters, which endanger life and health, and property, threaten the ecological environment, and cause major social impacts; Notifiable diseases such as plague and cholera occur from time to time. Sudden acute infectious diseases continue to appear globally. The risks of imported infectious diseases and misuse of biotechnology are increasing. The safety of food and medicine is still poor, making it increasingly difficult to control public health events. Social interests are intertwined,

---

[1] Hong Yi, *China Emergency Management Report in 2017*, Beijing: National Academy of Governance Press, 2017, p. 55.

giving rise to mass incidents, and foreign-related risks. Social security is facing new challenges. Emergencies are complicated, because different risks are intertwined, with contradictions between natural and human-induced factors, between traditional and non-traditional factors, and between existing social contradictions and new ones, etc. In the process of industrialization, urbanization, internationalization, and informatization, emergency incidents are growing to show correlation, repercussion, complexity and irregularity. The trend of trans-regional and internationalization has become increasingly obvious, and the harm is increasing. Rapid development of new media poses new challenge to emergency response as incidents happened offline get widely spread online. Meanwhile, in the process of building a well-off society in an all-round way, the public has higher expectations for the government to timely deal with emergencies and ensure public safety. But the state's response capabilities are not up to these demands. Therefore, disaster prevention, mitigation and relief, production safety, food and medicine safety, and emergency medical rescue, like the resolution of social conflicts and the handling of social security incidents, have become important tasks of social governance with increasingly prominent status and role.

10.4.3   Coordinating real-world social governance and network social governance

In the 21st century, Internet technology has developed rapidly, forming a huge and complex network. Due to its anonymity, equality, wide participation, and interaction, the network has developed much faster than people's imagination. It is independent of as well as closely connected with the real society, so it has become a new space and way of living and interacting in human history. Internet society has brought great convenience to people's production and life, learning and shopping, communicating and socializing, etc. However, it is difficult to distinguish real information from fake ones. The internet often teems with harmful information including violence, pornography, fraud, and rumors, imposing dangers on information security. Some information is irrational, irresponsible or even politically-oriented, posing a threat to social order and political stability, becoming tools for crimes and offering shelters to criminals. The network society runs like a highway. Without traffic police and traffic laws, every driver will do whatever he wants without restraint, posing risks to drivers and passengers on the road. According to The 40th China Statistical Report on Internet Development released by the China Internet Network Information Center, as of June 2017, the total number of China's Internet users accounted for 1/5 of the global total, reaching 751 million. The Internet availability rate was 54.3%, exceeding the global average by 4.6

percentage points. As a major user of the network, it is an urgent task to coordinate the governance of the real and the network societies. Since the 18th CPC National Congress, the CPC Central Committee has continuously strengthened the top-level design of Internet governance by establishing management institutions, formulating policies and laws to implement Internet governance by the law and promote a healthy and orderly development of the Internet. Since 2014, the government has carried out several special campaigns against online rumors and cybercrimes. On June 1, 2017, Cyber Security Law of the People's Republic of China was officially implemented, indicating that China has officially entered a new stage of governance for Internet space in accordance with the law.

10.4.4 Priority is given to the construction of social psychological service system

In modern society, the pace of work and life is getting faster. Pressure from work, study, competition, and life is increasing. While the support network relying on traditional family and acquaintance is shrinking, the new social support network is so unstable that it is difficult to meet people's emotional and psychological needs. Mental health problems are increasing and unavoidable. Some extreme cases of violent injuries and homicides, as well as some incidents of taking extremely negative measures against individuals are frequently reported. According to the results of mental illness epidemiological surveys in China's some areas, some experts estimate that among the population over 15 years old, more than 100 million people are suffering from mental diseases, of which 16 million are patients with severe mental disorders, and most of the rest are suffering depression, autism and other mental disorders or behavioral disorders.[1] Those who suffer setbacks in work, life, study and relationship but have no family or friends to communicate with, are often psychologically vulnerable, such as the unemployed, those used to be disciplined by law, mobile population and their families. Mental abnormalities and fragility not only seriously affect their normal work and life, the happiness and well-being of their families, but also social harmony and stability. General Secretary Xi Jinping said that the core of strengthening and innovating social governance is people. Only when people live in harmony can society be stable and orderly. Therefore, whether it is for the protection of human rights or the maintenance of social peace and harmony, psychological services must be paid close attention to, and

---

[1] "Are You Depressed?" (People's Livelihood Perspective: Addressing Mental Health Among Chinese Citizens (Part 1), *People's Daily*, Oct. 14, 2016.

the construction of the psychological service system should be given urgent priority to. The 18th CPC National Congress began to focus on mental health, and suggested "provide compassionate care and psychological counseling". Many localities have actively explored and accumulated a lot of good experiences. On this basis, the 19th CPC National Congress made a more systematic and scientific deployment, and proposed "we will improve the system of public psychological services, and cultivate self-esteem, self-confidence, rationality, composure, and optimism among our people", resulting in a more proactive, clear and specific psychological service, which transforms from post-intervention to prevention, and from scattered to systematic construction.

10.4.5   Urban and rural communities are the focuses of social governance

Due to the disintegration of the "*danwei system*" formed during the planned economy period and the profound changes in the urban and rural social structures, and with the deepening of social governance practices, people are increasingly aware that urban and rural communities are the basic units and core of social governance. The governance of urban and rural communities is closely related to the implementation of the Party and the country's major policies, people's immediate interests, and the harmony and stability of the urban and rural grassroots. General Secretary Xi Jinping pointed out that "the social governance must take root in urban and rural communities. With strong capacity for community service and management, social governance will be endowed with a solid foundation. We must conduct in-depth research on governance system issues, deepen and expand grid management, and equip communities with resources, service, and management, so that communities not only have duties and rights but also resources to provide more accurate and effective services and management for the people."[1] "Urban and rural communities are the 'last kilometer' on connection between the Party and the people. We should take strengthening the construction of the Party at the grassroots and consolidating the foundation of the Party's governance as a red line, which will run through social governance and grassroots construction. We should make efforts to strengthening the Part in the region. Besides, we should adjust and improve outdated management systems and mechanisms, promote the downward shift of management focus, implement regular specific services and management responsibilities, hand over human resources and funds, rights and responsibilities to the primary level

---

[1] Party Literature Research Center of the CPC Central Committee, *Excerpts from Xi Jinping's Discourses on Socialist Social Construction*, Beijing: Central Party Literature Publishing House, 2017, p. 127.

organizations; hand over the resources and power down to the grassroots organizations, and strengthen the influence of and trust in the grassroots organizations among the people."[1] During the "Two Sessions" in 2016, General Secretary Xi Jinping attended the group deliberations of the Shanghai delegation and delivered an important speech on social governance. He pointed out that the grassroots are the end point of all work, so the focus of social governance must take root in urban and rural areas and communities. We should improve the legalization, scientific level and organization of urban and rural community governance, and promote the modernization of urban and rural community governance systems and capacities. In June 2017, the Central Committee and the State Council promulgated Opinions on Strengthening and Improving Urban and Rural Community Governance. The Report to the 19th CPC National Congress proposed that we should strengthen the construction of the community governance system, promote the downward shift of the focus of social governance to the grassroots level, give full play to the role of social organizations, and realize the benign interaction among government governance, social regulation and residents' self-governance. These important policies and regulations will greatly elevate the status of urban and rural communities in social governance, and promote the modernization of the community governance system and capacities.

---

[1] Party Literature Research Center of the Central Committee, *Excerpts from Xi Jinping's Discourses on Socialist Social Construction*, Beijing: Central Party Literature Publishing House, 2017, p. 129.

Bibliography

[1] Ding Yuanzhu, *Basic Theory and Methods of Community*, Beijing: Beijing Normal University Press, 2009.

[2] Ding Yuanzhu, *Strategic Thinking and Basic Countermeasures for Social Construction in China*, Beijing: Peking University Press, 2008.

[3] Fei Xiaotong, *From the Soil: The Foundation of Chinese Society*, Shanghai: Shanghai Century Publishing Group, 2007.

[4] Gong Weibin, *Case Studies of Contemporary Chinese Social Governance*, Kunming: Yunnan Publishing Group Company, Yunnan Education Publishing House, 2014.

[5] Gong Weibin, Ma Xiheng, *Chinese Social Management Essays (2012): Social Management in Urbanization*, Beijing: National Academy of Governance Press, 2013.

[6] Gong Weibin, *Research on China's Social Governance*, Beijing: Social Sciences Academic Press (China), 2014.

[7] Gong Weibin, *Social Structural Change and Social Governance Innovation*, Beijing: National Academy of Governance Press, 2014.

[8] Gong Weibin, Wu Xu and Ge Yuqin, *Innovation in Community Associations and Social Management*, Beijing: China Society Press, 2012.

[9] Li Gao, Dan Tong, *Governance of the Grassroots*, Beijing: People's Publishing House, 2018.

[10] Li Peilin, Han Xiuji and Lu Yangxu, *Research on Social Governance in Developed Countries and Regions*, Kunming: Yunnan Publishing Group Company, Yunnan Education Press, 2014.

[11] Li Peilin, *Social Reform and Social Governance*, Beijing: Social Sciences Academic Press (China), 2014.

[12] Li Qiang, Hu Baorong, *A History of Chinese Social Governance*, Kunming: Yunnan Publishing Group Company, Yunnan Education Press, 2014.

[13] Li Wen, *Social History of the People's Republic of China (1949-2012)*, Beijing: Contemporary China Publishing House, 2016.

[14] Li Wen, *The Structure and Transformation of East Asian Societies*, Beijing: Social Sciences Academic Press (China), 2006.

[15] Lu Xueyi, *A Study of the Social Structure of Contemporary China* (Volumes I, II, III, IV), Beijing: Social Sciences Academic Press (China), 2018.

[16] Lu Yilong, *After "From the Soil"*, Beijing: The Commercial Press, 2017.

[17] Ma Fuyun, *Research on Household Registration System: Rights and Changes*, Beijing: China Society Press, 2013.

[18] Ma Qingyu, Liao Hong, *Development Strategies of Social Organizations in China*, Beijing: Social Sciences Academic Press (China), 2015.

[19] Party Literature Research Center of the Central Committee, *Excerpts from Xi Jinping's Expositions on the Construction of Socialist Society*, Beijing: Central Party Literature Publishing House, 2017.

[20] Qing Lianbin, *Seeking Solutions to China's Retirement Conundrums*, Beijing: Central Party School Press, 2017.

[21] Samuel P. Huntington, *Political Order in Changing Society*, Chinese Edition, translated by Wang Guanhua et al., Beijing: SDX Joint Publishing Company, 1989.

[22] Song Guilun, *Research Reports on Chinese and Foreign Social Governance* (Volumes I, II), Beijing: China Renmin University Press, 2015.

[23] Sun Yat-sen, *The General Plan of National Construction*, Beijing: China Chang'an Publishing House, 2011.

[24] Tang Zhongxin, *An Introduction to China's Urban Community Construction*, Tianjin: Tianjin People's Publishing House, 2000.

[25] The History Research Office of the Central Committee, *Ninety Years of the Communist Party of China*, Beijing: Central Party History Publishing House, Party Building Reading Material Publishing House, 2016.

[26] The Writing Group of *Comprehensive Creation and Development of China's Emergency Management (2003-2007)*, *Comprehensive Creation and Development of China's Emergency Management (2003-2007)* (Volumes I, II), Beijing: National Academy of Governance Press, 2017.

[27] Ulrich Beck, *Risk Society*, Chinese Edition, translated by He Bowen, Nanjing: Yilin Press, 2004.

[28] Wei Liqun, *New Ideas, New Practices, New Horizons in Social Governance*, Beijing: China Yanshi Publishing House, 2018.

[29] Wei Liqun, *Selected Cases of Innovative Social Governance (2014)*, Beijing: Social Sciences Academic Press (China), 2015.

[30] Wu Zhongmin, *On Social Justice*, Jinan: Shandong People's Publishing House, 2004.

[31] Xie Zhiqiang, Li Huiying, *Introduction to Social Policies* (2nd Edition), Beijing: Central Party School Press, 2017.

[32] Yu Keping, *Modernization and Innovation of Urban Governance*, Beijing: China Society Press, 2018.

[33] Zhang Linjiang, *Towards the "Community Plus" Era*, Beijing: Social Sciences Academic Press (China), 2018.

[34] Zhang Linjiang, *Twelve Lectures on Social Governance*, Beijing: Social Sciences Academic Press (China), 2015.

[35] Zhang Zhanxin, Hou Yafei et al., *The Floating Population in Urban Communities: A Survey of Beijing and Other Five Cities*, Beijing: Social Sciences Academic Press (China), 2009.

Postscript

This book is a collaborative effort by a team. Gong Weibin authored Chapters 1, 6, 9, and 10; Wang Tao wrote Chapters 2 and 4; Wu Chao contributed to Chapter 3; Chen Cai authored Chapter 5; Gong Chunming wrote Chapter 7, and Zhai Huijie wrote Chapter 8. Gong Weibin structured the book and edited the manuscripts for the entire work.